Guide to Medical School and the MCAT

DAVID A. HACKER, M.A.
Director of Medical Education
National Medical School Review

KENNETH IBSEN, PH.D.
Director of Faculty Development
National Medical School Review

Guide to Medical School and the MCAT

Williams & Wilkins

A WAVERLY COMPANY

BALTIMORE • PHILADELPHIA • LONDON • PARIS • BANGKOK
BUENOS AIRES • HONG KONG • MUNICH • SYDNEY • TOKYO • WROCLAW

Editor: Elizabeth A. Nieginski
Managing Editor: Amy G. Dinkel
Development Editor: Karla Schroeder
Production Coordinator: Cindy Park
Designer: Ellen B. Zanolle
Illustration Planner: Cindy Park
Cover Designer: Thomas Christopher Jones
Typesetter: University Graphics
Printer: Port City Press
Binder: Port City Press

Copyright © 1997 Williams & Wilkins

351 West Camden Street
Baltimore, Maryland 21201-2436 USA

Rose Tree Corporate Center
1400 North Providence Road
Building II, Suite 5025
Media, Pennsylvania 19063-2043 USA

Printed in the United States of America

First Edition,

Library of Congress Cataloging-in-Publication Data
Hacker, David A.
    Guidebook to medical school and the MCAT / David A. Hacker,
Kenneth Ibsen. — 1st ed.
        p.   cm.
    Includes index.
    ISBN 0-683-00679-7
    1. Medical colleges—United States—Admission.   2. Medical
colleges—United States—Entrance examinations.   3. Medical
colleges—United States—Entrance requirements.   I. Ibsen, Kenneth.
II. Title.
    [DNLM: 1. School Admission Criteria.   2. Schools, Medical—United
States.   3. Medicine—examination questions.   W 18 H118g 1997]
R838.4.H33   1997
610'.71'173—dc20
DNLM/DLC
for Library of Congress   96-20389
                                                           CIP

The publishers have made every effort to trace the copyright holders for borrowed material. If they have inadvertently overlooked any, they will be pleased to make the necessary arrangements at the first opportunity.

Call our customer service department at **(800) 638-0672** for catalog information or fax orders to **(800) 447-8438.** For other book services, including chapter reprints and large quantity sales, ask for the Special Sales department.

To purchase additional copies of this book or for information concerning American College of Sports Medicine certification and suggested preparatory materials, call **(800) 486-5643.**

Canadian customers should call **(800) 268-4178,** or fax **(905) 470-6780.** For all other calls originating outside of the United States, please call **(410) 528-4223** or fax us at **(410) 528-8550.**

Visit Williams & Wilkins on the Internet: **http://www.wwilkins.com** or contact our customer service department at **custserv@wwilkins.com.** Williams & Wilkins customer service representatives are available from 8:30 am to 6:00 pm, EST, Monday through Friday, for telephone access.

97 98 99
1 2 3 4 5 6 7 8 9 10

Dedication

To Paula, whose love, patience, and extra efforts at work and home made it possible for me to find the time to write this volume.

David A. Hacker

To Victor Gruber, M.D. and National Medical School Review. We appreciate the generous patronage and moral support that helped make the writing of this book feasible.

David A. Hacker and Kenneth H. Ibsen

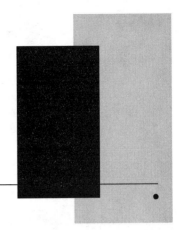

Contents

PART 1

Medical School Admissions

CHAPTER **9**

Not Accepted? The Options

PART **2**

The MCAT

CHAPTER **10**

Preparing for the MCAT

CHAPTER **11**

The MCAT

CHAPTER **12**

Practice MCAT

CHAPTER **13**

Scoring of the Practice MCAT

CHAPTER **14**

CHAPTER **15**

CHAPTER **16**

CHAPTER **17**

APPENDICES

INDEX

TABLES

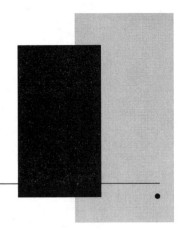

Preface

The information presented in this book is based on over 20 years of counseling, advising, and teaching thousands of premedical and medical students. Based on this experience, the authors have filled this guide with the essential information that will help students gain acceptance to medical school. The book is divided into two major parts. The first part fully describes the admission process, sources of financial aid, and facts about medical school and the medical profession. This information pinpoints the ways that students can optimize their chances for admission. Filled with practical advise and examples to aid the student in their premedical preparation, this part of the guide has one goal: making the student an attractive applicant for medical school.

The second part of the guide covers, in detail, methods to follow in preparing to take the Medical College Admission Test (MCAT). Starting with an overview of the MCAT, this section of the book continues will a full diagnostic MCAT examination, advice on how to review based on the results of the practice exam, proven test-taking strategies to use before and during the MCAT, and advice on how to deal with anxiety. In this part of the guide there are sample questions that show how to effectively analyze questions, which can substantially improve a student's scores on the MCAT. The methods defined in this part of the book are based on years of teaching students how to review for and take tests. The points described are presented in a clear, straightforward manner, and can immediately improve a student's test performance.

This guide provides the interested student with a reasoned and meticulous approach to the medical school admissions process. Starting with the premedical years and leading up to the application to medical school, this book will provide the student with information that can be tailored to individual educational experiences and personalities. Used properly, this combination of practical advice and training can substantially increase a student's chances of gaining admission to medical school.

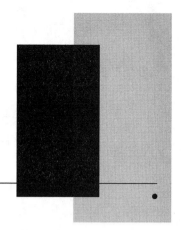

Acknowledgments

The authors wish to acknowledge the many individuals with whom we have worked over the years, who helped us formulate the concepts and insights that went into the formation of this volume. First among these are the professional staff with whom we worked at the University of California, Irvine, College of Medicine. These include former Deans Hutchinson Williams, Jon Sasson, Larry Silverberg, and Peter Coggan, as well as Susana Canett-Sandoval, Director of Educational and Community Affairs, Burt Winer, Counseling Psychologist, and Eileen Munoz, Administrative Assistant. We wish to give particular thanks to Leah Parker, Director of Admissions, for sharing with us her valuable insights on the medical school admission process.

We want to give special, posthumous, thanks to Ricardo Valdez whose unbounded enthusiasm and concern for students served as a lifelong inspiration to the both of us.

Thanks is also extended to the medical school staff and faculty at other institutions with whom we have interacted and from whom we have gained insights, too many to quantify. These include: Margie Beltran, Larry "Highpockets" Doyle, Roberto Piaz, Dr. Roberto Montoya, Gayle Currie, Mary Bush, Dr. Jacques Williams, Dr. Ron Garcia, Dr. Fernando Mendoza, Kathleen Healy, Saundra Kirk, Dr. Percy Russell, Patricia Pratt, Charolette Meyers, Dr. William Hooker, Althea Alexander, Beverly Guidry, Barbara Jarowsky, Dr. Anna C. Epps, and Dr. Alonzo Atencio.

Last but not least, we wish to acknowledge the professional editorial job performed by Karla Schroeder. We would also like to acknowledge the staff at Williams and Wilkins, particularly Melanie Cann, who served as our main contact throughout the editorial process.

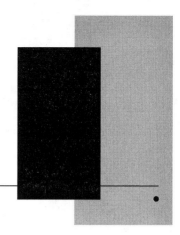

About the Authors

Kenneth Ibsen, Ph.D., worked as a teaching assistant with freshman medical students at the University of California, Los Angeles (UCLA) from 1956 to 1959, with residents in the Departments of Medicine and Surgery at UCLA from 1962 to 1965, and as a faculty member in the Department of Biochemistry at the University of California, Irvine, College of Medicine, (UCI-COM) from 1965 to 1993. While at UCI-COM he also served on the admission committee from 1968 to 1991 and as Assistant Dean of Student Affairs from 1986 to 1992. In 1993, Dr. Ibsen started working for National Medical School Review (NMSR), a nationally recognized test preparation company, as Director of Faculty Development. In this position he is responsible for the recruitment and training of medical school faculty to teach in programs that prepare medical students and physicians for the United States Medical Licensing Examinations (USMLE).

David A. Hacker, M.A., is a learning skills expert who worked as the Director of Medical Education at UCI-COM from 1985 to 1992. In this position he counseled, evaluated, conducted workshops and seminars and gave numerous presentations to high school, undergraduate, graduate, and medical students on a variety of topics related to the improvement of reading, writing, test-taking, time management, note-taking, comprehension, retention, and computer skills. He also developed, tested, and evaluated diagnostic and learning materials and methods for students preparing to take the MCAT and USMLE examinations. Since 1992, Mr. Hacker has performed similar duties as the Director of Medical Education for NMSR.

In addition, while at UCI-COM, Dr. Ibsen and Mr. Hacker co-directed several state and federally funded programs designed to assist disadvantaged premedical students in gaining admission to medical school. This included premedical and post-baccalaureate programs that provided advice to students on the medical school admission process and training in how to take the MCAT. Each of these programs was highly successful, with over 90% of the student participants eventually gaining admission to medical school. After leaving UCI-COM, Dr. Ibsen and Mr. Hacker also started a private MCAT preparation program for minority students that was partially funded by the state of California.

PART 1

Medical
School

CHAPTER 1

Is Medicine the Career for You?

- Advantages of a Medical Career
- Disadvantages of a Medical Career
- Minimal Requirements for Success in Medicine

The training needed to achieve an MD degree is extensive and demanding. Medicine is not for everyone; but if you can meet the demands of medical training and have clear reasons for pursuing a medical career, you will succeed as a medical student and later as a physician.

Each year, approximately 15,000 MD degrees are granted by United States medical schools.[1] The recipients of these degrees come from all walks of life and, although intelligent, usually are not geniuses. Many of them had the same doubts, fears, and questions that you have now. Not too far in the future, you too may earn an MD degree.

This book discusses the advantages and disadvantages of becoming a physician and provides guidelines for overcoming the obstacles.

● ● ●
ADVANTAGES OF A MEDICAL CAREER

Many people consider medicine an attractive career for a number of reasons.

Medicine is a socially significant, humanistic career. Few, if any, career choices offer as many advantages as medicine. Because medicine is one of

---

[1]Jolly P, Hudley DM: *AAMC Data Book—Statistical Information Related to Medical Education*. Association of American Medical Colleges, Washington, DC, 1995, Table B1.

the healing arts, many people regard physicians with awe and respect. Moreover, health care providers feel accomplishment and pride because they make a meaningful contribution to the lives of individuals and to society as a whole.

Physicians are the leaders of the health care team. The MD is normally considered to be at the top of the health professional hierarchy. A physician has the scientific training required to lead the team, make final patient care decisions, and assume responsibility for all aspects of patient care.

Medicine is a challenging career. As the member of the health care team with the highest level of scientific training, the physician is engaged in an educationally challenging career. Practicing physicians must keep abreast of scientific developments and understand their potential application to patient care. Because education is a constant factor in his life, a physician must enjoy learning.

Medicine offers a variety of professional experiences. Although caring for patients is often considered the primary task of a physician, many successful MDs make valuable contributions to society without seeing patients. The variety of potential experiences provides room for varied personality types in the profession. Experiences available to physicians include:

- *Primary care,* including family medicine, internal medicine, and pediatrics. Primary care physicians usually have the initial contact with patients, provide continuing comprehensive care, refer patients to other specialists when appropriate, coordinate the activities of the various members of a patient's health team, and advise patients on health issues.

- *Specialist,* including 24 subspecialties that range from anesthesiology to urology. Specialists undergo an additional 1–4 years of training, gaining in-depth knowledge of one field of medicine. They often see patients who have complex problems and are referred by a primary care physician. Specialists usually provide one-time, short-term care focused on a specific problem (e.g., a neurosurgeon performing surgery on a patient with a brain tumor).

- *Scientist.* Many physicians perform some type of research, but some perform extensive basic or clinical research in academic, governmental, or private business settings (e.g., performing clinical research on the effectiveness of a drug developed to control blood pressure). These physicians may work solely in the laboratory, without seeing patients, or may be indistinguishable from other physicians who work with patients in an office or a hospital.

- *Detective.* Forensic and epidemiology specialists work for governmental or international agencies, such as the United States Centers for Disease Control or the United Nations. These physicians often provide legal or expert testimony in congressional or international hearings on health issues. They also monitor the outbreak and spread of diseases across political or international borders. For example, they have been highly active in studying the spread of acquired immune deficiency syndrome (AIDS).

- *Pathologist.* All hospitals use the services of pathologists to identify disease states in patients. Most cities and counties also have pathologists who act as coroners. A coroner identifies the cause of death when a person dies under suspicious circumstances.

Medicine offers stable, but flexible employment. A physician may enter private or group practice, work for a state, or work for a health maintenance organization (HMO). As discussed in Chapter 5, current trends indicate that a greater proportion of physicians will become employees of HMOs or other organizations. However, now two-thirds of practicing physicians are self-employed, either as an individual or as part of a group.

A flexible work schedule is possible for physicians. Although some physicians work 20 hours a day, 7 days a week, most practitioners have more manageable schedules. An increasing number of practitioners now have part-time schedules. This flexibility is helpful for physicians with small children and those who are older, but not ready to retire.

Demand for physicians is high. Although the health industry is changing (see Chapter 5), it is likely that the demand for physicians will not diminish. Physicians normally do not face the layoffs that affect many other professional fields. However, because some specialties are becoming crowded, some physicians must redirect their practice into primary care or to different specialty areas.

Medicine offers good compensation. Remuneration for physicians will probably continue to be among the highest of the professions.

● ● ●
DISADVANTAGES OF A MEDICAL CAREER

Although a medical career offers many advantages, there are disadvantages as well. For some people, the disadvantages outweigh the advantages.

Entry is limited. Preparation for medical school requires hard work and provides no guarantee of success. In addition, increasing numbers of students apply for a static number of positions in medical school. For example, in 1995, more than 50,000 applicants competed for approximately 16,000 medical school positions.[2] Of the premedical students who apply to medical schools, 32% are accepted. Of the remaining 68%, some apply again and are accepted. Chapter 9 offers recommendations for students who are initially rejected.

The premedical program is difficult. Only approximately 30% of entering college freshmen who declare an interest in medicine ever apply to medical school. The rest are either discouraged by the competitive premedical program or realize that they lack the desire to perform the hard work involved. Other students find other interests more compelling. Still others are influenced by negative stereotypes promulgated by friends, instructors, and even academic advisors. These stereotypes often involve prejudices based on economic or ethnic conventions.

Some students do not complete medical school. The attrition rate in medical school is approximately 1.1%. Some students leave for social, psychological, or health reasons, and some fail academically.

A licensing examination is required. Although three licensing examinations are required, a very small percentage (1%–3%) of graduated physicians fail to become licensed.[3]

Medical school requires deferral of gratification. A consequence of the need to work hard and achieve academically is the concomitant need to defer gratification. Earning good grades requires attendance in class and studying with a clear head. Costs include tuition, books, and living expenses, and most students cannot afford luxuries, such as a new car. For students without an independent means of support, becoming a physician involves learning to defer gratification. However, many students are surprised to learn that deferring material acquisition leads to a deep sense of accomplishment. In addition, learning the principles

---

[2]Ibid.
[3]Barzansky B, Jonas HS, Etzel S: Educational programs in United States medical schools. *JAMA* 27(9):716–722, 1995.

of time management may lead to accomplishing more in less time.

The training period is long. The need to focus and work hard is not unique to a career in medicine. Success in any endeavor requires dedication; however, in medicine, the pressure never ceases. In addition to at least 4 years of undergraduate school, 4 years of medical school, and 3–7 years of residency training, the physician faces a lifelong challenge to stay abreast of new knowledge.

Psychological pressures are intense. Some physicians believe that they can accomplish more than is humanly possible. This belief is reflected in the high rates of suicide, among the highest of all professional groups; drug abuse, enhanced by increased temptation because of easy availability; and divorce among physicians.[4]

● ● ●
MINIMAL REQUIREMENTS FOR SUCCESS IN MEDICINE

The academic requirements for medical school admission are described in Chapter 6 and Appendix A. Most medical schools use two basic criteria to assess the intelligence and potential competence of applicants. These criteria are the grade point average (GPA) and the Medical College Admission Test (MCAT) score. Admission to medical school requires both good grades and a high MCAT score. Although earning As in college and a high score on the MCAT indicates academic competence, neither indicator provides a true measure of intelligence. For this reason, medical schools use noncognitive criteria as adjuncts to these measures (see Chapter 3).

A willingness to work hard and persevere is the single most important requirement for admission to medical school. Individuals who devote themselves fully to their studies, who use every opportunity to further their career goals, and who can focus their energies toward success are the ones who eventually are accepted into medical school.

---

[4]Martin, T: *How To Survive Medical School.* New York, Penguin Books, 1983.

CHAPTER 2

Preparing for Medical School

- High School—It's Not Too Early
- Choosing the Right College and Curriculum
- Prehealth and Premedical Clubs
- Summer Internships and Premedical Programs
- Premedical Advisors and Faculty
- Residency

HIGH SCHOOL—IT'S NOT TOO EARLY

Most students consider college the beginning of their premedical career. However, students who are seriously thinking about entering medicine can use their high school years to good advantage. For example, during the school year, a high school student can work as a volunteer in a hospital or a nursing home, work at a community health fair, or spend time observing the staff in a physician's office. Although these experiences are limited, they can help a student to determine whether medicine is the career for her and can also provide valuable contacts. During the summer, students may work in a hospital, nursing home, or physician's office.

Many local colleges and universities offer summer programs designed to give high school students exposure to college-level science and mathematics, and some have a medical orientation. *Table 2–1* lists some programs available to high school students. In addition to the programs listed, most major universities offer preadmission or high school programs.

High school offers students the opportunity to sharpen their study and test-taking skills. Students who want to study medicine should take a full load of academically challenging courses, including all of the mathematics courses that the school offers. Students can also prepare for college by taking advanced placement classes; reading; joining one or

●●●●

TABLE 2-1. High School and College Preparation Programs

Program	Description and Eligibility	Stipend	Time	Application Deadline
Summer Readiness Program San Joaquin Delta College Elliot Chambers, EdD 5151 Pacific Avenue Stockton, CA 95207 (209) 474-5672	Guidance and English courses; field trips; open to students with 12 college units	$400 to eligible students	6 weeks	Mid-May
Minority Research Apprentice Program MHSSPREP Student Services 13-154 CHS University of California, Los Angeles School of Medicine Los Angeles, CA 90024-1720 (310) 825-3575	Exposure to research and medicine; courses in math, critical thinking, and information processing; open to Los Angeles county minority high school students 16 years or older	None	6 weeks	April 1
Early Academic Outreach Program Bilal Shabazz, PhD Student Academic Programs University of California, San Francisco 145 Irving Street, Box 0943 San Francisco, CA 94143 (415) 476-4373	1 complete day at each University of California, San Francisco, school: dentistry, graduate, medicine, nursing, and pharmacy; applicants must be in an early academic outreach program at University of California, Berkeley, Davis, or Santa Cruz	None	1 week	April 1
Minority Research Apprentice Program Sandra Kirk Special Admission Support Programs University of California, San Diego, School of Medicine Medical Teaching Facility Room 162 9500 Gillman Drive La Jolla, CA 92093-0621 (619) 534-4170	Research with faculty, 5 days/week, 7 hours/day; research paper; lectures; field trips; open to San Diego area high school seniors who are United States citizens or permanent residents	Employed by the university	8 weeks	May 30
College Preparatory Program Anna Curtin or Boake Plessy, PhD University of Connecticut Health Center Office of Minority Student Affairs Farmington, CT 06030-3920 (203) 679-3483/4	27 hours formal lecture and laboratory time; covers college-level basic science, study, and test-taking skills; open to high school seniors and first- and second-year college students; applicants must submit transcripts and two recommendations	$800 and room and board	8 weeks	Mid-April
Headlands Indian Health Careers Summer Program Tom Hardy University of Oklahoma Headlands Indian Health BSEB, Room 200 PO Box 26901 Oklahoma City, OK 73126 (405) 271-2250	Miniblock courses (e.g., lecture, laboratory work, and tutorials) in mathematics, chemistry, physics, biology, and communication skills; prominent Native American health professional lecturers; open to Native American high school seniors and first-year college students with a 2.5 GPA	$350 stipend, $200 scholarship, and expenses; 4 semester credits, limited housing and travel expenses provided	8 weeks	Mid-March
Project Prepare Leslie Howard, PA University of Southern California School of Medicine 1975 Zonal Avenue KAM B-29 Los Angeles, CA 90033 (213) 342-1328	5-day program that introduces participants to the physician assistant's profession; includes afternoon visits to the hospital; open to high school seniors	None	1 week	May 1

Data from *Health Pathways,* Volume 17 #2, Fall, 1994.
GPA = grade point average.

more academically oriented clubs, particularly health-related clubs; participating in student government; and participating in community outreach programs. Although career-oriented activities are important, high school students need time for leisure activities, such as sports and hobbies.

Many high schools offer students the opportunity to earn college credit for advanced placement courses taken at local colleges. Earning college credit in high school gives students more time to explore other options while in college. Some students also earn college credits through the College-Level Examination Program (CLEP). For more information about this program, write or call:

CLEP
PO Box 6600
Princeton, NJ 08541-6600
(609)951-1026

Some medical schools provisionally admit high school seniors or first- or second-year college students. These programs guarantee admission to the medical school if the student maintains prescribed academic standards. The record of a student's performance in high school determines whether he is accepted into one of these programs. *Table 2–2* lists combined baccalaureate–medical degree programs. The primary advantage of entering one of these programs is that the student has assurance that he will obtain a medical degree if he meets the stated provisions. These provisions usually include maintaining a specified minimum grade point average (GPA). Some programs also reduce the total time required to earn a medical degree.

● ● ● ●
CHOOSING THE RIGHT COLLEGE AND CURRICULUM

The conventional route for entering medical school is to matriculate at a 4-year college or university and then to apply to medical school as graduation nears. Other students become interested in studying medicine after taking a health or science course or after graduating and working in another field. Students who complete their studies in a nonmedical field must return to college to complete their premedical requirements. A student's choice of college can affect the likelihood of acceptance to medical school. For instance, undergraduate campuses that have an affiliated medical school often matriculate more of their students at the affiliated medical school. Graduates of prestigious colleges, those that rank among the top 100 schools nationwide, are usually more successful at gaining admission than are students from less highly ranked colleges. Another reason for this trend is that top students often attend top-ranked colleges.

A student who wants to pursue a medical education should attend the best possible college. To prepare to enter a highly ranked school, students should do their best in high school classes and prepare thoroughly to achieve a high Scholastic Aptitude Test (SAT) score. They should apply to all of the top colleges in their state and 10 or 15 out-of-state schools. Although attending a top college or university may offer students advantages, it is important to remember that there are hundreds of accredited colleges and universities that successfully prepare students for medical school.

When choosing a college, talk to high school advisors and faculty, particularly science instructors; obtain catalogues of courses and schedules of classes; visit cam-

TABLE 2-2. Combined Baccalaureate–Medical Degree Programs

State	Medical School	Selection Level	Residency Requirements	Undergraduate School	Address for Inquiries
Alabama	University of South Alabama College of Medicine	High school seniors	None	University of South Alabama	Office of Admissions University of South Alabama Administration Building 182 Mobile, AL 36688 (800) 872-5247
California	University of California, Los Angeles, School of Medicine	High school seniors	None	University of California, Riverside	Student Affairs Division of Biomedical Science University of California, Riverside Riverside, CA 92521 (909) 787-4333
California	University of Southern California School of Medicine	High school seniors	None	University of Southern California	Office of College Academic Services College of Letters, Arts, and Sciences University of Southern California Los Angeles, CA 90089-0152 (213) 740-5930
District of Columbia	Howard University College of Medicine	High school seniors or first-year college students	None	Howard University	Center for Preprofessional Education PO Box 473 Administration Building Howard University Washington, DC 20059
Florida	University of Miami School of Medicine	High school seniors	Florida	University of Miami	Office of Admissions University of Miami PO Box 248025 Coral Gables, FL 33124 (305) 284-4323
Illinois	Northwestern University Medical School	High school seniors	None	Northwestern University	Office of Admissions Northwestern University 1801 Hinman Avenue Evanston, IL 60204 (708) 491-7271
Illinois	Finch University of Health Sciences Chicago Medical School	High school seniors	United States citizens or permanent residents	Illinois Institute of Technology	Director of Admissions BS/MD Program 10 West 33rd Street Chicago, IL 60616 (312) 567-3025 or (800) 448-2329
Louisiana	Louisiana State University School of Medicine, New Orleans	High school seniors	Limited to students from 4 local high schools	Louisiana State University	Office of Admissions Louisiana State University School of Medicine 1901 Perdido Street New Orleans, LA 70112 (504) 568-6262
Louisiana	Louisiana State University School of Medicine, Shreveport	High school seniors	Residents of Louisiana	Louisiana State University	Office of Admissions Louisiana State University School of Medicine PO Box 33932 Shreveport, LA 71130
Massachusetts	Boston University School of Medicine	Before college	None	Boston University	Associate Director of Admissions Boston University 121 Bay State Road Boston, MA 02215 (617) 353-2330
Michigan	University of Michigan Medical School	High school seniors	None	University of Michigan	Inteflex Program 5113 Medical Science I Building, Wing C University of Michigan Ann Arbor, MI 48109 (313) 764-9534
Michigan	Michigan State University College of Human Medicine	High school	None	Michigan State University	College of Human Medicine Office of Admissions A-239 Life Sciences Michigan State University East Lansing, MI 48824 (517) 353-9620

TABLE 2-2. Combined Baccalaureate–Medical Degree Programs *(Continued)*

Missouri	University of Missouri, Kansas City, School of Medicine	Before college	None	University of Missouri, Kansas City	Council on Selection University of Missouri, Kansas City School of Medicine 2111 Holmes Kansas City, MO 64108 (816) 235-1870
New Jersey	New Jersey Medical School	High school seniors	United States citizens or permanent residents	Boston University Drew University Montclair State College New Jersey Institute of Technology Stevens Institute of Technology Richard Stockton College of New Jersey Trenton State College	Office of Admissions C653 MSB UMDNJ-New Jersey Medical School 185 South Orange Avenue Newark, NJ 07103 (201) 982-4631
New Jersey	Robert Wood Johnson Medical School	Sophomores at Rutgers University	None	Rutgers University	Bachelor/MD Program Nelson Biology Laboratory Rutgers University Box 1059 Piscataway, NJ 08855 (908) 932-5270
New York	State University of New York, Brooklyn, College of Medicine	High school seniors	None	Brooklyn College	Director of Admissions 1602 James Hall Brooklyn College Brooklyn, NY 11210 (718) 951-5044
New York	New York University School of Medicine	High school seniors	None	New York University	Admissions Office New York University College of Arts and Sciences 22 Washington Square West Room 904, Main Building New York, NY 10003 (201) 998-4500
New York	Albany Medical College	High school seniors	None	Rensselaer Polytechnical Institute	Admissions Counselor Rensselaer Polytechnical Institute Troy, NY 12180 (518) 276-6216
New York	Albany Medical College	High school seniors	None	Siena College	Office of Admissions Siena College Route 9 Loudenville, NY 12211 (518) 783-2423
New York	Albany Medical College	High school seniors	None	Union College	Associate Dean of Admissions Union College Schenectady, NY 12308 (518) 388-6112
New York	University of Rochester School of Medicine and Dentistry	High school seniors	None	University of Rochester	Rochester Early Medical Scholars University of Rochester Undergraduate Admission Meliora Hall Rochester, NY 14627 (716) 275-3221
New York	All seven public medical school campuses	High school seniors	Residents of New York state	City College of New York	Sophie Davis School of Biomedical Education City University of New York Office of Admissions 138th Street and Convent Avenue New York, NY 10031 (212) 650-7700
Ohio	Case Western Reserve University School of Medicine	High school seniors	None	Case Western Reserve University	Office of Undergraduate Admissions Case Western Reserve University Cleveland, OH 44106 (216) 368-4450
Ohio	Northeastern Ohio University	High school seniors	None	Youngstown State University Kent State University	Associate Director of Admissions Northeastern Ohio University

(Table continued on the following page)

11

TABLE 2-2. Combined Baccalaureate-Medical Degree Programs *(Continued)*

	College of Medicine			University of Akron	College of Medicine 4209 State Route 44, PO Box 95 Rootstown, OH 44272 (216) 325-2511
Pennsylvania	Medical College of Pennsylvania-Hahnemann University	High school seniors	None	Gannon University	BS/MD Program Gannon University Office of Admissions University Square Erie, PA 16541 1 (800) GANNON-U
Pennsylvania	Medical College of Pennsylvania-Hahnemann University	High school seniors	None	Lehigh University	Office of Admissions 27 Memorial Drive West Lehigh University Bethlehem, PA 18105 (215) 758-3100
Pennsylvania	Medical College of Pennsylvania-Hahnemann University	High school seniors	None	Villanova University	Office of Admissions Villanova University Villanova, PA 19085 1 (800) 338-7927
Pennsylvania	Jefferson Medical College	High school seniors	None	Pennsylvania State University	Undergraduate Admissions 201 Shields Building Box 3000 Pennsylvania State University University Park, PA 16802 (814) 865-5471
Rhode Island	Brown University School of Medicine	High school seniors	None	Brown University	Program in Liberal Medical Education Office Brown University Box G-A134 Providence, RI 02912 (401) 863-2450
Tennessee	James H. Quillen College of Medicine	High school seniors	None	East Tennessee State University	Executive Associate Dean of Academic Affairs James H. Quillen College of Medicine East Tennessee State University Office of Academic Affairs PO Box 70,571 Johnson City, TN 37614 (615) 929-6327
Wisconsin	University of Wisconsin Medical School, Madison	High school seniors	Residents of Wisconsin	University of Wisconsin, Madison	Medical Scholars Program University of Wisconsin Medical School 1300 University Avenue Madison, WI 53706 (608) 263-7561

Data from Association of American Medical Colleges: *Medical School Admissions Requirements, 1996–1997,* 46th ed. Washington, DC, 1995.

puses and talk with students and prehealth advisors; and solicit the opinions of medical professionals. Factors to consider include:

Academic status. The school must be accredited and offer the courses required for acceptance to medical school. In addition, the school should have:

- a strong science department and adequate laboratory facilities

- a broad offering of courses to provide a good liberal arts background as well as a scientific education

- a number of premedical students each year who are accepted to medical school

- a viable prehealth advisory program

- a reputation for academic excellence
- a reputation for having a concerned teaching faculty

Cost. Financial worries can adversely affect college performance. For example, the need to work while attending school can lower a student's GPA. To save money, some students spend 1 or 2 years at a community or junior college, choose a state college instead of an out-of-state school, select a public school rather than a private one, or attend a local school and commute. Any of these approaches may require a compromise in the choice of a school. Although the ideal situation is to earn As at an institution recognized for its high academic standards, earning an A at a less prestigious college is better than earning a C or less at a prestigious school.

Comfort level. For example, a student who led a relatively sheltered life during high school probably should not move far away and live on the campus of a large, impersonal university. This student might prefer a smaller, more intimate college or a university that is close enough to home to permit weekend visits. For many students, it is advantageous to choose a school at which many students have similar cultural and social values. On the other hand, a student who has traveled extensively or who has friends or acquaintances of various backgrounds would likely feel comfortable at a large university that offers a diverse environment.

● ● ● ●
PREHEALTH AND PREMEDICAL CLUBS

Most colleges with a strong science program have prehealth or premedical clubs. These student-led groups usually have a faculty or staff advisor and sponsor informational, educational, and social activities. Students who want to study medicine should participate in these groups. These activities provide a chance to showcase leadership and organizational abilities and also may lead to health-related volunteer or employment opportunities.

● ● ● ●
SUMMER INTERNSHIPS AND PREMEDICAL PROGRAMS *(Table 2–3)*

Many medical schools and colleges with health or science programs offer summer programs designed to provide students with additional experience in health careers. These programs often provide students with an opportunity to meet medical school staff and faculty and are typically available to recent high school graduates or first- or second-year college students. Campus premedical or health advisors have information about these programs.

Most of these programs are competitive, and students should request an application at least 2–3 months before the deadline. These programs usually require a specific GPA, completion of certain science courses, and letters of recommendation from faculty.

TABLE 2–3. Summer Internships and Premedical Programs

Program	Description	Eligibility	Deadline
Honors Premedical Program Demetrium Pearson, EdD Senior Associate Dean Office of Admissions Baylor College of Medicine One Baylor Plaza Houston, TX 77030 (800) 633-6445	Participate in laboratory and clinical research with an MD or PhD mentor; counseling and MCAT preparation; 6 weeks long	Minority students with 1 year college or postbaccalaureate students; overall GPA > 2.75, science GPA > 3.0, SAT > 950, or ACT > 15	Early March
College Phase Summer Program Velma G. Watts, PhD Office of Minority Affairs Bowman Gray School of Medicine Medical Center Boulevard Winston-Salem, NC 27157-1037 (919) 716-4201	Residential program at several colleges in North Carolina; reinforces science and reading study skills in preparation for prehealth curriculum; 4 weeks long; stipend and limited travel paid	Disadvantaged college students interested in medicine or allied health; GPA > 2.5 or SAT > 800	March 1
Upper Level Premed Institute Velma G. Watts, PhD Office of Minority Affairs Bowman Gray School of Medicine Medical Center Boulevard Winston-Salem, NC 27157-1037 (919) 716-4201	Classes in science, writing, and MCAT preparation; mock admissions inter-view; 6 weeks long; stipend and limited travel paid	Disadvantaged junior or senior college students; science GPA > 2.5	March 1
Summer Science Program Robert Thomas, PhD Science Education Center, Building 438 Brookhaven National Laboratory Upton, Long Island, NY 11973 (516) 282-4503	Research training in a science area, working with staff; 10 weeks long, June to August; Stipend $225/week; limited travel paid; housing provided	Rising seniors with a B average or higher and a science major	Late January
Health Careers Enhancement Program for Minorities Rubens J. Pamies, MD Associate Dean for Academic Affairs Case Western Reserve University, School of Medicine 10900 Euclid Avenue Cleveland, OH 44106-4920 (216) 368-2212	Lectures, laboratory experience, counseling, drill in test-taking for the MCAT; 6 weeks long; stipend, housing, meals, and travel allowance provided	Underrepresented minorities	Mid-March
Summer Research Fellowship Program for Minority Premeds Bruce Ballard MD, Associate Dean Cornell University Medical College 1300 York Avenue, D-119 New York, NY 10021 (212) 746-1057	Laboratory or clinical research, lectures, discussions with physicians, hospital observation, and counseling; 7 weeks long; stipend of $120/week, free housing, and some travel support	Rising seniors with a B average or higher; premedical advisor recommendation, written essay, and transcript required	March 1
Summer Health Careers Advanced Enrichment Program Georgiana Aboko-Cole, PhD Center for Preprofessional Education Box 473, Administrative Building Howard University Washington, DC 20059 (202) 806-7231/2/3	Review of fundamental science principles; preparation for professional school examinations (DAT, MCAT, PCAT); mid-June to late July; no cost for program, tuition, housing, or meals; limited transportation paid	Disadvantaged students; GPA > 2.7; juniors and seniors must have completed basic science require-ments; two letters of recommendation needed	Late April

TABLE 2–3. Summer Internships and Premedical Programs *(Continued)*

Minority Summer Research Program Margaret Daniels Tyler MIT Summer Research Program Graduate School Office, Room 3-138 Massachusetts Institute of Technology Cambridge, MA 02139-4307 (617) 253-4869	Research laboratory experience; seminars; financial aid and graduate admissions counseling; 10 weeks long	Minority students who have completed 2 years of college; GPA > 3.0	February 1
Summer Scholars Program Pat Gyi, Director Ohio University, College of Osteopathic Medicine Student and College Relations Office 207 Grosvenor Hall Athens, OH 45701 (614) 593-2183	Anatomy, biochemistry, laboratory observation, principles of osteopathic medicine, study strategies, and seminars; financial aid and admissions counseling; room, board, and travel expenses paid	Minority students with at least 1 year of chemistry and biology; preference to rising seniors, postbaccalaureate students, and nontraditional students; two letters of recommendation needed	March 1
Pre-Entry Program Martha Suscheston MEDPATH 1072 Graves Hall Ohio State University, College of Medicine Columbus, OH 43210 (614) 292-3161	Lecture and laboratory experience in the basic sciences; test-taking and learning strategies and critical thinking; 6 weeks long; housing available; some stipends; fee-waiver program	Minority students who have been accepted to a medical school	June 1
HCOP Summer Academic Program Cynthia Lewis, PhD San Diego State University College of Sciences, LA 204 San Diego CA 92187-0277 (619) 594-4793	Precalculus, preparative general chemistry, and English; 7 weeks long; stipend and housing provided	Must complete education at San Diego State University in predental, premedical, preveterinarian, or pre-physician's assistant work	Mid-March
HCOP Summer Enrichment Program Herlisa Hamp, Coordinator San Jose State University College of Applied Science and Arts One Washington Square San Jose, CA 95192-0049 (408) 924-2911/2936	Participants meet with community health workers; preparation courses in biostatistics, health, physiology, writing, epidemiology, computers, and survival skills; 6 weeks long	Minority students who are matriculating at San Jose State University and have sophomore or junior status	May 1
Bridge to Medicine Summer Program for Minority/Disadvantaged College Students Thomas Bosquez, Coordinator Texas A&M University Health Center College of Medicine Office of Student Affairs and Admissions 106 Reynolds Medical Building College Station, TX 77843-1114 (409) 862-4065	Basic sciences, reading, writing, and study skills; full Kaplan MCAT preparation course; clinical preceptorships, counseling, and mock interviews; 6 weeks long; meals and lodging provided; no travel allowance	Minority or disadvantaged students with GPA > 2.8 and >60 hours undergraduate course work, including 8 hours of biology, organic chemistry, and physics, and 3 hours of mathematics	March 1
Summer Research Program for Undergraduate Minority Students Cathy Samson Tufts University Sackler School of Graduate Biomedical Science 136 Harrison Avenue Boston, MA 02111 (617) 956-6767	Laboratory research, seminars, field trips, symposia, and workshops on medical and graduate school admissions; 12 weeks long; stipend support, housing, and travel funds available	Minority students; transcript, two letters of recommendation, and application required	Mid-March

(Table continued on the following page)

TABLE 2-3. Summer Internships and Premedical Programs *(Continued)*

Summer Reinforcement and Enrichment Anna Cherrie Epps, PhD, Director Associate Dean for Student Services Office of MEDREP and Student Services Tulane University Medical Center 1430 Tulane Avenue SL40 New Orleans, LA 70112 (504) 588-5327	Basic sciences, clinical research, preceptorships, interviews, and counseling; 8 weeks long; stipend and shared apartments provided	Disadvantaged students with at least 2 years of college science; also premedical, postbaccalaureate, and unclassified graduate students	March 1
Summer Undergradaute Research Program in Science and Engineering Judy Sauer, SURPRISE Crocker Nuclear Laboratory University of California, Davis Davis, CA 95616 (916) 752-1460	Full-time laboratory work, research discussions, and written and oral reports as part of a research group; 8 weeks long; stipend of $2000 and room, board, and transportation; 5 units credit	Women and minority or disadvantaged students	March 1
Summer Academic Study Program Renée J. Maldonado, SASP Coordinator University of California, Davis, School of Medicine Office of Minority Affairs Davis, CA 95616 (916) 752-4808	Biology, chemistry, mathematics, reading, and writing skills; computer laboratory, study, and test-taking skills; anatomy and histology laboratories; AMCAS and MCAT; 6 weeks long; stipend, meals, and partial housing provided	Minority or disadvantaged students who are enrolled in a northern California campus; rising sophomore or junior; GPA > 2.0; personal statement and recommendations needed	Mid-February
Summer Premedical Program Eileen Muñoz Office of Educationalal and Community Programs University of California, Irvine, College of Medicine Irvine, CA 92717 (714) 824-8930	Physics, chemistry, molecular biology, clinical experiences, weekly rounds, learning skills, writing, and leadership skills; AMCAS; 6 weeks long; room, books, and didactic materials included	Rising minority second- or third-year college students	March 1
Summer Preentry Program Eileen Muñoz Office of Educational and Community Programs University of California, Irvine, College of Medicine Irvine, CA 92717 (714) 824-8930	Introduction to medical school courses; 6 weeks long; room, books, and didactic materials included	Disadvantaged students who have been accepted to a medical school	March 1
Pre-Medical Enrichment Program Raymond Prado, Director of UCLA PREP Office of Student Support Services 13-154 CHS UCLA School of Medicine Los Angeles, CA 90024-1720 (310) 825-3575	Tier 1: Problem solving, small group problem-based learning, clinical preceptorships, counseling, and networking; Tier 2: Similar to tier 1, plus MCAT preparation; 8 weeks long; stipend if student must travel >50 miles; materials and supplies provided	Tier 1: 1 year college chemistry; Tier 2: Minimum of 1 year college chemistry, biology, and mathematics, and two quarters physics; GPA > 2.5; transcripts, recommendations, and essay required	March 31
Summer Enrichment Program Kay Adams, MPH, Director University of California, Los Angeles, School of Public Health 41-240 CHS Los Angeles, CA 90024-1772 (310) 825-7449	Biology, mathematics, writing, test-taking, and study skills development; counseling; hands-on biomedical research; tutorials; 8 weeks long; room and board if needed	Minority students; rising seniors with an interest in public health or a health-related career	April 1

Summer Research Training Program for Undergraduate Minority Students Audrey Knowlton UCSF Graduate Division Summer Research Training Program University of California, San Francisco 513 Parnassus, S-140, Box 0404 San Francisco, CA 94143-0404 (415) 476-8134	Direct participation in research of senior faculty members; weekly research seminars; oral presentations; 10 weeks long; stipend, housing, health coverage, and some travel allowances	Minority students are encouraged to apply; students who have finished their junior year are preferred	February 1
Summer Premedical Enrichment Program Debbie Zorn University of Cincinnati, College of Medicine Office of Student Affairs and Admissions 231 Bethesda Avenue Cincinnati, OH 45267-0552	REACH Program: Comprehensive research, education, and experiences in cardiovascular, pulmonary, and hematologic sciences; 9 weeks long; stipend, housing, books, and up to $400 for travel provided; MARC/MBRS Scholars: Research experience, developmental seminars, admission workshops, and research symposium; 8 weeks long; stipend, housing, meals, travel allowances, and books provided	REACH: Minority undergraduate, graduate, or health professional students; transcripts, two letters of recommendation, and personal statement required; MARC/MBRS: Minority undergraduate students currently enrolled in a MARC or MBRS program; transcripts, one letter of recommendation, and personal statement required	March 15
Medical/Dental Preparatory Program Anna Curtin or Boake Plessy, PhD University of Connecticut Health Center Office of Minority Student Affairs Farmington, CT 60303-3920 (203) 679-3483/4	120 hours basic medical science; 60 hours MCAT or DAT preparation; interaction with clinical preceptors; 8 weeks long; stipend of $1000; room and board	Minority or disadvantaged juniors and seniors; preprofessional graduates; transcripts and two letters of recommendation required	Mid-April
College Preparatory Program Anna Curtin or Boake Plessy, PhD University of Connecticut Health Center Office of Minority Student Affairs Farmington, CT 60303-3920 (203) 679-3483/4	27 hours formal lecture and laboratory experience; college-level basic science; study and test-taking skills; 8 weeks long; stipend of $800; room and board	High school seniors and first- and second-year college students; transcripts and two letters of recommendation required	Mid-April
Summer Research Fellowship Program Anna Curtin or Boake Plessy, PhD University of Connecticut Health Center Office of Minority Student Affairs Farmington, CT 60303-3920 (203) 679-3483/4	Faculty-sponsored programs; 30 hours/week research and 10 hours/week clinical and experimental experience; 12 weeks long; stipend $1500; room and board	College juniors with biology and organic chemistry courses; SAT/ACT or MCAT/DAT scores (if available), transcripts, and two letters of recommendation required	Early February
Summer Enrichment Program Barbara Barlow Associate for Student Affairs University of Iowa, College of Medicine 124 Medicine Administration Building Iowa City, IA 52242-1101 (319) 335-8056	One medical science course for credit, plus noncredit instruction in other basic science courses, study and test-taking skills, time management, and personal development;	All matriculants in the entering class at the University of Iowa, College of Medicine	May 1

(Table continued on the following page)

	8 weeks long; covers tuition, living expenses, and books, if need is established		
Summer Enrichment Program Gladys Rodriguez-Parker, Director University of Massachusetts Medical Center Office of Minority Affairs 55 Lake Avenue North Worcester, MA 01655	Daily seminars on minority health issues, study skills, MCAT, AMCAS, and financial aid; 4 weeks long; stipend	Minority or disadvantaged students with at least 30 hours of college credit and 8 hours organic chemistry; limited to Massachusetts residents	March 1
General Chemistry and Precalculus or Calculus Program; Organic Chemistry and Precalculus or Calculus Program; Summer Biology Program; Summer Physics Program Michael Michlin, PhD 515 Delaware Street SE 1-125 Moos Tower University of Minnesota Minneapolis, MN 55455 (612) 624-5904	Noncredit intensive study with supplementary instruction; each program is 5 weeks long; stipend, limited housing, and travel provided	Minority students	April 30
Summer Premedical Academic Enrichment Program Ella M. Webster, MD Assistant Dean of Student Affairs M-27 Scaife Hall University of Pittsburgh, School of Medicine Pittsburgh, PA 15261 (412) 648-8987	Level 1: Enhances learning in science, written English, and speaking; interaction with physicians and medical students; Level 2: Provides exposure to medical school and hospital environments; test and interview training; 8 weeks long	Minority students; Level 1 first-year college students; Level 2 for other college students; two letters of recommendation and written essay required	Mid-March
Summer Research Fellowship (SURF) Mildred J. Reynolds Director, Minority Affairs University of Rochester, School of	Research with a faculty member, weekly seminars, and observation of clinical activities; June 5	Minority students with at least 2 years of college and a science background	Early January

●●●●

PREMEDICAL ADVISORS AND FACULTY

Premedical advisors are available to help students who are interested in health-related careers. At large schools, these advisors are generally staff, with or without a faculty adjunct. However, in some schools, faculty members play this role. Advisors often attend national or regional meetings of the Association of American Medical Colleges (AAMC) to remain abreast of developments in medical education. Although premedical advisors can provide valuable information and advice, students must gather information from a variety of sources, carefully consider the options, and make their own decisions.

Students at schools with undergraduate research programs should participate in them. In addition to providing an educational experience, research allows students to become acquainted with a faculty member. In some cases, this faculty member becomes the student's personal faculty advisor.

TABLE 2–3. Summer Internships and Premedical Programs *(Continued)*

Medicine and Dentistry 601 Elmwood Avenue, Box 601 Rochester, NY 14642 (716) 275-2175	to August 5; stipend of $150/week; $75 to MARC participants; free housing		
HEPP-Consortium for Health Professional Preparation Althea Alexander Assistant Dean of Minority Affairs University of Southern California, School of Medicine Office of Minority Affairs 1333 San Pablo Street MCH 51-C Los Angeles, CA 90033 (213) 342-1050	First year: College chemistry, biology, and mathematics; Second year: Physics, organic chemistry, and calculus; Third year: Clinicals, writing, medical ethics, and MCAT prepa- ration; Invited speakers discuss disciplines; question and answer sessions; 8 weeks long; no stipend; no expenses	First year is open to high school graduates; thereafter, participation is contingent on satis- factory progress	Mid-May
Medical Academic Advancement Program Moses Kwamena Woode, PhD Associate Dean of Academic Support Project Director, POSTBACC Program Office of Student Support University of Virginia, School of Medicine Box 446 Charlottesville, VA 22908 (804) 924-2189	Classes in biology, chemistry, physics, verbal reasoning, problem solving, stress management, and study skills; clinical lectures, mentoring, and counseling; 6 weeks long; housing paid out of stipend; maximum of $200 allowed for travel	Minimum of 1 year of college, including 3 hours biology, 6 hours chem- istry, and 3 hours physics; letter of recommendation required	May 1
Minority Medical Education Program Charlie Garcia, Director Minority Affairs Program, SM-22 University of Washington, School of Medicine Seattle, WA 98195 (206) 685-2489	Structured clinical research laboratory experience; MD/PhD mentor; biology, mathematics, physics, and communication; counseling in selecting and applying to medical school; MCAT review; 6 weeks long; stipend, housing, and travel expenses	Minority students with at least 1 year of college; two letters of recommendation and transcripts required	March 1

Data from *Health Pathways,* Volume 17 #2, Fall, 1994 and Association of American Medical Colleges: *Information on Schools Offering Post-Baccalaureate Premedical Programs,* March 1995.

ACT = American College Testing (assessment); *AMCAS* = American Medical College Application Service; *DAT* = Dental Admissions Test; *GPA* = grade point average; *MARC* = Minority Access to Research Careers; *MCAT* = Medical College Admission Test; *PCAT* = Podiatry College Admissions Test; *SAT* = Scholastic Aptitude Test.

RESIDENCY

Most states provide financial support for one or more medical schools. Those that do not support a specific school often participate in a regional program that allows students from states without a medical school to attend medical school in another state, with all or most of the funding paid for by the student's home state. States that fund their own schools usually offer preferred admission to residents of their own state or region. For this reason, on a per capita basis, more places are available for residents of some states than for residents of others. Therefore, a student might choose an undergraduate college and establish residency in a state with a greater number of first-year medical school openings per number of college graduates. However, it is important to weigh the possible advantages of this approach against the disadvantages in terms of academic standing and personal satisfaction. Further, residency requirements vary, and attending college in a given state may not establish residency.

Table 2–4 lists the numbers and percentages for admission of students within their home state. The percentage of students who are accepted by a medical school in their place of residence varies from 3.7% in the District of Columbia to 45.5% in Puerto Rico and West Virginia. This information, coupled with the fact that most state schools accept primarily in-state students, shows that where a student lives can have a significant effect on her chances of entering medical school.

● ● ● ●

TABLE 2-4. Admission of Applicants by State of Origin

State	Total Positions Available in State	Number of In-State Applicants	In-State Students Admitted	Percentage of Applicants Admitted to Medical School in Their Home State or in a Reserved Place
Alabama	232	588	210	35.7
Alaska*	10	63	10	16.4
Arizona	96	471	96	20.3
Arkansas	144	377	144	38.5
California	1026	5442	766	14.1
Colorado	130	602	117	19.6
Connecticut	180	522	172	33.3
District of Columbia	451	109	4	3.7
Delaware†	0	88	0	0
Florida	350	1597	324	20.4
Georgia	383	1054	315	30.3
Hawaii	56	189	54	28.6
Idaho*	15	128	15	9.5
Illinois	1062	2259	747	33.3
Indiana	283	702	265	38.5
Iowa	175	357	149	41.2
Kansas	175	433	164	38.5
Kentucky	234	573	208	37.0
Louisiana	423	929	301	32.2
Maine†	0	100	0	0
Maryland	289	1121	160	14.2
Massachusetts	586	982	216	22.0
Michigan	537	1617	450	27.0
Minnesota	277	767	243	31.2

TABLE 2–4. Admission of Applicants by State of Origin *(Continued)*

Mississippi	100	367	100	27.0
Missouri	456	622	234	38.5
Montana*	20	83	20	23.8
Nebraska	245	376	146	26.3
Nevada	52	146	48	33.3
New York	1711	3613	1056	29.4
New Mexico	73	267	67	25.0
New Jersey	312	1496	276	18.5
New Hampshire	87	91	9	9.9
North Dakota	58	151	42	27.7
North Carolina	440	995	299	30.3
Ohio	852	1907	702	37.0
Oklahoma	148	463	137	29.4
Oregon	92	388	80	20.8
Pennsylvania	1096	1772	554	31.2
Puerto Rico	221	475	217	45.5
Rhode Island	66	99	7	7.1
South Carolina	214	558	188	34.5
South Dakota	51	103	39	38.5
Tennessee	406	773	241	31.2
Texas	1123	2754	1022	37.0
Utah	100	380	77	20.4
Vermont	95	78	33	41.2
Virginia	408	1220	261	21.3
Washington‡	165	637	105	16.5
West Virginia	137	272	125	45.5
Wisconsin	346	651	225	34.5
Wyoming†	0	35	0	0
Total§	16,307	42,808	. . .	38.0

Data from Jolly P, Hudley DM: *AAMC Data Book—Statistical Information Related to Medical Education.* Association of American Medical Colleges, Washington, DC, 1995.
*Available positions reduced by those reserved for residents from Idaho, Alaska, and Montana.
†No medical school and no places reserved in other states.
‡Positions are reserved through the University of Washington School of Medicine.
§Includes foreign students and students from U.S. territories not identified elsewhere in this table.

CHAPTER 3

Medical Education: What's It All About?

- Traditional Versus Alternative Curricula
- MD Versus MD/PhD Programs
- Medical Licensing Examinations
- Specialties and Residencies
- Continuing Medical Education

● ● ●
TRADITIONAL VERSUS ALTERNATIVE CURRICULA

Although the United States has 124 medical schools, the experience of most medical students is similar. Medical school is designed to give students a broad, general education. Twenty years ago, a student could complete medical school, spend 1 year in an internship, pass the licensing board examinations, and practice medicine. Today, even physicians in family practice spend an additional 3 years in a postgraduate residency program before they can enter a practice.

Because medical school is followed by 3–7 years of specialty training, the goal of medical education is to give all students, regardless of their area of specialization, sufficient training in the basic and clinical sciences to allow them to enter a specialty. Which medical school a student attends is of little importance. However, lately much consideration has been given to the differences in medical school curricula. Three basic curricula are followed in the United States.

In the most common type, the traditional curriculum, the first 2 years focus on the basic sciences (with each discipline taught independently), and the last 2 years cover the clinical sciences. This model, based on recommendations made more than 80 years ago, assumes that all of the science content basic to medicine could be presented and learned during a 2-year period. This assumption is no longer true. The traditional curriculum uses faculty lectures as the main teaching modality and presents material from each discipline separately. This type of curriculum is best for students who learn well in a highly structured format, primarily by listening to lectures.

In the 1940s, the organ system approach was introduced to facilitate learning by integrating basic and clinical science information. This approach did not solve the information overload problem, however. The organ-centered curriculum requires students to integrate a large volume of information encompassing many topics. This information may be taught in lectures or small group seminars. Students who learn best by assimilating information from a variety of sources do well in this type of setting.

The newest type of curriculum is the problem-solving, or case management, curriculum, introduced by McMaster College of Medicine in the 1960s. The problem-solving curriculum uses simulations to involve students in the practice of medicine from the first day of medical school, and students are often responsible for their own training experience. Faculty are facilitators, not lecturers. Each department develops a set of learning objectives that each student must master. Students who master these objectives pass the course; those who cannot must repeat the course until they meet the criteria. This approach requires self-discipline and is not ideal for all students.

Most schools use a hybrid of the various approaches. An applicant who is accepted at several schools should investigate the dominant type of curriculum at each school and determine which best fits his needs. For example, a student who dislikes lectures should choose a school with a problem-solving approach. However, a student who does not like to solve problems, but prefers to have others provide the correct answer, may prefer a school that has a traditional, lecture-driven, discipline-oriented curriculum.

Students who have only one or two choices should not despair. All American medical schools are good, and all produce students who are among the finest in the world. Any American medical school provides a solid, substantial education.

● ● ●
MD VERSUS MD/PhD PROGRAMS

Over the next 10 years, approximately 40% of the physicians who teach in medical schools will retire. This situation will lead to a great demand for academic clinicians. To fill this gap, 116 medical schools offer some form of combined MD/PhD program. In addition, 33 schools offer combined MD and master's degree programs, 35 offer combined MD and master of public health programs, 10 offer combined MD and doctor of jurisprudence programs, and 13 offer combined MD and MBA programs.[1] The structure of these programs varies widely; however, all share some components. Most MD/PhD programs are 6 years long: 4 years for medical school and 2 years to complete the PhD requirements. Most students complete the first 2 years of medical school, spend 2 years performing research for the PhD degree, finish the last 2 years of medical school, and then write a dissertation. After graduation, many students apply for fellowships to perform more research, rather than immediately entering a residency program. After 2 or 3 years of research, these students usually begin a residency program.

Pursuing a combined MD/PhD degree is not for everyone. The time commitment and the difficulty involved in studying medicine and mastering laboratory techniques are daunting for many students. However, definite rewards are associated

[1] Barzansky B, Jonas, HS, Etzel S: Educational programs in United States medical schools. *JAMA* 27(9): 716–722, 1995.

with this process. Most graduate research students receive funding to help pay for medical school. Often, these students work in laboratories or facilities that conduct some of the most advanced research in the world. Finally, this path often leads to a career as an academic physician in a medical school.

●●●
MEDICAL LICENSING EXAMINATIONS

All physicians in the United States must pass a series of examinations for licensure. Until 1991, students could take a number of examinations: the National Board of Medical Examiners (NBME) Parts I, II, and III, which most United States medical students took; the Federation Licensing Examination (FLEX), which some United States medical students and most foreign graduates took; and the Educational Commission for Foreign Medical Graduates Examination (ECFMGE), which foreign medical graduates took before they could take the FLEX. The ECFMGE, which certified that foreign graduates had the minimum knowledge needed to apply for a residency position, included an English proficiency section.

In 1991, the NBME examination was renamed the United States Medical Licensing Examination (USMLE). This examination has three parts: Steps 1, 2, and 3. This change reflected a significant change in the way that the content was tested. Questions integrated the subjects tested, whereas previously, questions were written independently of each other. For example, on the new test, a question could test a student's knowledge of biochemistry, microbiology, and pathology. An additional change to the basic science test, Step 1, was to add more clinically relevant questions.

The USMLE also changed the way in which physicians are licensed. Starting in 1991, the other licensing examinations were gradually eliminated, and today, only the USMLE is used. To be licensed in the United States, a physician must complete all three steps of the USMLE.

Each test is administered twice a year, and each test takes 2 days to complete. The subjects covered on Step 1 are anatomy, biochemistry, behavioral science, microbiology, pathology, pharmacology, and physiology. The subjects covered on Step 2 are medicine, obstetrics and gynecology, pediatrics, psychiatry, preventive and public health, and surgery. Step 3 covers the same subject areas as Step 2, but requires more problem-solving and diagnostic skills. The average United States medical student usually takes Step 1 after the second year of medical school, Step 2 in the third or fourth year, and Step 3 after 1 year of residency. Today, some foreign medical students follow the same schedule as United States students, but many take the tests after they complete medical school. This requirement puts foreign students at a disadvantage because when they are tested, the material that they studied in medical school is several years old and may be out of date.

Graduates of United States medical schools usually take the Step 3 examination after the first year of postgraduate training, or residency, but approximately 10 states allow candidates to take the Step 3 examination before they start a residency program. Because only approximately 50% of foreign graduates are accepted into a residency program on the first attempt, as opposed to nearly 95% of United States graduates, some foreign graduates take the examination early because they hope their scores will be high enough to benefit them when they apply for a residency program.

All three USMLE tests are created by the NBME. The Step 1 and Step 2 examinations are administered by the NBME at medical schools for United States students and by the Educational Commission for Foreign Graduates at other sites nationwide and internationally for foreign graduates. The Step 3 examination is administered by the medical licensing board of each state at sites within the state.

The tests are scored by the NBME, but each state determines the passing score. Medical school graduates who pass all three examinations are granted a license to practice in the state in which they applied.

● ● ●
SPECIALTIES AND RESIDENCIES

Not long ago, physicians in the United States primarily trained to be general practitioners. However, with the explosion of medical knowledge over the last 20 years, medical specialties have emerged. A specialty is a separate field of medicine that requires an additional 3–7 years of training after medical school. There are approximately 24 specialties.

Obtaining a desirable residency at a prestigious hospital is the goal of most medical students. The ideal residency offers excellent academic training from clinicians who are leaders in the field as well as optimal access to and responsibility for patients. Achieving this goal requires a combination of good grades, good recommendations, and good USMLE scores. For this reason, in addition to serving as an examination for licensure, the USMLE can help a student to fulfill her career goals.

There are more residency positions than graduating seniors from United States medical schools. For example, in 1993, there were 15,466 graduates and 20,598 residency positions.[2] However, not every graduate of a United States medical school is guaranteed the residency of his choice, or even the discipline of his choice. The excess residency slots are filled by graduates of foreign medical schools and osteopathic schools.

The matching of residency positions with students is performed by the National Residency Matching Program (NRMP). Each student rank orders residency programs that she is interested in. The programs then select, again in rank order, the students that they want. The NRMP then matches the two lists. In 1993, a total of 82% of the residency positions were filled, 63.2% of these by students from United States medical schools.[3]

Unmatched students then "scramble" for the remaining residency slots. This is generally done with the assistance of the Dean of Student Affairs at the medical school they attend. Usually on the third Monday in March, 2 days before the matched students are informed that they did match, the schools receive a list of their unmatched students and of the residency programs still available. At noon [Eastern Standard Time (EST)] the following day, all schools in the country are free to start calling the available residency programs to place their unmatched students. By the end of the day, almost all United States students are matched. At noon (EST) on Wednesday, medical students learn which residency program they will enter. Most schools announce residency assignments, but no distinction is made between students matched via the NRMP and those matched by scrambling. Very few students are left without a residency program that is acceptable to them.

After completing residency training and passing a specialty board examination, physicians receive board certification in their specialty. Although board certification is not mandated, this additional credential is often required by hospitals before a physician can admit patients. One reason is the goal of hospitals to provide the best possible care; another is insurance liability. The assumption is that a well-trained physician is not likely to be involved in malpractice suits. In addition to the pressure exerted by hospitals, other physicians are more likely to refer patients to board-certified physicians. Without those referrals, many physicians would not have enough patients to survive economically.

---

[2] Jolly P, Hudley DM: *AAMC Data Book—Statistical Information Related to Medical Education.* Association of American Medical Colleges, Washington, DC, 1995, Table F3.
[3] Ibid.

• • •
CONTINUING MEDICAL EDUCATION

The field of medicine is changing rapidly. Because of new biologic science discoveries, new medical techniques, and new drugs or new uses for old ones, in addition to the sheer volume of scientific knowledge, no one can predict the future of medicine. Instead, physicians must specialize to reduce the amount of information that they must master. However, even completing a 7-year residency training program in surgery does not guarantee that a physician knows everything about the field. Therefore, each specialty has developed a process of continuing medical education (CME).

Although the time required for CME credit each year varies by specialty, each physician must undergo a minimum amount of training to maintain board certification. Physicians who lose their certification may be required to take both a specialty examination and a licensing examination. The licensing examination may be required by the state.

CME ensures a more informed, more competent medical profession. It also shows that any student of medicine must, in some ways, remain a student. Only those who are willing to commit to being lifelong learners should consider medicine as a career.

CHAPTER 4

What Is Medical School Like?

- Hard Work and Enlightenment
- The Basic Science Years
- The Clinical Science Years

HARD WORK AND ENLIGHTENMENT

Medical school may seem daunting. The necessary sacrifices take a toll, both financially and emotionally. The average student emerges from medical school with $50,000–$80,000 in debt. Equally important, the average age of a graduating medical student approaches 30 years, and several years of residency training still lie ahead.

Despite its demands, medical school can be a rewarding experience. Most medical faculty, even with their busy schedules, are happy to answer questions, help students to complete the many required forms, or offer advice. Many patients gladly undergo tests or answer the questions that students must ask as part of clinical training.

THE BASIC SCIENCE YEARS

In the United States, most medical schools require 4 years of basic and clinical science education. Despite curriculum revisions in the last decade, the first 2 years of medical school are still largely devoted to the basic sciences, including anatomy, neuroanatomy and neurophysiology, behavioral science, biochemistry, microbiology, histology, pathology, pharmacology, and physiology. Some first- and second-year medical students also have clinical experience and patient contact. The basic science years are composed of rigorous, time-consuming classes; all-night study sessions; and frequent comprehensive tests. During the first and second years of medical school, students spend approximately 35 hours per week in class. When combined with after-class study hours, the average student studies approximately 100 hours per week, leaving only about 70 hours for everything else. For this reason, time management is an important skill for medical students, who must manage their limited time to accommodate sleep and other needs, such as social activities.

During the first year, each class develops its own character. Many students form close bonds, and lifelong friendships are often established. After they adjust to the demands of medical school, most students look back on this time nostalgically.

At the end of the second year, most medical students have a 1- to 6-week break to prepare for the United States Medical Licensing Examination (USMLE) Step 1. Approximately 70%–80% of medical schools require students to pass this test before they progress to the third year of medical school. At several schools, students are subject to dismissal, dependent on faculty review, if they do not pass this examination after three attempts.

● ● ●
THE CLINICAL SCIENCE YEARS

The transition from the study of basic science to the clinical years is difficult. The class is divided into segments, and students rotate through clerkships in small groups. Only rarely does the class meet as a whole.

Clerkships are composed of the major clinical sciences: medicine, surgery, pediatrics, psychiatry, obstetrics and gynecology, and family medicine. Each clerkship has several rotations. For example, a student who is serving in a medicine clerkship may rotate through cardiology, general medicine, and nephrology. During this period, students learn to handle responsibility for patients and are involved, as part of a medical team, in making decisions. The time demands of each clerkship, or clinical rotation, may be double those of the first and second years of medical school. For example, a student may be on call for 72-hour periods while serving in a surgery or obstetrics rotation. Most students are exhilirated by these experiences but some have trouble coping. For students who need help, counseling is usually available through the Student Affairs office.

Near the end of the third year, or at the beginning of the fourth year of medical school, students are given 1 or 2 weeks to prepare to take the USMLE Step 2. Only 15%–20% of medical schools require students to pass this examination before they finish the fourth year, although most schools require students to take the examination.

In the fourth year of medical school, students are given large blocks of time, 10–15 weeks, to complete elective courses at other schools as well as at their school, and for vacation. Students choose their elective courses, which usually last 1–10 weeks. Many students use these courses to audition, or preapply, for residency positions. Students also use their vacation time to complete audition electives and apply for residency programs.

CHAPTER 5

The Future of Medicine

As the twenty-first century approaches, changes in the demographics of the United States, coupled with the likelihood of further modifications in the way in which physicians are reimbursed for their services, will have a significant effect on the practice of medicine. The United States population is aging. By 2020, approximately 18% of Americans, or 52 million people, will be 65 years old or older. Today, that figure is only 12%, or 32 million people.[1] Because older patients often have chronic conditions that require a great expenditure of dollars, a substantial increase is expected in both the number of patients requiring medical care and the cost of providing that care.

As the major providers of funding for medical care, the United States government and private insurers have a strong interest in containing the cost of care. In 1965, government at all levels and private insurers paid $21 billion for health care. By 1993, that figure had increased to $694.7 billion. At this rate of expansion, total health care costs are expected to increase to $1.7 trillion by the year 2000.[2] This figure is roughly 18% of the gross national product (GNP), making the health care industry the single largest force in the economy of the United States. In the past, to help curb these increases, the federal government imposed cost controls to restrict the fees charged by physicians and hospitals. Diagnosis-

---

[1] The Council on Long-Range Planning and Development of the American Medical Association: The future of medical practice—a 95-page report. American Medical Association. June, 1994.
[2] Ibid.

related groups (DRGs) were developed in the 1980s to limit the amount that hospitals or physicians nationwide can charge for similar procedures or treatments. For example, the government established a dollar figure that could be charged for an appendectomy. If the actual cost of the operation was lower than this figure, the hospital or physician could keep the difference; however, if the actual cost was higher, the physician or hospital would lose that amount.

Initially, this new reimbursement process rewarded hospitals or health organizations that moved patients into and out of the hospital rapidly. As hospital stays decreased, hospital profits increased. However, as a result of this change, physicians felt pressured to release patients quickly. In some cases, they were restricted in the number and types of diagnostic tests that they could prescribe. The resulting ethical dilemma is unresolved and will continue to affect physicians and patients as pressure increases to further limit health care costs. Future trends are likely to include:

Fewer physicians in private practice. Because of their success in managing hospital stays and their emphasis on preventive medicine, a growing number of health maintenance organizations (HMOs) are beginning to dominate the employment of physicians. HMOs enroll subscribers through businesses, who pay a monthly fee for all services. This situation creates a strong incentive for physicians to limit hospital admissions, referrals to specialists, and even the amount of time spent with each patient. In response to the restrictions imposed by HMOs, and with the goal of maintaining their autonomy, physicians have formed independent practice associations (IPAs) and preferred provider organizations (PPOs). Physicians who belong to an IPA see patients in their own offices. Because they are prepaid an annual fee, however, they are concerned with reducing costs. PPOs negotiate with health insurers to provide health care to plan members. Each patient chooses a physician from the practitioners who belong to the PPO.

Because of the development of these groups, more physicians will be employees of HMOs, IPAs, or PPOs. In 1992, approximately 30% of practicing physicians worked as employees, 30% worked in group practices, and the rest worked in solo practices. In contrast, in 1965, only approximately 10% of physicians worked as employees or in group practices.

Although these changes may lead to lower pay for physicians, they also bring benefits. These organizations relieve practitioners of the burden of establishing a practice, overseeing staff, and managing the day-to-day operation of a business. They also provide more opportunities for part-time employment, potentially reducing the stress associated with practicing medicine. Finally, although salaries may decrease, physicians will always be needed, and employment at a comfortable salary will still be the rule.

Continued cost containment. The government, private companies, and health insurers will continue to attempt to reduce the cost of medicine, with or without the approval of physicians and hospitals. It is probable that the defeat of health care reform in 1995 was not brought about by the desire to maintain the status quo, but rather was a reaction to the managed care emphasis of the legislation. There continues to be a consensus among all participants that health care costs are spiraling out of control and that unless changes are made, the cost of health care will destroy the economy, bankrupt the government, or both.

The form that these cost controls take will affect the role of the physician. For example, the number and types of tests that a physician can order may be limited, or some patients may be denied treatment based on their age or ability to pay. Many people worry that the quality of care will suffer in the name of cost savings unless an equable means of providing appropriate health care is found. Physicians must play an important part in these changes. They must speak out for patient rights and help to make the difficult choices required when the finite resources of medicine face the continuing need for medical care.

Increased need for primary care physicians. As the patient population ages and the emphasis on controlling costs increases, the role of the physician in preventing illness will grow. The first line in the prevention of illness will be primary care practitioners in family medicine, internal medicine, and pediatrics. Increasingly, primary care practitioners will advise patients about disease prevention and health promotion. Because this preventive care can significantly decrease health care costs, more resources may be allocated to these practitioners.

CHAPTER 6

Requirements for Admission to Medical School

- Criteria For Acceptance
- Required College Courses
- Required GPA
- Required MCAT Scores
- Volunteer or Work Experience
- Other Achievements
- Relative Importance of Academic Criteria and Personal Skills
- Skewed Admission Standards

CRITERIA FOR ACCEPTANCE

Medical schools publish their requirements for admission (see Appendix A), but a literal reading of the requirements may mislead an average premedical student. Some students with a high grade point average (GPA) or high Medical College Admission Test (MCAT) scores may not be admitted, whereas less academically gifted students may receive multiple acceptances. The reasons for the variability in acceptance criteria are related to the diverse skills needed by physicians and the importance of the medical profession to society. Medicine is both a science and an art. Therefore, a brilliant student with a sterling academic record may not be a successful medical candidate because she lacks the skills needed to work with people. Conversely, a personable student whose scientific background is weak would not likely be a successful diagnostician. Most admission committees look for candidates with both academic ability and social skills.

Medical schools seek to admit students of both sexes and all ethnic backgrounds. In addition, some schools are interested in admitting students who will become primary care practitioners; others, specialists; and still others, academicians. This training preference may be mandated by the state or may grow out of the tradition of a specific school. The desire to produce graduates who will enter a specific type of postgraduate training affects the preferred characteristics of candidates. For instance, a school that sees its primary mission as preparing students to enter academic medicine will probably prefer candidates who show a talent for research or teaching.

Because of this heterogeneity, medical school offers opportunities for candidates with a variety of personalities and skills. If they are motivated, even nontraditional students, such as those who majored in history, probably can study medicine.

REQUIRED COLLEGE COURSES

Most applicants to medical school major in biology or bioscience. All medical schools provide a list of the specific courses required for admission. In general, candidates need a bachelor's degree that includes 1 year of inorganic chemistry, 1 year of organic chemistry, 1 year of general biology, 1 year of general physics, 1 year of English, and 1 semester of calculus. A detailed description of the minimal requirements of each medical school is provided in Appendix A.

Although the average student accepted to medical school is a recent college graduate with a degree in biology or another science field, medical schools are also looking for students with training in other fields. Appendix B shows that a significant percentage of students with nontraditional majors also are accepted to medical school. For instance, although only 1.3% of all medical school positions were filled by history majors, more than 50% of students with history majors were eventually accepted to medical school. Clearly, students with nontraditional degrees can be highly competitive, provided they have also completed the core science courses required for admission to medical school.

REQUIRED GPA

No specific GPA is needed for admission to medical school. Medical schools evaluate GPA as one of many factors. However, most schools establish minimum GPA and MCAT scores for admission. In 1994, the mean GPA for admitted students was 3.46 (on a 4.0 scale) and 53% had a GPA of 3.5 or greater.[1] Conversely, 47% had GPAs below 3.5. The lowest noted was 2.8.[2] Thus, although a high GPA usually improves the chance of acceptance, some students are accepted despite a lower GPA. Mitigating factors include:

An increasing GPA. Many schools overlook prior poor grades if more recent work shows ability. This improvement may occur during a student's junior and senior years or during postbaccalaureate work. Graduate programs are evaluated by criteria other than GPA.

Higher GPA in selected courses. If a student has poor grades in social science or humanities courses and better grades in hard science courses (e.g., biology, chemistry), this difference may weigh in the student's favor.

[1] Barzansky B, Jonas HS, Etzel S: Educational programs in United States medical schools. *JAMA* 27(9):716–722, 1995.
[2] Association of American Medical Colleges: *Medical School Admission Requirements 1996–1997,* 46th ed. Washington, DC, 1995.

● ● ●
REQUIRED MCAT SCORES

For students accepted into medical school in 1994, the average overall MCAT score, combining the verbal reasoning and physical and biologic science sections, was 9.4. The range of scores for 66% of accepted students was 7.6–11.4. Thus, although the goal is to achieve a double-digit score, some students enter medical school with a lower score. High MCAT scores can compensate for a low GPA, although most schools prefer to see evidence of academic achievement in undergraduate courses. Thus, high MCAT scores and 1 year of good science grades may be a winning combination.

● ● ●
VOLUNTEER OR WORK EXPERIENCE

Because acceptance into medical school almost guarantees graduation with an MD degree, most medical schools encourage potential students to gain exposure to medicine before they are accepted. Medical schools want students to have a realistic understanding of the demands, frustrations, and rewards of a medical career. Potential students should seek clinical experience, in either a volunteer or paid capacity. For most students, opportunities of this type are limited; however, the more intense and focused this type of experience is, the more value it has. The ideal situation is to secure a position assisting staff in an emergency room at a large hospital. This environment provides the greatest exposure to the types of clinical problems that physicians encounter. By volunteering early (i.e., during high school), students have a better chance of working into a more meaningful position.

Students who cannot find a position in a hospital or another clinical setting can obtain experience in other ways. Examples include organizing a blood drive, participating in a community health fair, and planning an antismoking campaign.

● ● ●
OTHER ACHIEVEMENTS

Other academic achievements, such as earning an advanced degree or writing a scholarly article, are viewed favorably. Awards for excellence in scholarship are also valued, even if the work is not done in a medical or bioscience field. For example, recognition for athletic achievements, musical ability, or contributions to the arts can highlight a student's special talents. Participating in campus government, student affairs, and social and service clubs also can showcase a student's abilities.

Research experience is valuable, and many schools substitute research experience for clinical exposure. Committed participation in a research project provides training in critical thinking and offers students an opportunity to develop relationships with academic professionals. As a rule, you should start your research effort in the summer after your sophomore year. By this time, you have completed sufficient basic science work to be able to make a meaningful contribution to the laboratory with which you are associated.

● ● ●
RELATIVE IMPORTANCE OF ACADEMIC CRITERIA AND PERSONAL SKILLS

The importance of specific activities and skills varies from school to school and area to area. For example, a student who has a high GPA and high MCAT scores but shows no evidence of social commitment will be considered less favorably than a similar student who has a clear record of dealing effectively with people. At the other extreme, a person who has extensive clinical exposure (e.g., practice as a nurse) has a good chance of being accepted, even with an average GPA and average MCAT scores, compared with another candidate with a higher GPA and higher MCAT scores, but no clinical experience.

Personal characteristics associated with success in medical school include fortitude, compassion, leadership, and the ability to think and act quickly.

● ● ●
SKEWED ADMISSION STANDARDS

Many students wonder whether admission standards are ever skewed to benefit or reject certain members of society. As few as 25 years ago, there were barriers against the admission of women, minorities, and anyone over 26 years of age. On the other hand, deans were routinely provided with a percentage of admission positions to be used at their discretion. These positions generally went to children of alumni or individuals whose families could make sizable donations to the school or alumni association. In recent years, this type of patronage has become the exception rather than the rule, and gender, race, and age are no longer barriers to admission.

One might also wonder whether certain members of society are given unfair advantages with respect to admission. When considered globally with respect to the needs of society, the answer is no. Gender and age have little effect on admission standards. On the other hand, belonging to certain minority groups will provide some advantage with respect to admission. The Association of American Medical Colleges (AAMC) recognizes four groups of "underrepresented" minorities: African-Americans, Mexican-Americans, Native Americans, and mainland Puerto Ricans. These groups are underrepresented in two respects: the percent of health care providers is low in proportion to the percent of the toal population represented and these populations are, as a whole, underserved. That is , there tends to be a shortage of physicians and health care facilities in the ghettos, barrios, and reservations where many members of these minority groups live. Several studies have shown that a significant number of physicians will serve the population with which they identify.[3]

The goal of the AAMC is to have 3000 underrepresented minorities accepted into United States medical schools by the year 2000. It is unlikely that this goal will be reached because only 1377 underrepresented minorities (8.8% of the total United States freshman class) were admitted in the 1994–95 class and the acceptance rates have actually declined since the class of 1989–90.[4]

Local population pressures also affect admission policies. For example, California needs more Hispanic and Asian physicians. Special consideration may also be given to certain groups depending on the needs of individual schools.

However, it must be emphasized that whereas special consideration may be given, no admission committee will admit any person that is thought to be underqualified. Moreover, any admitted student has to pass all of his medical school course work as well as the licensing examinations in order to practice.

---

[3] Association of American Medical Colleges: *Minority Students in Medical Education: Facts and Figures VII*. November, 1994.
[4] Ibid.

CHAPTER 7

How to Pay for Medical School

- The Cost of Medical School
- Sources of Funding
- Scholarships
- Ethnic and Religious Funds
- Military and Paramilitary Programs
- Parents with Military Service
- Private or Organizational Loans
- Loans to Graduating Students
- Research Awards
- Loans Through Medical School
- Loan Repayment Programs
- Institutional Funds

THE COST OF MEDICAL SCHOOL

A medical education is expensive. For the 1994–95 academic year, tuition and fees paid by first-year medical students averaged $8760 for residents and $19,362 for nonresidents at public medical schools, and $22,873 at private medical schools.[1] These figures do not include costs for books and materials, housing, food, or transportation. The tuition and fees for medical schools in the United States and Puerto Rico are listed in Appendix C.

SOURCES OF FUNDING

Students with financial needs can obtain aid through government or institutional loans or scholarships. The primary source of financial aid is loans. Approximately 72% of the expenses of the average student are met by such loans. The graduating class of 1994 had an average indebtedness of $63,434; some students graduate with $100,000 in debts.[2] The cost

---

[1] Association of American Medical Colleges: *Medical School Admissions Requirements, 1996–1997,* 46th ed. Washington, DC, 1995.
[2] Ibid.

of a medical education is an investment in the future, and each student must assess whether the return is worth the investment.

Loans are offered at relatively low interest rates, and payments are deferred until graduation. In addition, federal programs permit students to repay all or part of their debt through military or social service. Some states and counties have repayment programs that involve primary care service, usually in an underserved area. Many of these programs also pay a salary.

Despite the availability of loans and repayment programs, it is prudent to minimize total indebtedness. The next section of this chapter lists scholarships, awards, grants, and loans that are available to premedical and medical students. This information was verified in August 1995, but is subject to change. This list is not complete; for example, only county medical societies in California are included. Many county societies in other states also provide funds. Students can contact their local medical societies to determine whether they offer similar scholarships.

When requesting applications, students should provide as much information as possible (e.g., grade level, area of residence, academic year funds) and note whether they meet any special requirements [e.g., grade point average (GPA), nationality, organizational affiliation]. A self-addressed stamped envelope should be enclosed with the application.

Students who receive a scholarship from an organization should write a thank you letter. Most people like to have their acts of generosity acknowledged, and the simple step of thanking the donor helps to ensure that funding will continue.

The following are potential sources of funds:

Parent's employer. Some companies sponsor scholarship programs for children of their employees.

Union, employee organization, fraternity/sorority, veterans group, or other organization. Many organizations offer scholarships or educational loans to members and children of members.

Residency. Many scholarship programs are offered to residents of various cities, counties, or states.

Alumni groups. Some county medical societies, auxiliaries, or local hospital auxiliaries offer scholarships to alumni of certain high schools or colleges.

Religious groups. Many religious groups sponsor scholarship programs.

Ethnic group or sex. Some scholarships are targeted toward specific ethnic groups or offered to women.

Many of these funds offer small amounts of money ($300–$1000), but some students receive multiple scholarships. Many scholarships are available for 1 year and may be renewed.

●●●
SCHOLARSHIPS

Almanor Scholarship Fund
Offers scholarships to graduates of Chester High School in Plumas County, California.
Applications: Almanor Scholarship Fund, c/o Collins Pine Company, PO Box 796, Chester, CA 96020.

B'nai B'rith Hillel Foundation
Offers scholarships of as much as $1000/year to students who are residents of California or who are attending California medical schools. A GPA of 3.0 is required.

Deadline: June 1.
Applications: Request in March or April from B'nai B'rith Hillel Foundation Medical Scholarship Program, 900 Hilgard Avenue, Los Angeles, CA 90024; (213) 208-6639.

Caldwell-Pitts Scholarship
Offers awards to students from the Biggs, California, area who attended and graduated from Biggs High School. Based on need.
Applications: Principal, Biggs High School, PO Box 397, Biggs, CA 95917; (916) 968-5825.

Carolina Freight Carriers Corporation
Offers four scholarships of $1000/year, two to children or close relatives of employees and two scholarships to other students from the Carolina service area.
Deadline: April 15.
Applications: Scholarship Committee, Carolina Freight Carriers Corporation, PO Box 697, Cherryville, NC 28021.

Chinese-American Physicians Society
Offers scholarships of $500–$1000 to medical students based on financial need, academic achievement, and community service record. Special consideration is given to students from the San Francisco metropolitan area who are willing to return to the area to serve the Chinese community.
Deadline: October 10.
Applications: Scholarship Committee, Chinese-American Physicians Society, c/o Lawrence Ng, MD, Chair, Scholarship Committee, Chinese-American Physicians Society, 345 Ninth Street, Suite 204, Oakland, CA 94607-4206; Fax (510) 357-4363.

Collins (Joseph) Foundation
Offers scholarships of as much as $2500/year to medical students who have an interest in arts and letters or other cultural pursuits outside of medicine and who intend to specialize in neurology, psychiatry, or general practice. Only one application per year may be forwarded from each medical school.
Deadline: February 15 to the Financial Aid office.
Applications: Collins Foundation, One Chase Manhattan Plaza, New York, NY 10005.

Elks Foundation Scholarship Awards
Offers numerous scholarships based on scholarship, leadership, and financial need. Availability determined by local Elks lodge.
Deadline: February 1.
Applications: Contact the Secretary or Lodge Foundation Chairman of the local BPO Elks Lodge.

Foundation for Exceptional Children
Offers educational scholarships to handicapped and gifted youths.
Deadline: February 1.
Applications: Foundation for Exceptional Children, 1920 Association Drive, Reston, VA 22091.

Fresno-Madera Medical Society
Offers scholarships of as much as $1000 to medical students who have been residents of Fresno or Madera County for 1 year or longer. Need and scholastic achievement are considered. Funds cover tuition, laboratory fees, and books only.
Deadline: May 15 to the medical school Financial Aid office.
Applications: Fresno-Madera Medical Society, Scholarship Foundation, PO Box 311, Fresno, CA 93707; (209) 224-4224.

Groff (Frank and Louise) Foundation

Offers scholarships of $500–$1000/year to medical students who graduated from a public high school in Monmouth County, New Jersey. Based on need.
Deadline: April 1.
Applications: Susan Rechel, Educational Advisor, Frank and Louise Groff Foundation, 15 Floyd Wycoff Road, Morganville, NJ 07751.

International College of Surgeons

Offers scholarships of $1000 to senior medical students who are accepted for residency in a surgical specialty and want to study abroad.
Applications: International College of Surgeons, US Section Headquarters, 1516 North Lake Shore Drive, Chicago, IL 60610.

Irvine (Richard B.) MD Scholarship

Offers scholarships of $200–$800 to medical students who graduated from a high school within the Mt. Diablo Hospital District in Concord and Pleasant Hill, California.
Deadline: February.
Applications: Deborah Kolhede, Medical Staff Assistant, Mt. Diablo Hospital Medical Center, 2540 East Street, Concord, CA 94250; (415) 674-2359.

Lakewood Medical Center Foundation

Offers scholarships to medical students whose permanent residence is within the Lakewood Medical Center Foundation service area (Lakewood, Long Beach, Bellflower, Norwalk, Artesia, Hawaiian Gardens, Paramount, Compton, and Signal Hill) in Los Angeles County, California. Awards range from $250–$5000 and may be renewed.
Deadline: March 30.
Applications: Kay Koford, Public Relations Director, Lakewood Medical Center Foundation, 3700 East South Street, Lakewood, CA 90712; (310) 602-6777.

MAP-Readers Digest International Fellowship

Pays 75% of airfare costs for senior medical students, interns, and residents to complete an overseas elective in a rural or outlying foreign medical center. The minimum period for an externship is 8 weeks.
Deadline: Applications are considered annually in September and should be received in the MAP office by June 1.
Applications: MAP-RDIF Coordinator, MAP International, PO Box 215000, Brunswick, GA 31521-5000; (800) 225-8550.

Mortar Board National Foundation

Offers fellowships of $1500 to alumni Mortar Board Members pursuing graduate or professional study.
Deadline: January 31.
Applications: Mortar Board National Office, 1250 Chambers Road, Suite 170, Columbus, OH 43212; (800) 989-6261.

Ramona's Mexican Food Products

Offers scholarships to graduates of high schools in the East Los Angeles area (Roosevelt, Garfield, and Lincoln).
Applications: Ramona's Mexican Food Products, Inc., Scholarship Foundation, 13633 South Western Avenue, Gardena, CA 90249; (213) 323-1950, extension 247.

Redding Medical Center Foundation

Offers a scholarship of $1000 to a medical student who is a permanent resident of Shasta County, California. Consideration is given to students from the immediate

surrounding counties in the Redding Medical Center service area. Based on scholastic achievement and financial need, with preference given to students who intend to return to the Memorial Hospital Service area.
Deadline: April 1.
Applications: Katryne Young, Redding Medical Center 1100 Butte Street, Redding, CA 96001; (916) 244-5454.

Riverside County Physicians Memorial Foundation

Offers grants to medical students who are residents of Riverside County, California, and are accepted at an accredited medical school. Based on need.
Applications: Riverside County Medical Association, 3993 Jurupa Avenue, Riverside, CA 92506; Theresa Herra: (714) 686-3342.

Sacramento-El Dorado Medical Society

Offers four grants $1000 annually to students who graduated from a high school in Sacramento County or El Dorado County, California, and are attending an accredited American medical school.
Deadline: June 15.
Applications: Scholarship Secretary, Sacramento-El Dorado Medical Society, 5380 Elvas Avenue, Sacramento, CA 95819; (916) 452-2671.

San Pedro Peninsula Hospital Auxiliary Health Grant

Offers renewable scholarships of $600 to students attending a community college and scholarships of $1000 to students attending California State University or the University of California. Students must be in at least the second semester of work in a health career field. Applicants must be from the San Pedro Peninsula Hospital Service area (San Pedro, Palo Verdes Peninsula, Lomita, Harbor City, and Wilmington), but may attend a school outside of this area.
Deadline: November 15.
Applications: San Pedro Peninsula Hospital Auxiliary, 1300 West Seventh Street, San Pedro, CA 90732; (310) 832-3311.

Teagle Foundation

Offers scholarships of as much as $5000/year to children or wards of current, retired, or deceased employees of the Exxon Corporation and its operating units and affiliates.
Deadline: November 1.
Applications: Contact the Annuitant Affairs Office or the Employee Relations Department of the Exxon affiliate that employs the parent.

Two/Ten International Footwear Foundation

Offers scholarships of $200–$2000 to children of full-time employees (with at least 1 year of service) in the footwear, leather, and allied industries or to students who have worked at least 500 hours in these industries in the year before the scholarship is used.
Deadline: January 15.
Applications: Two/Ten Foundation Scholarship Program, 56 Main Street, Watertown, MA 02172; (617) 923-4500.

Whittier Hospital Volunteers Scholarship Program

Offers funds to college students in health-related fields whose permanent address is in the greater Whittier, California, area (Whittier, La Habra, La Mirada, Fullerton, Buena Park, Brea, Santa Fe Springs, Pico Rivera, Hacienda Heights, Rowland Heights, El Monte, and La Puente). Based on financial need. Applicants must have a GPA of at least 2.5.
Deadline: May 31.
Applications: Whittier Hospital Volunteer Health Career Scholarship Program, 15151 Janine Drive, Whittier, CA 90605; (310) 907-7318.

● ● ●
ETHNIC AND RELIGIOUS FUNDS

American Association of University Women
Offers as much as $9500 to support ethnic women pursuing an MD or a DO degree.
Deadline: December 15.
Applications: American Association of University Women Education Foundation, 1111 16th Street NW, Washington, DC; (202) 828-0600.

American Association of Japanese University Women
Offers scholarships of $1000 to female junior, senior, or graduate students attending a college or university in California. Preference is given to students with a potential for contributing significantly to cultural exchange between the United States and Japan.
Deadline: September 15.
Applications: Tomie Woolsey, 7419 Calico Trail, Orange, CA 92669.

Business and Professional Womens Career Advancement Scholarships
Offers awards of $500–$1000, funded by the New York Life Foundation, to women seeking advancement within a health career at the undergraduate level and awards of $2000, funded by the Wyeth-Ayerst Laboratories Scholarship, to women enrolled in full-time health care programs at the graduate level. Based on need. Applicants must be older than 25 years and within 2 years of graduation.
Deadline: Applications are considered between October 1 and April 1.
Applications: Scholarships/Loans, BPW Foundation, 2012 Massachusetts Avenue NW, Washington, DC 20036.

Carr (Vikki) Scholarship Foundation
Awards fellowships to residents of California or Texas who are 17–22 years old and are of Latino heritage.
Deadline: April 1.
Applications: Vikki Carr Scholarship Foundation, PO Box 5126, Beverly Hills, CA 90210, or PO Box 780968, San Antonio, TX 78278.

Forssgren Scholarships
Offers scholarships to full-blooded Native American students who are enrolled in a California college.
Applications: Forssgren Scholarships, c/o Pacific Trust Co., PO Box 1855, Santa Cruz, CA 95061; (408) 688-4700.

Gulbenkian (Calouste) Foundation
Awards scholarships of as much as $1600/year to students of Armenian origin, regardless of their legal nationality.
Deadline: July 15.
Applications: Calouste Gulbenkian Foundation, Department of Armenian Affairs, Avenida de Benna 45-A, 1093 Lisbon Codex, Portugal.

Hovorka (James and Helen) Endowment Fund
Offers scholarships to students of Czechoslovakian background who have completed 1 full year of full-time coursework at an accredited college or university and who need financial assistance to continue their education. Student loans of as much as $500/semester are also available.
Deadline: July 1.
Applications: Council of Higher Education, James and Helen Hovarka Endowment Fund, 8738 Washington Avenue, PO Box 136, Brookfield, IL 60513.

Indian Fellowship Program

Offers fellowships to students of Native American descent. Fellowships to cover tuition and fees are available for as long as 4 years. Stipends of $600/month and a dependency allowance of $90/month/dependent are also available. Based on financial need, academic background, evidence of potential success, and likelihood of service to others of Indian descent.

Deadline: February 6.

Applications: US Department of Education, Indian Fellowship Program, 400 Maryland Avenue SW, Room 2177, Mail Stop 6267, Washington, DC 20202; (202) 732-1887.

Indian Health Employees Scholarship Fund, Inc.

Offers scholarships to students of documented Native American descent who are entering a health care field. Priority consideration is given to students from the Dakotas and Minnesota.

Deadlines: January 1, June 1, and October 1.

Applications: Executive Secretary, Indian Health Employees Scholarship Fund, Inc., Federal Building, Room 215, Aberdeen SD 57401; (605) 226-7451.

Indian Health Service/Clinical Clerkships

Offers clinical clerkships of 2–8 weeks to third- and fourth-year medical students on a reservation or at an Indian Health Service facility. Availability of stipends, housing, and travel money varies from site to site.

Deadline: Varies.

Applications: Health Professions Support Branch, Indian Health Service, 5600 Fishers Lane, 6-39, Rockville, MD 20857; (301) 443-4242.

International Order of the King's Daughters and Sons, Inc.

The Health Center Scholarship program offers awards, usually of $1000, to second-year medical students. Preference is given to students with a Christian background.

Deadline: April 1.

Applications: Merle D. Raber, Health Careers Director, 602 East Chicago Road, Jonesville, MI 49250-9752.

Jackson (Agnes Jones) Scholarship

Offers awards to students who have been members of the National Association for the Advancement of Colored People (NAACP) for at least 1 year or are fully paid life members. Applicants must be younger than 25 years and from a financially needy background (i.e., family of four with an annual income of <$35,000) and must have a graduate GPA of 3.0 or an undergraduate GPA of 2.5.

Deadline: April 30.

Applications: Dr. Beverly P. Cole, Director of Education, National Office, NAACP, 4805 Mt. Hope Drive, Baltimore, MD 21215-3297; (301) 358-8900.

Kosciuszko Foundation

Offers scholarships and interest-free loans of varying amounts to medical students of Polish descent with evidence of identifying with the Polish community.

Deadline: March 1.

Applications: Grants Office, Kosciuszko Foundation, 15 East 65th Street, New York, NY 10021; (212) 734-2130.

Le Flore (Miss Louie) and Foremand (Mr. Grant) Scholarship

Offers scholarships of $100–$300 to students who are members of one of the Five Civilized Tribes of Oklahoma and are enrolled in a health-related curriculum.

Deadline: July 1.

Applications: Sarah Morgan, Financial Aid Office, Bacone College, Muskogee, OK 74403.

Lutheran Church Women Awards

Offers several scholarships, including some targeted toward health professionals and women of color, to women who are members of the Lutheran Church in America. Award amount is determined on an individual basis. The maximum award is $2000, and awards may be given for 2 consecutive years. Preference is given to women who have not completed their baccalaureate degree and who have had a significant interruption in their studies since high school.

Deadline: February 15.

Applications: Mailed after October 1. Women of the ELCA Scholarship, 8765 Higgins Road, Chicago, IL, 60631-4189; (312) 380-2730.

Maple Creek Willie Scholarship Fund

Offers scholarships of as much as $1250/year to California college students who are of Native American descent (at least one grandparent).

Deadline: July 1.

Applications: Mailed after May 1. Request from Maple Creek Willie Scholarship Selection Board, State Department of Education, 721 Capitol Mall, Room 205-DTP, Sacramento, CA 95814; (916) 322-9744.

Medellas Scholarship: Medical, Dental, Legal Ladies Society of Orange

Offers scholarships of $1000–$2000 to students of Chinese, Japanese, Korean, or Filipino descent who live in Orange County, California. Based on scholastic achievement, leadership, and character.

Deadline: December 31.

Applications: Mrs. Allan Yin, 277 Skylark Circle, Costa Mesa, CA 92626; 835-8806.

National Medical Fellowships (NMF), Inc.

Offers awards of $500–$6000 for first- and second-year medical school students who are black, Mexican American, Native American, or mainland Puerto Rican. Based on need.

Deadline: May 31 for reapplicants. August 31 for new matriculants. Students are encouraged to apply immediately after receiving their first medical school acceptance. Applications are available after January 1.

Applications: National Medical Fellowship, Inc., 110 West 31st Street, 8th Floor, New York, NY 10001; (212) 714-1007. Awards and fellowships include the following:

- **Fellowship Program in Academic Medicine—Bristol-Myers Squibb Co. Fellowship.**
  Offers 35 scholarships of $6000 to second- and third-year minority students who are enrolled in an accredited US medical school. Candidates are nominated by the dean.

- **Irving Graef Memorial Scholarship**
  Offers scholarships of $2000 to rising third-year minority medical students who received NMF assistance during the second year of medical school.

- **James H. Robinson, MD, Memorial Prizes in Surgery**
  Offers one scholarship of $500 to a minority student nominated by the dean and the chair of the surgery department.

- **Metropolitan Life Foundation Awards**
  Offers as many as 10 scholarships of $2500 to second- and third-year minority students who attend school or have a legal residence in cities designated by MetLife. Students are nominated by the dean.

- **William and Charlotte Cadbury Award**
  Offers a stipend of $2000 to one senior underrepresented student enrolled in a US medical school. Based on academic achievement. Students are nominated by the dean.

- **Franklin C. McLean Award**
  Offers an award of $3000 to a senior minority student enrolled in a US medical school. Based on academic achievements, leadership, and community service. Students are nominated by the dean.

- **Henry G. Holladay Awards**
  Offers five awards of $760 to African-American men who have been accepted at a United States medical school.

- **Aura E. Severinghaus Award**
  Offers stipend of $2000 to a minority student attending Columbia University College of Physicians and Surgeons.

- **Clinical Training Fellowship for Substance Abuse**
  Offers 10 awards of $5000 to second- and third-year minority students who have shown academic achievement and promise for a career in biomedical and clinical research, epidemiology, and health policy.

- **Ralph W. Ellison Prize**
  Offers one stipend of $500 to a graduating minority medical student. Applicants are nominated by the dean.

- **Gerber Prize for Excellence in Pediatrics**
  Offers one scholarship of $2000 to a senior minority student enrolled in an MD or DO program in Michigan. Based on excellence in pediatrics. Applicants are nominated by the deans and the chair of pediatrics and must have been accepted to a pediatric residency.

- **George Hill Memorial Scholarship**
  Offers one 4-year scholarship of $4000 to an African-American resident of Westchester County, New York, who has been accepted to a United States medical school. Based on need.

- **Slack Awards for Medical Journalism**
  In 1995, awarded three scholarships of $2500 to students with demonstrable skill in journalism. Based on academic achievement and leadership.

- **NMA Merit Scholarship**
  In 1995, awarded eight scholarships of $2500 to African-American medical students enrolled in accredited United States MD or DO programs. Based on academic achievement.

Navajo Nation Scholarship Assistance
Offers scholarships of $1000–$2500 to legally enrolled members of the Navajo tribe with one-fourth or more Native American blood.
Deadline: June 30 for fall, November 30 for winter/spring, and April 30 for summer.
Applications: Navajo Department of Higher Education, PO Drawer S, Window Rock, AZ 86515; (602) 871-5544.

Northern California Medical, Dental, Pharmaceutical Association
Offers scholarships of $500 to black medical students. Based on financial need and academic record.
Deadline: December 3.
Applications: NMDPA Scholarship Committee, 1238 Felton Street, San Francisco, CA 94134.

Osage Tribal Education Scholarships
Offers scholarships of $300–$1000 to students who are of Osage descent.
Deadline: July 1 for fall, December 31 for spring, and May 1 for summer.

Applications: Osage Tribal Education Committee, c/o Bureau of Indian Affairs, Oklahoma Area Education Office, 4149 Highline Boulevard, Suite 380, Oklahoma City, OK 73108.

Reformed Church in America/Minority Educational Scholarship

Offers grants to minority students who are members of a Reformed Church in America congregation.
Applications: Office of Human Resources, Reformed Church in America, 18th Floor, Room 1897, 475 Riverside Drive, New York, NY 10115.

Sierra Nevada Region Soroptimists

Offers grants of as much as $1000 to female medical students who are entering the third or fourth year of studies.
Deadline: February 28.
Applications: Liz Hiller, 2584 Butano Drive, Sacramento, CA 95821.

Wellesley College- M.A. Shackford Medical Fellowship

Offers an award of $3500 for the study of medicine to a female graduate of any American institution who intends to enter general practice.
Applications: Secretary to the Committee on Graduate Fellowships, Career Center, Wellesley College, 106 Central Street, Wellesley, MA 02181.

Sarah Perry Wood Medical Fellowship

Offers an award of $24,000 to alumnae of Wellesley College for the study of medicine.
Deadline: December 1.
Applications: Secretary to the Committee on Graduate Fellowships, Career Center, Wellesley College, 106 Central Street, Wellesley, MA 02181.

●●●
MILITARY AND PARAMILITARY PROGRAMS

Army National Guard

Contact the Army National Guard recruiter for information about the Student Loan Repayment program.

COSTEP

Offers paid externships of 31–120 days in the commissioned Corps of the Public Health Service to students who have completed 1 year of medical school. Transportation is paid to and from the location of the assignment, and students are paid at the level of a junior assistant health service officer (approximately $1580/month).
Deadline: October 1 for January–April assignments, February 1 for May–August, and May 1 for September–December.
Applications: COSTEP, Commissioned Personnel Operations Division, Parklawn Building, Room 4–25, 5600 Fishers Lane, Rockville, MD 20857; (415) 982-2400, extension 215.

National Health Service Corps

Offers a monthly stipend of $580 plus the cost of books, fees, and expenses. Service obligation of 1 year for each year of receipt of scholarship, with a minimum commitment of 2 years.
Applications: US Public Health Recruitment, 8201 Greensboro Drive, Suite 600, McLean, VA 22102; (301)443-4513.

Navy Officer Health Professions Scholarship Program (HPSP)
The Navy pays full tuition; fees; cost of books; expenses, except housing and meals; and a monthly stipend of at least $824 to physically qualified, matriculated students of an accredited medical or osteopathic school in the United States or Puerto Rico. Applicants must be 21–40 years old when commissioned. Training and service obligations are incurred. Contact the Navy recruiting office, or call 1-800-USA-NAVY. In Puerto Rico, call 1-800-872-6289.

US Air Force Medical Scholarship
Similar to the US Army program. Contact the United States Air Force Recruiting Service, Medical Recruiting Division, Rudolf Air Force Base, TX 78148.

US Army Medical Scholarship
Offers full tuition, cost of books, fees and reimbursables, a monthly stipend for 10.5 months, and full second lieutenant salary and allowances for 1.5 months to physically qualified, matriculated students at an accredited medical or osteopathic school in the United States or Puerto Rico. Training and service obligations are incurred. Contact the Army Medical Department (AMEDD), or call 1-800-USA-ARMY.

● ● ●
PARENTS WITH MILITARY SERVICE

Students with a parent who served in the Army, Navy, Marines, or Coast Guard are eligible for educational assistance programs. Most programs are available only to dependents of military personnel whose death or permanent total disability is related to military service, but some programs are also available to children of retired personnel. For Army service, request DA Pamphlet 352-2 from the Department of the Army, HQDA DAAG-ED, Alexandria, VA 22331. For Navy, Marines, or Coast Guard service, contact Commander, Naval Military Personnel Command, NMPC-121D, Navy Dependent, Washington, DC 20370.

California Veterans Dependents Educational Assistance Program
Offers college fee-waiver programs to children and dependents of veterans with service-related disability or death.
Applications: Educational Representative, California Department of Veterans Affairs, Division of Veteran Services, 1227 O Street, Room 101, Sacramento, CA 95814; 1-800-952-5626.

Society of the Daughters of the US Army
Offers grants of as much as $1000/year to daughters, stepdaughters, or granddaughters of retired or deceased officers of the regular Army.
Deadline: Applications accepted between November 1 and March 1. A stamped, self-addressed envelope is required.
Applications: Janet B. Otto, DUSA Memorial and Scholarship funds, 7717 Rockledge Court, West Springfield, VA 22152-3854.

Society of the 1st Division Foundation
Awards scholarships of $3000 to high school seniors who are children or grandchildren of a member of the 1st Infantry Division of the US Army. Based on scholastic achievement and an essay.
Deadline: June 1.
Applications: Scholarship Committee, Society of the 1st Division, 5 Montgomery Avenue, Erdenheim, PA 19038.

●●●
PRIVATE OR ORGANIZATIONAL LOANS

Many private or organizational loans are available at a lower interest rate than some loans that are offered as part of financial aid packages. Students who apply for and receive an outside loan may request that it be used to meet the expenses normally funded by a Health Education Assistance-Loan (HEAL) (i.e., minimum self-help expectation or unmet need).

Armenian General Benevolent Union (AGBU) of America, Inc.

Offers a loan program for full-time students of Armenian heritage who are pursuing their first professional degree in medicine. Candidates must be enrolled in a highly competitive college and have an undergraduate GPA of 3.5 or higher. Loans range from $5000–$7500/year. Repayment begins within 12 months after the completion of full-time study and extends for 5–10 years. The interest rate of 3% starts when repayment of the loan is initiated.
Deadline: May 15.
Applications: AGBU Education Department, 31 West 52nd Street, New York, NY 10019-6118.

California State PTA Loan

Offers student loans to high school seniors for use at an accredited college or university in California. Available between December 1 and March 15.
Applications: California State PTA Loan, 930 Georgia Street, PO Box 15015, Los Angeles, CA 90015. Applicants should indicate college, course of study, grade level, and loan period.

Drew (Charles) Scholarship Loan Fund

Offers loans of as much as $2500/year to minority third- and fourth-year medical students who are residents of California. All loans require a cosigner. Loans accrue interest at 3% less than the current prevailing loan rate and are due after the completion of the internship.
Deadline: May 30.
Applications: Charles Drew Scholarship Loan Fund, PO Box 431427, Los Angeles, CA 90043.

Eddy (Royal A. and Mildred D.) Student Loan Trust Fund

Offers loans of as much as $2000/year to students who have completed at least 2 years of college. Loans are made only to students who will begin to earn money and repay the loan within 2 years. Interest is 10% on the unpaid balance and begins as of the date of the loan. Two cosigners are required. No payments are due until 5 months after graduation.
Applications: NBD Bank Trust Department, 8585 Broadway, Suite 396, Merrillville, IN 46410.

Hebrew Free Loan Association

Offers loans of as much as $1500/year ($4500 cumulative amount, interest-free) to Jewish students from the greater Bay area, including Sacramento and San Jose, with employed cosigners in Northern California. Repayment begins 1 month after the loan is received, and the repayment period is 24–28 months.
Applications: Mr. Blackman, Hebrew Free Loan Association, 703 Market Street, Suite 445, San Francisco, CA 94103. In Los Angeles, contact the Jewish Free Loan Association, 6505 Wilshire Boulevard, Suite 515, Los Angeles, CA 90048. Call for an appointment; (213) 655-6922.

Knights Templar Educational Foundation
Offers loans of as much as $1500/year ($2500 cumulative amount) to full-time students who are California residents. Interest accrues 5%/year. Repayment over a 4-year period begins 90 days after graduation. A cosigner is required.
Applications: Knights Templar Educational Foundation, Inc., 801 Elm Avenue, Long Beach, CA 90813; (310) 436-8271.

Monterey County Medical Society Auxiliary
Offers loans to medical students who are residents of Monterey County, California.
Applications: Teria Marie Holmes, Scholarship Chairperson, c/o Monterey County Medical Society, PO Box 80308, Salinas, CA 93912; (408) 455-1693.

San Diego Association for Medical and Paramedical Education and Research
Offers the AMPER loan of as much as $2000/year for first- through third-year medical students. Loans are interest-free until the degree is obtained, and then interest is charged at 9% during the repayment period. The loan is repaid at $100/month. Applicants are interviewed at the April or July board meeting.
Deadline: Applications filed between February 1 and March 15 are considered at the April board meeting, and those filed between May 1 and June 15 are considered in July.
Applications: San Diego Association for Medical and Paramedical Education and Research, PO Box 23105, San Diego, CA 92123; (714) 565-8888.

San Joaquin Medical Society
Offers loans of as much as $10,000/year to a maximum of $40,000 to students who are residents of San Joaquin, Amador, and Calaveras Counties, California, or who attended high school in these areas. Loans are interest-free until 1 year after graduation, when repayment begins. The interest rate is 1%–3% above the prime rate, depending on the term of the loan, which may not exceed 7 years. All loans require a cosigner and life insurance for the amount of the loan.
Deadline: June 1 for the fall semester and December 1 for the spring semester.
Applications: San Joaquin Medical Society, PO Box 230, Stockton, CA 95201; (209) 948-1334.

Sonoma County Medical Association
Offers loans of as much as $2000/year to medical students from Sonoma County, California. The interest rate is currently 6%. Repayment begins 1 year after graduation, and the loan must be repaid within 3 years.
Deadline: August 15.
Applications: Sonoma County Medical Association, 3033 Cleveland Avenue, Santa Rosa, CA 95401; (707)925-4359.

Strickler (Albert) Memorial Fund
Offers loans of $400–$800/year to medical students. Based on need.
Deadline: July 15.
Applications: After April 1, contact Endowment Director, Federation of Jewish Agencies, 226 South 16th Street, Philadelphia, PA 19102; (215) 893-5600.

Strong (Hattie M.) Foundation
Offers interest-free loans of as much as $2500/year to baccalaureate or medical students in their final year. Based on need.
Deadline: Request applications between January 1 and March 31.
Applications: Hattie M. Strong Foundation, Suite 700, 1620 Eye Street NW, Washington, DC 20006; (202) 331-1619.

Yuba-Sutter County Medical Society Auxiliary
Offers no-interest loans of as much as $3000 cumulatively over the educational period to medical students from Yuba and Sutter Counties, California. Loan repayment begins 45 days after graduation, and the loan must be repaid within 3 years. If the recipient practices in Yuba or Sutter County for at least 1 year, $500 of the loan is forgiven.
Deadline: July 31.
Applications: Loan Fund Chairperson: (916) 674-2018 or (916) 673-6894.

●●● LOANS TO GRADUATING STUDENTS

Loans are available to senior medical students who have been accepted into a residency program.

National Association of Residents and Interns (NARI)
Offers loans of as much as $10,000 to senior medical students, residents, and fellows who have matched for residency. Students who owe more than $50,000 are not eligible. An interest-only option is available during residency.
Applications: (800) 221-2168.

●●● RESEARCH AWARDS

Information on current research opportunities and awards is often available at university basic and clinical science department offices.

American Academy of Allergy, Asthma and Immunology Summer Fellowships
Offers stipends of $1500/summer to medical students who are interested in pursuing research in allergy and immunology.
Deadline: March 15.
Applications: Summer Fellowships, American Academy of Allergy, Asthma and Immunology, 611 East Wells Street, Milwaukee, WI 53202.

American Academy of Neurology
Four awards are offered: (1) clinical neurology award ($350); (2) experimental neurology award ($350); (3) historical aspects of neurology award ($350); and (4) extended neuroscience award ($1000). Applicants must be United States medical students in good standing and must submit an original essay targeted toward general neurologists. For all awards but the extended award, the student should spend less than 1 year on a project leading to the essay; for the extended award, the student should spend more than 1 year. In addition, all recipients receive a 1-year complimentary subscription to *Neurology,* airfare, and expenses (including 1 night's lodging) to attend the American Academy of Neurology annual meeting in San Francisco.
Deadline: October.
Applications: Essay Award Contest, American Academy of Neurology, 2221 University Avenue SE, Suite 335, Minneapolis, MN 55414; (612) 623-8115.

American Association for the History of Medicine
The William Osler Medal is awarded for the best unpublished essay on a medical–historical subject written by a medical student. The winning contestant is invited to attend the annual meeting of the American Association for the History of Medicine and receives a stipend of $500 to defray traveling expenses.

Deadline: February 1.
Applications: Dr. Edward Hundert, Associate Dean for Student Affairs, Harvard Medical School, 25 Shattuck Street, Boston, MA 02115.

American Congress of Rehabilitation Medicine

Sponsors an annual essay contest for cash awards based on the merits of manuscripts submitted on physical medicine and rehabilitation.
Applications: Consult the January through April issues of *Archives of Physical Medicine and Rehabilitation.*

American Heart Association, California Affiliate

Offers 10-week summer research opportunities in cardiovascular research to undergraduate students who will be juniors or seniors in the fall immediately after they complete the program. Students are assigned to leading research laboratories in California under the direct supervision of an experienced investigator. A grant of $2500 is provided for this period. A good GPA is helpful.
Deadline: January 15.
Applications: Request by December 15 from Student Research Committee, American Heart Association, California Affiliate, 1710 Gilbreth Road, Burlingame, CA 94010; (415) 259-6720.

American Osler Society

Offers a stipend of $1000 for 8 weeks of researching the broad areas of medical history and medical humanism.
Deadline: February 1.
Applications: Larry D. Longo, MD, Secretary-Treasurer, Osler Society, c/o Center for Perinatal Biology, Loma Linda University, Loma Linda, CA 92350; (909) 824-4325.

American Society of Clinical Nutrition (ASCN)

National Clinical Nutrition Internships are sponsored by ASCN and the American Medical Student Association (AMSA) to increase interest in and awareness of nutrition for physicians. Applicants must have completed at least 1 year of medical school. A stipend of $2000 is provided to cover living expenses.
Deadline: March 1 for research beginning between June 1 and October 1.
Five runner-up applicants receive a $750 travel award and a plaque. The overall winner receives an additional $500. Research papers are presented by young investigators still in graduate or medical school. Rules for submitting abstracts are included in the *Experimental Biology* annual meeting announcements.
Deadline: November 24.
Applications: ASCN National Clinical Nutrition Internship, 9650 Rockville Pike, Bethesda, MD 20814; Telephone (301) 530-7110; Fax (301) 571-1863; E-mail secretar@ascn.faseb.org.

American Urological Association

Offers 10 fellowships with a stipend of $2000 to medical students to work in a urology research laboratory during the summer.
Deadline: April 15.
Applications: Research Scholar Division, American Foundation for Urological Disease, 300 West Pratt Street, Suite 401, Baltimore, MD 21201; Fax (410) 528-0550.

Barron Neurological Institute

Offers 10-week clerkships in neurology, neurosurgery, neuropathology, neurobiology, neuroradiology, and neuroanesthesiology. A stipend of $1000 for first- and sec-

ond-year students or $1500 for third- and fourth-year students is available.
Applications: BNI Medical Student Clerkships, c/o Catherine Ellering, Barrow Neurological Institute, 350 West Thomas Road, Phoenix, AZ 85013-4496; (602) 266-3355.

Children's Hospital of LA/USC Summer Oncology Fellowships

Offers a weekly stipend of $110 to students who participate in a research or clinical oncology program. Fellowships are completed between May 15 and September 15 and are 8–12 weeks long.
Applications: Robert Adler, MD, MSEd, Children's Hospital of Los Angeles, PO Box 54700, Los Angeles, CA 90054-0700; (213) 669-2110.

Chinese Hospital Medical Student Research Fund

Offers stipends of as much as $2000 to students of any ethnic background who are currently attending an accredited United States or Canadian medical or public health school. Applicants should be full-time students and must be able to spend 8 weeks at the Chinese Hospital in San Francisco during the summer. Starting and ending dates are flexible. No housing assistance is available. The program emphasizes epidemiologic, rather than clinical, laboratory research. Research preceptors are commonly community-based primary care private practitioners.
Applications: Patricia Chung, Coordinator of Medical Staff Services, Chinese Hospital, 845 Jackson Street, San Francisco, CA 94133; (415) 677-2480.

Commonwealth Fund Fellowship for Academic Medicine

Provides 20 awards of $5000 to academically gifted (black, mainland Puerto Rican, Mexican American, or Native American) third-year medical students who are interested in a career in biomedical research and academic medicine. Each Fellow spends 8–12 weeks in a major research laboratory.
Deadline: December 1.
Applications: Commonwealth Fund Medical Fellowship Program, Inc., 254 West 31st Street, 7th Floor, New York, NY 10001.

Diabetes Research and Training Center at Vanderbilt University

The summer Student Research Program provides a stipend for transportation and living expenses for a 12-week program. The program provides training experience in biomedical research. Students select a research project and work under the supervision of a faculty preceptor. A seminar series provides a comprehensive review of diabetes and related research topics. Applicants should have completed the first year of medical school.
Deadline: Early February.
Applications: Director, Summer Student Research Program, Vanderbilt Diabetes Research and Training Center, Vanderbilt University, Nashville, TN 37232; (615) 322-7001.

Epilepsy Foundation of America

Offers fellowships of $2000 to enable medical students to participate in a 3-month project related to an ongoing program of research, service, or training in epilepsy.
Deadline: February 28.
Applications: Epilepsy Foundation of America, 4351 Garden City Drive, Suite 406, Landover, MD 20785.

Ewing (James) Foundation

Offers seven fellowships of $2000 to students in the first 3 years of medical school. Students work for 2–3 months in oncology. Applicants must be sponsored by a

Society of Surgical Oncology member.
Deadline: March 15.
Applications: James Ewing Foundation, 85 West Algonquin Road, Suite 550, Arlington Heights, IL 60005; (708) 427-1400.

Giannini Foundation

Offers fellowships of $25,000 for 12 months for students to perform research projects after graduation from one of the eight accredited California medical schools.
Deadline: December 1.
Applications: Caroline Boitano, Administrator, Bank of America, Giannini Foundation, PO Box 37000, San Francisco, CA 94137; (415) 953-3175.

Kramer (Simon) Externship in Radiation Oncology

Provides a stipend of $1200 for living expenses in addition to partial travel expenses to a United States medical student. Students perform a 6-week externship in a clinical radiation oncology facility in the continental United States and Hawaii.
Deadline: March 7.
Applications: Ruth Levine, Department of Radiation Therapy, Thomas Jefferson University Hospital, 11 South 11th Street, Philadelphia, PA 19107; (215) 955-6700.

Los Angeles Society of Neurology and Psychiatry

Offers an award of $500 for a paper in the clinical neurosciences.
Deadline: October 1.
Applications: Secretary-Treasurer, Los Angeles Society of Neurology and Psychiatry, PO Box 3465, Los Angeles, CA 90051-1465.

Minority Research Training and Career Development Programs Sponsored by the National Institutes of Health (NIH), National Heart, Lung and Blood Institute (NHLBI)

Offers research opportunities to encourage research training among minority students.
Applications: US Department of Public Health and Human Services, Minority Scholarships Programs, Parllawn Building, 17A-31, 5600 Fishers Lane, Rockville, MD 20857; (301) 443-4513.

Montefiore Medical Center Program in Occupational Health

Offers opportunities for medical students to work with labor union locals and employers to prevent disease through worker education and investigation of health hazards. Most placements are in New York City. Full-time opportunities are available from mid-June to mid-August, with limited opportunities during the academic year. Stipends may be available.
Applications: David Michaels, MPH, Department of Epidemiology and Social Medicine, Montefiore Medical Center, 111 East 210th Street, Bronx, NY 10467; (212) 920-4321.

National Medical Fellowships (NMF)

The Fellowship Program in Academic Medicine for Minority Students offers awards of $6000 to 2nd- or 3rd-year minority medical students to complete research projects for 8–12 weeks.
Applications: National Medical Fellowships, Inc., 110 West 32 Street, 8th Floor, New York, NY 10001; (212) 714-1007.

National Student Research Forum

Offers medical and graduate students, interns, and residents an opportunity to present biomedical research and compete for awards at a national meeting.

Deadline: November 1.
Applications: Shannon Womacht, National Student Research Forum, University of Texas Medical Branch, 301 University Boulevard, Galveston, TX 77555-1317; (409) 772-3763.

Parenteral Drug Association for Pharmaceutical Science, Inc.

Offers an award of $1000 to a student for the best unpublished manuscript based on original laboratory research in pharmaceuticals, clinical pharmacy, hyperalimentation, parenteral nutrition, and related disciplines. The award includes as much as $1000 for travel and lodging expenses to attend the annual Association meeting.
Deadline: July 15.
Applications: PDA Foundation for Pharmaceutical Sciences, Inc, PO Box 242, Garden City, New York, NY 11530; (212) 889-3109.

Pharmaceutical Manufacturers Association (PMA) Foundation

Offers a fellowship for 3–12 months and a stipend of $500/month for full-time research within a pharmacology or clinical pharmacology unit to a second- through fourth-year medical student. The student must be sponsored by the program in which the investigative project is undertaken.
Deadline: January 15.
Applications: PMA Foundation, 1100 15th Street NW, Washington, DC 20005; (202) 296-2427.

Roswell Park Cancer Institute

Offers an 8-week summer oncology research program. Fellowships and a weekly stipend of $250 are awarded to first- and second-year medical students.
Deadline: March 15.
Applications: Dr. Edwin A. Mirand, Director, Summer Oncology Research Program, Roswell Park Cancer Institute, Elm and Carlton Streets, Buffalo, NY 14263; (716) 845-2339.

Society for Biomaterials

Offers an award to a student with an outstanding research paper in biomaterials. The student presents the paper at the annual meeting and receives complimentary membership in the Society.
Deadline: November 3.
Applications: Dr. P. K. Bajpai, 325 Applehill Drive, West Carrollton, OH 45449-1562; (513) 229-2135; Fax (513) 229-2021.

Society for Clinical Vascular Surgery

Offers an award of $1000 plus transportation and accommodations for the Society's annual meeting for an essay by a medical student, resident, or fellow on vascular surgery.
Deadline: September 15.
Applications: Society for Clinical Vascular Surgery, 13 Elm Street, Manchester, MA 01094; (508) 526-8330.

Society of Nuclear Medicine

Offers a stipend of as much as $3000 for medical or graduate students to spend elective quarters or a summer (at least a 2-month time block) in a department of nuclear medicine assisting in clinical and basic research activities.
Deadline: December 15 and May 1.
Applications: Student Fellowship Award, Education and Research Foundation, Society of Nuclear Medicine, 1850 Samuel Morse Drive, Reston, VA 22090-5136; (312) 880-4416.

University of Minnesota, Minneapolis

Offers predoctoral fellowships and stipends at $12,000/year to students who have completed 2 or more years at an accredited medical school. The fellowships are usually for 1 year, beginning July 1. Applications for shorter periods are also considered. A fellowship usually consists of time spent in autopsy and surgical pathology, working with pathology residents. Work in clinical pathology, hemopathology, transfusion medicine, immunology, clinical chemistry, molecular diagnostics, cytogenetics, and health informatics may also be elected. Diverse research opportunities are available, and fellows are encouraged to undertake a scholarly project during the year.

Deadline: 3 months before the requested starting date.

Applications: Sue A. Bartow, MD, Director, Residency and Clinical Fellowship Training Programs, Department of Laboratory Medicine and Pathology, Box 609 UMHC, University of Minnesota, 420 Delaware Street, SE, Minneapolis, MN 55455-0392; (612) 625-8952; Fax (612) 626-0617.

University of Pennsylvania Clinical Research Training Program

Through the Charles A. Dana Foundation, offers medical students an opportunity to participate in a year long in-depth clinical research training program at the University of Pennsylvania. Topics are epidemiology, clinical research, methodology, and the delivery of health care services. The program offers a stipend of $11,000.

Deadline: December 31.

Applications: Barbara Koalsky, Samuel P. Martin, MD, Charles A. Dana Foundation, Clinical Research Training Program, University of Pennsylvania, School of Medicine, Philadelphia, PA 19104-6094; (215) 662-3350.

Williams (William Carlos) Poetry Competition

Sponsored by the Human Values in Medicine program at the Northeastern Ohio Universities College of Medicine, offers prizes of $100–$300 to medical and osteopathic students in the United States. Winners are also invited to visit Northeastern Ohio Universities and read their poetry. Travel and lodging expenses are paid. Poems may not exceed 750 words and are judged on the basis of craftsmanship, originality, and content.

Deadline: December 31.

Applications: Human Values in Medicine, Northeastern Ohio Universities College of Medicine, Rootstown, OH 44272.

●●●
LOANS THROUGH MEDICAL SCHOOL

Some loans are available through medical school financial aid offices. Often, only one application is required to apply for all of these loans. The federal loans listed in this section are often determined on the basis of need as prescribed by federal regulation. University financial affairs officers determine student needs and distribute loans so that each student receives an equitable share at the lowest possible repayment rate. Federal guidelines offer financial affairs officers little leeway.

Loans often account for most of the funds obtained by medical students, and they must be repaid. Because of the time needed to process applications, it is wise to start the process as soon as possible. Many institutions allow students to submit a completed loan application at the time of the medical school interview. Forms are usually sent to all applicants in January or February.

The best approach is to secure funding through the school or the Association of American Medical Colleges (AAMC) program listed in the following section. The programs listed in the previous sections can be used to obtain scholarship money. These funds decrease total indebtedness from nongovernmental sources and have a lower interest rate or a more liberal payback schedule than government loans. However, any funds secured, except those for research and similar projects, lower a student's need assessment and concomitant eligibility for government-sponsored loans. In other words, one type of money replaces another, but the amount received rarely exceeds the established need. The following section lists the major federal loan programs.

The AAMC MEDLOANS Program
Permits students to apply for several types of loans, including the major federal programs, in a single package. The AAMC maintains an Alternative Loan Program (ALP) that is based on federally determined need. This program offers students an opportunity to obtain a loan, even if they do not meet the federal guidelines.
Applications: AAMC, Division of Student Affairs and Education Services, 2450 N Street NW, Washington, DC 20037-1126.

Financial Assistance for Disadvantaged Health Professional Students (FADHPS) Programs
Offers loans of as much as $10,000/year to disadvantaged students. Based on need. The family contribution is not to exceed the lesser of $5000 or one-half the cost of education.
Applications: Contact the medical school financial affairs office.

Health Education Assistance Loan Program (HEAL)
The primary source of financing for medical school. Administered through the Department of Health and Human Services. Students may borrow as much as $20,000/year for 4 years. Interest rates are variable, set at the Treasury bill rate plus 3%. Interest accrues while the student attends school. The payback period is 10–25 years and begins 9 months after graduation, but may be deferred as long as 4 years for residency, 3 years for active military duty, and an additional 3 years for most primary care physicians.

Perkins Loans
Provides loans of as much as $5000/year, for a total of $30,000 as an aggregate for both undergraduate and graduate school. Funded through the United States Office of Education. Payback, at a minimum of $40/month, begins 9 months after graduation. The interest rate is 5%. Interest begins to accrue after graduation. Some students use all of the available funds from this source for undergraduate study.

Primary Care Loan
Pays tuition plus $2500. This loan is of particular value to students attending schools with high tuition rates. The interest rate is 5% for recipients who enter primary care; otherwise, it is 12%, computed from the time the loan is granted. Payback begins 1 year after graduation, and the loan must be paid off in 10 years. Deferment is possible. If the recipient does not enter primary care, payback is in 3 years.

Scholarship Program for Students of Exceptional Financial Need (EFN)
Pays tuition and other educational expenses. Based on need. The family contribution is not to exceed the lesser of $5000 or one-half the cost of education.
Applications: Contact the medical school financial affairs office.

Subsidized Stanford Loan
Pays as much as $18,500/year aggregate undergraduate and graduate. The interest rate is based on the 1991 Treasury bill rate plus 2.5%, capped at 8.25%. Payback begins 6 months after graduation, with allowable deferments, and is completed within 10 years. The minimum payment is $50/month.

Unsubsidized Stanford Loan
Pays as much as $138,500 aggregate undergraduate and graduate. The interest rate is based on the 1991 Treasury bill rate plus 2.5%, capped at 8.25%. Payback

begins 6 months after graduation, with allowable deferments, and is completed within 10 years. The minimum payment is $50/month.

● ● ●
LOAN REPAYMENT PROGRAMS

Debt can be reduced through participation in a federal, state, or county repayment program. Contact the financial affairs office for information about local programs.

National Health Service Corps (NHSC)
Pays as much as $25,000/year for the first 2 years and $35,000/year thereafter toward educationally derived loans from most sources. Students commit to a minimum of 2 years of service in the Corps. In addition to the loan reduction, students receive a salary and benefits. The Corps sponsors some state programs.
Applications: Ask for the handbook *State and Other Loan Repayment/Forgiveness and Scholarship Programs.* Contact NHSC Scholarship Programs, US Public Health Recruitment, 8201 Greensboro Drive, Suite 200, McLean, VA 22102; (301) 443-4513.

● ● ●
INSTITUTIONAL FUNDS

Most medical schools have funds available through university or college foundations, state scholarships or financial aid programs, endowments, alumni, or other sources. These funds are distributed to students as scholarships, awards, or loans, depending on the requirements of the source. Students apply for these funds through the medical school. The application deadline for these loans usually occurs in February or March, which is before many students are admitted. Financial affairs officers can help students to maximize the amount that they receive. The goal is to graduate from medical school with the lowest possible indebtedness. Using the available resources effectively can substantially reduce the amount of debt.

CHAPTER 8

The Application Process

AMCAS SCHOOLS

All but 16 medical schools in the United States subscribe to the American Medical College Application Service (AMCAS). This service simplifies the application process for both schools and students. With one standard application form, students can apply to one school or all AMCAS schools. Students mail this form to AMCAS with the appropriate fees. The fees increase with each school selected. Medical College Admission Test (MCAT) scores and academic transcripts are also sent to AMCAS. AMCAS confirms the validity of the transcripts and mails copies of the full application packet to each school selected by the student. AMCAS also provides a one-page cover sheet that summarizes the information about the student. This transmittal notification is sent to the student, and a slightly modified version is sent to each selected school. This page can be the most important part of the application.

Figure 8–1 shows an AMCAS application cover page. The following points are important: identifying information (e.g., name, residence, birth date); minority status and ethnicity; financial status; schools attended, including major and degree earned; breakdown of the grade point average (GPA); MCAT scores; and the AMCAS school or schools selected. The most important items on this form are the schools attended, the GPA breakdown, and the MCAT scores.

The schools attended can make a difference in medical school acceptance, largely based on the relative

AMERICAN MEDICAL COLLEGE APPLICATION SERVICE

ASSOCIATION OF AMERICAN MEDICAL COLLEGES

AMCAS

Section for Student Services

2450 N Street NW, Suite 201
Washington, D.C. 20037-1131
Telephone (202) 828-0600

TRANSMITTAL NOTIFICATION (TN)

Your AMCAS application has been forwarded to the schools listed below, with the biographic and academic information and MCAT scores which appear on this Transmittal Notification (TN). Please check all items carefully and notify AMCAS in writing immediately of any discrepancies. In all correspondence with AMCAS or medical schools, be sure to indicate your complete name, cycle/file number, social security number, and telephone number.

10/23/95   Cycle: 090-NEW

TO: VUONG D. NGUYEN   Soc. Sec. #: 000-62-3896
       1345 DEVLIN CIRCLE   Cycle/File #: 090-00144
       WESTMINSTER, CA 92670   Entering Class: 1996

       Phone: 714-845-2659   Self-Desc: Vietnamese
       Leg. Res.:   Minority/Consider-Ethnic: No
           ORANGE, CA   Financial: Yes
       Citizenship: UNITED STATES   Fee Waiver: Yes
       Visa Type: Military Service: No
       Birth Place: SAIGON, VIETNAM   Previous Med School: No
       Birthdate: 11/3/73   Age: 23   Institution Action: No
       Sex: Male   Num of Dep: Early Decision: No
                                          Advisor Information Release: Yes

Colleges Attended	Major	Program	Degree	Degree Dates	Attended
CERRITOS COLLEGE	GENERAL	UNDERGR	ND		90–92
UC LOS ANGELES	BIOLOGY	UNDERGR	B.A.	92–93	92–93
CSU LONG BEACH	PSYCH	GRADUAT	M.A.	93–94	93–94
UC IRVINE	POSTBAC	UNDERGR	ND		94–95

	BCPM GPA	BCPM HOURS	AO GPA	AO HOURS	TOTAL GPA	TOTAL HOURS
FR	3.08	20.0	3.51	18.0	3.28	38.0
SO	2.97	19.5	3.85	6.0	3.18	25.5
JR	2.83	17.3	2.18	22.3	2.46	39.6
SR	3.36	14.0	2.00	4.0	3.06	18.0
PBU	4.00	16.5	4.00	3.3	4.00	19.8
CUG	3.22	87.3	2.91	53.6	3.10	140.9
GRD	3.24	6.6	4.00	42.3	3.90	48.8

MCAT Scores

Test Date(s)	04/95	09/94
Series #	07	06
Verbal Reasoning	9	7
Physical Sciences	10	8
Writing Sample	P	O
Biological Sciences	12	10

Number of MCAT(s) Taken: 2
Next MCAT Date: 04/96

Supplementary Hours:
Pass/Fail-Pass: 3
Pass/Fail-Fail: 1

Your application was Transmitted to: Code School	Date of Application	Yr(s) Prev Applied
849 XYZ School	101895	95
850 ABC School	101895	94

● ● ●

FIGURE 8–1. Sample AMCAS student transmittal notification sheet. Reprinted with permission of the Association of American Medical Colleges.

weighing of the schools by admission committee members. Schools that are considered academically challenging or are not subject to grade inflation may be rated higher than schools that demand less of students or practice some form of grade inflation. This weighing process can have a significant effect on the evaluation of a student's GPA. For example, a student who earned an undergraduate degree at the University of California, Berkeley, and who has a science GPA of 3.0 might be rated higher than a student who has a science GPA of 3.4–3.5, but attended a less well known or less demanding school. The weighing of academic difficulty is subjective and is largely determined by the prejudices of admission committee members.

The GPA breakdown is divided into three parts. The first part lists the student's GPA, by academic year, for the sciences (BCPM—biology, chemistry, physics, mathematics). The second part lists all other courses taken (AO—all other), and the third part lists the total GPA. An additional breakdown is given for the hours, or units, in each of these areas.

Admission committee members consider several factors when evaluating this information. First, they consider the science GPA and its consistency from year to year. Some inconsistency between years can be explained by an exceptionally heavy science course load in a year in which the GPA is lower. If the difference between the lower GPA in 1 year and the average in other years is not too great (e.g., 3.1 in the junior year, with an average of 3.5), and if the student completed a heavy course load that year, this lower GPA would not be held against the student. However, to some committee members, a great discrepancy (e.g., 2.8 in the sophomore year versus an average of 3.4) suggests that the student cannot handle a demanding course load.

Second, committee members consider the other courses on a student's transcript. Although nonscience courses are not weighed as heavily as the science GPA, the nonscience GPA should show year-to-year consistency. Variations in the nonscience GPA can be explained by an especially heavy course load. However, again, too much variation can indicate the potential for failure in medical school. To avoid excessive variability in the GPA, a student should not take too many demanding courses during any one undergraduate semester or quarter. In the long run, it is better to remain in college for an extra year than to earn lower grades because of an especially demanding course load.

A GPA that is initially low and increases from year to year can counterbalance a lower overall GPA. For example, a student who has a science GPA of 2.6 in his freshman year, followed by a GPA of 2.9 in the sophomore year, 3.4 in the junior year, and 3.9 in the senior year, with an overall science GPA of 3.1, has a good chance of admission. Admission committees understand that some students have a difficult adjustment period. From the example just given, it could be argued that the student struggled at first, but mastered the demands of an academic setting by the time he was ready for medical school.

If a student experienced a traumatic event (e.g., the death of a loved one, an accident), during a year in which her GPA declined, she should explain the situation in her personal statement. A student's ability to overcome such an obstacle can be a positive factor in her acceptance.

Finally, admission committees consider the student's postbaccalaureate or graduate school experience. On the AMCAS form, the postbaccalaureate units (PBU) are listed just above the cumulative undergraduate grade (CUG), the average grade point earned prior to receiving a baccalaureate degree. The GPA for any postbaccalaureate work undertaken is listed in this section. The postbaccalaureate GPA is added to the CUG. A student who had a low undergraduate GPA but earns better grades in a postbaccalaureate program can improve his bottom line GPA by several tenths of a point.

On the other hand, the graduate school GPA is reported separately as "GRD." Although earning an advanced degree is usually viewed positively, the graduate school GPA is not usually considered as important as the undergraduate GPA. Nearly all graduate programs require a GPA of 3.0 or greater, and graduate students are often given Bs and As for performing research. As a result, the GPA may be inflated. Moreover, medical school is more similar to undergraduate study than to graduate school. For this reason, graduate school performance is less predictive of success in medical school than undergraduate performance.

The next important section of the cover page is the MCAT scores. Scores for the two most recent attempts are reported. In addition, the number of times that a student took the MCAT is listed. Obviously, committee members are looking for evidence that a student can do well in medical school. Therefore, committee members usually place the most weight on the scores for the Biological Sciences and Physical Sciences sections. If these scores are adequate and the other scores are not too low, then a student will meet the criterion established for the MCAT scores. After the MCAT was revised in 1991, admission committees relied slightly more on GPA than on MCAT scores because they were unsure how to evaluate the new test. However, committees have become more familiar with the new format and scoring scales, and the MCAT has largely regained its significance. The section of the new MCAT that is least useful to many admission committees is the Writing Sample. There has been a recent trend, however, to use this section as a criterion for automatic rejection. That is, if a student does not score above a certain minimum level, he is given no further consideration because communication is considered an essential skill for medical professionals.

To apply to medical school through AMCAS, consult a premedical advisor or write to:

AMCAS
Association of American Medical Colleges
Section for Student Services
2450 N Street NW, Suite 201
Washington, DC 20037-1131
(202) 828-0600

● ● ●
NON-AMCAS SCHOOLS

AMCAS simplifies the medical school application process; however, 16 schools still require students to apply individually. Fortunately, these application forms are similar to the AMCAS application form. Call or write the admission offices of these schools to request an application. Their complete addresses and telephone numbers are listed in Appendix A.

The following schools require a separate application: Yale; Johns Hopkins; Harvard; University of Missouri, Kansas City (6-year program, with admission from high school); Columbia; New York University School of Medicine; University of Rochester; University of North Dakota; Brown University (only relevant for MD/PhD candidates, plus some postbaccalaureate students because most students are selected at lower grade levels). In addition to these nine schools, all seven medical schools in Texas subscribe to their own application service. To apply to a school in Texas, contact:

University of Texas System Medical Application Center
702 Colorado, Suite 620
Austin, TX 78701

● ● ●
THE APPLICATION

The AMCAS application packet contains more than 11 items. The most important is the AMCAS application form (*Figure 8–2*). This form includes the personal statement and the student's name, address, other personal information, and academic record. Because the forms may change slightly from year to year, it is important

1. SSN 000-62-3896	**AMCAS® APPLICATION** **FOR THE 1996 ENTERING CLASS**	**AMCAS USE ONLY**

2A. Last Name NGUYEN	2B. First Name VUONG	2C. Middle Name DINH	2D. Suffix

3A. Permanent Address - Street 1345 Devlin Circle	3B. City Westminster	3C. St CA	3D. Zip 92670

3E. County (if in U.S.A.) Orange	3F. Country (if not U.S.A.)	4. Telephone (714) 845-2659

5. PARENTS OR GUARDIAN

Name	Living? Yes	Living? No	Occupation	Legal Residence	Education/College (highest level)
Father Tri Tuan Nguyen		X	Army Officer	—	B.S.
Mother Bich Than Nguyen	X		Restaurant owner	Yes	High School
Guardian					

6A. Ages of your Brothers 17, 13	6B. Ages of your Sisters 15, 11	7A. Secondary School—Name Cerritos, H.S.	7B. City, State Cerritos, CA	7C. Grad Yr. 1990

8. ALL COLLEGES, GRADUATE AND PROFESSIONAL SCHOOLS ATTENDED (list in chronological order)

Name	Location (City & State)	Dates of Attendance MM/YY MM/YY	Check if summer only	Check if Jr/Comm College	Major	Degree Granted or Expected (with date)
Cerritos College	Cerritos, CA	9/90 to 6/92		X	General	None
University of Calif	Los Angeles, CA	9/92 to 12/93			Biology	B.A.
Calif. State Univ.	Long Beach, CA	2/93 to 6/94			Psychology	M.A.
University of CA.	Irvine, CA	9/94 to present			Post BACC	—
		to				

9. Post-Secondary Honors/Awards:

Certificate of Merit - Asian Health Society of Long Beach

10. Extracurricular, Community, and Avocational Activities:

Flying Samaritans

Volunteer Orange County Community Clinic

11. Chronological Post-Secondary History, including Volunteer, Part-Time and Full-Time Employment

7/91 - 9/94 Waiter/Cook - family restaurant

summers - 20 hrs. per week during school

7/93 - 9/93 Lab Assistant Biological Chemistry

See AMCAS Instruction Booklet before completing this form. Type in dark black ink; if possible, use an Elite (12 pitch) typewriter.

● ● ●

FIGURE 8–2. Sample AMCAS application. Reprinted with permission of the Association of American Medical Colleges.

SSN 000-62-3896				ACADEMIC RECORD						AMCAS USE ONLY		

LAST NAME NGUYEN				FIRST NAME VUONG			MIDDLE NAME DINH			SUFFIX		

COLLEGE NAME LOCATION	ACADEMIC STATUS	BCPM/A	ACADEMIC YEAR	TERM	COURSE NAME	NUMBER	TYPE	OFFICIAL TRANSCRIPT GRADE	SEMESTER HOURS ATTEMPTED	AMCAS GRADE	AMCAS USE	
Cerritos College	Fr.	A	90	S1	Spanish Conver.	5		B	3	B		
Cerritos		C			Chem. I & Lab	101A		A−	4	A−		
		A			Swimming	50		A+	1	A		
		A			Anthropology Intro.	106		A+	3	A		
		A			Writing Skills	102		A−	3	A−		
		P			Physics I	101A		B	4	B		
		M			Calculus I	120A		B−	4	B−		
		A		S2	English Lit. I	110A		A	3	A		
		C			Chem. II & Lab	101B		B	4	B		
		A			Health	102		B	2	B		
		A			American History	110A		B	3	B		
		M			Calculus II	120B		B	4	B		
	So.	C	91		Analytical Chem.	115		B	4.5	B		
		A			American Lit.	125		A−	3	A−		
		A		S1	English Lit.	110B		A	3	A		
		B			General Biology	200A		B+	4	AB		
		C			Organic Chem.	210A		B	3	B		
		C			Organic Chem. Lab.	210		C	1	C		
		B		S2	General Biology	200B		B	4	B		
		C			Organic Chem.	210B	PF	S	3	P		
		C			Organic Chem. Lab	210	PF	U	1	N		
		P			Physics II	101B		C+	3	BC		
Univ. of Calif.	Jr.	A	92	Q1	Philosophy	250		B+	2.7	AB		
Los Angeles		A			American History	210		C	2.7	C		
		C			Elem. Biochem.	56		B+	3.3	AB		
		B			Comp. Vertebrate Ant.	110		D	3.3	D		
		A			Swimming	40		A		A		
		B		Q2	Ecology	110		A	3.3	A		
		A			Medical Ethics	150		C	2.7	C		
		M			Statistics I	200A		C+	2.7	BC		
		A			Modern Literature	225		D+	2.7	CD		
		A		Q3	Astronomy	150		C	2.7	C		
		B			Zoology - Seminar	307		B	2.0	B		
		A			Music Appreciation	100		F	2.7	F		
		M			Differential Equa.	220		B	2.7	B		
		A			European History	235		A	2.7	A		
		A			Medieval History	240		C	2.7	C		
	Sr.	M			Statistics II	200B		C	2.7	C		
		B			Cell Biology	210		B	3.3	B		
		B			Physiology	217		A	4.0	A		
		M			Statistics/Research	235		A	4.0	A		
		A			Business Math	5		C	4.0	C		

● ● ●

FIGURE 8–2. Sample AMCAS application. *(Continued)*

COLLEGE NAME LOCATION	ACADEMIC STATUS	BCPM/A	ACADEMIC YEAR	TERM	COURSE NAME	NUMBER	TYPE	OFFICIAL TRANSCRIPT GRADE	SEMESTER HOURS ATTEMPTED	AMCAS GRADE	AMCAS USE	
Calif. State Univ.	GR	A	93	02	Psych. Research	317B		A	3.3	A		
Long Beach		A			Physiol. Basis/Psych	307		A	2.7	A		
		A			Educ. Psychology	305		A	3.3	A		
		A			Abnormal Psych.	317		A	3.3	A		
		A		03	Psych. Research	317C		A	3.3	A		
		A			Seminar in Psychol.	350C		A	3.3	A		
		A			Social Psychology	312		A	3.3	A		
		A	94	Q1	Psych. Research	317A		A	3.3	A		
		A			Seminar in Psych.	350A		A	3.3	A		
		A			Deathbed & Dying	317		A	3.3	A		
		A		Q2	Psych. Research	317B		A	3.3	A		
		A			Seminar in Psych.	350B		A	3.3	A		
		B			Epidemiology	255		B+	3.3			
		A		Q3	Psych. Research	317C		A	3.3	A		
		B			Neuroanatomy			B	3.3	B		
Univ. Ca. Irvine	PB	B	95	Q1	Psychobiology	210		A	3.3	A		
		B			Immunology	250		A	3.3	A		
		B			Biology of Disease	50		A	3.3	A		
		B			Microbiology	265		A	3.3	A		
		B			Human Anatomy	275		A	3.3	B		
		A			Humanities	200		A	3.3	A		
		B			HIV and AIDS	55	CC		3.3			
		B			Virology	255	CC		3.3			
		B			Biology of Cancer	267	CC		3.3			

14. MCAT Testing Status

Number of MCATs taken since April 1991 — [2]

Have you taken, or do you plan to take, the August 1995 MCAT?

YES ☐   NO ☒

15. Medical School
You must answer this Question

Have you ever matriculated at or attended any medical school as a candidate for the M.D. degree?

YES ☐   NO ☒

16. Institutional Action
You must answer this Question

[Refer to *Instruction Booklet* before answering.] Were you ever the recipient of any action (e.g., dismissal, disqualification, suspension, etc.) by any college or medical school for: (1) unacceptable academic performance or (2) conduct violations? If "YES," explain fully in the "Personal Comments" section (page 2).

YES ☐   NO ☒

Certification Statement and Signature

I have read and understand the instructions and other information in the *AMCAS Instruction Booklet*. I certify that the information submitted in this application and associated materials is current, complete, and accurate to the best of my knowledge.

SIGNATURE (BLACK INK ONLY) DATE

DATE

● ● ●

FIGURE 8-2. Sample AMCAS application. *(Continued)*

to use the form for the correct year. In addition to the application form, the packet includes the instruction booklet, a postcard to acknowledge receipt, the school designation form, an additional designation form, a transcript inventory form, transcript matching cards, a fee wavier request packet, a biographic change form, a personal computer survey, a MEDLOANS information sheet, a brochure entitled *31 Questions,* and a return envelope.

All applications must be neatly typed. Many students obtain several copies of the AMCAS application so that they can prepare more than one draft. Students should also ask someone who is familiar with medical school applications (e.g., a premedical advisor, an admission counselor from a medical school, or a medical student) to review their application.

The first step in completing the application is to read the instruction booklet. This booklet provides most of the information needed to complete the application; however, many students also seek professional assistance in completing the forms. The most important form is the application, which includes the personal statement and academic record. The next section discusses the personal statement in detail. On the academic record, it is important to list all college-level or equivalent courses, regardless of where or when they were taken or whether credit was awarded. Some students mistakenly exclude courses taken at schools where they did not complete a degree or other program. Although AMCAS has no access to information that is not listed, a student who intentionally omits courses to artificially increase her GPA would be viewed as committing fraud, which could lead to dismissal from medical school.

Another point to consider in completing the academic record is the assignment of AMCAS grades and the calculation of GPA. A table for converting grading systems is provided in the instruction booklet. This table should be used to convert the school's assigned grade to the AMCAS grade equivalent. Until recently, the student had to complete a laborious process of calculating his GPA using a sheet in the application packet. AMCAS now computes the GPAs that appear on the transmittal notification, performing the needed calculations based on the student's assignment of the AMCAS grades on the academic record. Therefore, this section must be completed accurately. It is important for the student to calculate her GPA using the chart in the booklet, so that any discrepancies between the GPA on the transmittal notification and the GPA calculated by the student can be reported to AMCAS immediately.

The AMCAS designation form is used to identify the schools the student has selected. The fee is based on the number of schools the student selects. More important, the schools the student selects can make a significant difference in whether he is accepted. The information provided later in this chapter describes how to select schools based on the likelihood of acceptance. Most students should apply to 15–20 schools. All students should apply to all of the schools in their state as well as to out-of-state schools that accept a high percentage of students from other states. Applying to 15–20 schools through AMCAS costs between $380 and $480.

Students who cannot afford to pay the application fees should complete the fee waiver request packet included in the AMCAS packet. Students who qualify for this waiver are not required to pay to apply to the first 10 medical schools, although they must pay to apply to each subsequent school. Only students who believe that they qualify should apply for fee reduction.

The acknowledgment postcard is returned to the student after AMCAS receives his completed application forms. This postcard is only an acknowledgment that the forms were received, not an indication that the application is complete or final. Many students contact AMCAS a few weeks after receiving this postcard to ask whether anything else must be done. If there are no problems with the application, the student receives a copy of the transmittal notification in a few weeks. Any errors or discrepancies should be reported to AMCAS immediately because medical schools use a similar sheet to evaluate students initially. Incorrect information on this page may cost an acceptance.

• • •
THE PERSONAL STATEMENT

The personal statement asks the student to write a one-page essay about herself. It is the student's opportunity to highlight her personality characteristics and educational experiences. Many students write a chronologic autobiography, showing how their experiences have led to the decision to become a physician. The personal statement allows the student to explain who he is, why he wants to be a physician, and why the committee should consider him. A well-written personal statement can convince an admission committee to interview a student, even if his academic record is weak.

After they complete a rough draft of the personal statement, many students ask someone else to read it. Good resources include advisors, faculty members, and others who are familiar with the application process. Many students write a long rough draft and shorten the statement to one page in later revisions. Keep all drafts for later use when completing secondary applications. A personal statement should address the following points:

1. State why and when you decided to study medicine. Many students state that they want to help others. This is necessary but not sufficient. It is best to provide concrete examples of how you have, or how you feel you can, help others. The single most important factor in writing the personal statement is honesty. Write about what you think or feel, not what you think admission committees want you to think or feel.

2. Explain how a career in medicine fits your needs, desires, and personality. Medicine offers a variety of career choices. If you feel strongly drawn to a particular field or specialty, explain why.

3. Identify the factors that influenced you to choose medicine as a career.

    Many students choose a career in medicine because a family member or close friend is or was a physician. Deciding to follow in the footsteps of a friend or relative is a natural reason for wanting to be a physician. When writing about the effect your friend or relative had on your decision, emphasize the qualities she exhibited that fit your personal reasons for choosing medicine. Did she allow you to visit her office and observe her working with patients? Did she perform charity work with low-income patients?

    Other students choose medicine because they or a relative or friend had contact with physicians because of an illness. Sometimes this experience is positive, such as when someone is cured of a disease. In this case, students often write that they want to be like Doctor X who was caring, skilled, and intelligent. In other cases, the experience is negative, as when someone dies while receiving care from a physician. Under these circumstances, students often write about wanting to become a physician to help cure disease or stop its spread. Both of these experiences are legitimate reasons to want to become a physician. However, it is important not to be too optimistic about the effect you can have as a physician, or too negative about physicians you view as incompetent.

4. Analyze your personal qualities and beliefs that are appropriate for a career in medicine. This process requires introspection. In addition, many students talk to family, friends, faculty, advisors, and others who know them well. For example, do you or others feel that you possess leadership skills, teamwork abilities, problem-solving skills, physical endurance, or an empathic personality? List these qualities, and identify examples. For instance, to demonstrate leadership skills, a student might cite that he was president of his freshman class in college. Students are asked to write about their personal qualities to give admission committees some insight into who they are. A student's academic

record is shown by his GPA and MCAT scores, but these numbers do not say anything about the student as a person.

5. You can use the personal statement to explain academic weaknesses, such as a low GPA or low MCAT scores. As much as possible, be positive in describing these problems. Explain how you have learned, grown, or matured as a result of whatever factor caused a decline in GPA. Also explain any legitimate reasons (e.g., illness, family emergency) for a low GPA in one semester or quarter.

6. Explain your philosophy of medicine and health care, and provide examples. In other words, state how you believe medicine will change over the next decade or so as well as how you see yourself participating in those changes.

7. Summarize why you want to study medicine, and indicate that you are eager to begin. However, do not thank the committee for reading your essay.

Be selective in what you include in the personal statement. Because of the need for brevity, focus on your abilities, not on other persons or issues, and follow these guidelines:

1. Do not use the personal statement to discuss your research projects in detail. However, provide an overview of the research projects in which you have participated. If you asked the principal investigator or another member of the research team for a letter of recommendation, mention his name to provide the reviewer a means of verifying your statements. Mention any presentations or other significant academic milestones.

2. Do not apologize for mistakes (e.g., poor grades).

3. Do not attempt to demonstrate artistic or creative skills (e.g., no poems, songs, jokes, or quotes). Attempts at cleverness detract from the personal statement, and committee members usually are not amused by an attempt to make some witty point.

4. Do not attack Western medical practices, even if you believe that some of them are cold or indifferent to patients. If you feel strongly that changes should be made in medical practices, then state your beliefs positively, emphasizing how you will help to effect change.

5. Do not state your race, religion, or sexual orientation, unless it is necessary to make a point about an extracurricular activity (e.g., you volunteered at a blood drive run by your church).

Examples

This section shows personal statements written by students who eventually were admitted to medical school. Note the style of writing, the information that is included, and how each student approaches the points described earlier. There is no formula for writing a personal statement. Some students enjoy research, and some do not. Some are athletes, and some are not. Do not concern yourself with what you are not, but concentrate on what you are.

Example 1

Example 1 is a rough draft that contains major errors, followed by a revision of the same personal statement.

Rough draft:

I have decided to become a doctor because, in reviewing the features of a good doctor, the mastery of traditional skills in the art of clinical diagnosis, along with the ability to then deal with the problem in a direct and definitive manner, is what especially appeals to me and what sets medicine apart from all other disciplines.

In deciding on a career in medicine, I also have considered what the qualities are that make me particularly well suited to and happy to be a doctor. From early on, I was taught that it was up to no one but myself, what I was to make of the rest of my life. Be it in my blood or upbringing, I have always been high both on myself and those around me, and I continue even when there is no one to come along. It was my intellectual curiosity that brought me toward medicine and my exposure to clinical research was enough to establish within me the desire to conduct my own research to eventually benefit those patients that I could not currently offer anything to. I do not, however, consider the medical school years to be the appropriate time for this. I would have neither the clinical experience nor perspective for the limited time available to permit me to see it through to completion, a situation that my drive to complete tasks could not tolerate. I consider the goal of these years to be the accumulation of as broad a base of knowledge as possible to allow us to become competent physicians. My appreciation of teaching and love of learning, instilled in me early in my education, have evolved such that I now derive tremendous satisfaction and further stimulation from teaching others what I have just learned.

Academic pursuit of excellence, however, is only one aspect of my personality. I actually need to see or feel the product of my efforts to be truly satisfied. This started with my interest in drawing—my goal always being the realistic depiction of nature. This developed in me observational skills and a sense of self that comes out of measuring yourself against what you want to be and no one else. In contrast to this more solitary side of me, I work well with others within a team as well as in a leadership position when that is appropriate. My personal integrity has gained me the trust and confidence of those I come in contact with, both in the clinical setting and elsewhere.

Although I prefer to use my ability to make use of all the data to arrive at as logical and practical a decision as possible, I do not hesitate to make a decision in spite of limited data when the situation demands it, guided by good instincts that are tempered by common sense. Despite my confidence, I recognize my limitations and times when I need to seek help.

Having presented the qualities that I consider relevant in consideration as an applicant to medical school. I am hoping to train at an institution that provides a balance of practical teaching in the care of patients, exposure to the advances in medicine with training in research techniques, and pride in passing on the craftsmanship of fine medical practice.

Revision:

I have decided to become a physician. What especially appeals to me, and what sets medicine apart from all other professions, is its dual emphasis on the mastery of traditional interpersonal skills used in the art of clinical diagnosis and on the breadth of scientific knowledge needed to deal with health problems in a direct and definitive manner. It is this combination of elements that motivates me to become a physician.

In deciding on a career in medicine, I have also considered what qualities make me particularly well suited for that career. From early on, I was taught that it was up to me to make the most of my life. Be it in my blood or upbringing, I have always striven for perfection. However, it was my intellectual curiosity that brought me into medicine, and my prior exposure to clinical research established within me the desire to conduct my own research that would eventually benefit patients who were considered untreatable. Once in medical school, I consider my goal to be the accumulation of as broad a base of knowledge as possible to allow me to become a competent physician. Additionally, my appreciation of teaching and love of learning, which were instilled in me early in my educational experience, have evolved to such an extent that I now derive tremendous satisfaction and stimulation from teaching others what I have learned.

My academic pursuit of excellence, however, is only one aspect of my personality. I actually need to see or feel the product of my efforts to be truly satisfied. This started with my interest in drawing. My goal as an artist, the realistic depiction of nature, developed in me observational skills and a sense of self that comes out of measuring yourself against what you want to do and can do. In contrast to this more solitary side of myself, I work well with others within a team as well as in a leadership position when that is appropriate. My personal integrity has gained me the trust and confidence of those I come in contact with, both in the clinical setting and elsewhere.

Although I prefer to use my ability to make use of all pertinent data to arrive at a logical and practical decision, I do not hesitate to make a decision in spite of limited data when the situation demands it, especially when I am guided by good instincts that are tempered by common sense. However, despite my confidence, I recognize my limitations and know when I need to seek help.

These are the personal qualities that I possess that I consider relevant to my pursuit of a career in medicine. I am hopeful that I will be accepted to train at an institution that provides a balance of practical teaching in the care of patients, exposure to advances in medicine, advanced training in research techniques, and pride in passing on the craftsmanship inherent in the practice of medicine. If I am selected, I can guarantee that I will do all that I can to further excellence in medicine by being prepared to complete my studies enthusiastically.

Example 2

Medicine appeals to me as a humanistic, challenging field offering the opportunity to help people in the most vital aspect of their lives: their health. Aspiring to become a physician since childhood, I have verified my interest by several activities, notably volunteer work, first aid and emergency life support training, medical research, and continuous medically oriented education.

My hospital volunteer work began while I was attending high school and continued well into my college career; this experience was an early indicator that a hospital environment is compatible with my needs as a place to learn.

I have successfully completed several extracurricular health delivery courses, including Advanced First Aid and Emergency Care by the American Red Cross as well as Basic and Advanced Cardiac Life Support by the American Heart Association.

My latest research experience includes clinical investigation of the use of transcutaneous PO_2, PCO_2, and thoracic impedance cardiac output monitoring in critically ill patients. Past projects include several experiments dealing with the elucidation of the nature of the various transport mechanisms of the blood–brain barrier.

I enjoy the pursuit of knowledge and acknowledge my responsibility to teach what I have learned. In addition to a successful and uninterrupted medically oriented academic career, I have enjoyed tutoring students in mathematics, chemistry, physics, and physiology. My background also includes participation as a behavior modification therapist in the Los Angeles Young Autistic Project. Teaching has been a rewarding experience. I have learned patience and perseverance while enriching someone else's life. Likewise, my clinical training has been rewarding because I have witnessed the healing of disease and injury as a direct result of medical intervention.

The field of medicine appeals to me particularly because of the opportunity to combine intellectual and technical skills. I have enjoyed performing the procedures I've learned through my volunteer work; however, there has been little chance to emphasize the other effects a disabling illness has on a patient, whether they are psychological, socioeconomic, or on the patient's family. I consider myself an empathic, concerned individual who will truly care for his patients as whole persons; these facets of my personality will help me fill this vacuum. When my medical school training is completed, I will most likely pursue teaching or research at a university hospital as a career.

As a medical student, I can offer you an enthusiastic, motivated, well-rounded individual who is eager to support and promote the fine reputation of your institution.

This personal statement shows that the applicant has seriously considered medicine and has tested his interest by several means. It reveals that he has done research and, without going into detail, suggests that he knows something about the subject. The applicant also reveals that he has worked with other students, suggesting that he is a team player. He has also indicated goals for the future and ends with a strong positive sentence.

Example 3

As I apply to medical school, everyone from my mother to complete strangers asks me, "What kind of doctor are you going to be?" I always answer, "Probably a pediatrician." By the time I complete my medical school training, I hope that this will still be my answer. I have already heard about some of the negative things about pediatrics, such as patients who cry loudly, making it difficult to examine them, and the problem of having to deal with overanxious parents or, worse yet, the death of a child who is your patient. But I believe that the positives far outweigh the negatives.

What attracts me to medicine, and pediatrics in particular? For me, the most compelling reason is the combination of both science and clinical practice that medicine provides. I find science exciting; I am excited by the quest for knowledge and the exhilarating, but demanding work needed to find solutions to clinical problems. My past experiences as a volunteer in the emergency room, in doctors' offices, and my extensive research training have shown me that medicine can satisfy my desires. What attracts me to pediatrics is simply that I love to work with children. Instead of following an adult patient with the same disease for years, administering the same effective treatment, I will have patients who are rapidly developing, requiring constant reassessment and redirection of their care. In general, I will be working with children and their parents who are motivated and interested in the child's health. I will not be working with patients whose diseases are brought on by their own unhealthy lifestyles, but rather will be involved in preventive medicine, a process that I find more rewarding. Furthermore, in working within the entire range of pediatrics, from newborns to young adults, I will encounter a large variety of clinical situations. Finally, I look forward to interacting with patients and their parents. Putting complex medical terms into lay people's language not only is enjoyable to me, but also is one of my strengths.

Lifelong continuing education and the challenge of a variety of patient problems are essential to me. For this reason, I eventually hope to work in or near a major university in a metropolitan area, both as a resident and as a practicing physician. I enjoy teaching and hope to interact with medical students as I combine a predominantly clinical career with academic endeavors. I do realize that our health care system is deficient in primary care practitioners, and I intend to contribute to the alleviation of this problem as a weekly volunteer at a free clinic.

Regardless of where my career takes me, I plan to continue pursuing my outside interests, which include dance, piano, creative writing, and experiencing as many theatrical works, symphonies, and art exhibits as I can afford, in terms of both time and money. I am a hopelessly eternal student, and enjoy studying languages, such as Spanish, German, and American Sign Language, as well as history, literature, and fine arts. Playing racquetball and taking aerobic dance classes help keep me in shape. My favorite pastime, however, is travel—experiencing other cultures and reading a good novel on the trains.

The strength of this personal statement lies, in large part, with the strong positive feeling it imparts to the reader. The applicant presents herself as a warm, positive person, one who might be expected to excel in the art of medicine. The writer also reveals her experiences in a positive light and suggests an ability to think.

Action Words

One way to improve the personal statement is to use positive, active words and phrases. This section lists some examples.

A

accomplished

achieved

accustomed, used to

administered

an administrator

affected (influenced)

analytical

analyzed

approved

arranged

assisted

attained

awarded

B

broad gauge

C

catalogued

communicated

(possess)
   communication skills

competent, capable, able

composed

conceived

conducted

consistent record (of progress, growth, achievements, promotion)

contracted

contribute

contributor

controlled

converted

convinced

coordinated

created

D

dedicated

delegated

demonstrably
   (successful, capable)

designed

developed

directed

disapproved

distinguished

distributed

dynamic

E

economized

educated, schooled, trained

effected (brought about)

effective

efficient

enlarged

established

examined

exceptional

expanded

G

(a) generalist

governed

grouped

guided

H

handled

harmonized

I

imaginative, conceptual

implemented

improved

increased

indexed

ingenious, inventive

initiated

innovative, creative

installed

instituted

introduced

invented

investigated

L

(a) leader

learn, work well with
others

M

managed

moderated

modernized

motivated

multilingual, bilingual

N

negotiated

O

obtained

organized

originated

outstanding

P

performed

planned

prepared

presented

presided

produced

Q

qualified

qualify for

R

recommended

recruited

rectified

reduced

reliable

reorganized

reshaped

responsible for

S

saved

scheduled

secured

set up

served in, served on

skilled

sold

solved problems

sorted

(a) specialist

straightened

strengthened

stress resistant

structured

student of

succeeded

supervised

systematized

T

teach, taught

trained

traveled

U

understood

W

worked

wrote

● ● ●
APPLICATION SCHEDULE

A number of factors determine when to submit a medical school application. The AMCAS schools start accepting applications between June 15 and June 17 for enrollment the next year. For example, students applied in June 1995 for admission in September 1996. Most schools stop accepting applications by November 1 or 15. The latest date at some schools is December 15. The acceptance dates for all schools are given in Appendix A. In theory, it is best to apply as early as possible. However, students with the best GPA and MCAT scores often send in their applications at the earliest possible date, so students who apply early are compared with these students. For this reason, students with weaker academic records sometimes wait to apply. Also, students who have a personal milestone (e.g., award, publication of a paper) that will occur before November may delay their application so that this information can be included.

One factor to consider in deciding when to apply is the recent upward trend in the number of medical school applicants. Until 1989, the number of applicants to medical school showed a decline (e.g., the 1989 entering year applicant pool was 26,915). In 1993–94, the applicant pool increased to 42,808, and in 1995 the total number of applicants was 46,591. This trend means that competition for medical school positions is increasing. As more students compete for the same number of slots, a smaller percentage of applicants will be accepted. A student who has a high GPA, high MCAT scores, and a strong personal profile probably will not be affected by this trend. On the other hand, many students with average grades or MCAT scores gain admission to medical school. A later section of this chapter discusses school requirements and shows how most students have the potential to enter medical school, regardless of their academic performance.

As discussed in Chapter 2, some students are accepted to a medical school program immediately after high school. At the other end of the spectrum, some students apply to medical school after having participated in another career. Medical schools have recently begun to admit older students. Many of these students did not pursue an undergraduate degree in the biologic sciences. Nevertheless, the typical medical school applicant has a bachelor's degree in the sciences and is approximately 23 years old.

With all of these factors to consider, the ideal application schedule is described below:

Fall of the Junior Year

1. Start to write your personal statement.

2. Review sample personal statements.

3. Attend conferences or workshops to meet admission advisors or counselors. Subscribe to Health Pathways (see the sources listed at the end of this chapter) for more information.

4. Continue to do well in your classes, especially science classes.

5. Ask a professor or an advisor to review a rough draft of your personal statement.

6. Ask for letters of recommendation from faculty. Give them copies of your personal statement and your AMCAS application, if you have completed it.

Spring of the Junior Year

1. After March 15, arrange to have all of your high school and college (including junior or community college) transcripts sent to AMCAS.

2. Take the April MCAT. This is the best time to take the MCAT because students who are disappointed in their scores can take the MCAT in August and not delay their application for another year.

3. Begin to assemble your formal AMCAS application and identify appropriate medical schools.

Summer of the Junior Year

1. Complete and send the AMCAS application as well as non-AMCAS school applications.

2. Complete and return the early decision packet, if applicable.

Fall to Winter of the Senior Year

1. Complete and return secondary applications.

2. Send letters of recommendation.

3. Begin the interviewing process.

4. Complete financial aid need analysis forms (see Chapter 7). These forms are provided by the schools that send secondary applications between November and March.

Spring of the Senior Year

1. Complete interviews.

2. Send thank you letters to interviewers.

3. Complete the financial aid packet for each medical school at which you interviewed. Need analysis forms are usually due between March and May.

4. Apply for housing at each medical school at which you interviewed.

Spring to Summer of the Senior Year

1. Of the medical schools that have accepted you, decide which medical school you would like to attend.

2. Send letters to the schools that you reject.

● ● ●
EARLY DECISION PROGRAMS

Approximately 70% of United States medical schools offer some type of early decision program. These programs simplify the application process for students who have selected a medical school and who clearly have the academic skills, as shown by excellent GPA and MCAT scores, to succeed. Students who apply through an early decision program normally have a high GPA and high MCAT scores, residence status in the state, and someone in the state who will sponsor them at the school. Sponsorship is most important if the sponsor is a prominent person (e.g., state senator, city mayor, medical school dean). The sponsor may write a supportive letter that will result in early consideration and an interview.

Applicants to an early decision program apply to only one school. The school reviews the application, evaluates the candidate, conducts an interview, and notifies the applicant of acceptance, usually between June and mid-August. The obvious benefit of this process is that the student knows fairly early whether he has been accepted and therefore has time to plan for the next year. Additionally, the student does not participate in multiple interviews or submit secondary applications, activities that take time and money. If the school does not accept the student, he has time to apply to other schools through the regular AMCAS process.

Table 8–1 lists medical schools with early decision programs as well as schools that limit these programs to state residents. Full addresses of medical schools are given in Appendix A.

● ● ●

TABLE 8-1. Schools With Early Decision Programs

Medical School	Accept State Residents Only
University of Alabama	Yes (Alabama)
University of South Alabama	Yes (Alabama)
Loma Linda University	
University of Southern California	
Stanford University	
University of Colorado	
University of Connecticut	
Yale University	
George Washington University	
Georgetown University	
University of Miami	Yes (Florida)
University of South Florida	Yes (Florida)
Medical College of Georgia	Yes (Georgia)
Mercer University	Yes (Georgia)
Morehouse School of Medicine	Yes (Georgia)
University of Hawaii	Yes (Hawaii)
University of Chicago-Pritzker	
Chicago Medical School-Finch	
University of Illinois	
Loyola University of Chicago	
Northwestern University	
Rush Medical College	
Southern Illinois University	
Indiana University	
University of Iowa	
University of Kansas	
University of Kentucky	
University of Louisville	
Louisiana State University	Yes (Louisiana)
Johns Hopkins University	
University of Maryland	
Boston University	

● ● ●

TABLE 8-1. Schools With Early Decision Programs *(Continued)*

University of Massachusetts	Yes (Massachusetts)
Tufts University	
Michigan State University	
University of Michigan	
Wayne State University	
Mayo Medical School	
University of Minnesota, Duluth	
University of Minnesota, Minneapolis	
University of Mississippi	Yes (Mississippi)
University of Missouri, Columbia	Yes (Missouri)
St. Louis University	
Creighton University	
University of Nevada	
University of Medicine and Dentistry of New Jersey, New Jersey Medical School	
University of Medicine and Dentistry of New Jersey, Robert Wood Johnson Medical School	
University of New Mexico	
Albert Einstein College of Medicine	
Cornell University	
Mt. Sinai School of Medicine	
New York Medical College	
State University of New York, Brooklyn	
State University of New York, Buffalo	
State University of New York, Syracuse	
State University of New York, Stoney Brook	
Bowman Gray School of Medicine	
East Carolina University	Yes (North Carolina)
University of North Carolina	
Case Western Reserve University	
University of Cincinnati	
Medical College of Ohio	Yes (Ohio)
Northeastern Ohio Universities	
Ohio State University	
Wright State University	

(Table continued on the following page)

● ● ●

TABLE 8-1. Schools With Early Decision Programs *(Continued)*

Jefferson Medical College	
Medical College of Pennsylvania	
Pennsylvania State University	
University of Pittsburgh	
Temple University	
Universidad Central Del Caribe	Yes (Puerto Rico)
Ponce School of Medicine	Yes (Puerto Rico)
Medical University of South Carolina	
University of South Carolina	
East Tennessee State University	
Meharry Medical College	
Vanderbilt University	
Baylor College of Medicine	
Texas Tech University	
University of Utah	
University of Vermont	
Eastern Virginia Medical School	
Virginia Commonwealth University	
University of Virginia	
Marshall University	Yes (West Virginia)
West Virginia University	Yes (West Virginia)
Medical College of Wisconsin	
University of Wisconsin	Yes (Wisconsin)

● ● ●

SELECTING SCHOOLS TO APPLY TO

Deciding which medical schools to apply to can be difficult and frustrating. Students can make this process more predictable by applying to medical schools that are likely to accept someone with their qualifications.

Some students apply to 50–60 medical schools, although the norm is 15–20 schools. Most students apply to all of the medical schools in their state or those that have made special arrangements with residents of their state. Many also apply to schools in states where they or their family previously lived. Public medical schools in most states preferentially admit students who are, or were, state residents. Sometimes a student who has a relative who lives in one of these states can establish residency by using the relative's address. The issue of residency is important. In 1994, 68.1% of entering medical students were accepted at schools within their state. For public schools, the percentage was 87.1%; for private schools, it was 40.7%. Clearly, at an out-of-state school, the odds are better at a private school than at a public school. However, it is not wise to artificially limit the number of prospects based on residency status because more than 30 schools have classes composed of 50% or more out-of-state students, and approximately 60 schools have classes composed of 20% or more out-of-state students.

Tables 8–2, 8–3, and *8–4* can help you identify the schools whose requirements most closely match your qualifications. *Table 8–2* shows the mean MCAT scores that students had on acceptance at 110 of the 124 United States medical schools. *Table 8–3* lists the class size and percentage and number of out-of-state students accepted by United States medical schools. *Table 8–4* lists schools that enroll 10% or more of minority students. In 1991, only 52 schools admitted 10% or more minority applicants to their freshman class. The increase to the 89 schools listed in *Table 8–4* probably reflects the 3000 by 2000 campaign of the Association of American Medical Colleges (AAMC). The goal of this campaign is to have 3000 minority students accepted to United States medical schools by the year 2000. This campaign has succeeded in increasing not only the total number of minority matriculants, but also the choices available to them.

When using these tables to help select medical schools, students must consider their individual circumstances. First, determine the overall mean MCAT score (not including the Writing Sample) by adding all of the numeric scores and dividing the total by three. Consult *Table 8–2* to determine which schools accept students with MCAT scores in that range. For instance, a student whose mean MCAT score is at or near the median national score of 9.4 will have scored at or above the mean score accepted by 56 of the United States medical schools. A mean MCAT score of 10 will make a student's application welcome at 89 of the 110 schools listed.

Table 8–2 lists the mean score, not the minimal acceptable score, at each school. It is nearly impossible to extrapolate the lowest possible acceptable score from the mean score. However, a student whose mean score is within one point of the mean for a given school probably will be considered for admission to that school. For example, a student with a mean score greater than 10 is a potential candidate at

● ● ●

TABLE 8–2. Medical Schools Accepting Students by Range of Mean MCAT Scores*

Medical Schools Accepting Students	Mean MCAT Score of Accepted Students
MCAT 11–11.9	
Washington University, Missouri	11.4
University of California, Davis	11.0
University of California, San Francisco	11.0
Yale University, Connecticut	11.0
MCAT Range 10–10.9	
Columbia University, New York	10.8
Vanderbilt University, Tennessee	10.8
Stanford University, California	10.7
Harvard Medical School, Massachusetts	10.7
New York University	10.7

(Table continued on the following page)

• • •

TABLE 8-2. Medical Schools Accepting Students by Range of Mean MCAT Scores* *(Continued)*

University of Pennsylvania	10.5
Cornell University, New York	10.4
University of Utah	10.4
University of Vermont	10.4
University of Michigan	10.3
Ohio State University	10.3
University of Pittsburgh	10.3
University of Texas, Dallas	10.3
University of Chicago, Illinois	10.2
University of Virginia	10.2
University of California, Irvine	10.1
New York Medical College	10.1
Georgetown University, DC	10.0
University of Massachusetts	10.0
Mayo Medical School, Minnesota	10.0
Case Western Reserve University, Ohio	10.0
Oregon Health Sciences University	10.0
Baylor College of Medicine, Texas	10.0
University of Washington	10.0
MCAT Range 9-9.9	
University of Colorado	9.9
St. Louis University, Missouri	9.9
University of Connecticut	9.8
Emory University, Georgia	9.8
University of Maryland	9.8
Uniformed Services University, Maryland	9.8
Albert Einstein College of Medicine, New York	9.8
University of Alabama	9.7
University of Southern California	9.7
George Washington University, DC	9.7
Northwestern University, Illinois	9.7
University of Minnesota, Minneapolis	9.7
State University of New York, Buffalo	9.7
University of Miami, Florida	9.6
University of South Florida	9.6

● ● ●

TABLE 8-2. Medical Schools Accepting Students by Range of
Mean MCAT Scores* *(Continued)*

MDNJ, Newark, New Jersey	9.6
Bowman Gray School of Medicine, North Carolina	9.6
Medical College of Wisconsin	9.6
University of Iowa	9.5
Tulane University, Louisiana	9.5
Tufts University, Massachusetts	9.5
Mt. Sinai School of Medicine, New York	9.5
State University of New York, Brooklyn	9.5
University of Cincinnati, Ohio	9.5
University of Wisconsin	9.5
Medical College of Georgia	9.4 (Median)
Indiana University	9.4
UMDNJ, Robert Wood Johnson, New Jersey	9.4
University of North Carolina	9.4
Temple University, Pennsylvania	9.4
University of South Alabama	9.3
University of Illinois	9.3
Dartmouth Medical School, New Hampshire	9.3
Jefferson Medical College, Pennsylvania	9.3
Texas Tech University	9.3
Virginia Commonwealth University	9.3
University of Florida	9.2
University of Missouri, Columbia	9.2
University of Nevada	9.2
Eastern Virginia Medical School	9.2
University of Arizona	9.1
Loma Linda University, California	9.1
Boston University, Massachusetts	9.1
Michigan State University	9.1
Albany Medical College, New York	9.1
Northeastern Ohio University	9.1
University of Oklahoma	9.1
Pennsylvania State University	9.1
Chicago Medical School, Illinois	9.0

(Table continued on the following page)

• • •

TABLE 8-2. Medical Schools Accepting Students by Range of Mean MCAT Scores* *(Continued)*

Rush University, Illinois	9.0
University of Kentucky	9.0
University of Mississippi	9.0
University of New Mexico	9.0
University of Rochester, New York	9.0
State University of New York, Syracuse	9.0
Medical University of South Carolina	9.0
University of Tennessee	9.0
University of Texas, San Antonio	9.0
West Virginia University	9.0
MCAT Range 8–8.9	
Wayne State University, Michigan	8.9
University of Minnesota, Duluth	8.9
University of Hawaii	8.8
Southern Illinois University	8.8
University of Louisville, Kentucky	8.8
Louisiana State University, Shreveport	8.8
University of Nebraska	8.8
University of South Dakota	8.8

any school in the United States, and a student with a mean score of 8.0 is considered competitive at 35 schools. However, other factors, such as GPA and other achievements, are also considered by admission committees.

After determining which schools accept students with a specific MCAT score, students should compare this list of schools with *Table 8–3*. Students who reside in a highly competitive state should apply to schools in other states that accept significant numbers of out-of-state students. For example, a mean MCAT score of 8.0 is a competitive score at 35 schools. Of these 35 schools, 15 have entering classes that include 10% or more out-of-state students. Thus, a student with a score of 8.0 should apply to these 15 schools.

Table 8–4 lists schools that accept significant numbers of minority students. Students can use these three tables to identify which schools are most likely to accept them. For instance, if a minority student has a mean MCAT score of 7.5, then nine schools would consider him a potential candidate (i.e., the schools' mean MCAT score for matriculated students is 8.5 or less). Four of these nine schools—Morehouse, Howard, Meharry, and the Medical College of Pennsylvania—both accept 10% or more out-of-state students and have a high rate of minority student acceptance. Clearly, the student should apply to these four schools.

• • •

TABLE 8-2. Medical Schools Accepting Students by Range of Mean MCAT Scores* *(Continued)*

East Tennessee State University	8.8
University of Kansas	8.7
Creighton University, Nebraska	8.7
University of North Dakota	8.7
Medical College of Ohio	8.7
University of Texas, Houston	8.7
Louisiana State University, New Orleans	8.6
Mercer University, Georgia	8.5
Medical College of Pennsylvania	8.4
University of Arkansas	8.3
East Carolina University	8.2
Marshall University, West Virginia	8.0
MCAT range <8.0	
Meharry Medical College, Tennessee	7.6
Howard University, DC	7.4
Morehouse University, Georgia	7.0
University of Puerto Rico	6.7

*See Appendix A for the complete address of each school.

These recommendations focus on the school side of the equation, or which schools are likely to accept a specific student. On the other side of the equation are factors that a student should consider in choosing a school. These factors include:

- The school's curriculum
- Support services offered by the school (e.g., tutorials, learning assistance, career counseling)
- Availability of fully-paid scholarships
- Clinical training or experience (e.g., what type of hospitals provide training for students)
- Social and recreational activities
- Availability of affordable housing on campus or in the community

A student should evaluate which schools are likely to accept her and which schools are attractive to her. Ideally, each student should have a list of 15–25 schools. At this point, some students rank the schools according to their personal preference. For instance, a student's first choice might be a school that is in-state, which usually means lower tuition, and offers a specific curriculum. Although it is important to choose schools carefully, students should not limit themselves. A student who really wants to attend Harvard, for instance, should apply there, even if

● ● ●

TABLE 8-3. Medical Schools Accepting Out-of-State Students*

Medical School	Percentage of Students Accepted from Out of State	Class Size	Number of Out-of-State Students
Georgetown University, DC	98	185	181
Harvard Medical School, Massachusetts	93	168	156
George Washington University, DC	98	157	154
New York Medical College	77	183	133
Tulane University, Louisiana	84	148	124
Jefferson Medical College, Pennsylvania	55	223	123
University of Southern California (1991 data)	80	150	120
Tufts University, Massachusetts	73	168	119
Chicago Medical School, Illinois	71	165	117
Washington University, Missouri	92	123	113
Howard University, DC	92	122	112
Johns Hopkins University, Maryland	88	118	104
Columbia University, New York	69	150	104
St. Louis University, Missouri	68	151	103
Creighton University, Nebraska	90	112	101
Medical College of Wisconsin	47	213	100
Hahnemann University, Pennsylvania	52	171	89
University of Pennsylvania	66	150	99
Albert Einstein College of Medicine, New York	56	177	99
Boston University, Massachusetts	66	135	89
Yale University, Connecticut	88	100	88
Vanderbilt University, Tennessee	86	102	88
Northwestern University, Illinois	51	173	88
Dartmouth Medical School, New Hampshire	86	88	76
Albany Medical College, New York	58	131	76
New York University	47	160	75
Meharry Medical College, Tennessee	89	80	71
Temple University, Pennsylvania	38	182	69
Duke University, North Carolina	68	100	68
Loma Linda University, California	43	159	68
Medical College of Pennsylvania	50	131	66
University of Rochester, New York	65	98	64

● ● ●

TABLE 8-3. Medical Schools Accepting Out-of-State Students*
(Continued)

Loyola University, Illinois	49	130	64
Cornell University, New York	60	101	60
Emory University, Georgia	52	114	59
University of Chicago, Illinois	55	104	57
University of Vermont	62	91	55
University of Pittsburgh, Pennsylvania	42	131	55
Virginia Commonwealth University	31	173	54
Bowman Gray School of Medicine, North Carolina	48	108	52
University of Michigan Medical School	43	122	52
Pennsylvania State University	48	107	51
Baylor College of Medicine, Texas	30	167	50
Case Western Reserve University, Ohio	35	136	48
Mt. Sinai School of Medicine, New York	40	115	46
Stanford University, California	50	86	43
Ohio State University	20	210	42
Eastern Virginia Medical School	40	100	40
University of Virginia	29	139	40
Mayo Medical School, Minnesota	88	42	37
University of Alabama	20	166	33
University of California, San Francisco	22	141	31
Wayne State University, Michigan	12	256	31
University of Cincinnati, Ohio	17	162	28
University of Utah	25	100	25
University of Maryland	17	145	25
University of Texas, Dallas	12	200	24
University of Illinois	8	300	24
Medical University of South Carolina	17	140	24
Medical College of Ohio	17	135	23
State University of New York, Brooklyn	10	199	20
University of Texas Medical School, Houston	10	200	20
Michigan State University	16	116	19
UMDNJ, Robert Wood Johnson, New Jersey	14	138	19
University of Colorado	14	126	18
University of Wisconsin Medical School	13	143	18

(Table continued on the following page)

• • •

TABLE 8–3. Medical Schools Accepting Out-of-State Students*
(Continued)

University of Tennessee, Memphis	11	165	18
Indiana University	6	265	16
University of Minnesota Medical School, Minneapolis	8	185	15
University of Washington (excludes contracted students from Alaska, Montana, and Idaho)	10	165	15
University of Iowa	8	175	14
University of Missouri, Kansas City	13	99	13
University of North Dakota (includes contracted positions)	23	57	13
Rush Medical College, Illinois	11	120	13
Morehouse School of Medicine, Georgia	35	34	12
University of Kansas Medical Center	7	175	12
UMDNJ, New Jersey Medical School, Newark	7	170	12
University of Texas, Galveston	6	209	12
University of Texas Medical School, San Antonio	6	203	12
University of Connecticut	14	81	11
Oregon Health Sciences University	11	91	10
University of California, Los Angeles	7	145	10
University of Oklahoma	7	148	10
University of North Carolina	6	160	10

*See Appendix A for the complete address of each school.

• • •

TABLE 8–4. Medical Schools Accepting Significant Numbers of Minority Students*

Medical School	Percentage of Minority Students in Entering Class (1994-95)
Morehouse School of Medicine, Georgia	94
Meharry Medical College, Tennessee	80
Howard University, Washington, DC	58
University of Texas, Dallas	37
University of Florida	34
University of California, San Francisco	31

• • •

TABLE 8-4. Medical Schools Accepting Significant Numbers of
Minority Students* *(Continued)*

University of New Mexico	30
Wright State University, Ohio	27
University of Illinois	27
University of Texas, Galveston	26
Emory University, Georgia	26
University of Texas, Houston	26
University of California, Los Angeles	23
Harvard Medical School, Massachusetts	22
University of Tennessee	21
Louisiana State University, New Orleans	21
Medical College of Georgia	20
Temple University, Pennsylvania	20
Michigan State University	20
UMDNJ, Robert Wood Johnson, New Jersey	20
UMDNJ, New Jersey Medical School	19
University of Southern California	19
University of Mississippi	19
University of California, Davis	18
Wayne State University, Michigan	18
University of Minnesota, Duluth	18
Medical University of South Carolina	17
Texas Tech	17
East Carolina University, North Carolina	17
University of Colorado	16
University of Wisconsin	16
Mt. Sinai School of Medicine, New York	16
Brown University, Rhode Island	16
University of Texas, San Antonio	16
University of Kansas	16
University of Virginia	16
University of Michigan Medical School	15
State University of New York, Brooklyn	15
University of Oklahoma	15

(Table continued on the following page)

• • •

TABLE 8-4. Medical Schools Accepting Significant Numbers of Minority Students* *(Continued)*

Medical College of Ohio	15
University of Maryland	15
Mayo Medical School, Minnesota	15
University of Pennsylvania	15
Yale University, Connecticut	15
Case Western Reserve University, Ohio	14
University of Southern Illinois	14
University of North Dakota	14
Stanford University, California	14
University of Connecticut	14
University of Chicago, Illinois	13
University of Cincinnati, Ohio	13
University of South Alabama	13
Medical College of Pennsylvania	13
University of North Carolina	13
University of South Carolina	13
Cornell University, New York	13
Washington University, Missouri	12
Bowman Gray University, North Carolina	12
Loma Linda University, California	12
Tufts University, Massachusetts	12
Georgetown University, Washington, DC	12
Boston University, Massachusetts	12
Duke University, North Carolina	11

her GPA and MCAT scores are not outstanding. The selection process is not a science, and many students are accepted to medical schools on the basis of criteria other than GPA or MCAT scores. The ideal situation is for a student to apply to 15–20 schools at which he knows he is a viable candidate and to 3–5 schools that he really wants to attend, regardless of GPA and MCAT scores.

● ● ●

TABLE 8-4. Medical Schools Accepting Significant Numbers of Minority Students* *(Continued)*

State University of New York, Buffalo	11
University of Rochester, New York	11
Baylor University, Texas	11
University of Massachusetts	11
Columbia University, New York	11
University of California, San Diego	11
East Tennessee State University	11
University of Arizona	11
University of Washington	11
Pennsylvania State University	11
University of Alabama	10
Virginia Commonwealth University	10
University of California, Irvine	10
Ohio State University	10
Johns Hopkins University, Maryland	10
Tulane University, Louisiana	10
Rush University, Illinois	10
University of Iowa	10
Medical College of Wisconsin	10
Eastern Virginia University	10
Creighton University	10
University of Louisville, Kentucky	10
University of Missouri	10
University of Nebraska	10

*African-American, Mexican-American, Native American, and Mainland Puerto Rican.

● ● ●

THE SECONDARY APPLICATION

Approximately 3–15 weeks after the completed application is sent by AMCAS to the medical schools, the school sends a secondary application. Students who are asked to complete this second application are also asked to send faculty letters of recommendation and a processing fee (usually $50–$75). Not all schools request a secondary application, but being asked to submit one is a good sign. Although some schools routinely send most applicants secondary applications, most schools first evaluate whether the student has the minimal GPA and MCAT scores required. Thus, a student who receives a secondary application is probably being seriously considered for a position at that medical school.

Secondary applications vary by school, but most ask three to five questions. Common questions include why you chose to apply to this school and what special qualities or abilities you possess that qualify you for a career in medicine. Most secondary applications direct students not to simply copy points from the personal statement.

The interview is the most important part of the selection process. To improve their chances of being asked to interview at a school, students should put adequate thought and effort into completing secondary applications. The secondary application must be neatly typed and carefully written. Some students do not complete their secondary applications; others submit them after the deadline. These students are not accepted.

The most important question on the secondary application is why the student chose this particular school. Reviewing any available literature, brochures, or curriculum descriptions can help you answer this question. An ideal source of information about medical schools is the *AAMC Curriculum Directory,* published by the Association of American Medical Colleges (Washington, DC). The best approach is to say that you chose a particular school because of the nontraditional curriculum, the chance for clinical experience in the first year, the diversity of patients, or something to this effect. Although some students ultimately choose a medical school for geographic reasons (e.g., proximity to ski slopes), it is best to focus on academic considerations at this point.

Many students have trouble identifying the traits that they possess that make them suited to a medical career. Reviewing the personal statement can help. Consistency is important. Information from early versions of the personal statement can be used to amplify important points. Basically, the school wants insight into each applicant as a person. At this point, the school has weighed the student's quantitative academic record (e.g., GPA and MCAT scores) and is now assessing the more subjective qualities that a physician must possess. Many students emphasize the compassion they feel toward the ill. Examples are helpful (e.g., experiences with sick family members). Be clear in stating the desire to aid them, but do not be trite. Statements such as, "I have always felt a deep sorrow for those in pain," can be appropriate, but statements such as, "I want to see that no one dies," are unrealistic.

Minority students may be asked to identify a commitment to serving "underserved minority or ethnic communities." The simplest, most straightforward way to answer this question is to express a preference to practice in these communities. It is helpful to provide examples of previous contributions to the community. For some minority students, this type of question is insulting because it appears to force them to make choices based on their ethnicity alone. However, students whose goal is to help serve these groups are more likely to be admitted to medical school. The decision to state the wish to serve these communities is up to each applicant, but this interest is what medical schools are often looking for in a special-admit minority student candidate.

● ● ●
LETTERS OF RECOMMENDATION

Typically, accompanying the secondary application is a request to submit three to five letters of recommendation. These letters play a minor, but significant, role in the application process. The admission committee knows about the student's grades from the AMCAS application or transcripts. The personal statement is on file, as is a description of extracurricular activities. Letters of recommendation may simply corroborate and expand information presented elsewhere; sometimes they present new information. Students should ask persons to write these letters who know them well enough to attest to their character and abilities. In addition, the authors should have some stature so that the committee members will not question their word. For this reason, medical schools usually prefer letters that are written by a faculty member rather than a staff member. Schools normally request a minimum number of letters, but students can send as many as they want. However, quality is more important than quantity. A few strong letters are better than many that merely state the same facts.

What points can a potential letter writer verify, expand, or add? A common topic is the student's academic potential. Typically, a student chooses a science faculty member in whose class he earned an A. This strategy can be effective. The letter will likely say nothing detrimental. However, if the faculty member does not know the student, the letter may not be helpful. It may say, in effect, that the student was a member of the faculty member's class and earned an A, a fact that is already recorded. A more specific letter is more helpful, for example, one stating that the student earned one of the highest grades in the class or has good work habits. Even an instructor who did not award the student an A can write a letter attesting to the student's diligence or some other positive quality.

Because the strongest letters of recommendation describe specific qualities of the student, students should increase their contact with faculty outside the classroom or laboratory. Opportunities include meeting in the faculty member's office, having lunch together, and attending conferences or seminars. These meetings give students the opportunity to express their opinions and communicate their hopes of pursuing a medical career. The faculty member can base her letter of recommendation on these conversations. Although letters from science faculty are the most relevant, letters from other faculty (e.g., social sciences, arts) can also be helpful.

A letter of recommendation can also include information about the student's personality. Although your instructors may be able to make statements that attest to your character, their knowledge generally is limited and superficial. It is advantageous to include a letter from someone who knows you well and has seen you in a variety of settings. However, this person must have sufficient professional stature to bear weight with members of the admission committee. A relative or peer is inappropriate. Appropriate persons include physicians with whom you have worked, either for pay or as a volunteer; members of the clergy; and professionals who have worked with you in civil or social organizations (e.g., United Way, Red Cross, Boy Scouts).

Ideally, letters of recommendation discuss the student's educational potential. The ideal physician is both intelligent and creative. An ideal person to assess your innate cognitive ability is a faculty member with whom you have done research. Research offers students an opportunity to become well acquainted with a faculty member or a member of the research team.

Sample Letters

This section shows examples of letters of recommendation that illustrate some of the points discussed in the previous section. They are written about the same two students by two different recommenders. In the first set of letters, the recommenders knew the students well; in the second set, they knew them less well; and in the third set, they had little knowledge of the students. In the first case, the recommender knew the student in an academic setting, and in the other case, in an extracurricular setting.

Analysis of exceptional letters

Figures 8–3 and *8–4* show letters that are outstanding because the writers observed the applicants over time and sincerely believe in their abilities. Although the title of professor and chairperson can lend more stature to a letter than the title of registered nurse, a nurse is a professional whose opinion is likely to be seriously considered by the admission committee. Both writers came to favorable conclusions about the work and personal ethics of the respective applicants.

However, only Dr. Jacblonski can make comments about the student's cognitive ability and, by implication, her academic potential. Therefore, Ms. Spellman's letter will bear less weight if Mr. Miller does not also have a good GPA and high MCAT scores. If he has these qualifications, then Ms. Spellman's letter would help to qualify him as a desirable candidate for most medical schools. However, if Mr. Miller's academic record is not strong, the committee may be concerned about his academic qualifications. In contrast, Dr. Jacblonski's letter may offset a poor academic record.

Analysis of good letters

Figures 8–5 and *8–6* show letters that are weaker than the previous letters because the writers did not know the applicants as well. For this reason, Dr. Jacblonski could not comment on Ms. Jones' cognitive abilities, and Ms. Spellman's letter was more formal. However, these writers knew the applicants better than the average student and conveyed nothing but praise.

Analysis of average letters

Figures 8–7 and *8–8* show letters that are not negative, yet manage to convey a feeling of restraint about the respective applicant. The writers are not particularly enthusiastic, and the letters suggest that the writer has reservations about the student. A writer rarely states negative feelings toward an applicant. Some people feel pressured into writing a letter for a student against their better judgment, and then feel obligated not to be too negative. Others may fear that a negative letter might become the basis for a lawsuit. In both cases, they express their uneasiness indirectly. Some faculty members tell a student honestly that they cannot write a positive letter and recommend that the student ask someone else to write a letter.

●●● THE INTERVIEW

Some simple, common sense rules go a long way toward making the interview a success. First, be on time for the interview. If necessary, take a practice run to locate parking areas and the interviewer's office. No excuse can compensate for lateness. If possible, determine who will conduct the interview, and try to learn something about her (e.g., what type of research she does, where she received her degrees, her philosophy of medicine). Consult the biographic and informational sources listed at the end of this chapter to obtain this type of information.

Each medical school has its own method of interviewing. A student may be interviewed by one person, by a small committee, or more than once. Either faculty members or students may conduct interviews. Each situation requires a different approach. Additionally, some schools provide the interviewer with all of the information from the student's application; at other schools, the interviewer has little or no information about the student (i.e., she is conducting a blind interview).

The Faculty Interviewer

Faculty members may use two basic styles of interviewing, relaxed and forceful. Most interviewers use a hybrid approach. The faculty member who uses a relaxed approach usually introduces himself and then asks an open-ended question, such as, "Tell me about yourself." This question should be interpreted as, "Tell me those things about yourself that would lead me to accept you to medical school." The student's performance is judged on the relevance of her response and her ability to ar-

University of Alaska
Department of Biology
1400 Mary Lane
Fairbanks, Alaska 19077
907-475-8955

July 15, 1996

To whom it may concern:

I have been asked by Ms. Alice Jones to write a letter recommending her to medical school. It gives me great pleasure to do so.

I first met Alice two years ago as a student in my organic chemistry class. She was an outstanding student, ranking fifth in a class of 165. More importantly, she attended all discussion sessions and asked probing questions. Ultimately I accepted her into my laboratory as an undergraduate research student for the remaining two quarters of the year. She worked closely with one of my post-doctoral fellows and showed great diligence in her work and quickly learned techniques new to her. We were impressed enough to hire her as a research assistant during the summer and assigned her to her own project. She researched the background literature in a thorough fashion, rapidly learning how to use a computer generated data base. This alone impressed me. However, she then devised an outstanding and creative experimental protocol and attacked it with great energy. She continued the project this academic year, again as an undergraduate student. Unfortunately, she has not yet been able to come to an unambiguous conclusion due to the lack of time. However, the originality of her approach and level of energy convince me that Alice will be successful in any profession.

During this almost two year period I've also had a chance to get to know Alice as a person. In addition to interacting with her in the laboratory, my wife and I have had her and her husband over to dinner several times. She has also participated in our weekly departmental seminar. She is well read, articulate and not afraid to express her opinion on a wide variety of subjects. On a personal level she is pleasant, gets along well with all the laboratory personnel, other undergraduates, the technicians and post-docs. She is also a talented musician and had seriously considered becoming a professional musician.

She appears to have the highest ethical values. She subjects all her data to the closest scrutiny and has acted in an honest straightforward manner in all my dealings with her.

I feel that I can give Ms. Jones the highest possible recommendation without any reservation. Should you desire any further information, do not hesitate to call or write.

Yours truly,

Reginald Jacblonski, Ph. D.
Professor and Chair

● ● ●

FIGURE 8–3. Example of an exceptional academic letter.

Mercy General Hospital
3463 Florence Avenue
Shreveport, LA 44444
504-378-6029

July 12, 1995

Dear Admissions Committee:

It gives me real pleasure to recommend Mr. James Miller to your medical school. Mr. Miller works at our hospital as a volunteer. For the past year and a half he has worked as a ward attendant on Tuesday evenings in the pediatric wing I supervise.

Despite his heavy work load at the university, Mr. Miller is always punctual and has never missed a scheduled day. He works hard and performs the most menial tasks, even emptying the bedpans, with good cheer and enthusiasm. Most importantly, he is able to establish a true rapport with the children. He reads them stories, plays games with them and has that rare ability to calm their fears and make them feel good.

I have enjoyed my conversations with him. He shared his ambitions and plans with me. It is his fervent ambition to become a pediatrician and practice in a rural area similar to where he grew up. I have no doubt that he has the personality, the warmth and dedication required to make him an outstanding pediatrician. His patients will love him.

Please contact me should you desire any additional information.

Yours truly,

Joyce Spellman, R.N.

● ● ●

FIGURE 8–4. Example of an exceptional extracurricular letter.

University of Alaska
Department of Biology
1400 Mary Lane
Fairbanks, Alaska 19077
907-475-8955

July 15, 1996

To whom it may concern:

I have been asked by Ms. Alice Jones to write a letter recommending her to medical school. It gives me great pleasure to do so.

I first met Alice two years ago as a student in my organic chemistry class. She was an outstanding student, ranking fifth in a class of 165. More importantly, she attended all discussion sessions and asked probing questions. In this way I got to know her better than the average student in my classes.

During the subsequent two years, Ms. Jones chose to seek me out as an advisor and I have had several extended discussions with her. She appears to be well read, articulate and not afraid to express her opinions on a wide variety of subjects. She is pleasant, and I would imagine, gets along well with her peers. I think she is honest and has high ethical values.

I feel that I can recommend Ms. Jones without reservation.

Yours truly,

Reginald Jacblonski, Ph. D.
Professor and Chair

● ● ●

FIGURE 8–5. Example of a good academic letter.

Mercy General Hospital
3463 Florence Avenue
Shreveport, LA 44444
504-378-6029

July 20, 1995

Dear Admissions Committee:

I am pleased to recommend Mr. James Miller to your medical school. Mr. Miller works at our hospital as a volunteer. He and I have frequently crossed paths during the past year. He worked as a ward attendant in the pediatric wing that I supervise.

Despite his heavy academic work load at the university, Mr. Miller is usually punctual and seldom misses a scheduled day. He works hard and will perform the most menial task, such as emptying the bedpans. He appears to get along well and has established a good rapport with the children. He reads them stories and plays games with them.

I understand he wishes to become a pediatrician and practice in a rural area similar to where he grew up. Judging by the fact that he volunteered to work on a pediatric ward, I believe him to be sincere.

Yours truly,

Joyce Spellman, R.N.

● ● ●

FIGURE 8–6. Example of a good extracurricular letter.

University of Alaska
Department of Biology
1400 Mary Lane
Fairbanks, Alaska 19077
907-475-8955

July 15, 1996

To whom it may concern:

I agreed to write Ms. Alice Jones a letter recommending her to medical school.

Alice was a student in my organic chemistry class some two years ago. She did very well, ranking fifth in a class of 165. My teaching assistant informs me that she attended the discussion sessions with some regularity.

During the subsequent two years Ms. Jones apparently did seek me out once or twice to ask for advice on which classes to take. She seemed fairly pleasant, and I would imagine she gets along well with her peers. She very likely is honest and has high ethical values.

I have no reason to believe that Ms. Jones will not get along well in medical school and would therefore recommend her to you.

Yours truly,

Reginald Jacblonski, Ph. D.
Professor and Chair

● ● ●

FIGURE 8-7. Example of an average academic letter.

Mercy General Hospital
3463 Florence Avenue
Shreveport, LA 44444
504-378-6029

July 20, 1996

Dear Admissions Committee:

Mr. James Miller asked me to write a letter of recommendation to your medical school. Mr. Miller works at our hospital as a volunteer. He and I have crossed paths during the past year. He worked as a ward attendant in the pediatric wing that I supervise.

Unfortunately, due to his heavy academic work load at the university, Mr. Miller was sometimes late and on several occasions had to call in to inform us that he would have to miss a scheduled day. When on the ward, he works hard and will perform the most menial task, such as emptying the bedpans when asked. He reads the children stories and plays games with them and manages to hold their attention.

I was told that he wishes to become a pediatrician and practice in a rural area similar to where he grew up. Judging by the fact that he volunteered to work on a pediatric ward, I believe him to be sincere.

Yours truly,

Joyce Spellman, R.N.

● ● ●

FIGURE 8–8. Example of an average extracurricular letter.

ticulate her thoughts clearly. The interviewer then leads the interview in whatever direction he feels is most appropriate. Usually, the student has the opportunity to ask questions at the end of the interview. This approach is often used by older, more confident faculty members or those with training in interviewing skills.

To prepare for this type of interview, think about why you want to study medicine, what will make you a successful medical student, and what talents you have to contribute to the profession. If you have been involved in a research project, make sure that you know what you did, why you did it, and the significance of the project. Know the names of the other researchers involved in the project and what they contributed. However, do not pretend that you know more than you do. An experienced interviewer can lead a student into an unfamiliar subject and reveal the student's ignorance and lack of sincerity. Ironically, the student often leaves such an interview feeling good because he was articulate and expansive.

The interviewer who uses a forceful approach usually introduces herself, may chat amiably for awhile, and then asks a direct and challenging question. In a blind interview, the question may concern a moral or ethical issue, such as, "Do you feel it is appropriate for doctors to perform abortions?" If the interviewer has access to the student's application, the question usually focuses on some information contained in the application, such as, "I see from your personal statement that you feel you can help make medicine more humane. Does this mean that you think it is not humane now?"

An inexperienced interviewer who uses a forceful approach may ask closed-ended questions that can be answered with a yes or no. In this situation, a student should give fully developed answers and strive to convey his thoughts sincerely. Otherwise, the interview may be short and essentially meaningless. The interviewer's evaluation of the interview will reflect this outcome, and the committee will have little sense of the student.

The committee member who is faced with two essentially equivalent applications, one of which depicts a real human being and one of which does not, often votes in favor of the former. It is the applicant's responsibility to show his humanness to the interviewer so that she can convey it to the committee.

Some experienced interviewers also prefer the forceful technique. They tend to probe, not necessarily to see what the student believes, but to see how well and sincerely she defends her beliefs. Again, respond sincerely, without waffling in an attempt to please the interviewer.

A student may leave the interview feeling that it was negative or that she did poorly. These impressions can be inaccurate. Sometimes an interviewer seems negative when he is simply playing devil's advocate. In the written summary of the interview, which nearly all schools require, the interviewer may praise the student's persistence and willingness to take a strong or forceful position. On the other hand, a student who genuinely believes that the interviewer was prejudiced against him or treated him unfairly should request another interview.

The Student Interviewer

At many schools, medical students act as interviewers. The difficulty of the interview often decreases as the interviewer progresses through medical school. The toughest interviewers are often first-year medical students, whereas third-year students seem to be the easiest. As time passes, medical students learn how demanding medical school can be, and they may become more forgiving.

Medical students know all of the dodges and evasions because they may have used them. As a result, applicants may have to be more frank with a student interviewer than with a faculty interviewer. Student interviewers can tell quickly when an applicant is stretching the facts, but they are also sympathetic to anxiety and nervousness. An applicant can learn a great deal by asking a student interviewer what the school is looking for in a prospective student. Student interviewers may provide helpful information that could affect the applicant's acceptance.

Committee Interviews

Few medical schools use committee interviews. These interviews can be intimidating, yet many follow a set pattern of questioning in which each interviewer is preassigned a question or a set of questions to ask. During a committee interview, the student must remember several names and make eye contact with all of the interviewers. However, the applicant will probably not be bombarded with questions from all sides. Also, interview committees usually include a mix of the faculty types described earlier.

Making the Most of the Interview

If possible, arrive at the medical school a day or two early. Use this time to become familiar with the school and surrounding area. Talk to some of the medical students, ask if you can sit in on a lecture, and try to determine the school's strengths. Find out how the curriculum works, and visit the clinical facilities. This information can help you to decide whether the school is for right for you and may be useful during the interview.

Some schools give the applicant the name of the interviewer in advance, but most do not. If the school does not, visit the admissions office the day before the interview and ask who will conduct the interview and where it will be held. If this information is available, learn as much as you can about the interviewer. This opportunity is not always available; for example, some schools schedule special interview days that include a group orientation, after which the applicants are given specific information about the interview.

If the faculty interviewer is a clinician, your first contact may be with a receptionist or secretary. Always state your full name and that of the person with whom you have an appointment. Be courteous, but do not engage in a long conversation with the secretary.

When you meet the interviewer, establish eye contact, smile, and offer a firm handshake. These gestures show interest. Many interviewers may be inexperienced and therefore nervous. While the interviewer reads your personal statement, or if there are interruptions in the meeting, wait quietly. Avoid drumming your fingers, swinging your leg, adjusting your clothing, cracking your knuckles, or playing with your hair. Do not handle anything on the interviewer's desk unless you are invited to do so, and do not stand when someone else enters the room, unless you are introduced. Do not swear or use slang, even if the interviewer does. Speak clearly and carefully, and avoid expressions such as "like," "um," and "you know." Do not interrupt the interviewer while she is speaking or reviewing your personal statement or application. If she needs clarification, she will ask.

During the interview, be respectful, but do not use flattery. Use the interviewer's title and last name (i.e., Dr. Smith) unless she asks you to call her by her first name. In either case, do not overuse the interviewer's name. If the interviewer receives a telephone call, indicate that you can leave if she needs privacy.

If you have researched the medical school by reading about it or visiting it, you should be able to ask detailed, intelligent questions. An interview is a give-and-take process, and both parties should come away from the meeting feeling that they have learned something.

An interviewer often asks open-ended questions to encourage the applicant to talk about himself. In this case, one- or two-word answers are not helpful. Answer questions fully without straying from the point. The next section describes typical interview questions.

When asked about your qualifications, provide specific examples. Quoting others lends objectivity to your answers and enhances your credibility. Describe yourself positively, yet honestly and concisely. If the interviewer asks you to defend or explain something in your personal statement or application (e.g., GPA, MCAT scores), briefly answer the question and move on to the next. However, do not volunteer negative information. If the interviewer asks a question that you believe is too personal, politely tell him so, and do not answer the question.

At the end of the interview, ask the interviewer when you will be contacted. This information will help you to decide when you should call the admissions office if you do not hear from them. When the interview is over, write down the questions that were asked, your responses, and any other information that may be of use when talking to the interviewer later. Finally, write a brief letter of thanks for the interviewer's time.

Typical Interview Questions

The following questions are commonly asked during a medical school interview. Following each question are some points to consider in preparing an answer. One question is not the entire interview, so do not worry if you mishandle a question. Also, there is no right or wrong answer to an open-ended question.

- Why do you want to be a physician?

   This standard question has lost some validity because so many applicants have been coached in how to answer it. However, you must clearly understand why you want to become a physician. Before the interview, refer to your personal statement to see how you addressed this point.

- Why did you choose this medical school?

   If you have researched the school, this question is easy to answer. Possible answers include, "I chose it because of your innovative curriculum," "I like your student support system," "I understand that you have one of the best (fill in the blank) of any medical school," "You accept a lot of out-of-state students, and I thought I had a good chance of being accepted."

- Where do you see yourself in 10 years?

   This question helps the interviewer to determine how much thought you have given to your future and whether you have a realistic view of medical training. If you have chosen a specialty, then state it and explain why you have chosen this field of medicine (e.g., "I plan to be working as a surgeon in an emergency clinic").

- Tell me about yourself.

   This question is designed to see how concisely, yet informatively, you can describe your personal and academic history, current status, and goals. Students make two common errors when answering this question; some ramble, jumping from one point to another without a clear focus or direction, and some are too brief, focusing on their academic record, research, or desire to study medicine. An effective answer gives the interviewer a sense of who you are and some insight into your personality and character.

- What are your plans for residency?

   Many students have no definite plans, and it is fine to say so. This question offers an opportunity to ask the interviewer about residency programs. However, you should have some general knowledge of residencies (e.g., types available, lengths).

● What are you looking for in a medical school?

This question is an opportunity to discuss what attracts you to the school (e.g., "I mostly want the chance to work with patients, and I understand that your school offers a class in the first year that has the students spend one afternoon a week at an outpatient clinic").

● What are your interests outside of medicine?

This question is a chance to shine if you excel in any outside activities. Talking about your interest in sports, music, or gardening allows you to describe your abilities outside the academic area.

● How do you feel about working in a group setting, and have you had any such experience?

This question is an attempt to determine whether you are a team player. In most cases, physicians work as part of a team, and the ability to work cooperatively and effectively with others is important. More immediately, in many medical school classes, students work closely with each other.

● Do you have any concerns about our medical school?

This question provides a chance to demonstrate what you know about the school and its curriculum. Although the question is phrased negatively, your response can be positive (e.g., "At first I was worried that there were not enough opportunities built into the curriculum to meet with patients, but I realize that I need a good grounding in the basic sciences before I can work meaningfully with patients").

● What can I say to convince you to come here?

This question is an attempt to determine what you think a desirable educational experience should be. This question may or may not mean that the interviewer thinks that you are worthy of recruiting.

● We have many applicants. Why should we choose you?

This question is difficult to answer. Think of what makes you special. Because you have been granted an interview, you have been deemed academically acceptable. To answer this question, focus on the nonacademic talents, skills, or abilities that make you a valuable addition to the entering class.

● What books have you read recently?

The answer to this question provides a clue to your personality. There is no one type of material that is undesirable. President Kennedy, for example, enjoyed reading James Bond novels.

● How do you plan to pay for medical school?

You should be able to show that you have made plans to manage your finances while in medical school. However, a school is not likely to reject you because you do not have a great deal of money. Most medical students borrow money to pay for their education, and you can state that you plan to apply for loans and grants through the financial aid office.

- What are your major strengths and weaknesses?

  You should prepare for this question before the interview. Your strengths are easier to pinpoint. However, everyone has weaknesses, and the ability to recognize them shows the capacity for introspection and the potential for improving yourself. When discussing your weaknesses, describe how you are working to overcome them (e.g., "One of my greatest weaknesses is that I can't say no to people. When a friend asks me to help him with his studies or go to a social function, I usually say yes, even if it means that I have to take time away from another task. Recently, though, I have been trying to say no more often, since I realize that I must prioritize what is important").

- Do you really want to move here?

  This question is a test of your sincerity in applying to the school. It is fine to admit that this location is not your first choice because, for example, you dislike cold weather or would miss your family or friends. However, you should state that you know that you would receive a good education.

- Please discuss the future of medicine

  You should be familiar with health maintenance organizations, preferred provider organizations, private practice plans, and potential legislation that may affect how physicians will practice in the future (see Chapter 5).

- How do you feel about (AIDS patients, abortion, access to health care, passing out condoms in high school)?

  Interviewers often use socially and emotionally charged issues to encourage students to take a stand on an issue. You should state your opinion honestly, and not try to give the answer you think the interviewer wants. Sometimes the interviewer may argue against your point of view, but you should hold firm. The interviewer may not actually care how you feel about the topic, but is attempting to determine whether you have the strength of character to defend your position.

- Where else have you applied?

  This question is asked to see how realistic your expectations are. If you have applied to only four or five schools, the interviewer may conclude that you are not aware of the highly competitive nature of the admissions process. This question is also a chance for you to point out how many schools have granted you interviews and how many have accepted you. Admission committees are more likely to accept an applicant who is a desirable commodity at other schools.

- Have you had any role models?

  You need not have role models, but identifying admirable qualities in others can help you to describe why you want to study medicine or how you formed your values and ethics. In answering this question, you can discuss your parents, a family physician, a teacher, or anyone else you admire.

- What clinical experience have you had?

  This question is important. Your answer should be brief, but complete (e.g., "I have worked as a volunteer in the pediatrics ward at St. Johns Hospital in Seattle for the last 3 years"). You should also state what you learned or what insights you gained (e.g., "I love working with children, and I'm fascinated by the treatment methods the doctors, nurses, and therapists use"). Research experience can often substitute for clinical experience.

- What are your plans for a family? Are you married?

  This question is inappropriate and probably illegal. You can answer it if you like, but if you are uncomfortable, you can say, "I don't think that this has a bearing on my application to medical school."

- What subject did you find the most difficult as an undergraduate?

  Give an honest answer. If there is a specific reason for this difficulty, state the reason (e.g., "My worst subject was physics. Unfortunately, I was unable to attend a pre-physics course at my high school, which I think put me at a disadvantage.").

- With what type of people do have trouble working?

  This question could be a probe of your prejudices or an attempt to see if you can be honest in describing your relationships with others. No one gets along with everyone, so do not be afraid to answer honestly.

- What do you plan to do if you are not accepted to medical school?

  This question is another attempt to determine whether your expectations are realistic. You should have considered the possibility of not being accepted and made alternative plans. It is fine to say that you would reapply to medical school. However, you should state a plan of action to improve your chances of acceptance (e.g., take additional science courses).

- Tell me about your family life.

  This question is also inappropriate. It is appropriate, however, to discuss your upbringing and how it influenced your decision to study medicine and helped or hindered your premedical career.

Questions to Ask

A successful interview typically becomes a dialogue in which the student has an opportunity to ask questions. However, either before or after the interview, the applicant can ask questions of current medical students, faculty, or administrative staff. This section lists questions that can open a further dialogue and provide useful information that can help you decide which school is the best choice for you.

- What diagnostic and treatment equipment is available at the medical school and teaching hospital?
- How have students performed on the medical licensing examinations?
- What specific clinical experiences are available at the teaching hospitals?
- What are the affiliated institutions of the teaching hospitals?
- Does the academic schedule allow time for outside research, vacations, or other activities?
- What subspecialties are particularly strong here?
- Is there much turnover of faculty?
- What happens on a typical day?

- Are students happy here? (This is a question to ask a currently enrolled student.)

- What is the typical patient population? Are the beds usually full?

- What is the experience of alumni? (e.g., Did they receive fellowships? Where did they establish practice?)

- Can you tell me anything about this city and the surrounding area?

- What are the educational objectives of the medical school?

- What learning opportunities does the school offer to achieve the stated objectives?

- How are the medical school and the students evaluated to determine whether the learning objectives have been achieved?

- What are the strengths and weaknesses of the medical school?

- What do you like about this school?

- Is housing available at or near the school?

- How can I improve my chances of being selected?

- What qualities do you feel that a medical student should possess?

Sources of Information about Interview Committee Members and Medical School Programs

This section lists sources of information about medical schools and medical school faculty. You can use these sources to help select schools and to learn more about schools and interviewers when you are granted interviews.

Primary sources

- *Medical School Admission Requirements*. Association of American Medical Colleges. Purchase from AAMC, Membership and Publication Orders, 2450 N Street, NW, Washington, DC 20037-1126; (202) 828-0416.

- *Minority Student Opportunities in United States Medical Schools*. Association of American Medical Colleges. Purchase from AAMC, Membership and Publication Orders, 2450 N Street, NW, Washington, DC 20037-1126; (202) 828-0416.

- *AAMC Curriculum Directory*. Association of American Medical Colleges. Purchase from AAMC, Membership and Publication Orders, 2450 N Street, NW, Washington, DC 20037-1126; (202) 828-0416.

- *AAMC Directory of American Medical Education*. Association of American Medical Colleges. Purchase from AAMC, Membership and Publication Orders, 2450 N Street, NW, Washington DC 20037-1126; (202) 828-0416.

- *The Hospital Phone Book: A Complete Name and Address Book of Hospitals in the U.S.A.* U.S. Directory Service, New Providence, NJ. Updated yearly.

- *Dictionary of American Medical Biography*. M. Kaufman, S. Galishoff, and T. Savitt.

- *American Medical Directory*. American Medical Association. Updated yearly.

● Catalogs, available from each school's admissions office.

Secondary sources

● J. Pekkanen: *The Best Doctors in the U.S.: A Guide to the Finest Specialists, Hospitals, and Health Centers*. Wide View Books.

● *Directory of Medical Specialists.*

● *Who's Who in Medicine*. Marquis, Chicago, IL (800-521-8110).

● *Directory of Women Physicians in the U.S.* American Medical Association. Updated yearly.

● *Health Pathways*. Quarterly newsletter of the Health Professions Career Opportunity Program. Order a free subscription from the Office of Statewide Health Planning and Development, Health Professions Career Opportunity Program, 1600 Ninth Street, Room 441, Sacramento, CA 95814; (916) 654-1730.

Other sources

American Academy of Family Physicians
8880 Ward Parkway
Kansas City, Mo 64114-2797
(800) 274-2237

American Board of Family Practice
2228 Young Drive
Lexington, KY 40505
(606) 269-5626

American Board of Internal Medicine
3624 Market Street
Philadelphia, PA 19104
(215) 243-1500

American College of Emergency Physicians
PO Box 619911
Dallas, TX 75261
(214) 550-0911

American College of Surgeons
55 East Erie Street
Chicago, IL 60611
(312) 664-4050

American Medical Student Association
Resource Center
1890 Preston White Drive
Reston, VA 22091
(703) 620-6600, extension 217

American Society of Contemporary Medicine and Surgery
233 East Erie Street
Chicago, IL 60611
(312) 951-1400

CHAPTER 9

Not Accepted?
The Options

- Reapplication: How to Increase the Chances of Acceptance
- Postbaccalaureate and Alternative Programs
- Osteopathy and Other Health-Related Fields
- Foreign Medical Schools

Each year, more than 50% of the applicants to medical school are not accepted. What happens to these students? This chapter discusses their options.

●●●
REAPPLICATION: HOW TO INCREASE THE CHANCES OF ACCEPTANCE

After recovering from the shock of rejection, most students reapply to medical school. However, successful reapplying does not simply entail resubmitting your application and paying fees. Successful reapplicants do everything possible to make the reapplication process more effective.

The first step is to determine why the initial application was not accepted. A student whose grade point average (GPA) is 2.0–3.0 range and whose Medical College Admission Test (MCAT) score is 7 or below has little chance of acceptance. However, most rejected applicants in the last few years had a competitive academic record and believed that they were qualified for a career in medicine. How can these applicants determine what the medical schools thought they were lacking?

The first thing to do is to look for some pattern to the rejections. If a significant number of schools reject a student without asking for a secondary application, the problem is probably apparent in the American Medical College Application Service

(AMCAS) application and is most likely the academic record; however, the personal statement may be the culprit as well. If most schools asked for secondary applications, but few granted an interview, the problem is probably associated with the student's nonacademic record, such as insufficient volunteer or research experience or, less likely, an unfavorable letter of recommendation. A student who received more than three interviews and was not even placed on an alternate list most likely interviews poorly. Conversely, a student who received several interviews can feel secure about her academic record and extracurricular activities.

In addition to self-analysis, it is important to contact the schools and ask the reasons for rejection and also to talk with your prehealth advisor. A pattern will probably emerge, and you may be able to identify your weak points. Knowing them will help you to design a course of action to make subsequent application stronger.

Some deficiencies are more easily corrected than others. Applying to inappropriate schools, applying to too few schools, a poorly drafted personal statement, and poor interviewing skills account for many rejections. Fortunately, these problems can be easily overcome. A low MCAT score can also be overcome within the next application period. However, a low GPA and the absence of suitable extracurricular activities cannot be quickly rectified.

What course of action should you take to raise your MCAT score, improve your GPA, or overcome a nonacademic deficiency? If a student has a low MCAT score, he should ask himself why he scored poorly. Does he lack content knowledge, are his reading or problem-solving skills deficient, was he overly anxious, or did he simply have a bad day?

A student whose GPA is adequate probably does not lack content knowledge. A student who typically has problems with standardized tests, such as the Scholastic Aptitude Test (SAT), probably has a skills or anxiety problem. One way to overcome any of these problems is to take an MCAT review course.

It is important to choose a review program that best fits your needs. If you have a content problem, you would benefit from a course that provides didactic material and review. On the other hand, if the problem is with test-taking or reading skills, you should choose a course that provides feedback from a trained study skills expert, not just another student. For most students, the best programs use content material to hone test-taking and reading skills. These programs also provide mock examinations.

If the problem is with the GPA, it is important to convince the admission committees that you can do well academically in a competitive situation. The best approach is to take more classes. As discussed in Chapter 8, the most helpful courses are at the undergraduate level, preferably in association with a postbaccalaureate program. In general, these programs help to improve MCAT scores and provide an opportunity to participate in volunteer or other activities.

● ● ●
POSTBACCALAUREATE AND ALTERNATIVE PROGRAMS

Postbaccalaureate programs are of several types. Formal structured programs require a formal application and acceptance process. Some students prefer informal alternative programs that they can set up themselves with the aid of academic advisers. Students who decide to develop their own programs should seek guidance about the number and types of courses they should take and the undergraduate school they should attend. To design a postbaccalaureate program, it is usually necessary to declare a second undergraduate major. The alternative, entering a graduate program, has some value, but its impact is limited (see Chapter 8).

A major advantage of a structured postbaccalaureate program is that the director or the staff counselors are often experienced and may be known to admission committee members at one or more medical schools. For this reason, a recommendation from them can bear significant weight. However, these formal programs are usually highly competitive, with few positions available nationwide. Students who are accepted may need to move to another city or state.

There are two types of formal postbaccalaureate programs. Most programs are for students who have earned a degree in another field, have worked in that field, and have decided to pursue a career in medicine. The participants take the basic premedical course requirements. These programs are not appropriate for reapplicants who have already fulfilled these requirements. The other type of program is designed to help students improve their chances of acceptance. *Table 9–1* lists postbaccalaureate programs for reapplicants. Most of these programs provide classroom work, training in learning skills, academic counseling, and MCAT preparation. Many are free, although some are limited to state residents or disadvantaged students, or have other admission requirements. The primary goal of these programs is to help students who are late achievers demonstrate an ability to do well in a competitive academic environment, and most, therefore, require participants to take academic courses for several quarters or semesters.

• • •
OSTEOPATHY AND OTHER HEALTH-RELATED FIELDS

The following discussion is limited to health provider occupations that require a doctorate degree. As a rule, the doctorate degree permits the recipient, once licensed, to practice professionally without supervision. There are many allied health professions that do not require a doctorate degree; the *Allied Health Directory 1995–1996,* published by the American Medical Association (AMA), is a useful reference for students considering careers in the allied health fields. Copies can be obtained by contacting the AMA at PO Box 109051, Chicago, IL 60610 or calling (800) 621-8335.

Osteopathy

The Doctor of Osteopathy (DO) degree is almost indistinguishable from the MD degree in most respects. After they finish their training, DOs receive a license to practice medicine in the same way as MDs. The primary difference between the MD and DO degrees is the training DOs receive in manipulation of the musculoskeletal system. Osteopathic medicine is based on the belief that misalignment of the musculoskeletal system as a result of stress or disease can cause pathologic responses in the internal organs. Therefore, these practitioners believe that manipulation of the musculoskeletal system alleviates primary pain and may promote healing of the whole body by returning it to a more normal homeostatic state. DOs receive at least 1 year of training in the holistic and manipulative aspects of medicine in addition to the standard medical procedures of drug and surgical therapy.

The DO degree is not as widely known as the MD degree. Also, osteopathic schools are not usually as prestigious or as well funded as MD schools. Students and their advisors often overlook osteopathy as a viable option to medicine. As a result, these schools receive only approximately 14% of the number of applications that allopathic schools do. However, because fewer positions are available in osteopathic schools, the ratio of applicants to acceptances is similar to that for allopathic schools, with about 43% of applicants accepted.

Because DOs practice manipulation as an adjunct to traditional medical techniques and emphasize holistic medicine, colleges of osteopathy tend to be more concerned with the art of medicine than with developing a reputation based on research. As a consequence, their admission committees tend to focus on noncognitive

●●●

TABLE 9-1. Postbaccalaureate Programs for the Reapplicant

State	School and Contact	Comments
California	Richard McFarland, PhD Health Professions Office California State University, Fullerton 800 State College Boulevard Fullerton, CA 92634 (714) 773-3980	Duration: up to 2 years
	Robert M. Schmidt, Chair Health Professions Program School of Science TH323 California State University, San Francisco 1600 Holloway Avenue San Francisco, CA 94132 (415) 338-2410	
	Post-baccalaureate Program Coordinator Office of Minority Affairs University of California, Davis, School of Medicine Davis, CA 95616 (916) 752-1852	For minority or disadvantaged students; must be a resident of California, unsuccessful in applying to medical school, and have a bachelor's degree; costs covered during the summer; some loans available during the academic year; duration: summer plus 2 quarters
	Eileen Muñoz, Coordinator Educational and Community Programs Office of Student Affairs University of California, Irvine, College of Medicine PO Box 4089 Irvine, CA 92717 1 (800) 824-6442	For minority or disadvantaged students; must be a resident of California, unsuccessful in applying to medical school, and have a bachelor's degree; costs covered during the summer; some loans available during the academic year; duration: summer plus 3 quarters
	Saundra Kirk, Director Special Admissions Support Programs Reapplicant Summer Course Medical Teaching Facility, Room 162 University of California, San Diego, School of Medicine 9500 Gilman Drive La Jolla, CA 92093-0621 (619) 534-4170	For minority or disadvantaged students; must be a resident of California, unsuccessful in applying to medical school after interviewing, have a bachelor's degree, and have a GPA > 2.7; stipend and housing during the summer (8 weeks); some loans available during the academic year; duration: summer plus 3 quarters
Connecticut	Keat Sanford, Director University of Connecticut Postbaccalaureate Program University of Connecticut, School of Medicine 263 Farmington Avenue Farmington, CT 06030-1905	Must have a bachelor's degree with a minimum of a B− average; duration: 1 year
District of Columbia	Georgiana Aboko-Cole, PhD Pre-Medical Advisor and Director Center for Professional Education PO Box 473, Administration Building Howard University Washington, DC 20059 (202) 806-7231	
Florida	Kathleen S. Smith Program in Medical Science Florida State University R-115, 34 Montgomery Tallahassee, FL 33124 (904) 644-1855	Open only to residents of Florida
	Suzette Rygiel-Abella, Co-chair Committee on Premedical Studies University of Miami PO Box 248004	Must have a bachelor's degree and a GPA > 3.3; duration: up to 2 years

TABLE 9-1. Postbaccalaureate Programs for the Reapplicant *(Continued)*

	Coral Gables, FL 33124 (305) 284-5174	
Illinois	Robert Roth, PhD, Chair and Chief Health Professions Advisor Department of Biology Illinois Institute of Technology Chicago, IL 60616 (312) 576-3480	
	Vera Felts, Admission Coordinator MEDPREP Southern Illinois University School of Medicine Carbondale, IL 62901-4323 (618) 536-6671	For disadvantaged students; GPA > 2.0; Illinois residents given priority; duration: usually 18 months to 2 years
	P. James Nielsen, Premed Advisor Department of Biology Western Illinois University Macomb, IL 61455 (309) 298-1483	Illinois residents only
Indiana	Ralph Ockerse, PhD, Premed Advisor Biology Department Indiana University-Purdue University at Indianapolis 723 West Michigan Street Indianapolis, IN 46202-5132 (317) 274-0586	
Louisiana	Walter Durio, Department Administrator Department of Biology University of Southwestern Louisiana PO Box 42451 Lafayette, LA 70504 (318) 231-6748	
Michigan	Joyce Mitchell, MD, Assistant Dean Office of Student Affairs 5109 Medical Science Building I, C-Wing University of Michigan, Medical School 1301 Catherine Street Ann Arbor, MI 48109-0611 (313) 764-8185	For disadvantaged students; must have a bachelor's degree, a GPA > 2.45, and a MCAT score > 4.5; Michigan residents preferred; conditional acceptance to medical school offered
	Wanda Lipscomb, PhD Prematriculation Programs A254 Life Science Building Michigan State University, College of Human Medicine (MSU-CHM) East Lansing, MI 44824-1317 (517) 353-5440	Limited to MSU-CHM, AMCAS applicants placed in a "hold" category; stipend of $40/day for eligible students; conditional admission to MSU-CHM; some medical school courses waived
Missouri	C. Larry Sullivan, PhD, Premed Advisor Avila College 11901 Wornall Road Kansas City, MO 64145 (816) 942-8400, extension 255	For disadvantaged students
Nebraska	John T. Elder, PhD Pharmacology Department Creighton University, School of Medicine 24th and California Omaha, NE 68178 (402) 280-3185	For minority or disadvantaged students; must have a bachelor's degree or foreign equivalent; duration: September to April; must take MCAT in April; links to several Midwestern medical schools
	J. S. Johar, PhD Head, Mathematics and Science Division Wayne State College Wayne, NE 68787 (402) 375-7329	

(Table continued on the following page)

TABLE 9-1. Postbaccalaureate Programs for the Reapplicant *(Continued)*

New Jersey	John M. Maiello, PhD, Chair Prehealth Advisory Committee Department of Biological Sciences Smith Hall, Room 135 Rutgers University-Newark 101 Warren Street Newark, NJ 07102 (201) 648-5705	
New York	Steve Wallace, Coordinator Post-baccalaureate Program SUNY, Buffalo, School of Medicine and Biomedical Sciences 3435 Main Street, 40 CFS Building Buffalo, NY 14214 (716) 829-2811	For disadvantaged students; must have a bachelor's degree; must have been interviewed and rejected by one of the Associated Medical Schools of New York; duration: two summers plus 1 academic year; stipends for spring and fall; summer housing and board; tuition and fee waiver
	C. Howard Krukofsky, Professor Preprofessional Office College University of New York, Hunter 695 Park Avenue New York, NY 10021 (212) 772-5244	
North Carolina	Pinapaka Murthy, PhD Chair and Premed Advisor Department of Natural Sciences Fayetteville State University 1200 Murchison Road Fayetteville, NC 28301-4298 (919) 486-1691	
	Velma G. Watts, PhD Office of Minority Affairs Bowman Gray School of Medicine Medical Center Boulevard Winston-Salem, NC 27157-1037 (910) 716-4201	For minority or disadvantaged students; must have a bachelor's degree, a GPA > 2.5, a mean MCAT score > 7, and a score of N on the writing section; duration: 1 year; stipend; no cost to student; tuition waived

traits when evaluating applicants. As a result, osteopathic schools accept a greater percentage of nontraditional students. If you show an affinity for holistic medicine, an osteopathic school might consider you a viable candidate, even if you have a lower GPA or MCAT score. For this reason, you may wish to apply to colleges of osteopathy when you reapply to medical school.

The following 16 osteopathic schools are accredited by the American Osteopathic Association (AOA):

● **Chicago College of Osteopathic Medicine of Midwestern University,** 555 West 31st Street, Downers Grove, IL 60515

● **College of Osteopathic Medicine of the Pacific,** 309 East College Plaza, Pomona, CA 91766-1889

● **Kirksville College of Osteopathic Medicine,** 800 West Jefferson Avenue, Kirksville, MO 63501

● **Lake Erie College of Osteopathic Medicine,** 1858 West Grandview Boulevard, Erie, PA 16509

● **Michigan State University College of Osteopathic Medicine,** East Fee Hall, East Lansing, MI 48824

TABLE 9-1. Postbaccalaureate Programs for the Reapplicant *(Continued)*

Ohio	Madeline Hall, PhD Associate Professor Department of Biology Cleveland State University 24th and Euclid Cleveland, OH 44115	
	Robert A. Wood, Director Office of Preprofessional Advising College of Liberal Sciences Wright State University 445 Millett Hall Dayton, OH 45435 (513) 873-3181	
Pennsylvania	Tata Subhas, PhD Director, Undergraduate Health Programs Room 241, Mellon Hall Duquesne University Pittsburgh, PA 19345 (412) 434-6335	Pennsylvania residents only
Tennessee	Paul Langford, PhD, Chair Premed Committee David Lipscomb University 3901 Grannywhite Pike Nashville, TN 37204-3951	
Texas	Sandra Williams, Director of Medical Student Recruitment Ashbel Smith, G120 University of Texas Medical School, Galveston Galveston, TX 77555-1317 (409) 772-3256	For disadvantaged students who applied to, but were not accepted to, a University of Texas medical school; conditional acceptance to medical school offered

AMCAS = American Medical College Admission Service; GPA = grade point average; MCAT = Medical College Admission Test.

- **New York College of Osteopathic Medicine of New York Institution of Technology,** PO Box 8000, Old Westbury, NY 11568-8000

- **Nova Southeastern University College of Osteopathic Medicine,** 1750 NE 167th Street, North Miami Beach, FL 33162

- **Ohio University College of Osteopathic Medicine,** Grosvenor Hall, Athens, OH 45701

- **Oklahoma State University College of Osteopathic Medicine,** 1111 West 17th Street, Tulsa, OK 74107

- **Philadelphia College of Osteopathic Medicine,** 4150 City Avenue, Philadelphia, PA 19131

- **University of Health Sciences College of Osteopathic Medicine,** 2105 Independence Boulevard, Kansas City, MO 64124-2395

- **University of Medicine and Dentistry of New Jersey School of Osteopathic Medicine,** 301 South Central Plaza, Stratford, NJ 08084

- **University of New England College of Osteopathic Medicine,** 11 Hill Beach Road, Biddeford, ME 04005

- **University of North Texas Health Science Center at Fort Worth, Texas College of Osteopathic Medicine,** 3500 Camp Bowie Boulevard, Fort Worth, TX 76107

- **University of Osteopathic Medicine and Health Sciences College of Osteopathic Medicine and Surgery,** 3200 Grand Avenue, Des Moines, IA 50312-4198

- **West Virginia School of Osteopathic Medicine,** 400 Lee Street, Lewisburg, WV 24901

Admission requirements for osteopathic schools are similar to those for traditional medical schools. For instance, all applicants must take the MCAT. Although only 3 years of college study is required by osteopathic schools, 97% of matriculants have a minimum of a bachelor's degree. In 1994, a total of 2602 students matriculated at an osteopathic medical school. Of these, 37% were women. In the same year, 1771 students graduated from an osteopathic college. Students can apply to osteopathic schools through a central application service that is analogous to AMCAS, the American Association of Colleges of Osteopathic Medicine Application Service (AACOMAS). For an application package, contact:

American Association of Colleges of Osteopathic Medicine Application Service
6110 Executive Boulevard, Suite 405
Rockville, MD 20852

Osteopathic college curricula vary from school to school, but are similar to the traditional medical school curricula. However, a greater emphasis is placed on the interrelation of structure and function in health and disease. Students are also trained to manipulate skeletomuscular structures.

Graduates of an osteopathic college may enter a variety of residency programs and are not limited in their career choices. In 1995–96, there were 150 internship training programs, 2270 approved intern positions, 510 residency training programs in 62 specialty and subspecialty areas, and 3687 approved residency training positions. Although there remains some prejudice against them, DOs are eligible for MD residency programs. To increase their eligibility for these programs, osteopathic students sometimes take the United States Medical Licensing Examination (USMLE) as well as their own board examination. DOs can obtain admitting privileges at allopathic hospitals. In addition, there are 140 AOA-accredited hospitals in 26 states.

All 50 states license osteopathic physicians and surgeons. The examinations of the National Board of Osteopathic Medical Examiners (NBOME) are accepted in 48 states and the District of Columbia. They are not accepted in Louisiana and Texas. For more information on licensing, contact:

AOA Division of State Government Relations
142 Ontario Street
Chicago, IL 60611-2864
1 (800) 621-1773, extension 7441, or (312) 280-7441

In December 1994, there were 36,492 DOs. Of these, 10,333 were AOA board certified in a specialty area. Although some specialize without board certification, 65% to 75% of practicing DOs are primary care practitioners. Many practice in rural areas.

Osteopathic students are eligible to receive financial aid from most of the same sources as medical students (see Chapter 7). In addition, several sources are specifically designated for them. These include:

National Osteopathic Scholarships
Twenty-five awards of $1500 to entering freshmen; $750 is applied toward tuition for 2 years. **Contact:** Office of Education, American Osteopathic Association, 142 East Ontario Street, Chicago, IL 60611.

Health Professional Educational Assistance Scholarships

Awards as much as $2000 to financially disadvantaged students. Available to 10% of each entering class. **Contact:** Dean.

Florida Osteopathic Medical Association

Offers scholarships of $1000 to osteopathic students who are residents of Florida. **Contact:** Florida Osteopathic Association, PO Box 896, Palmetto, FL 33561.

Kansas Osteopathic Foundation

Offers two scholarships to Kansas residents who are students of osteopathy. **Contact:** Executive Vice President, Kansas Osteopathic Foundation, 853 Western Avenue, Topeka, KS 66606.

Maine Osteopathic Association

Offers two scholarships of $750 to osteopathic students who received their undergraduate education in Maine. **Contact:** Maine Osteopathic Association, 491 Stevens Avenue, Portland, ME 04103.

Michigan Osteopathic College Foundation

Offers scholarships to students attending the College of Osteopathic Medicine, Michigan State University. **Contact:** Executive Director, Michigan Osteopathic College Foundation, 306 Penobscot Building, Detroit, MI 48226.

Minnesota State Osteopathic Association

Offers scholarships of $550 to osteopathic students who are residents of Minnesota. Recipients must agree to practice in Minnesota for 5 years after graduation. **Contact:** Chairperson, Minnesota Osteopathic Association Scholarship Fund, 1595 Selby Avenue, St. Paul, MN 55104.

New Jersey Association of Osteopathic Physicians and Surgeons

Offers three scholarships of full tuition for first-year osteopathic students who are residents of New Jersey. **Contact:** Executive Director, New Jersey Association of Osteopathic Physicians and Surgeons, 1212 Stuyvesant Avenue, Trenton, NJ 08618.

New York State Scholarships

Scholarships of $350–$1000 are available to New York students of osteopathic medicine. Eligibility based on an examination given annually in Albany, New York. **Contact:** Regents Examination and Scholarship Center, University of the State of New York, State Education Department, Albany, NY 12201.

Texas Osteopathic Scholarships

Two scholarships of $750 and one scholarship of $1000 are available to osteopathic students in Texas. **Contact:** Texas Osteopathic Association, 512 Bailey Street, Ft. Worth, TX 76107.

Canadian Osteopathic Scholarship

A scholarship of $3000 is available to a first- or second-year Canadian student at an osteopathic school. **Contact:** Canadian Osteopathic Education Trust Fund, 3545 Cote des Neiges Road, Suite 126, Montreal 25, Quebec, Canada.

National Osteopathic Foundation Student Loan Fund

Offers a loan of as much as $1000 annually to approved candidates. **Contact:** National Osteopathic Foundation Student Loan Fund Committee, 142 East Ontario Street, Chicago, IL 60611.

Other Doctoral Programs

Students who do not believe that they will be accepted to either an MD or a DO school should consider the other health-related doctoral degrees. These students might consider applying to one or more of these other programs while applying to allopathic or osteopathic schools. Other doctoral degrees in the health sciences include the following:

Doctor of dentistry (DDS). Although limited to treating the mouth and jaw area, modern dentistry offers many practice possibilities. The general dentist, who fills teeth and oversees general dental hygiene, is the typical image of the dentist. However, several specialty options are available, ranging from orthodontist to maxillary surgeon. For information about educational opportunities, contact one of the following:

American Dental Association
Council on Dental Education
211 East Chicago Avenue
Chicago, IL 60611

American Association of Dental Schools
1625 Massachusetts Ave, NW
Washington, DC 20036

Doctor of Podiatric Medicine (DPM). Podiatric medicine is devoted to the study and medical care of the ankle and foot. A DPM makes independent judgments, prescribes medication, and may perform surgery. There are six accredited schools of podiatric medicine in the United States. For information, contact:

American Association of Colleges of Podiatric Medicine Application Service (AACPM)
1350 Piccard Drive, Suite 322
Rockville, MD 20850-4307
1 (800) 922-9266; in Maryland, 1 (301) 990-6882

Doctor of Optometry (OD). The doctor of optometry treats the eye, but unlike the ophthalmologist (an MD or DO), cannot prescribe drugs or perform surgery. Although they are licensed to practice without supervision, some ODs work in conjunction with ophthalmologists. For more information, contact one of the following:

American Optometric Association
Student Recruitment
243 North Lindbergh Boulevard
St. Louis, MO 63141

Association of Schools and Colleges of Optometry
6110 Executive Boulevard
Rockville, MD 20852

Doctor of Chiropractic Medicine (DC). Chiropractors are licensed in all 50 states, but their practice is limited to manipulation and natural remedies. Chiropractors cannot prescribe drugs or perform surgery. For information, contact one of the following:

American Chiropractic Association
1701 Clarendon Boulevard
Arlington, VA 22209

International Chiropractic Association
1901 L Street NW, Suite 800
Washington, DC 20036

Council on Chiropractic Education
3209 Ingersoll Avenue
Des Moines, IA 50312

Doctor of Naturopathic Medicine (ND). Naturopathic physicians are primary health physicians who generally serve in private practice. They are trained in the conventional tools of diagnosis and in the use of natural therapeutics. They are not permitted to prescribe drugs or perform surgery other than minor, in-office procedures. Acupuncture and homeopathy are taught as part of the curriculum. NDs are licensed to practice without supervision in seven states (Alaska, Arizona, Connecticut, Hawaii, Montana, Oregon, and Washington) and in five Canadian provinces (Alberta, British Columbia, Manitoba, Ontario, and Saskatchewan). They may also practice in other states, but generally under the supervision of an MD or a DO. For more information, contact:

American Association of Naturopathic Medicine
PO Box 20386
Seattle WA 98102
(206) 323-7610

Doctor of Clinical Psychology (PhD). Clinical psychologists play an important role in the delivery of mental health care. Many clinical psychologists have their own practices, whereas others practice as part of a team in an office or a hospital setting. Unlike psychiatrists (MD or DO), they cannot prescribe drugs, and they often refer severely affected patients to a psychiatrist. Unlike other health care providers, clinical psychologists earn a doctoral degree in an academic program rather than at a health professional school. For more information, contact the psychology department at a major university.

●●●
FOREIGN MEDICAL SCHOOLS

Some students who are not accepted by a United States medical school but do not want to pursue an alternative health career apply to a foreign medical school. An MD degree from a foreign school is as valid as one awarded by a United States school, provided that the graduate passes the licensure examinations and is accepted to a residency program in the United States. Two types of foreign medical schools accept United States students.

The first type accepts only residents of the country and United States residents who are connected by birth, ethnicity, or language to the country of the school. For example, a foreign school might accept a student whose parents were born in that country. The second type of foreign medical school actively recruits and accepts United States students.

Foreign medical schools that exist for their own nationals are usually inaccessible to the average United States student because of residency restrictions, language barriers, or differences in the educational system. However, students who have close ties to a specific country may investigate the possibility of attending a school in that country. Traditionally, United States citizens have found it easiest to attend schools in Mexico, Italy, Belgium, Spain and, more recently, Poland and Hungary. For the addresses of foreign medical schools, consult the *World Directory of Medical Schools,* 6th ed. Geneva, World Health Organization, 1988.

Certain medical schools, primarily those located in the Caribbean, accommodate United States students. Many of the matriculants at these schools were rejected by United States medical schools, and the GPA and MCAT score required for acceptance are not as high. These schools provide a second chance for students who are rejected by United States schools.

The disadvantages of attending these schools include culture shock, often associated with living in a third-world country, and the expenses of living abroad. The graduates of these schools often have a disadvantage when sitting for United States licensing examinations and when applying for a residency position. This problem also occurs with other graduates from medical schools outside the United States.

These problems occur because the level of training at these schools varies greatly. Although many are similar to United States schools, difficulties still arise. Differences in philosophy, culture, governmental demands, and patient populations may cause these schools to emphasize some basic and clinical science areas to the exclusion of others.

In addition to an emphasis on different subject matter, many foreign medical schools teach a different philosophy of medicine to their students. In the United States, the dominant philosophy is treatment of diseases after they occur. Many foreign medical schools place a greater emphasis on preventing disease. Also, because of the lack of high-tech equipment and facilities in many underdeveloped countries, physicians there do not receive training in the use of this equipment for diagnosis or treatment.

Most Canadian medical schools conduct classes in English and are accredited by the same agency that accredits United States schools, the Liaison Committee for Medical Education (LCME). Thus, completion of a Canadian program is almost equivalent to completion of a United States program. However, access is a problem for non-Canadian applicants. McGill University Faculty of Medicine accepts more United States students than any other Canadian medical school. Traditionally, approximately 25% of its class of 100 comes from foreign countries, primarily the United States. Requirements for entrance are similar to those for United States schools, including the MCAT. The McGill curriculum is problem based (see Chapter 3). For more information, contact the admissions office at:

McGill University Faculty of Medicine
3655 Drummond Street
Montreal, Quebec, Canada H3G 1Y6
(514) 398-3517

Most other Canadian schools also teach in English and accept a limited number of foreign applicants. In general, the admission policies, procedures, and prerequisites are similar to those of United States schools, but access is limited for students who do not have a Canadian connection, and sometimes a connection to a specific province. For information, contact one of the following:

Admissions Office
University of Alberta Faculty of Medicine
2-45 Medical Sciences Building
Edmonton, Alberta, Canada, T6G 2H7
(403) 492-9350

Office of Admissions
University of Calgary
Faculty of Medicine
3330 Hospital Drive NW
Calgary, Alberta, Canada T2N 4N1
(403) 220-6849

Chairman, Committee on Admissions
Memorial University of Newfoundland
Faculty of Medicine
St. John's, Newfoundland, Canada A1B 3V6
(709) 737-6615

Brenda L. Detienne
Admissions Coordinator, Room C-23
Lower Level, Clinical Research Centre
5849 University Avenue
Dalhousie University
Halifax, Nova Scotia, Canada B3H 4H7
(902) 494-1874

Admissions and Records
HSC Room 1B7-Health Science Centre
McMaster University
1200 Main Street West
Hamilton, Ontario, Canada L8N 3Z5
(905) 525-9140

Admissions
University of Ottawa
Faculty of Medicine
451 Smyth Road
Ottawa, Ontario, Canada K1H 8M5
(613) 787-6463

Admissions Office
Queen's University
Faculty of Medicine
Kingston, Ontario, Canada K7L 3N6
(613) 545-2542

Jan Murray
Admissions Officer
University of Toronto
Faculty of Medicine
Toronto, Ontario, Canada M5S 1A8
(416) 978-2717

The schools listed in *Table 9–2* accommodate United States students, teach in English, and have a basic 4-year curriculum. Although their programs are not LCME-accredited, several have made arrangements with hospitals in the United States that permit the students to complete some or all of their clinical work in the United States.

All foreign medical graduates, whether United States citizens or foreign nationals, face additional difficulties when they either attempt to return to the United States or immigrate. The first task is passing the USMLE licensing tests. Many foreign-trained medical students and graduates, including United States citizens, have difficulty passing these examinations. This difficulty is reflected in the national pass rates for foreign-trained medical students and graduates. The average passing rate for these individuals is less than half the rate for United States–trained medical students and graduates. For example, in June 1995, 92% of United States medical students passed the USMLE, Step 1, whereas only 45% of foreign students and 27% of United States students who were trained abroad passed on their first attempt.

Besides the differences in testing results, there are other differences between foreign-trained medical students and United States–trained medical students. In the United States, before they are licensed to practice medicine, medical students must graduate from an accredited medical school, complete at least 1 additional year of residency training, and pass all three steps of the USMLE. To be licensed, foreign-trained students must complete the same requirements, pass an English proficiency examination (even if they are United States citizens), and will soon be required to pass a special clinical proficiency examination.

Foreign graduates may have trouble entering a residency program. In 1995, 93% of United States graduates secured a place in a residency program on their first attempt, compared with 56% of foreign graduates. These added hurdles sometimes take years to overcome, and may cause economic hardship and personal anguish. Students who are considering applying to a foreign medical school should bear these factors in mind.

• • •

TABLE 9-2. Foreign Medical Schools That Accept a Large Number of United States Citizens

Country	School and Address
Belize	American University of the Caribbean, School of Medicine Belize City, Belize or Suite 201 901 Ponce de Leon Boulevard Coral Gables, FL 33134-3036 (305) 446-0600 or (305) 442-1421
Dominica	Ross University School of Medicine and Veterinary Medicine Dominica or 460 West 34th Street New York, NY 10001 (212) 279-5500 or 5443 Vista Del Arroyo La Cresenta, CA 91214 (818) 248-0812
Grenada	St. George's University School of Medicine Grenada or 1 East Main Street Bay Shore, NY 11706 (800) 899-6337 or (809) 444-4562
Israel	Sackler Faculty of Medicine Tel Aviv University Ramat Aviv 69 978 Tel Aviv Israel
Mexico	Universidad Autónoma de Guadalajara School of Medicine 8801 Callaghan Road San Antonio, TX 78230 (210) 366-1611 Escuela de Medicina Universidad México-Americana del Norte Guerrero No. 1317 Colonia del Prado, 88630 CIUDAD Reynosa Tamaulipas, Mexico
Netherlands-Antilles	Saba University School of Medicine PO Box 1000 Saba, Netherlands-Antilles 011-599-46-3456 or (800) 825-7754
Saint Lucia	Spartan Health Sciences University PO Box 324 Vieux Fort Saint Lucia, West Indies (809) 454-6128 or Suite C 7618 Boeing Drive El Paso, TX 79925 (915) 778-5309

PART 2

The MCAT

CHAPTER 10

Preparing for the MCAT

For the student who is planning to apply to medical school, the Medical College Admission Test (MCAT) is the single most important hurdle. Unlike the other requirements for admission, the MCAT is largely out of the control of students. As undergraduates, students can choose to take difficult or time-consuming courses all at once or over a period of several years and can allocate their time and effort to optimize their grades and volunteer experiences. However, students have far less control over the MCAT. Although a student may try to plan her course load to allow time to review for the MCAT, because the test is administered only twice a year (in April and September), a conflict often arises between regular class study time and MCAT review.

In addition, the MCAT covers many subjects and skills areas. Reviewing for the MCAT requires intensive study of biology, physics, and chemistry, as well as the development of timed essay-writing and reading comprehension skills. The breadth of knowledge and abilities needed to do well on this test can challenge the best of students. In addition, to prepare effectively, each student must carefully assess his strengths and weaknesses in each area that is tested.

One of the purposes of this guide is to help students who are planning to take the MCAT to identify their strengths and weaknesses. Part II of *Guide to Medical*

School and the MCAT explains the structure and purpose of the examination and is broken down into five components:

Overview and description of the MCAT. This section focuses on how the examination is structured, with an emphasis on important areas to study (Chapter 11).

Diagnostic testing. A practice MCAT helps students to assess their mastery of subjects covered on the examination (Chapters 12 and 13). The practice test in this guide differs from other commercially available tests in that the scoring strategy identifies deficiencies in knowledge or skills to guide student review for the MCAT.

Study methods. This section describes methods for study and retention of information, including the use of mnemonic devices, time management, and the development of problem-solving skills (Chapter 14).

Test-taking techniques. This section discusses specific methods to improve test scores. Additional practice MCAT-type questions are included to strengthen the ability to analyze and work effectively with the types of questions on the MCAT (Chapter 15).

MCAT review courses and materials. This section summarizes other sources of help for preparing for the MCAT (Chapter 16).

Anxiety reduction. This section describes techniques designed to overcome the anxiety that can impair performance on the examination (Chapter 17).

CHAPTER 11

The MCAT

OVERVIEW

Purpose of the MCAT

The Medical College Admission Test (MCAT) is a test developed by the Association of American Medical Colleges (AAMC) to offer admissions committees a standarized reference point for the comparison of academically similar candidates. The test is administered at most major colleges and universities in the United States, and in some foreign countries. Each year, the AAMC refines the MCAT to ensure that it is a valid predictor of student performance in medical school.

The MCAT has four sections: Verbal Reasoning, Physical Sciences, Writing Sample, and Biological Sciences. Medical schools often place the greatest emphasis on the science sections. A student who earns high scores on the Biological Sciences or Physical Sciences sections of the MCAT is more likely to do well with similar science material in medical school. However, high scores on these sections do not negate the effect of low scores on the Verbal Reasoning or Writing Sample sections. A student who wants to enter medical school should prepare for all of the sections of the MCAT.

Applying to Take the MCAT

If it is not available from your bioscience advisor, you can call or write for the MCAT application:

MCAT Program Office
P.O. Box 4056
Iowa City, IA 52243
(319) 337-1357

The fee for taking the MCAT is $155.00. The fee is reduced to $55.00 for qualified applicants. A separate application is required for the fee-reduction program. The MCAT application materials include the fee-reduction application, the MCAT application, and other required forms. Applicants are required to attach a photograph to the application form. The section that asks the applicant to indicate whether the MCAT scores should be released to the student's bioscience advisor and to selected medical schools is important; releasing these scores can eliminate delays in the application process.

Structure of the MCAT

The MCAT is a timed, standardized, multiple-choice test that includes an essay component. The multiple-choice section of the test assesses knowledge of biology, organic and inorganic chemistry, and physics, as well as verbal reasoning skills. The MCAT is a day-long test with morning and afternoon sessions (*Table 11–1*). In the morning, verbal reasoning skills are tested, followed by knowledge of physical sciences. In the afternoon, applicants complete two essays and the biologic sciences section.

● ● ●
VERBAL REASONING SECTION

Structure

The verbal reasoning section contains nine reading passages of 500–600 words each. Each passage is accompanied by six to ten questions. Students have 85 minutes to read the passages and answer the questions.

Preparation

This section of the MCAT requires a broad, comprehensive overview of a number of nonscience topics. To prepare for the verbal reasoning section, students should gain general knowledge of a variety of topics by taking classes in the nonmedical areas tested on the MCAT or by reading widely. The best source of general information is often magazines. For example, *National Geographic* is an excellent source of information about anthropology, archeology, art history, natural history, geology, ecology, and sociology. Other popular magazines contain similar diverse topics. *Table 11–2* lists topics covered on the MCAT.

• • •

TABLE 11-1. MCAT Schedule

Section	Number of Questions	Time Allotted (minutes)
Verbal Reasoning	65	85
Break	...	10
Physical Sciences	77	100
Lunch	...	60
Writing Sample	2	60
Break	...	10
Biological Sciences	77	100

Writing Styles Used in the Passages

The verbal reasoning subtest uses four distinct writing styles: (1) argumentative, which presents and defends a position (e.g., supporting the death penalty); (2) expository, which explains a situation (e.g., why social systems tend to collapse); (3) informative, which discusses a controversial subject (e.g., environmentalism); and (4) narrative, which describes a series of events (e.g., the rise and fall of slavery in the American South).

Each type of writing requires a different analytical approach, and each lends itself to a different type of question. Argumentative passages tend to have a clear beginning, middle, and end. In many cases, conclusions are found in the last paragraph and descriptions in the middle paragraphs. The introductory paragraph is usually some type of gambit or misdirection. Therefore, this type of passage tends

• • •

TABLE 11-2. Verbal Reasoning Topics for the MCAT

Humanities	Social Science	Natural Science
Architecture	Anthropology	Astronomy
Art and art history	Archeology	Botany
Dance	Business	Computer Science
Ethics	Economics	Ecology
Literary criticism	Government	Geology
Music	History	Meteorology
Philosophy	Politics	Natural history
Religion	Psychology	Technology
Theater	Sociology	

to have questions that ask the reader to draw conclusions or determine whether the author would agree with an additional interpretation. These questions also ask the reader to analyze the writer's message, thesis, or claim, so it is important to look for evidence, assumptions, and conclusions. The answers to most questions connected with these passages are found in the middle and final paragraphs.

Expository passages are often a section of an argumentative passage. They contain the middle parts of the argument, where data to support the argument are presented. These passages usually do not offer conclusions, nor do they present much background information. The most important information is often found in the beginning paragraphs. Questions associated with these passages generally ask the student to test the author's explanation against other interpretations or to evaluate the writer's message. It is important to look for accuracy, consistency, and relevance in the writer's statements. The answers to many questions are found in the opening paragraph.

Informative passages include a variety of styles and types. These passages may be taken from a chapter in a book, a journal article, or a monograph. Informative passages are usually densely packed with facts, details, and definitions. These passages usually present both sides of a controversial topic. Questions are usually about specific points presented in the passage. Because so much information is presented, it may be difficult to locate the data needed to answer a question. However, it is important to note dates, names, and other proper nouns when reading the passage because these details often appear in the questions. Questions also ask the reader to extend the writer's message to solve a problem or interpret a hypothetical situation.

Narrative passages often have a beginning, middle, and end. The narrative passage is a hybrid of the argumentative passage and the informative passage, and some of the same types of questions are used. Additionally, questions for these passages ask the reader to incorporate new information and reevaluate the content of the passage. Answers to questions are often found in the concluding paragraph.

● ● ●
BIOLOGIC AND PHYSICAL SCIENCE SECTIONS

Structure

Each science section of the MCAT consists of 77 questions. These questions are divided into two types: problem sets and individual questions.

Each section usually has 10 problem sets, each with five to eight questions. Each set focuses on a specific biology, chemistry, or physics topic. For example, a problem set in the physical science section may deal with thermodynamics, whereas one in biologic science may deal with genetics. The five to ten questions that accompany the problem sets are linked to a reading passage that may be combined with graphs or tables. Each passage is approximately 250 words long. Four types of passages are used:

1. Information presentation (from a textbook passage or journal article)

2. Problem solving (word problems similar to those in textbooks)

3. Research study (presentation of raw experimental data)

4. Persuasive argument (attempts to convince the reader or change her point of view, can be either positive or negative)

Questions based on the passages ask you to: recall basic science concepts; show comprehension of concepts presented in the text; interpret data presented in graphic, tabular, or diagram form; use concepts in the passage to solve problems; or evaluate methods, evidence, and conclusions.

Approximately 15 independent, stand alone questions are also included in each section. Chapter 15 describes the process for answering questions in the science subtests.

Preparation

The MCAT evaluates the student's ability to analyze and interpret basic science concepts in a problem-solving format. For this reason, the best way to prepare for the MCAT is to study the basic principles of each subject. For instance, when studying mendelian genetics, it is important to understand that autosomal genes can be either dominant or recessive and that the dominant gene controls the expression of the gene. Understanding this concept allows you to answer many questions on simple genetics.

The science sections require students to interpret data that are presented in tabular, statistical, or raw form. In most cases, numeric information is combined with textual explanations. These passages require students to perform four tasks:

1. Compare components of tables, figures, or diagrams. For example, does Table A contradict the data in Table B?

2. Identify trends and relations in data. For example, do values increase or decrease over time?

3. Identify relevant background knowledge. For example, what do you know about the incidence of malaria in developing countries?

4. Select an appropriate format to represent information. For example, is it best to define the result by expressing the mean or the median value?

Only simple arithmetic operations are needed to solve the mathematical and graphic questions in the science sections. Calculus is not required. The basic mathematics concepts needed for the MCAT are arithmetic (i.e., proportions, ratios, square root); algebra (i.e., logs, exponents, reciprocals); trigonometry (i.e., sine, angles, length relations); metric units (i.e., balancing equations); error (i.e., estimates, effects of experimental error); probability (i.e., simple calculations); vectors (i.e., addition, subtraction); and statistics (i.e., mean, standard deviation, correlation coefficients).

Tables 11–3 and *11–4* list the science subject areas covered on the MCAT.

● ● ●
WRITING SAMPLE

For many students, the most intimidating section of the MCAT is the writing sample, or essay subtest, which requires applicants to write two essays on different topics in 60 minutes. Concerns about this part of the MCAT are largely based on the fact that, unlike the other sections, it is impossible to anticipate the question topics. Although the topics for the essay questions are drawn from an array of subjects, there is a strategy that students can use to prepare and practice for this section of the MCAT.

Certain topics are not addressed in the writing sample section: biology; chemistry; physics; the medical school application process; reasons for choosing a career in medicine; unfamiliar social or cultural issues; and emotionally charged issues. The questions usually present hypothetical situations in which an ethical problem

• • •

TABLE 11-3. Topics on the MCAT

General Chemistry
   Stoichiometry
   Electronic structure and the periodic table
   Bonding
   Phases and phase equilibria
   Solution chemistry
   Acids and bases
   Thermodynamics and thermochemistry
   Rate processes: kinetics and equilibrium
   Electrochemistry

Physics
   Translational motion
   Force and motion: gravitation
   Equilibrium and momentum
   Work and energy
   Wave characteristics and motion
   Sound
   Fluids and solids
   Electrostatics and electromagnetism
   Electronic circuits
   Light and geometric optics
   Atomic and nuclear structure

or dilemma has two clearly opposing sides. The passage usually contains a statement of opinion, philosophy, or policy. For example:

An American writer described a difficult moment in his life, saying, "The test of a first-rate intelligence is the ability to hold two opposing ideas in the mind at the same time, and still retain the ability to function. One should, for example, be able to see that things are hopeless and yet be determined to make them otherwise." Write an essay in which you explain how the author's example applies to his "test of a first-rate intelligence." In your essay, provide another example that either supports or refutes the author's definition of a first-rate intelligence.

• • •

TABLE 11-4. Biologic Science Topics on the MCAT

Biology
   Molecular biology
   Microbiology
   Eukaryotic cells
   Specialized cells and tissues
   Nervous and endocrine systems
   Circulatory, lymphatic, and immune systems
   Digestive and excretory systems
   Muscle and skeletal systems
   Respiratory and skin systems
   Reproductive systems and development
   Genetics and evolution

Organic chemistry
   Biologic molecules
   Oxygen-containing compounds
   Amines
   Hydrocarbons
   Molecular structure of organic compounds
   Separation and purification
   Use of spectroscopy in structural identification

What does this question say about the typical MCAT essay question? First, the stem, or informational passage, of the question presents an either/or situation. The reader either agrees or disagrees with the author. Second, these topics are usually broad and subject to more than one interpretation. *Table 11–5* shows sample essay topics.

Students can use three strategies when writing essays for this section of the MCAT.

1. Agreeing with the author is the safest approach. If you agree that a "first-rate intelligence can hold two opposing ideas at the same time," then your answer may be considered correct by the readers of your essay, and you will be given at least an average score.

2. Disagreeing with the statement requires the use of examples or background information. If adequately defined and defended, this position can lead to a higher score. For example, if you can support the argument that "it does not take a first-rate intelligence to hold two opposing ideas at the same time," then your essay will stand out from other essays, and your score will probably be higher.

3. Both agreeing and disagreeing with the author is the most difficult approach. A student who does not create the ideal balance between the two views may be considered too eager to please the essay readers. The readers usually prefer essays that present a strong case for one side of the argument. Attempting to encompass both sides requires a special understanding of the topic or a level of writing skill that is beyond the abilities of most students. However, because most students write essays that agree with the author's view, the arguments supporting their positions are usually similar. A student who writes an essay that presents a different view often receives a high rating and a higher score.

The writing sample assesses the student's skill in the following areas: (1) developing a central idea, (2) synthesizing concepts and ideas, (3) expressing ideas cohesively and logically, and (4) writing clearly, according to accepted practices of

● ● ●

TABLE 11–5. Sample Essay Topics

Truth is great, and its effectiveness endures.

Criticism comes easier than craftsmanship.

Every science and every inquiry, and similarly every activity and pursuit, is thought to aim at some good.

Law is order, and good law is good order.

To like and dislike the same things, that is indeed true friendship.

Force without wisdom falls of its own weight.

It is quality rather than quantity that matters.

What is not good for the swarm is not good for the bee.

The deed is everything, the glory nothing.

Every nation has the government it deserves.

Liberty consists in doing what one desires.

grammar, syntax, and punctuation. To achieve a high score, a student must argue for or against the idea clearly and concisely. The best approach is to either refute the argument presented in the passage or show the strengths and weaknesses of both sides of the argument. The least effective approach is to simply agree with the author and support her ideas without creating a strong argument for them.

To write an effective essay, a student must state the hypothesis, or main idea, of the passage; antithesis of the passage, or the arguments that can be presented against it; and how two conflicting ideas can be reconciled. Chapter 15 offers additional suggestions for writing essays.

● ● ●
SCORING

Verbal Reasoning, Physical Sciences, and Biological Sciences Subtests

With the exception of the writing sample, the subtests of the MCAT are scored on a scale of one to fifteen, with fifteen representing the highest score. The final scaled scores are determined by statistically converting the total raw score for each subtest to the scaled score. This conversion is performed for a number of reasons, most significantly, to compensate for differences in the level of difficulty of the questions on different administrations of the MCAT. This conversion also allows for other forms of test validation that are necessary for a nationally normed examination.

Every MCAT includes questions that are not considered in the final scoring process because they are statistically invalid or, less frequently, experimental. On any MCAT administration, 5%–8% of the questions are either invalid or experimental.

Because the MCAT is scored using a percentile factor, the conversion from the raw to scaled score is nonlinear. More correct answers are required in the midpoint range (7–9) than at either extreme to increase the scaled score. Therefore, once a student has reached a certain scaled score, fewer correct answers are required to increase his score by a digit than would be required at a lower score. This process is considered in greater detail in Chapter 13.

Writing Sample

Writing samples are scored according to an alphabetical scale that ranges from J through T. J is the lowest score, and T is the highest. The way in which the final scaled scores are derived for the writing sample is also different from that for the other sections of the MCAT. For the other sections, the raw score is derived by computing the number of questions answered correctly. The writing sample is evaluated and scored after the essays are read by professional readers.

Each essay is scored by two professional readers who use a holistic approach. The student's ideas or arguments are weighed more heavily than the punctuation, spelling, or grammar used. Very poor language skills may lower the overall score, but points are not deducted for accidental mistakes.

The raw scores given the two essays by the two readers are combined to form a final raw score. Because the highest raw score that each reader can give a single essay is six, then the highest possible total raw score is twenty-four (six points for each essay times two readers). The raw score is converted to a scaled score based on statistical weighing of the raw scores against previous MCAT administrations. *Table 11–6* shows the raw scoring scale.

● ● ●

TABLE 11–6. Scoring Scale for Essays

Raw Score Scale	Interpretation
6	Excellent
5	Adept
4	Proficient
3	Competent
2	Weak
1	Inadequate
0	Illegible, foreign language, or obvious effort to ignore the purpose of the writing sample

CHAPTER 12

Practice MCAT

This chapter contains a full-length practice Medical College Admission Test (MCAT) examination, a multiple-choice answer sheet, and blank pages to use to write the essays. Each section is marked with the allotted time and the question numbers. It is important to follow the time line strictly when taking the practice examination. Chapter 13 contains a complete answer key and analysis form to use in interpreting answers.

Verbal Reasoning

Time: 85 Minutes
Questions 1–65

Passage I (Questions 1–5)

Once upon a time there were no lies and no liars. The world was still too new, and mankind had not learned of the social and cultural implications of not telling the truth. In fact, it was very important that people told each other whether a lion or tiger was in the vicinity, for their lives and the lives of their families depended on it. It was only after people had gained control of their environment that they were able to afford the luxury of lying.

The lie is a common social phenomenon, but only the most sophisticated of cultures could have produced the big lie, or propaganda. In modern times, this was best exemplified by Nazi Germany. The Nazis rose the lie past mere braggadocio into the stratified heights of military and political strategy. The big lie became so convincing that the propagandists came to believe it themselves.

Today, the big lie is called disinformation, not propaganda. Accusations of wrongdoing in China, Bosnia, Somalia, Iraq, and other hot spots have filtered back and forth across the world at such a hectic pace that just keeping up with the story of who's doing what to whom has become a full-time affair. We would like to believe that our government does not participate in this whole mess, but we know from experience that, given an opportunity, any bureaucrat or diplomat would rather lie than tell the truth if the lie seems to serve a purpose at the time.

Of course, a lie saves time and discomfort. It makes it possible for us to be on speaking terms with individuals and nations that would not like us, or us them, if it were not for the intervening buffer of the lie. We plead ignorance, lack of planning, or some other fault, rather than acknowledge culpability at being caught in a lie. We confuse ourselves and our friends with changes brought about because of some new reality that must be falsified. Old lies become old truths, and new lies become policy. The most recent example of this in the United Stated was the Iran–Contra affair, where some members of President Reagan's administration attempted to supply weapons illegally to the Contras in Nicaragua. To accomplish this, they had to lie to Congress and the President. The ultimate question regarding this issue was not whether these men were evil, but how they used patriotic slogans and ideals to justify their actions. Once again, individuals in the government came to believe their own lies about the need for immediate action, even when those actions were not in the best interest of the people.

Governments believe that they need to lie because they must protect their citizens. Any government would lie if it believed that it could benefit from the lie. That is probably where most governments go wrong. They may gain security, but in the process, they lose freedom.

1. The main idea of this passage is:

    A. lying is beneficial.
    B. lies hurt more than they help.
    C. governments lie to protect their interests.
    D. government lies lead to fear, distrust, and a loss of freedom.

2. Nazi Germany:

    A. made lying into governmental policy.
    B. did not believe its own propaganda.
    C. is an example of a government that used disinformation only for peaceful ends.
    D. never used propaganda.

3. The author would agree that:

    A. lying can be justified.
    B. lying cannot be justified.
    C. lying is wrong only for governments, not for people.
    D. lying leads to greater security.

4. Which of the following statements would NOT be supported by the passage?

    A. Lies are used by governments to control opinion.
    B. Lying is a natural part of life.
    C. All governments would lie if necessary.
    D. Confusion can occur if lies are told.

5. The passage states that:

A. Iran received military supplies from the United States.

B. the Contras received military supplies from the United States.

C. Nicaragua sold planes to Iran.

D. the United States sold planes to Iran.

Passage II (Questions 6–12)

Today, the Japanese are viewed as the ultimate business success story. As a people and as a nation, they have constructed a society that can produce quality goods for competitive prices. Some authorities credit the unusually cooperative nature of Japanese society for its phenomenal economic growth. They believe that, in contrast to America's goal orientation, where efficiency, output, and productivity are highly valued and the primary objective is to win or to achieve success, the Japanese are more norm oriented. They prize how things are done and the means of interaction to accomplish them. For this reason, playing according to the rules is just as important as winning the game. Clearly, this norm orientation of Japanese culture implies that some form of social control must exist. Over time, the Japanese codified these controls as verbal expressions in their language, creating a sort of moral and cultural shorthand that is understood and followed by all.

One of the most pervasive of these expressions, *enryo*, relates to feelings of modesty or obeisance in the presence of one's superior. Two other expressions stem from enryo. *Hige* holds that self-praise or praise of one's family in public is in bad taste, and *hazukashi* refers to the idea that one might make a fool of oneself in front of others. Thus, enryo, hige, and hazukashi define one's responsibility within the wider community.

Other expressions, such as *giri* and *on,* refer to being in the right place. Giri relates to role position, with a connotation of moral obligation or duty to family and community; *on* relates to ascribed obligation, or the specific obligations one feels toward other people. In the family, those obligations are defined by *oyakoko,* which means filial piety or the obligation of the child to the parent. *Chu* also deals with obligation to others; however, it specifically means loyalty to one's superior and therefore relates to authority structuring.

Two final expressions, *gaman* and *shikataganai,* represent the philosophical view of Japanese culture. *Gaman* means that one bears up under pain or adversity by suppressing emotions. *Shikataganai* refers to the idea that one's fate is tied to forces beyond individual control. Thus, life is uncontrollable, but one must endure and never lose the sense of obligation that gives each individual a clearly defined position and role in the family and community.

Nearly all of these expressions deal with obligation or, in essence, control. The obligations of the individual are defined by the culture, transmitted by the family, and enforced by the community. The transition from family obligation to corporate obligation was a slight one for most Japanese. Through the use of group exercises, singing of the corporate song, and waving of the corporate flag, a sense of community and family was fostered.

Japan's executives have followed the natural inclination of their culture and created an efficient and productive employment structure. For Americans, this abject loyalty to the corporation is both alien and distasteful. The American worker is

GO ON TO NEXT PAGE.

leery of the corporate establishment and knows from experience the struggles that have been necessary to provide a safe and fair working environment. An American could never embrace the concept of shikataganai because Americans believe that it is possible to master any situation.

Japan's success, based as it is on cultural controls, is probably not transferable to American shores. Rather, the unique American reliance on goals must be channeled into similar pathways. The American worker should be encouraged to find goals that lead to increases in productivity. Americans do have one thing in common with the Japanese: they too believe in gaman.

6. According to the passage:

   A. the Japanese are successful because they work together.
   B. the Japanese are successful because they have been able to adopt American business practices.
   C. the Japanese are successful because their culture made loyalty to the company easier.
   D. American business could learn a great deal from Japan.

7. The controlling expression that is cited as the most common in the passage is:

   A. *hige.*
   B. *oyakoko.*
   C. *gaman.*
   D. *enryo.*

8. The author's statement that the Japanese are concerned about norms means that:

   A. Japanese society is prone to conformity.
   B. the Japanese are more normal than other people.
   C. all Japanese follow the same set of rules.
   D. Japan does not have the same problems with deviant behavior as America does.

9. What lesson could American businesses learn from Japanese culture?

   A. Have all workers share the same beliefs.
   B. Make workers exercise together and pledge allegiance to the company.
   C. Use the American workers' cultural goal orientation to develop worker incentives.
   D. Develop a series of expressions to control worker behavior.

10. Obeisance of the child to the parent is inferred in which expression?

    A. *Chu*
    B. *On*
    C. *Oyakoko*
    D. *Giri*

11. The author of this passage would agree that:

    A. the Japanese have developed the perfect working philosophy.
    B. America needs to become more like Japan.
    C. what works for Japan will not necessarily work for America.
    D. the lessons to be learned from Japan are directly transferable to America.

12. *Gaman* relates to:

    A. feelings of obligation to others.
    B. a stoic outlook on life.
    C. modesty in the presence of others.
    D. being in the right place.

The refracting telescope uses lenses that bring the light from a distant object into focus by refraction. The principal lens, called the objective, collects the parallel rays of light from a body and brings them to a point, called the focus, where they may be examined by the eye of the observer at a second lens or combination of lenses, called the eyepiece. Sometimes the rays of light are photographed by a light-sensitive film placed in the focus. In this case, no eyepiece is used.

The distance from the center of the objective to the focus is called the focal length (F). The diameter of the objective is called the aperture (a). In the typical visual refractor, the focal length is approximately 15 times the aperture. The focal ratio (F/a) is therefore approximately 15. This figure varies from telescope to telescope and sometimes is as great as 20.

The function of the eyepiece is to magnify the image formed by the objective. There are two principal types of eyepieces—positive and negative—with various modifications. The positive eyepiece consists of two plano-convex lenses of the same focal length placed with the curved sides facing each other. The larger of the two is called the field lens; the other is the eye lens. The eyepiece is placed so that the image is in front of the field lens. This eyepiece can also be used as a hand magnifier.

13. The focus:

    A. reflects light to the eyepiece.
    B. refracts light.
    C. is the place where light converges.
    D. is adjusted by hand.

14. The refracting telescope:

    A. is used to observe small objects.
    B. is used to observe distant objects.
    C. is made up of two primary lenses.
    D. both B and C.

15. As used in this passage, refraction of light:

    A. is a process unique to the telescope.
    B. involves bringing parallel light rays to a point.
    C. involves spreading parallel light rays.
    D. is the opposite of reflection.

16. The focal ratio is:

    A. always preset at 15.
    B. the distance from the center of the objective to the focus.

C. the ratio between the focal length and the aperture.
D. the ratio between the focal length and the focus.

17. Which part of the telescope is made up of two lenses?

    A. The objective
    B. The eyepiece
    C. The focus
    D. The aperture

18. The author would agree that:

    A. a refracting telescope is better than a reflecting telescope.
    B. light focused on the lens of a refracting telescope would contain some images too faint for the human eye to see.
    C. light focused on the lens of a refracting telescope is best studied with a large aperture.
    D. all light contains the same spectrum.

GO ON TO NEXT PAGE.

Passage IV (Questions 19–23)

Linguistics is the science of language. Many linguists view their discipline as a completely autonomous science, and there is a growing trend in American universities to establish independent departments of linguistics. However, languages are aspects of cultures, intimately interacting with all of the other manifestations of culture, and are therefore best understood in the cultural context. Consequently, among the social sciences, the scientific study of languages is widely held to be a branch of cultural anthropology. In the United States, at least, all of the larger departments of anthropology include linguistic analysis as a part of their programs. Anthropologists, once they had begun to base their studies on objective fieldwork, were forced to learn many primitive languages from scratch, with no book of grammar to guide them. As a result, a universal system of phonetic writing had to be developed so that records could be kept of what native informants were saying in tongues that had no system of writing. Development of this system soon led to a realization that different cultures organize speech in accordance with principles different from those that govern the familiar Indo-European languages. Some anthropologists, fascinated by their new discoveries, began to concentrate their efforts on recording and analyzing primitive languages, and linguistics as a specialized branch of anthropology developed in a way that is revolutionizing all language study.

19. Which statement about linguistics is **NOT** true?

A. It is universally recognized as a part of anthropology.
B. Anthropologists believe that it is a part of anthropology.
C. It is the study of language.
D. It is best understood in a cultural context.

20. Anthropologists:

A. are all linguists.
B. developed a universal system of phonetic writing.
C. found no differences between languages.
D. believe that Indo-European languages are better than other languages because they are based on writing.

21. The author of this passage would agree that:

A. language is not important to study.
B. language and culture are best studied separately.
C. cultures without a written language are inferior.
D. language is best studied in connection with other aspects of culture.

22. It can be inferred from the passage that:

A. all languages came from the same source.
B. a scientific study of language is best done from written sources.
C. languages are different because of cultural differences.
D. Indo-European languages are completely understood.

23. Linguistics is:

A. a part of the humanities.
B. a physical science.
C. a social science.
D. a part of the fine arts.

Passage V (Questions 24–30)

Fluorescent lights are ideally suited to grow any plant indoors. The light from fluorescent tubes contains much of the light that plants need for growth. Sunlight contains the full spectrum of useful light; the spectrum runs from low (red) to high (blue) energy. Visible light has a range of 3800 to 7000 angstroms. The best range for plants is 6100 to 7000 angstroms. Red light tends to make plants mature more rapidly (tall, spindly growth), whereas blue light tends to make plants short, with thickened stems and dark green leaves. Fluorescent lights used alone are good for most plants, although sometimes it is useful to include as much as 10% incandescent light.

Fluorescent lamps are classified as cool to warm. The terms refer to the amount of red light emitted by the lamp. Cool lamps emit little red light, and warm lamps produce significantly more light at the red end of the spectrum. Because fluorescent lamps work by exciting gases within the tube, they achieve the best light in the 11 inches in the middle of the tube. Thus, it is best to start plants under the middle of the lamp and then move or transplant them to the outside of the lamp as they grow.

Seedlings and young plants that need maximum light can be placed 1 to 4 inches below a pair of suspended 40 watt lights. Older plants can be placed approximately 11 inches away from the lamps. Plants with leaves that lean toward the light or with weak stems that trail the plant over the edge of the growing box are not receiving enough light. This situation can be corrected by raising the box, increasing the length of exposure, or increasing the wattage of the lamps. Plants with bunched leaves and hard centers and leaves that show a loss of color or burned areas may be receiving too much light. This problem can be solved by moving the lamps away or decreasing the length of exposure.

24. Fluorescent lights:

   A. emit light in all colors of the spectrum.
   B. emit light in the range of 6100 to 7000 angstroms.
   C. emit light in most of the colors of the spectrum.
   D. emit more red light than blue light.

25. For young plants, the optimum distance from fluorescent lamps is:

   A. 15 inches.
   B. 20 inches.
   C. 2 inches.
   D. 1 to 4 inches.

26. Plants that appear bunched are receiving:

   A. too little light.
   B. too much light.

C. too little blue light.
D. too much blue light.

27. To be most effective, fluorescent light should be mixed with:

   A. natural light.
   B. candlelight.
   C. incandescent light.
   D. starlight.

28. A fluorescent lamp labeled as cool would:

   A. emit less blue light.
   B. emit less red light.
   C. emit more blue light.
   D. emit more red light.

29. A good title for this passage would be:

   A. Fluorescent Lights Are Best.
   B. Fluorescent Lights Improve Growing.
   C. Fluorescent Lights From A to Z.
   D. Growing Indoors.

30. Fluorescent lights:

   A. produce light by irradiation.
   B. produce light equally.
   C. produce light by exciting gases.
   D. produce light and heat equally.

GO ON TO NEXT PAGE.

Passage VI (Questions 31–38)

Since the birth of radio broadcasting in the 1920s, the networks have shaped the thinking of broadcasters, politicians, and the American public. Television replaced radio, but in the transformation, the radio networks became the major American television syndicates. Today, with the advent of cable TV, videocassette recorders, subscription TV, pay TV, superstations, and other forms of alternative television, the future of the networks is in question.

Part of the reason for the development of network broadcasting is the nature of the broadcast medium, or spectrum. Because of the way the medium works, individual broadcasters interfere with other programs by transmitting on wavelengths that other broadcasters are using. Order was imposed on the broadcast system by the United States Congress. Working with other governments, Congress established a series of regulations that led to the creation of the Federal Communications Commission (FCC) under the auspices of the Communications Act of 1934. The FCC created order by assigning individual stations a frequency, or wavelength, on which to transmit. The power, or output, of each station was also limited. To enforce these regulations, the FCC was given the authority to license each station and to revoke the license.

Another major provision of the Act was the assertion that the broadcast spectrum, or airways, is public property. The FCC has predicated most of its subsequent decisions on the principle of public ownership of the broadcast medium. It has mandated the number of stations that an individual or group may own, established guidelines for commercials and political advertising, and generally served as the watchdog of the airways in the name of the people.

Recently, the FCC began to exercise greater flexibility in its interpretation of what is in the public interest. It has recognized the rights of pay TV and subscription TV, allowing these non-network services to compete on an equal footing with the networks. Of course, those who most vigorously opposed the FCC's actions were the networks. They realized that unrestrained competition with these services would mean reduced profits and eventual loss of the near-monopoly that they enjoyed.

Because of the limitations imposed by the FCC on station ownership and the equally compelling economic realities of producing television shows, the networks established a system of affiliate stations firmly based on a core of network-owned stations. The networks paid for, produced, and delivered to the affiliates high-quality programs. In turn the networks were allowed to charge sponsors fantastic sums for commercials aired during popular programs.

Today, the trend seems clear: greater diversity in available TV services will place more control in the hands of the viewer. As a result, the viewer may choose one of the other services over network TV. A profound change in the viewing habits of Americans has begun. The outcome of this change may bring forth a worthy successor to the American network system.

31. The FCC bases its power on:

  A. the assumption that without control, there will be chaos over the airways.
  B. the assumption that the airways are public property.
  C. the assumption that television is likely to espouse morally or socially unacceptable views.
  D. the Communications Act of 1920.

32. Network television:

  A. is made up of network-owned stations and affiliate stations.
  B. was created by the Communications Act of 1934.
  C. has a complete monopoly in America.
  D. should be disbanded and replaced by pay TV.

33. The title for this passage might be:

  A. The End of the Networks.
  B. The Birth of Alternative TV.
  C. The FCC and the Networks.
  D. The Communications Act of 1934.

34. The author would agree that:

  A. the changes occurring in television are positive.
  B. the FCC should not allow new forms of television.
  C. the changes occurring in television are negative.
  D. subscription TV is better than network TV.

35. Congress set up the FCC to:

  A. guarantee the networks a monopoly.
  B. bring order to the broadcast spectrum.
  C. stop other governments from taking over America's airways.
  D. increase competition between networks.

36. As part of its mission, the FCC has:

  A. mandated the number of stations that can be owned by an individual or group.
  B. censored commercials and political advertising.
  C. assigned stations frequencies and power limits.
  D. all of the above.

37. The initials FCC stand for:

    A. Federal Commerce Commission.
    B. Federal Civil Commission.
    C. Federal Communications Commission.
    D. Federal Cable Control.

38. The term airways refers to:

    A. the networks.
    B. the broadcast spectrum.
    C. the FCC.
    D. pay TV.

Passage VII (Questions 39–46)

There are two limiting conditions of historical phenomena with which the historian must deal: the effect of those phenomena and the artifact that is used to interpret the effect. The effect and the artifact are merely parts of historic events and serve as representation of the true events in history, which are continual processes. Those processes emanate from the real events of history and have remained unfathomable. The effect those processes have on the historical scene, once recorded or preserved, become the artifact. Thus, the historian is unable to recreate for study the actual event or historical moment and must rely instead on the artifacts strewn throughout history to interpret it.

An artifact can vary in dimension, physical attributes, and quantity to such an extent that the historian often becomes an arbiter of the artifact. Judgment of the relative worth of an artifact means selection under duress because even the most rigorously recorded and documented event will exclude a multitude of historic minutiae that may have great moment without apparent purpose or, worse yet, without artifact.

The historian must ferret out from written, oral, and other sources the artifacts left after the event. This process of artifaction is the primary work of the historian. By reconstructing the past through artifacts generated by the effects of history, the historian creates a more or less distorted version of history. This process points out the absurdity of ever hoping to gain the true story of history.

However, we can still gain a great deal of knowledge from the artifaction of history. The major theoretic underpinning of artifaction is that events create effects that are recorded or preserved as artifacts. This process can allow for the creation of new artifacts, such as is occurring with oral history today. Artifaction becomes a method of inquiry based on the availability of artifacts and the historian's understanding of the nuances related to them.

39. History:

    A. can never be truly recreated.
    B. is the true story of the past.
    C. is studied to learn how to deal with current problems.
    D. is best understood by studying what people said.

40. The effects of history are:

    A. constantly being changed by historians.
    B. caused by the true events in history.
    C. without apparent purpose.
    D. created by artifacts.

GO ON TO NEXT PAGE.

41. The author implies that:

A. history is useless.
B. history is a process of selection and interpretation of artifacts.
C. effects in history are the sole source of historical knowledge.
D. historical knowledge leads to a greater understanding of today's world.

42. Historians are unable to recreate the true past because:

A. all of the people involved are dead.
B. the effects of history are unclear.
C. many of the events of history are not documented through artifacts.
D. the past is beyond our comprehension.

43. The author would probably title this passage:

A. The Truth About History.
B. History and Facts.
C. The Artifactualization of History.
D. The Historian as Detective.

44. The difference between effects and artifacts is that:

A. effects are undocumented.
B. artifacts must be discovered.
C. effects are the direct result of events.
D. artifacts are the direct result of events.

45. Oral history is:

A. the study of opera.
B. the study of the recording industry.
C. the study of radio.
D. the study of history using verbal testimony.

46. Artifaction:

A. is the science of discovery.
B. is the primary work of the historian.
C. always reveals new information about history.
D. leads to confusion.

Passage VIII (Questions 47–55)

Computers are really quite old. The Chinese abacus, a hand-held calculator that uses round beads on string or wire, was arguably the first use of a machine to perform mathematic work. However, the first successful use of an electronic computer occurred in the 1950s with the UNIVAC I, which was as large as a warehouse and contained thousands of vacuum tubes. These machines were mainly number crunchers used to perform massive and laborious calculations such as those needed to plot the projection of spacecraft.

Today's handheld calculator is the equivalent of the original UNIVAC in computing power. This dramatic improvement was largely made possible through the discovery of the transistor in the 1950s and the development of the integrated circuit in the 1960s. The size of computers has been decreasing while their power and speed have been increasing.

There are three major types of computers. Mainframes, the largest, are used to store vast amounts of data and to perform tremendously complicated calculations. Mainframes are equipped for access by many users on terminals. Minicomputers are smaller, but still have many of the capabilities of mainframes. Microcomputers, or personal computers, are the most recently invented computers. These computers are increasingly able to perform functions that only mainframes could do previously, such as provide access to multiple users (through networks).

A computer operates through a combination of hardware and software (the programs that perform calculations, word processing, etc.). Hardware is all of the actual mechanical and electronic parts that form the "guts" of a machine. A computer has three major hardware components. The central processing unit, also called the motherboard, is the heart of the computer, where processing and calculations actually occur. The screen, or monitor, is where the user sees what is taking place in the computer and what has been typed, drawn, or graphically entered. The keyboard is the final component of the computer. It is used to interface with the computer and input data, words, and numbers.

In addition to these three basic components, other hardware, known as peripherals, may be attached to the computer. First among these are printers, which print out what is entered or computed. Second are plotters, which draw out what is entered or computed. Last are modems or FAX/modems, which are used to communicate with other computers over telephone lines or using microwave relays.

Computer chips, especially memory chips, make the micro-computer possible. Two types of memory chips are used in these computers. ROM (read-only memory) chips are hard-wired, which means that they cannot be erased, even when the computer is turned off or there is a loss of power to the machine. RAM (random access memory) chips store information or data electronically, and when the power is turned off, everything stored in them is lost. For instance, when a software program is loaded into the computer, it goes into RAM chips, or memory. In most cases, there is a maximum amount of RAM

142

(640 kilobytes) that can be used. However, extended and expanded memory, which can exceed 640 kilobytes is now available. For every program that is put into RAM, some storage space, or memory, is lost. If a program of 250 kilobytes is loaded then 390 kilobytes of RAM will be available. As information is entered, it is stored in RAM, which further reduces available memory. If a user runs out of RAM when working in a program, the computer will lock up, or freeze.

47. The difference between RAM and ROM is that:

   A. RAM is unchanging, whereas ROM changes.
   B. RAM changes, whereas ROM does not.
   C. ROM can be altered to include new information, whereas RAM cannot.
   D. ROM is fixed in size, and RAM is not.

48. The passage implies that:

   A. personal computers are inferior to mainframe computers.
   B. personal computers will probably become more powerful than mainframe computers.
   C. minicomputers are better than mainframe computers.
   D. mainframes will always be used for larger, more complex tasks.

49. The author suggests that the most important component of the personal computer is the:

   A. central processing unit.
   B. keyboard.
   C. monitor.
   D. memory chips.

50. Based on the information in the passage, if a personal computer has 640 kilobytes of regular RAM and 1046 kilobytes of expanded memory, how much memory would be left for other programs if a program uses 780 kilobytes?

   A. 805 kilobytes
   B. 600 kilobytes
   C. 906 kilobytes
   D. Cannot be determined from the information given

51. The author would agree that:

   A. the speed of computers increases because they are smaller.

   B. the size of the machine determines how fast it can work.
   C. the speed and size of computers are changing primarily because of an increase in memory.
   D. the speed of computers has increased because of innovations in electronic technology.

52. As defined in the passage, all of the following could be called computers **EXCEPT** a:

   A. slide rule.
   B. adding machine.
   C. cash register.
   D. telephone.

53. The passage implies that the term lock up means:

   A. a loss of information, or data.
   B. a conflict in memory that leaves the computer unable to function.
   C. too many programs running at the same time.
   D. cannot be determined from the passage.

54. Based on the passage, it can be inferred that:

   A. computers perform mathematic functions better than humans.
   B. computers are used only for laborious tasks.
   C. computers will be used to solve all of the world's problems.
   D. cannot be determined from the passage.

55. Another definition of memory is:

   A. electronic storage.
   B. storage.
   C. hardwired.
   D. processing.

GO ON TO NEXT PAGE.

Passage IX (Questions 56–65)

The need for the early development of competence in analytic reading and reasoning, written communication, and test taking as essential skills for survival at the university and professional school level has developed over time. Recently, greater emphasis has been placed on the development of reading and writing skills, which is summed up in the phrase, "back to basics." Much concern about this problem is a reflection of the continually declining scores posted by students on standardized tests such as the Scholastic Aptitude Test (SAT), Graduate Record Examination (GRE), Law School Admission Test (LSAT), and Medical College Admission Test (MCAT). Most of these examinations are configured as multiple-choice tests. For a variety of reasons, most multiple-choice questions assess cognitive function only at the two lowest levels of Bloom's taxonomy of cognition: knowledge and interpretation. It appears that the ability to read and write is secondary to the ability to memorize material and understand the literal meaning of words and facts.

It seems inconsistent to bemoan the lack of reading and writing skills exhibited by today's students when those deficiencies are based on scores derived from standardized tests that do not actually test reading or writing skills. However, students who do well on these tests do so by using advanced reading skills. These students are using critical reading skills to assess answers based on the close reading of questions. In effect, although test makers seem content to test students at the lower levels of cognition, an effective test taker uses higher cognitive skills. Higher cognitive skills imply more advanced reading skills, and the use of those skills translates to higher scores on standardized tests. Therefore, the ability to read at advanced levels is a necessary component of any student's academic preparation. Unfortunately, many students do not acquire these skills, and as a result, they are often unable to pass standardized tests. Even if they have memorized every textbook on the subject or reviewed and practiced every test, they will not be able to pass these tests because they cannot analyze the questions or answers with sufficient understanding to determine what the question is really asking. Therefore, some students who seem to be likely candidates for admission to college and have A or B averages in high school courses are unable to pass a standardized test.

Reading and writing skills are the most underestimated and least understood skills that students need to succeed in an academic environment. Students reason that all that they need to gain admittance to an undergraduate or graduate program is the proper number of classes in the subject matter, adequate scores on admission tests, and the ability to present themselves well to admission committees. Faculty often believe that students must perform well in their classes and have the right core course load.

Many of these beliefs are basically true, but success in a college or graduate program depends on how well the student masters and understands the ideas, theories, concepts, and opinions presented in the classroom and through the assigned written materials. It is not simply the ability to memorize and regurgitate facts that constitutes an education. The ability to assess and weigh facts out of context and apply new information is at the core of education. Students must be made aware that learning and education are not dispensed only in schools; they occur throughout a person's lifetime. The most important skill that a lifelong student needs is the ability to read and think critically about both facts and opinions.

56. From the passage, Bloom's taxonomy appears to be:

   A. related to the amount of reading a student does.
   B. a hierarchic arrangement of thinking abilities.
   C. a method of defining reading tests.
   D. a scale of difficulty for making multiple-choice questions.

57. The author's intent in writing this passage is:

   A. to convince students to read more.
   B. to eliminate standardized tests.
   C. to emphasize the need for the development of critical thinking and reading skills.
   D. to stop the spread of reading programs.

58. If the author were told that all academic programs were going to include instruction in critical thinking skills, would he agree that this change was positive?

   A. He would agree.
   B. He would disagree.
   C. He would neither agree nor disagree.
   D. He would not comment.

59. When the author writes that "test makers seem content ... to test ... lower levels of cognition ... an effective test taker uses higher cognitive skills," he means that:

   A. test takers are superior to test makers.
   B. effective test takers use skills beyond those intended to be used by the test makers.
   C. to be an effective test taker, one must learn the tricks of the test.
   D. the average or poor student cannot perform better on these tests.

60. As used in the passage, the term cognitive means:

   A. test-taking skills.
   B. reasoning abilities.

C. reading skills.
D. knowledge.

61. Why does the author believe that current concerns about lower scores on standardized tests are misplaced?

   A. Standardized tests are not meant to measure the reading and writing skills that are considered important for lifetime success.
   B. Most of these tests are used to assess potential for college, and most students do not go to college.
   C. Standardized tests eventually will be improved to solve these problems.
   D. Poor students will always perform poorly on these tests.

62. The author would define an education as:

   A. the ability to memorize and recall facts.
   B. learning from one's mistakes.
   C. the ability to evaluate new facts and apply this information in new ways.
   D. performing well on standardized tests.

63. If the author were asked to identify the single most important element of learning, he would say:

   A. knowledge.
   B. understanding.
   C. critical thinking.
   D. the right core course load.

64. Assume that standardized test scores have increased dramatically in the last year, without any change in the tests or the curriculum. The author would point to this change as evidence that:

   A. students are becoming smarter.
   B. students have acquired better test-taking skills.
   C. the students cheated.
   D. previous students lacked proper motivation.

65. A title for this passage would be:

   A. Raising Standardized Test Scores.
   B. Bloom and His Theories.
   C. Be a Lifelong Learner.
   D. How to Succeed in College.

STOP. IF YOU FINISH BEFORE TIME IS CALLED, CHECK YOUR WORK. YOU MAY GO BACK TO ANY QUESTION IN THIS TEST BOOKLET.

Physical Sciences

Time: 100 Minutes
Questions 66–142

DIRECTIONS: Most questions in the Physical Sciences test are organized into groups, each preceded by a descriptive passage. After studying the passage, select the one best answer to each question in the group. Some questions are not based on a descriptive passage and are also independent of each other. You must also select the one best answer to these questions. If you are not certain of an answer, eliminate the alternatives that you know to be incorrect and then select an answer from the remaining alternatives. Indicate your selection by blackening the corresponding circle on your answer sheet. A periodic table is provided for your use. You may consult it whenever you wish.

PERIODIC TABLE OF THE ELEMENTS

IA																	VIIIA
1 H 1.0	IIA											IIIA	IVA	VA	VIA	VIIA	2 He 4.0
3 Li 6.9	4 Be 9.0											5 B 10.8	6 C 12.0	7 N 14.0	8 O 16.0	9 F 19.0	10 Ne 20.2
11 Na 23.0	12 Mg 24.3											13 Al 27.0	14 Si 28.1	15 P 31.0	16 S 32.1	17 Cl 35.5	18 Ar 39.9
19 K 39.1	20 Ca 40.1	21 Sc 45.0	22 Ti 47.9	23 V 50.9	24 Cr 52.0	25 Mn 54.9	26 Fe 55.8	27 Co 58.9	28 Ni 58.7	29 Cu 63.5	30 Zn 65.4	31 Ga 69.7	32 Ge 72.6	33 As 74.9	34 Se 79.0	35 Br 79.9	36 Kr 83.8
37 Rb 85.5	38 Sr 87.6	39 Y 88.9	40 Zr 91.2	41 Nb 92.9	42 Mo 95.9	43 Tc 98.0	44 Ru 101	45 Rh 102	46 Pd 106	47 Ag 108	48 Cd 112	49 In 115	50 Sn 119	51 Sb 122	52 Te 128	53 I 127	54 Xe 131
55 Cs 133	56 Ba 137	57 La 139	72 Hf 179	73 Ta 181	74 W 184	75 Re 186	76 Os 190	77 Ir 192	78 Pt 195	79 Au 197	80 Hg 201	81 Tl 204	82 Pb 207	83 Bi 208	84 Po 209	85 At 210	86 Rn 222
87 Fr 223	88 Ra 226	89 Ac 227															

58 Ce 140	59 Pr 141	60 Nd 144	61 Pm 145	62 Sm 150	63 Eu 152	64 Gd 157	65 Tb 159	66 Dy 163	67 Ho 165	68 Er 167	69 Tm 169	70 Yb 173	71 Lu 175
90 Th 232	91 Pa 231	92 U 238	93 Np 237	94 Pu 244	95 Am 243	96 Cm 247	97 Bk 247	98 Cf 251	99 Es 252	100 Fm 257	101 Md 258	102 No 259	103 Lr 260

GO ON TO NEXT PAGE.

Passage I (Questions 66–72)

When one mixes an acid solution with a basic solution, a salt is formed, e.g., $HCl + NaOH \rightarrow NaCl$. Because the chloride ion obviously came from the acid and the sodium ion came from the base, the alchemists defined cations as bases and anions as acids. At the turn of the century, Brönsted introduced the concept that an acid was any compound that yielded an H^+ in solution and a base was any compound that could accept an H^+. His colleague at the Carlsberg institute, Sörensen, introduced the use of the pH scale. This scale was defined as the negative log of the $[H^+]$. This scale was based on the dissociation of water, which has a dissociation constant (K_d) of 10^{-14}, or $[H^+][OH^-] = 10^{-14}$. Thus, if the $[H^+]$ is 1, $[OH^-]$ is 10^{-14}, and vice versa. Sörensen used a log term to reduce the wide range of numbers to a more manageable scale and the negative log to make the numbers, which are always less than 1, positive. Thus, the pH scale extends from 1 to 14. The pH at neutrality is 7.0. At this point, the acid HOH is one-half dissociated (i.e., $H^+ = OH^-$) at pH 7.0.

Henderson and Hasselbalch used the pH scale and the Brönsted concept of acid and base to define the action of buffers. The generalized acid HA dissociates to yield a proton and the acid's conjugate base A^-, i.e., $HA \rightleftharpoons H^+ + A^-$. Therefore, according to the law of mass action, $K_{eq} = [H^+][OH^-]/HA$. By converting this statement into the log form, Henderson and Hasselbalch obtained the following: $\log K_{eq} = \log [H^+] - \log [A^-]/[HA]$. By multiplying through by -1, it becomes $-\log K_{eq} = -\log [H^+] - (\log [A^-]/[HA])$ or, in other terms, $pK = pH + \dfrac{\log [A^-]}{HA}$. This Henderson-Hasselbalch equation describes buffer capacity in quantitative terms. The graph below represents the titration of phosphoric acid (H_3PO_4) with 1 mmol NaOH.

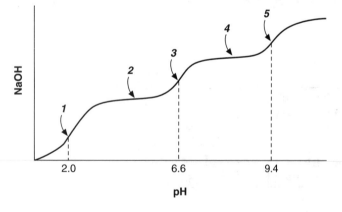

66. At approximately what pH(s) will H_3PO_4 act as a buffer?

    A. 7 only
    B. 5 only
    C. 2, 6.6, and 9.4
    D. 5, 10, and 14

67. According to the graph, $H_2PO_4^-$ is a Brönsted:

    A. acid.
    B. base.
    C. acid and base.
    D. There is no way to tell whether it is an acid or a base.

68. In millimoles per liter, the concentration of H_3PO_4 is:

    A. 2.
    B. 4.
    C. 6.
    D. 8.

69. In milliequivalents per liter, the concentration of H_3PO_4 is:

    A. 2.
    B. 4.
    C. 6.
    D. 8.

70. The elements in the second column of the periodic table are referred to as the alkali earths. This name is derived from concepts introduced by:

    A. alchemists.
    B. Brönsted.
    C. Sörensen.
    D. Henderson and Hasselbalch.

71. An acid buffers most effectively at the pH at which it is:

    A. 25% titrated.
    B. 50% titrated.
    C. 75% titrated.
    D. 100% titrated.

72. Which of the following is **NOT** an acceptable definition of the pKa?

    A. The negative log of the K_{eq}
    B. The pH at which the concentration of an acid equals that of its conjugate base
    C. The pH at which H^+ equals A^- for the generalized acid HA
    D. The pH at which an acid is one-half titrated

148

Passage II (Questions 73–80)

The atoms in molecules are held together by covalent, or ionic, bonds in which electrons are shared. Of equal importance in explaining the behavior of substances are the weaker inter- and intramolecular interactions. These fall into three categories: van der Waals forces, hydrogen bonds, and hydrophobic effects. van der Waals forces and hydrogen bonds arise because of the polarity of molecules. Hydrophobic attraction occurs between molecules, or domains of macromolecules, that lack polarity. Hydrophobic and polar molecules, or domains, repel each other.

Polarity arises because of the difference in electronegativity of different atoms in a molecule. The most electronegative atoms are fluorine > oxygen > nitrogen ~ chlorine. Insertion of one of these atoms into an organic molecule creates polarity (e.g., C-O or C-F) in which the carbon atom has a partial positive charge and the fluorine or oxygen atom has a partial negative charge. Intramolecular attraction occurs when the positive elements of one molecule, or domain, associate with the negative elements of another. Individually, these attractions are weak, but collectively, as in certain macromolecules, they can add up to significant attractions. Conversely, like charges repel. These forces of attraction and repulsion play important roles in orienting molecules in both the liquid and solid states.

A hydrogen bond may be thought of as a special, more stable type of polar attraction. These bonds occur when a hydrogen atom is sandwiched between two electronegative atoms, one of which is a coordinate covalent bond, e.g.:

$$-\overset{\underset{\|}{O}}{C}-O-H\cdot\cdot N<$$

or

$$-\overset{\underset{\|}{O}}{C}-O-H\cdot\cdot F-$$

Optimally, hydrogen bonds are at least an order of magnitude stronger than ordinary van der Waals forces, and they have a strong vectorial effect. They are most stable when the bonds are at a 180° angle to each other, that is, when the two electronegative atoms are in direct opposition. An important consequence of this phenomenon is that a macromolecule with many hydrogen bonds will be at its lowest energy level when as many of its hydrogen bonds as possible are lined up in a straight configuration. This configuration provides the macromolecule with definite orientation among its domains and, when supported by many van der Waals forces and hydrophobic effects, accounts for the precise orientation of enzymes and other biologically active proteins. That this alignment is stabilized by weak bonds means that any perturbation that disturbs the initial conformation, such as binding of a substrate or an allosteric effector by an enzyme, can induce a shift in bonding and stabilize a new conformation, which is determined with equal precision. These factors account for the large entropy component and the resulting great catalytic effect characteristic of enzyme-catalyzed reactions.

Hydrophobic bonds are attractive forces, with a bonding strength similar to that of van der Waals forces, generated by the absence of polarity on molecules. These bonds exist in aqueous solution because they and polar substances, such as water, repel each other. Therefore, nonpolar substances tend to come together and avoid association with polar substances, such as water, to as great a degree as possible. In thermodynamic terms, the entropy of the system increases and the free energy is decreased.

Increasing the temperature increases the kinetic energy of compounds. When the energy becomes high enough, solids melt and liquids vaporize. These weak forces are overcome when a compound passes from the solid to the liquid phase or from the liquid to the gaseous phase. The greater the contribution of these bonds, the higher the melting or vaporization temperature.

73. Which of the following compounds has the highest dipole moment?

   A. Ethane
   B. Acetylene
   C. Ethanol
   D. Fluormethane

74. Which of the following is NOT an intramolecular force that influences the freezing point of liquids?

   A. van der Waals forces
   B. Hydrogen bonds
   C. Covalent bonds
   D. Hydrophobic forces

75. The stabilization of precise, yet pliable, conformational dimensions in the tertiary structure of some macromolecules is primarily caused by:

   A. van der Waals forces.
   B. hydrogen bonds.
   C. covalent bonds.
   D. hydrophobic forces.

76. Hydrophobic forces depend on:

   A. coulombic attractions between molecules.
   B. repulsion of polar solvents.
   C. precise vectorial alignment of molecules.
   D. sharing of electrons.

GO ON TO NEXT PAGE.

77. Hydrogen bonds can be formed between the hydrogen atom of a hydroxyl group and which of the following atoms?

A. Carbon
B. Nitrogen
C. Sulfur
D. Silicon

78. The vectorial alignment that best stabilizes hydrogen bonds is:

A. 180°
B. 135°
C. 90°
D. 45°

79. The strongest of the following weak intramolecular forces is the:

A. van der Waals force.
B. hydrogen bond.
C. dipolar force.
D. hydrophobic attraction.

80. All other factors being equal, the melting and freezing points of compounds increase with molecular weight. Water and methanol are compounds with similar molecular weights; however, water freezes and vaporizes at much higher temperatures than methanol. This difference occurs primarily because water, but **NOT** methanol, forms:

A. van der Waals attractions.
B. hydrogen bonds.
C. covalent bonds.
D. hydrophobic attractions.

Passage III (Questions 81–88)

Niels Bohr is generally credited with being the father of the modern concept of atomic structure. He pictured a system analogous to the solar system, in which the positively charged nucleus took the place of the sun, around which negatively charged electrons traveled in well-defined orbits, similar to the planets. This general concept has stood the test of time, but it is a gross oversimplification. Bohr's concepts have been refined by the work of several subsequent scientists.

In Bohr's model, the coulombic forces of attraction between the negative electron and the positive nucleus are balanced by the centrifugal force that tends to tear the electron away from the nucleus. This action results in a perfectly balanced system in which the electrons travel in discrete orbits. This situation can be described mathematically as follows:

$$E = -2\pi m Z^2 e^4 n^2 h^2$$

In this equation, n is a whole number integer (e.g., 1, 2, 3) that describes the energy state of the electron, m is the mass of the electron, e is the charge on the electron, Z is the nuclear charge and is equal to the atomic number, and h is Planck's constant. With this equation, Bohr predicted the major spectrum lines of hydrogen. This achievement indicated that he was on the right track, but because his equation could not explain more complicated atoms, it needed some refinement.

Heisenberg hypothesized that it is impossible to determine the position and momentum of an atom simultaneously, as required by Bohr's theory. This concept became known as the Heisenberg uncertainty principle. Schroedinger used this concept to expand Bohr's idea by using probabilities of an electron being at a given place in time while moving. According to this concept, electrons exist in clouds rather than as discrete particles with discrete orbits. Schroedinger also used the concept of quanta. According to this idea, the energy of electrons exists in packages that cannot be subdivided. In other words, there is not a continuous spectrum of energy levels, but the energy increases in jumps, each jump being a quantum.

With these ideas, plus Pauli's exclusion principle, which states that no two electrons can have identical values, it became possible to devise a system to describe each electron in all of the atoms. In this system, each electron is defined in terms of its orbital size, orbital shape and orientation, and direction of spin. The orbital size is given a whole number integer (e.g., 1, 2, 3), as Bohr did. These are called the principal quantum numbers and are basically a function of the distance of the electron from the nucleus. Those closer to the nucleus have less energy and are therefore filled before those further from the nucleus. Each orbital can have a limited number of electrons. For example, orbital 1 can have only two electrons. These account for the first two elements in the periodic table, hydrogen and helium. Helium, the first noble gas, is inert because all of its available orbitals are full. The orbital shape and orientation of electrons in this orbital are termed s. The first three orbitals of the first three principal quantum numbers are called s or p and, as seen, the s orbital can carry two electrons, but the p configurations can carry as many as six electrons. Therefore, the electronic configuration of helium can be described as $1s^2$. In other words, principal quantum number 1 is filled with two electrons in an s orbital. In accordance with Pauli's exclusion principle, these two electrons differ with respect to spin, the only option open. The shape and orientation of the s orbital is essentially spheric, similar to Bohr's concept, except spread out in all dimensions (i.e., a cloud) rather than in a discrete circular orbit. The next principal quantum number has two potential orbital configurations, s and p. This second principal quantum number starts the second row of the periodic table with lithium, atomic number 3, and is filled in neon, atomic number 10. The electronic configuration for neon is then $1s^2$, $2s^2$, $2p^6$. The spheric s orbitals are full, with two electrons with opposite spins, but the p orbital fills with six electrons. These are three sets of orbitals in a figure eight shape. One set is oriented along the x-axis, the second along the y-axis, and the third along the z-axis. See the diagram below:

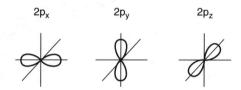

The two electrons in each set again have opposite spins. Similarly, the next noble gas in the third row, argon, atomic number 18, has all of its orbitals full with 18 electrons. The electronic configuration of argon is $1s^2$, $2s^2$, $2p^6$, $3s^2$, $3p^6$.

Implicit in this discussion is the idea that each row of the periodic table represents a principal quantum number. Obviously, the first element in each column has only one electron in its principal quantum orbital system, the second element has two, and so on. The discussion above covered the first three rows, called the representative elements. These are atomic numbers 1 through 18, or hydrogen through neon, and involve just two types of orbitals, s and p.

To reiterate, the s orbital can carry only two electrons because a sphere leaves no room for extra configurations and there are only two types of electromagnetic spin, + and −. A p orbital can carry six electrons because the figure eight configuration can be aligned along one of three axes—x, y, or z—and again each alignment has the potential for two directions of spin. The fourth row introduces a new type of orbital called d, which can carry 10 electrons. Thus, the noble gas that follows neon, krypton, atomic number 36, carries 36 electrons. The first 18 electrons are filled, as for neon, and the fourth principal quantum is filled as follows: $4s^2$, $4p^6$, $4d^{10}$. The next orbital is called f, and it takes 14 electrons. It is generally sufficient to comprehend only the representative elements, the first three rows of the periodic table.

81. All of the noble gases:

A. contain only s orbitals, p orbitals, or s and p orbitals.
B. are the first elements in a row in the periodic table.
C. have all of their orbitals full.
D. have no neutrons in their nucleus.

82. A fundamental difference between Bohr's and Schroedinger's views of the electron orbit around hydrogen is that:

A. Bohr visualized a circular orbit, but Schroedinger conceived it to be elliptic.
B. Bohr labeled the principal quantum numbers with whole integers, but Schroedinger used letters of the alphabet.
C. Bohr visualized discrete orbits, but Schroedinger conceived a spheric cloud.
D. Bohr visualized the electron as a discrete particle in motion, but Schroedinger concluded that it is impossible to define the position and momentum of an electron simultaneously.

83. The following figure represents which type of orbital configuration?

A. s
B. p
C. d
D. f

84. The maximum number of electrons that can have the configuration of the figure below is:

A. 1.
B. 2.
C. 3.
D. 4.

GO ON TO NEXT PAGE.

85. The minimum number of electrons in a shell with a principal quantum number of 3 is:

    A. 3.
    B. 9.
    C. 11.
    D. 8.

86. Aluminum has how many electrons in its 3p orbitals?

    A. 1
    B. 2
    C. 3
    D. 4

87. The electronic configuration of chlorine is:

    A. $1s^2, 2s^2, 2p^5$.
    B. $1s^2, 2s^2, 2p^6, 3s^1$.
    C. $1s^2, 2s^2, 2p^6, 3s^2, 3p^5$.
    D. $1s^2, 2s^2, 2p^6, 3s^2, 3p^6, 4s^1$.

88. Pauli's exclusion principle states that:

    A. no two electrons can have identical quantum values.
    B. the position and momentum of an electron cannot be determined simultaneously.
    C. no two electrons will have the same orbital.
    D. all electrons in a given orbital shell have different spin values.

Passage IV (Questions 89–92)

Mechanical energy, a scalar, may be divided into potential and kinetic energy.

Potential energy is the energy of position. It may be a position in a gravitational or electromagnetic field or compressed energy against a spring. It is important to realize that an object does not have an absolute quantity of this energy; it has only an amount measured against some reference point. The formula for potential energy is:

Eq. 1. $PE = mgh$,   where PE = potential energy, m = mass, g = acceleration by gravity, and h = height above the reference point.

Consider an object suspended above a table. It has a certain potential energy reference to the table, but a different potential energy reference to the floor. What is inviolate is a change in potential energy. If the object falls through a distance $y < h$ (so that it does not hit the table or floor), the change in potential energy is mgh, regardless of its reference point.

Kinetic energy is energy of motion. Because motion is relative, an object in motion can have only a relative amount of kinetic energy. However, if the object changes its velocity, its corresponding change in kinetic energy is the same, regardless of reference.

In a mechanical system in which only one type of energy is present, the other type is "waiting." For instance, if one drops the object suspended above the table, the object obviously moves. As it falls, it loses potential energy, but gains kinetic energy as it moves faster. The law of conservation states that the increase in kinetic energy is exactly equal to the loss of potential energy, neglecting friction and other dissipating factors. Any energy lost as a result of these dissipating factors is equal to the difference between the gain in kinetic energy and loss of potential energy. In other words, the energy changing from potential to kinetic is conserved. If one reverses the process and throws the object up, the potential energy increases in the same amount as the kinetic energy decreases. This example is called a simple system and, without dissipative forces, a conservative system.

89. Suppose a 1-kg mass and a 5-kg mass are dropped from equal heights in a vacuum. If they have been falling for 1 second, their:

    A. kinetic energies are equal.
    B. potential energies are equal.
    C. mechanical energies are equal.
    D. velocities are equal.

90. If the 1-kg mass is given an initial velocity of 5 m/sec downward, after 1 second, their:

   A. kinetic energies are equal.
   B. potential energies are equal.
   C. potential energies are greater than their kinetic energies.
   D. kinetic energies are greater than their potential energies.

91. Suppose the two masses are 5 kg each and are dropped from the same height. Mass A is dropped, but mass B has an initial velocity of 5 m/sec downward. The respective mechanical energies of masses A and B after 1 second are (in joules):

   A. 480 and −480.
   B. −788 and 480.
   C. 240 and 548.
   D. 480 and 788.

92. Mass A is still dropped, but now mass B has an initial velocity of 5 m/sec upward. The mechanical energies of masses A and B after 1 second are, respectively:

   A. 480 and −480.
   B. −788 and 480.
   C. 240 and 548.
   D. 480 and 788.

Passage V (Questions 93–100)

Momentum (P) is the product of mass (m) and velocity (v).

Eq. 1. $P = mv$

Although related to kinetic energy, momentum is itself not an energy. It is a conserved vectorial. Momentum is closely related to inertia, the resistance of an object to a change in motion. The more massive an object, the more momentum it has, in direct proportion. It also has more kinetic energy, but the increase in kinetic energy is not linear. Momentum is also a relative quantity because it is tied to velocity. Conservation of momentum means that the amount of momentum present before an event equals that present after the event. This event is called a collision.

A collision is not necessarily a catastrophic event that occurs between two vehicles. It could be one billiard ball striking another or a dog catching a ball. Each of these events describes a type of collision. The types of collisions are:

● Elastic: a collision in which neither object is deformed permanently by the collision, such as in billiards. In this case, kinetic energy as well as momentum is conserved.

● Inelastic: a collision in which one or both objects are permanently deformed by the collision. Momentum is conserved, but kinetic energy is not, because energy is required to deform the object.

● Perfectly inelastic: a collision in which one or both objects are permanently deformed and they stick together. Again, momentum is conserved, but kinetic energy is not.

The conservation equation for a perfectly inelastic collision is:

Eq. 2. $m_1v_1 + m_2v_2 = (m_1 + m_2)v'$, where m_1 is the mass of the first object, m_2 is the mass of the second object, v_1 is the velocity of the first object; v_2 is the velocity of the second object, and v' is the speed of the combined masses after the collision.

Because the objects stick together, their masses are summed on the right side of the equation. If m_2 is stationary after the collision, the product $m_2v_2 = 0$.

93. Momentum is directly proportional to:

   A. kinetic energy.
   B. potential energy.
   C. inertia.
   D. mass.

GO ON TO NEXT PAGE.

94. Conservation of momentum means that the amount of momentum present before an event equals:

    A. that present after the event.
    B. the loss of kinetic energy.
    C. the work done because of the event.
    D. the inertia present before the event.

95. A car with mass m_1, speeding at 70 mph, runs into a concrete wall, with mass m^2. The wall remains intact and does not move. The force of the impact sticks the car to the surface of the wall. The conservation equation for this collision is:

    A. $m_1v_1 + m_2v_2 = (m_1 + m_2)v'$.
    B. $m_1v_1 = (m_1 + m_2)v'$.
    C. $m_1v_1 + m_2v_2 + (m_1 + m_2) = v'$.
    D. $m_1v_1 + m_2v_2 + (m_1 + m_2)v' = 0$.

96. If two equal masses traveling in opposite directions with the same velocity collide in an elastic collision, then:

    A. both rebound with velocities opposite those they had before.
    B. both stop so that the final momentum is zero.
    C. the masses will stick together and stop.
    D. the masses stick together and move off in an oblique direction.

97. Two masses collide elastically. Mass A is twice the mass of mass B, and both are traveling with equal velocities in opposite directions. After the collision:

    A. mass A comes to a halt, and mass B rebounds with twice its original velocity.
    B. both masses move off in the same direction with equal velocities.
    C. mass A rebounds with one-half its original velocity, and mass B rebounds with twice its original velocity.
    D. mass B comes to a halt, and mass A rebounds with one-half its original velocity.

98. Two air hockey pucks are of equal mass. Puck A is moving to the left with a velocity of 1 m/sec; puck B is stationary. After a glancing collision, puck A moves up at an angle of 30°, and puck B moves down at an angle of 60°. Momentum is conserved in all dimensions. What are the velocities of pucks A and B, respectively?

    A. 1.73 m/sec and −1 m/sec
    B. 0.87 m/sec and 0.5 m/sec

C. 0.5 m/sec and 0.87 m/sec
D. 1 m/sec and 1 m/sec

99. If two equal masses traveling in opposite directions with the same velocity collide in a perfectly inelastic collision, then:

    A. both rebound with velocities opposite those they had before.
    B. mass A stops, and mass B rebounds with twice its original velocity.
    C. the masses stick together and stop.
    D. the masses stick together and move off in an oblique direction.

100. A 2000-kg car moving east at 10 m/sec collides with and sticks to a 1500-kg car moving north at 15 m/sec. The final velocity and angle of the two cars is:

    A. 0.7 m/sec at 56°.
    B. 8.6 m/sec at 56°.
    C. 0.7 m/sec at 48°.
    D. 8.6 m/sec at 48°.

According to Newton, an object in motion tends to stay in motion unless acted on by an external force. He makes no qualification about linear or rotational motion. The resistance to change in linear motion from an accelerating force is called inertia, and it is directly proportional to the mass of the object. The object has the same inertia, regardless of the direction of the induced motion. The same cannot be said of rotational inertia. Rotational inertia is directly proportional to mass, but it is more dependent on the distribution of the mass around the axis of rotation. In fact, it is dependent on the square of the distance between a differential mass element and the axis of rotation. For this reason, rotational inertia is a power relation, with all of the commensurate implications. Because the choice of the axis of rotation is critical in this concept, and because any object can have an infinite number of arbitrary axes of rotation, one must specify around which axis rotational inertia will be calculated. This choice and the inertial result is called the moment of inertia (I). Thus, I is the resistance to a change in rotational motion around a specific axis. It has units of mass times length squared: $I = mr^2$, where m = mass of the object and r = distance between the object and the axis. Because there are many axes from which to choose, and all but a few yield easy moment of inertia calculations, we shall choose our axis of rotation to be an axis of symmetry. Calculations of moments of inertia usually require integration. However, a simple summation approach can be used to find the moment of inertia of a thin hoop. Consider a point mass m on the x-axis, at a distance r from the origin. It has a momentum of inertia equal to mr^2. Now, add to this system another mass m on the negative axis at point $-r$. The moment of inertia for the system is now $mr^2 + mr^2$, or $(m + m)r^2$. The two masses need not be connected, and we can add moments of inertia without any special considerations as long as the masses have a common axis of rotation. Place similar masses on the y-axis, at y = $+r$ and y = $-r$. The moment of inertia for the system about an axis through the origin is $(m + m + m + m)r^2$. Extending this method until a circle with radius r is described about the origin, we have a thin hoop whose moment of inertia is $(m + m + m)r^2$. If we let M be the sum of all of the differential mass elements, then $I = Mr^2$.

101. A moment of inertia is:

   A. the exact moment when an inert element subjected to a force begins to move.
   B. the exact moment when a moving object subjected to a force comes to a stop.
   C. the resistance to a change in rotational motion around a specific axis.
   D. directly proportional to the mass of the object in motion.

102. Inertia is:

   A. a power term.
   B. directly proportional to the mass of the object.
   C. indirectly proportional to the mass of the object.
   D. a form of work.

103. The moment of inertia of a hoop with a mass of 5 kg and a radius of 2 m is:

   A. one-half that of a hoop of mass 5 kg and radius 1 m.
   B. equal to that of a hoop of mass 5 kg and radius 1 m.
   C. one-fourth that of a hoop of mass 5 kg and radius 1 m.
   D. four times that of a hoop of mass 5 kg and radius 1 m.

104. The kinetic energy of a rotating object is still $^1/_2\ mv^2$. If $v = \theta v^2$, then the equation becomes $^1/_2\ I\theta^2$. Assuming that both hoops have the same angular velocity, the kinetic energy of the larger hoop in the previous question is related to the kinetic energy of the smaller hoop by a factor of:

   A. 0.5.
   B. 1.
   C. 2.
   D. 4.

105. The moment of inertia of a sold disk is $^1/_2\ Mr^2$. If a disk and a hoop of equal mass and radius roll down a hill:

   A. they will reach the bottom at the same time.
   B. the hoop will always beat the disk to the bottom.
   C. the disk will always beat the hoop to the bottom.
   D. the winner of the race to the bottom will be determined by the steepness of the slope.

106. A disk and a hoop of equal radius and mass are placed on top of each other and rotated about a common axis through the center of each. The energy required to rotate this system is related to that required to turn each separately by a factor of:

   A. 4.
   B. 2.
   C. 1.
   D. 0.5.

GO ON TO NEXT PAGE.

107. Two equal masses are connected to each other by a massless rod. It can be rotated either about an axis passing through the center of the rod and perpendicular to it, or about one end.

    A. Rotating about the end requires more energy than rotating about the center.

    B. Rotating about the center requires more energy than rotating about the end.

    C. Both rotations require equal energy.

    D. Neither requires any energy.

Passage VII (Questions 108–112)

Any charge source (q) is surrounded by an electric field. This field is represented by lines called electric field lines, which extend out from the charge source. If the charge source is positive, the field lines (noted by arrows) extend away from the source. If the charge is negative, the lines point inward. These electric field lines are always perpendicular to the surface of the source, never intersect, and always terminate in another charge source. They can be parallel if the source is infinitely flat and extensive, or perfectly radial in the case of a point source. Parallel lines indicate constant field strength; radially diverging lines indicate a weakening of electric field strength, depending on the distance (r) from the source. The formula for electric field strength is:

Eq. 1. $E = KQq/r^2$,   where K, a constant, is approximately 9×10^9 Nm^2/C^2, E is the electric field, Q is the charge generated by the field, q is the charge placed into the field, and r is the distance between the charges

If a charge is placed in an electric field, the charge will be acted on by a force.

Eq. 2. $F = Eq$

If the charge accelerates because of this force, work will be done on this force.

Eq. 3. $W = Fr$

Therefore, within the electric field, there is the potential for work to be done. This potential is dependent on the electric field strength and the distance (r) covered. Dividing by q, one obtains V, the potential measured in volts:

Eq. 4. $V = W/q$

The distance must be in the direction of the field lines. A charge will not experience a change in potential if it is moved perpendicularly to the field and maintains the same distance from the source because the electric field strength does not change. We can draw lines representing these areas of no potential change. These lines are called equipotential lines. They are always parallel to the surface of the source and never intersect each other, but always intersect the electric field lines at right angles.

108. The work done in moving a charge perpendicularly to the electric field lines is equal to:

    A. the product of E and V.

    B. the product of V and q.

C. zero.

D. the quotient of *V* divided by *E*.

109. A charge experiences a force of 8 *N* in an electric field of strength 2 *V/m.* The magnitude of the charge is:

A. 4 C.
B. $\frac{1}{4}$ C.
C. 2 C.
D. $\frac{1}{2}$ C.

110. A potential of 100 V exists over a distance of 5 cm. The electric field strength is:

A. 20 V/m.
B. 500 V/m.
C. 2000 V/m.
D. 5 V/m.

111. The work necessary to move a charge of 5 μC through a potential of 25 V is:

A. 125 J.
B. 125×10^{-6} J.
C. 1.25×10^{-6} J.
D. 5 J.

112. The electric field strength 500 km from 1 mole of electrons (in V/m) is:

A. 3.47×10^{9}.
B. 3.473×10^{6}.
C. 3.476×10^{3}.
D. 3.473×10^{-3}.

Passage VIII (Questions 113–117)

The photoelectric effect is the condition in which incident light liberates electrons from certain metals and semiconductors. The peculiarity of this effect is that the more intense the incident light, the more electrons are liberated; however, their individual energies are the same. If the wavelength of the incident light is changed, the electrons have different kinetic energies on release. This result indicated to Planck and Einstein that somehow energy is related to wavelength. The equation Planck derived was:

Eq. 1. $E = h\nu$, where h = Planck's constant and ν = frequency

Further, unless the light was at least a certain wavelength, no electrons were produced. This finding indicates that some minimum amount of energy is needed to liberate an electron. This amount of energy is called the work function, (Φ), and is a property of the metal or semiconductor. It is similar in function to ionizing energy. Therefore, any excess kinetic energy (*KE*) an electron has after escaping is the difference between the incident light's energy and the work function:

$$\text{Eq. 2.} \quad KE = h\nu - \Phi$$

If we shine light of a certain wavelength (λ) onto a metal (a cathode), electrons will be kicked off toward a wire (the anode), and a current will be established. If we apply a potential in the opposite direction, we can force the electrons back into the cathode, or just prevent them from escaping. The energy required to perform this task is the product of the voltage (*V*) and the charge on the electron (*e*). Combining this factor with equation 2 yields:

$$\text{Eq. 3.} \quad eV = h\nu - \Phi$$

You have performed an experiment to determine Planck's constant. The following data were obtained:

λ nm	V
38	-30.70
47	-24.05
61	-19.15
77	-15.04
167	-6.38
170	-6.32
177	-5.97

GO ON TO NEXT PAGE.

| 178 | -6.09 |
| 194 | -5.60 |

113. What is the average value for Planck's constant (in joules)?

    A. 4.9×10^{-3}
    B. 6.4×10^{-34}
    C. 5.9×10^{-34}
    D. 5.1×10^{-34}

114. What is the standard deviation of the mean?

    A. 5.9×10^{-34}
    B. 6.3×10^{-34}
    C. 4.5×10^{-35}
    D. 2.3×10^{-35}

115. If the electrons leave a metal with 3 eV of kinetic energy when light of 200 nm is incident, what is the work function of the metal?

    A. 1.26 eV
    B. 2.55 eV
    C. 3.00 eV
    D. 5.09 eV

116. It is postulated that the core of the planet Jupiter is composed of metallic hydrogen. What wavelength light would just liberate an electron with work function = 13.6 eV?

    A. 8.16 nm
    B. 81.6 nm
    C. 38 nm
    D. 167 nm

117. If silicon has a work function of 2.9 eV, what is the energy of an electron liberated under 15-nm light?

    A. -15 eV
    B. 13 eV
    C. 30 eV
    D. 71 eV

Passage IX (Questions 118–122)

Salts are stabilized by ionic attraction and result when a metal with low ionization energy is mixed with a nonmetal that has a high ionizing potential. The resulting ionic compound is more stable than the elements in solution because the elements can be neatly packed into a lattice. The fundamental unit of a crystal is called a unit cell. The better the ions fit into the lattice, the more stable the resulting crystal and the larger each individual crystal can grow (the greater the number of unit cells that can be packaged together). The larger the crystal, the less surface area it has.

Because crystals are ionic in nature, the external surface is polar, if not charged. Therefore, a crystal formed in an aqueous environment has a shell of hydration, which can attract other ions.

The solubility product (Ksp) of ions in a solution that precipitate to form solid salts (i.e., crystals) depends primarily on their attraction for each other, that is, how readily the positive ion can accept the unpaired electron of the negative ion. The initial precipitate is not necessarily the most stable, and it may change into a more complex structure that has a better packed lattice and is, therefore, at a lower energy level. This situation occurs, for example, when calcium phosphate is precipitated from alkaline aqueous solutions. The initial product is brushite $[Ca_3(PO_4)_2]$, which evolves into hydroxyapatite $[Ca_{10}(PO_4)_6(OH)_2]$. This evolution can be bypassed by the process of nucleation, in which the more stable crystalline substance grows on a template. The nucleating material may be either the crystal itself or some other substance that has the proper surface pattern of charge structure.

The mineral part of bone consists of hydroxyapatite. The apatites are a family of crystals that have their constituent ions arranged similarly in a three-dimensional symmetric pattern. Among the members of the apatite family are crystals with radium or strontium substituted for calcium and fluoride substituted for the hydroxyl group. The hydroxyapatite of bone is a particularly small and somewhat amorphous crystal. Fluorapatite, a naturally occurring mineral, has a unit cell structure of $Ca_{10}(PO_4)_6(F)_2$. It is a large, well-formed crystal.

118. Fluorapatite forms a larger crystal than hydroxyapatite because:

    A. the Ksp of the fluorapatite is less.
    B. the Ksp of the fluorapatite is greater.
    C. fluoride fits into the crystal lattice better than hydroxide.
    D. there is less room in bone for hydroxyapatite crystal to grow.

119. Hydroxyapatite is used as an ion-exchange resin for protein purification. Bone is known to attract several foreign ions to its surface. Fluorapatite has little ion-exchanging potential. This difference in properties arises from the fact that:

A. fluoride forms a more stable crystalline structure than hydroxide.
B. the hydroxyl ion is more electronegative than the fluoride ion.
C. the fluoride ion is more electronegative than the hydroxyl ion.
D. the hydroxyl ion is more basic than the fluoride ion.

120. Hydroxyapatite dissolves most readily at pH:

A. 10.5.
B. 8.5.
C. 7.5.
D. 6.5.

121. Small amounts of fluoride decrease tooth decay. This phenomenon may be attributed to the fact that fluoride:

A. is more electronegative than hydroxide.
B. poisons the bacteria in the mouth.
C. stabilizes the apatite lattice structure.
D. decreases the size of enamel crystals.

122. Which of the following halides most readily forms a crystalline salt with sodium?

A. Fluorine
B. Chlorine
C. Bromine
D. Iodine

Passage X (Questions 123–127)

Gases can be assumed to be composed of particles of infinitesimal extent and infinite hardness. This assumption yields a simple mechanism with perfectly elastic collisions and conservation of mass and momentum. The ideal gas is essentially a set of BBs bouncing around in a sealed container. This model suggests certain questions.

Question 1. How fast do the molecules bounce? Each gas particle has a speed, and because it also has mass, each particle has kinetic energy. We can therefore change the speed of the particle by adding or subtracting from this reserve of energy. Adding heat to the gas adds to the kinetic energy of each particle, which increases its speed. Because an increase in temperature accompanies added heat, the speed of the particle is related to the temperature. Of course, removing heat from the gas reduces the speed of the particle.

Question 2. How often do they collide? This answer depends on three factors: how fast they are going (see previous question), how many particles there are (we assume a fixed amount), and in what volume they are free to move. If the same number of particles are bouncing about at the same speed, more collisions occur if they are packed into a small volume than if they have more space.

Question 3. How do they interact with their container? Because our particles are perfectly elastic, they interact with the container by bouncing off the walls. Each particle has a speed, direction, and mass. In a container of finite dimensions, each particle will inevitably bump into a wall and change its direction. The product of velocity times mass is momentum. A change in momentum (e.g., when the particle strikes the wall) over time is a force. Because many particles strike an area of the wall and change their momentum over a given time, pressure (force over area) is produced.

Therefore, four qualities are related: temperature, number of particles, volume, and pressure. These come together in the ideal gas law:

$PV = nRT,$ where P = pressure, V = volume, n = number of moles of particles, R = the ideal gas constant (8.314 J/mol; K, a constant of proportionality), and T = temperature in degrees Kelvin

123. Changes to a system that do not change the temperature are called isothermal. In an isothermal process, if the pressure is doubled, then the:

A. number of particles doubles.
B. ideal gas constant doubles.
C. volume doubles.
D. volume is halved.

GO ON TO NEXT PAGE.

124. Changes to systems that do not change the pressure are called isobaric. In an isobaric system, if absolute temperature is doubled, then the:

A. number of particles is halved.
B. ideal gas constant is halved.
C. volume doubles.
D. volume is halved.

125. Changes to systems that do not change the volume are called isochoric. In an isochoric system, if pressure is doubled, then the:

A. number of particles doubles.
B. ideal gas constant is halved.
C. temperature doubles.
D. temperature is halved.

126. The product PV has units of:

A. momentum.
B. energy.
C. force.
D. mass.

127. How many moles of an ideal gas exist at $T = 150°C$ in a volume of 2 L at a pressure of 5 atm?

A. 7.784
B. 3.482
C. 1.285
D. 0.287

Questions 128–142 are **NOT** based on a descriptive passage.

---

128. Which of the following is **NOT** an endothermic process?

A. Melting of a solid
B. Vaporization
C. Increasing the temperature of a gas
D. Condensation of water vapor

129. Which response places the following acids in order of increasing acid strength?

1. C_6H_5COOH ($K_a = 6.5 \times 10^{-5}$)

2. HNO_2 ($K_a = 4.5 \times 10^{-4}$)

3. HCN ($K_a = 4.9 \times 10^{-10}$)

A. $2 > 1 > 3$
B. $2 > 3 > 1$
C. $1 > 2 > 3$
D. $3 > 1 > 2$

130. Which of the following species has the highest standard entropy ($S°$) at 25°C?

A. CH_3OH (1)
B. CO (g)
C. $MgCO_3$(s)
D. H_2O (1)

131. Calculate the molality of a 15% solution of $MgCl_2$ in water given that the density of this solution is 1.127 g/ml.

A. 0.157 M
B. 11.8 M
C. 1.85 M
D. 0.134 M

132. Calculate the H^+ concentration in a solution of 0.010 moles/liter HCN. Ka $= 4.9 \times 10^{-10}$.

A. 4.9×10^{-10} m/l
B. 4.5×10^{-9} m/l
C. 4.9×10^{-12} m/l
D. 2.2×10^{-6} m/l

133. The pH at the equivalence point of a titration may differ from pH 7.0 because of:

A. the initial concentration of the standard solution.
B. the indicator used.
C. the self-ionization of water.
D. hydrolysis of the salt formed.

134. The overall reaction:

$$2Co^{3+} (aq) + 2Cl^- (aq) \rightarrow 2Co^{2+} (aq) + Cl_2(g)$$

has the standard cell voltage, $E^0 = 0.46$ V.

Given: $Cl_2(g) + 2e^- \rightarrow 2Cl^- (aq)$ $E^0 = 1.36$ V.

160

Calculate the standard reduction potential (E^0) for the half-cell reaction $Co^{3+} + e^- \rightarrow Co^{2+}$ ($Co^{3+}/Co^{2+} = ?$) at 25°C.

A. 1.82 V
B. −0.90 V
C. 0.90 V
D. −1.82 V

135. Compare two springs. Spring 1 has a spring constant of 1000 N/m. Spring 2 has a spring constant of 500 N/m. When both springs are stretched an equal amount, the energy stored in spring 1 differs from that stored in spring 2 by a factor of:

A. 2.
B. 0.5.
C. 1.
D. 4.

136. A sample of radioisotope shows an activity of 999 disintegrations per minute because of beta decay. If after 1.1 years, the activity is 952 disintegrations per minute, what is the half-life of the radioisotope?

A. 0.0438 years
B. 11.4 years
C. 0.25 years
D. 15.8 years

137. A bird is standing with one foot on a high-voltage power line. What would happen if the bird put the other foot down on the same line? The bird would be:

A. electrocuted.
B. unharmed.
C. polarized.
D. ionized.

138. In a gymnasium, a boy who weighs 40 kg is asked to climb a rope that is 8 m long. He does so in 15 seconds at a constant speed. In watts, how much power does he expend in getting to the top?

A. 120
B. 209
C. 320
D. 600

139. You are standing on a railroad track and hear the horn of an oncoming train. As the train approaches you, how do the frequency and wavelength change?

A. The frequency becomes higher, and the wavelength becomes shorter.
B. The frequency becomes lower, and the wavelength becomes shorter.
C. The frequency becomes higher, and the wavelength becomes longer.
D. The frequency becomes lower, and the wavelength becomes longer.

140. Ultrasonic sound is characterized by frequencies:

A. greater than 20 Hz.
B. less than 20 Hz.
C. greater than 20,000 Hz.
D. less than 20,000 Hz.

141. Which color represents the wavelength of the highest frequency visible to the naked eye?

A. Violet
B. Blue
C. Green
D. Red

142. Light waves from a smooth concave mirror:

A. diverge.
B. are parallel.
C. converge.
D. are scattered.

STOP. IF YOU FINISH BEFORE TIME IS CALLED, CHECK YOUR WORK. YOU MAY GO BACK TO ANY QUESTION IN THIS TEST BOOKLET.

Writing Sample

Time: 60 Minutes
(2 essays, separately timed, 30 minutes each)

ESSAY TOPIC 1

Consider this statement:

Truth is great and will always endure.

Write a unified essay in which you perform the following tasks. Explain what you think the above statement means. Describe a specific situation in which truth might not be great or might not endure. Discuss what you think determines when truth is great and how it can endure.

ESSAY TOPIC 2

Consider this statement:

Power in defense of freedom is greater than power on behalf of tyranny and oppression.

Write a unified essay in which you perform the following tasks. Explain what you think the above statement means. Describe a specific situation in which power used in defense of freedom might not be as great as power used on behalf of tyranny and oppression. Discuss what you think determines when power in defense of freedom is greater than power on behalf of tyranny and oppression, and when it is not.

STOP. IF YOU FINISH BEFORE TIME IS CALLED, CHECK YOUR WORK.

Biological Sciences

Time: 100 Minutes
Questions 143–219

DIRECTIONS: Most questions in the Biological Sciences test are organized into groups, each preceded by a descriptive passage. After studying the passage, select the one best answer to each question in the group. Some questions are not based on a descriptive passage and are also independent of each other. You must also select the one best answer to these questions. If you are not certain of an answer, eliminate the alternatives that you know to be incorrect and then select an answer from the remaining alternatives. Indicate your selection by blackening the corresponding circle on your answer sheet.

Passage I (Questions 143–149)

During normal respiration, CO_2 is carried to the alveoli of the lung, where it diffuses out and O_2 diffuses in. The CO_2 is carried in the blood in various chemical forms. Approximately 70% is found in the plasma as HCO_3^-, 23% is carbaminohemoglobin, and only the final 7% exists as dissolved CO_2.

The diffusion gradient drives the CO_2 from the plasma into the alveolar space. The diffusion of CO_2 into the lung reduces the concentration of dissolved CO_2 in the blood and drives the following equations to the right, toward CO_2:

$$\text{Eq. 1.} \quad H^+ + HCO_3^- \rightleftharpoons H_2CO_3$$

$$\text{Eq. 2.} \quad H_2CO_3 \rightleftharpoons CO_2 + H_2O$$

where CO_2 = carbon dioxide, H_2CO_3 = carbonic acid, and HCO_3^- = bicarbonate.

Although most of the bicarbonate is carried in the plasma, the red blood cells contain carbonic anhydrase. This enzyme requires zinc ions for activity and catalyzes the reversible formation of carbonic acid from carbon dioxide and water (Eq. 2). Because of the intracellular location of this enzyme, the bicarbonate in the red cell is converted to carbon dioxide more rapidly than is the bicarbonate in plasma. This situation creates a concentration gradient, and the ion diffuses into the cell from the plasma. The decreased bicarbonate levels in the red cell as well as the accompanying pH shift and oxygenation of hemoglobin also cause the carbaminohemoglobin to dissociate, freeing more bicarbonate. The net result is that expired carbon dioxide is regenerated from both bicarbonate and carbaminohemoglobin.

Oxygen diffuses in the reverse direction from the lung into the blood, where it binds to deoxyhemoglobin to form oxyhemoglobin. In the tissues, the reverse reactions occur because CO_2 diffuses into the blood and O_2 diffuses out.

143. Individuals who have a substantial zinc deficiency would tend to have:

A. more water in the plasma.
B. more CO_2 in the lungs.
C. less bicarbonate (HCO_3^-) in the plasma.
D. more CO_2 in the tissues.

144. An increase in dissolved CO_2:

A. increases the pH.
B. decreases the pH.
C. decreases the bicarbonate concentration.
D. deceases the carbonic acid concentration.

145. The pH is:

A. lower in arterial blood than in venous blood.
B. lower in venous blood than in arterial blood.
C. the same in arterial and venous blood.
D. lower in patients who hyperventilate.

146. Which of the following is NOT true? The concentration of:

A. bicarbonate is greater in venous blood than in arterial blood.
B. bicarbonate is greater in arterial blood than in venous blood.
C. dissolved CO_2 is greater in venous blood than in arterial blood.
D. oxygen is greater in arterial blood than in venous blood.

147. The tissue capillaries may be so narrow that the red cells are squeezed, further elongated, and forced to pass through in single file. This situation:

A. permits the oxygen to have direct contact with the tissues.
B. helps squeeze the oxygen off of the hemoglobin, promoting its diffusion into the tissues.

GO ON TO NEXT PAGE.

C. brings the zinc ion and the carbonic anhydrase closer together, enhancing binding and further activating the enzyme.

D. increases the effective surface area of the red cell, enhancing the exchange of CO_2 and O_2 across the red cell membrane.

148. Oxygen is transported across biologic membranes by which of the following processes?

A. Active transport
B. Facilitated transport
C. Simple diffusion
D. An enzyme-catalyzed reaction

149. The principal constituents from which carbonic anhydrase is formed are:

A. amino acids.
B. sugars.
C. zinc atoms.
D. lipids.

Passage II (Questions 150–154)

Carcinogens are compounds that cause cancer. Compounds that are converted to carcinogens after ingestion are called procarcinogens. The liver is an organ that actively converts procarcinogens to carcinogens.

The Ames test is used as a simple screening technique for suspected carcinogens. The test uses a mutated strain of *Salmonella typhimurium* that lacks both enzymes for DNA repair and an enzyme required for the synthesis of histidine (His⁻). This strain can grow only if histidine is added to the medium or if a back mutation restores the capacity to synthesize histidine.

Carcinogens stimulate the growth of His⁻ strains of *S. typhimurium* on histidine-deficient agar plates. The addition of liver enzymes to the medium enhances the reliability of the test.

150. This test is based on the assumption that carcinogens:

A. bind to DNA.
B. are mutagens.
C. activate reverse transcriptase.
D. for mammalian cells will also cause cancers in bacteria.

151. Carcinogens act by altering the chemical structure of:

A. the DNA sugar.
B. the DNA nucleotide.
C. the RNA sugar.
D. the RNA nucleotide.

152. Relative to control plates, agar plates seeded with His⁻ *S. typhimurium* in a medium rich in carcinogens will:

A. have a greater number of colonies.
B. contain fewer colonies.
C. have colonies with a rougher surface.
D. have an equal number of morphologically indistinguishable colonies.

153. Reliability is enhanced by the addition of liver enzymes because:

A. these enzymes supply a source of histidine.
B. these enzymes convert procarcinogens to carcinogens.
C. the added liver enzymes code for the required DNA molecules.
D. the bacteria mutate liver enzymes easily.

166

154. The Ames test is based on the assumption that cancer cells have an aberration in their:

A. mitochondria.
B. nucleus.
C. ribosomes.
D. endoplasmic reticulum.

Passage III (Questions 155–160)

Retroviruses contain RNA and reverse transcriptase. Viruses in this family are absorbed into host cells through specific cell receptors. Once in the cell, the reverse transcriptase catalyses the synthesis of a complementary (minus) DNA strand from the viral RNA core. Even before this strand is completed, the synthesis of the plus DNA strand is begun. Between 6 and 9 hours after infection, synthesis of a linear double-stranded DNA molecule containing the information coded in the RNA virus is completed. This DNA then moves into the nucleus of the host cell, where it becomes cyclic. By 24 hours, several copies have integrated at random sites into the host's DNA, as a provirus. The viral DNA does not replicate independently. Progeny viral RNA is generated by regular transcription with host RNA polymerase II. Six genera of retroviruses are recognized. Three of these are oncoviruses (i.e., they directly induce cancers).

The lentiviruses are another genus within the retrovirus family. They are distinguished from the other genera by having a slightly larger genome and by inducing disease only after a long latent period. The human immunodeficiency virus (HIV) belongs to the lentivirus genus and causes acquired immune deficiency syndrome (AIDS). In establishing an infection, the glycoprotein envelope of HIV binds to a CD4 receptor found on the surface of T4 helper leukocytes and monocyte-macrophages. The T4 cells are part of the immune system and activate other T cells, natural killer cells, macrophages, and some B cells. The infection remains latent until the HIV-infected T4 cells are activated, causing them to transcribe more viroid particles that form new HIV cells and eventually kill the host cell, liberating virus into the bloodstream and infecting other T4 cells. The long-term result is acute immunosuppression that permits the development of opportunistic diseases that eventually kill the patient.

HIV is transmitted only through the exchange of bodily fluids. Transmission through the blood occurs in intravenous drug users who share needles, hemophiliacs who receive blood concentrates, patients receiving transfusions, and health care workers who accidentally stick themselves with a contaminated needle. Sexual transmission occurs among both homosexuals and heterosexuals. Anal sex appears to increase the risk of transmission. Mothers may transmit the virus during childbirth or perinatally. In contrast, persons simply living or working with an infected person have a low chance of infection.

155. Azidothymidine (AZT) is a drug used in the treatment of AIDS. It inhibits the reverse transcriptase to a greater degree than it does mammalian transcriptases. It can also be used as a prophylactic to prevent the establishment of the disease in exposed individuals, for example, after a needlestick from a patient with the disease. From information contained in the passage, the effectiveness of AZT as a prophylactic decreases:

GO ON TO NEXT PAGE.

A. 2 hours after exposure.
B. 6 hours after exposure.
C. 24 hours after exposure.
D. no relevant data are given in the passage.

156. Patients with AIDS are prone to malignancies such as Kaposi's sarcoma because:

A. HIV is an oncovirus.
B. the host has become more susceptible.
C. both A and B are correct.
D. neither A nor B is correct.

157. HIV infects only:

A. B cells.
B. T4 helper cells.
C. T4 helper cells that have been compromised by other infections.
D. cells that have a CD4 receptor site.

158. Reverse transcriptase lacks the editing functions associated with mammalian transcription. Therefore, a great number of transcriptional errors and a high mutation rate occur. As a result, which of the following is **NOT** true?

A. Infection with HIV is generally self-limiting because the new mutants are most often defective.
B. HIV cells are highly adaptable to new environments.
C. The virus avoids reacting with specific antibodies.
D. The strain has a high degree of variability.

159. Information presented in the passage supports the idea that the spread of AIDS will **NOT** be decreased by:

A. screening blood before transfusions.
B. practicing safe sex.
C. denying patients with AIDS access to their normal work environment.
D. education.

160. T4 cell clones become activated whenever the immune system is summoned to fight an infection. This observation suggests that the latent period between infection with HIV and the onset of frank symptoms of AIDS would be:

A. decreased in patients who are exposed to many infections.
B. increased in patients who are exposed to many infections.
C. increased in patients who take AZT.
D. unaffected by the number of subsequent infections.

Passage IV (Questions 161–167)

Blood pressure (*BP*) is a function of the product of cardiac output (*CO*) and peripheral resistance (*PR*), i.e., *BP* γ *CO* × *PR*. The resistance through a vessel varies inversely as the fourth power of the radius (*r*) (resistance γ $1/r^4$) and is also dependent on the volume of fluid in the arterial side of the circulatory system at the time of contraction. Normally, the blood is ejected from the heart when the ventricles contract. The arterial pressure obtained during this contractile phase is called systolic. After the contraction, the ventricles relax and are refilled with blood in the atria. The pressure obtained during this relaxation phase is called diastolic.

It is important to regulate blood pressure. If it is too low, tissues do not receive sufficient blood. If it is too high, the danger of an aneurysm increases and, over time, damage occurs to the vessels, possibly resulting in small leaks or enhancement of the arteriosclerotic process. Two interdigitating systems maintain blood pressure within the normal range. One functions directly through the central nervous system, which receives signals from baroreceptors located in the major arteries. The second is the humoral renin-angiotensin-aldosterone system.

The baroreceptors respond to an increase in blood pressure by sending a signal to the medullary regulatory center in the brain, which responds by stimulating the vagus nerve to send an inhibitory signal to the heart, decreasing cardiac output. Simultaneously, the regulatory center decreases excitatory sympathetic activity to both the heart and the adrenal medulla. Sympathetic signals induce the heart to increase cardiac output and the adrenal medulla to produce catecholamines. The catecholamines cause the arterioles to contract. Accordingly, a decrease in sympathetic activity further reduces cardiac output and also decreases peripheral resistance.

Renin is an enzyme stored in the juxtaglomerular cells of the kidney. The release of renin responds directly to blood pressure and is also under sympathetic control. A decrease in pressure increases renin release and vice versa. Renin converts another peptide, angiotensinogen, to angiotensin I, which is then converted to angiotensin II. Angiotensin II induces vascular constriction and increases aldosterone secretion. Aldosterone causes retention of sodium and water, thereby increasing blood volume.

161. In diastole, the:

- **A.** ventricle is contracting.
- **B.** arterioles are dilating.
- **C.** arterial blood pressure is at its lowest.
- **D.** veins are pulsating.

162. A drug that inhibits the formation of angiotensin II would:

- **A.** increase blood pressure.
- **B.** decrease blood pressure.
- **C.** increase heart rate.
- **D.** decrease heart rate.

163. It may be deduced from the passage that sympathetic impulses:

- **A.** increase cardiac output and decrease peripheral resistance.
- **B.** decrease cardiac output and decrease peripheral resistance.
- **C.** increase cardiac output and increase peripheral resistance.
- **D.** decrease cardiac output and increase peripheral resistance.

164. Diuretics are sometimes prescribed for patients to help reduce their blood pressure. The data in the passage suggest that diuretics act by:

- **A.** decreasing cardiac output.
- **B.** permitting arterioles to relax, thereby increasing their radius and decreasing resistance.
- **C.** reducing blood volume.
- **D.** increasing heart rate.

165. In the humoral system, the order of activation is:

- **A.** aldosterone, angiotensin I, angiotensin II, renin.
- **B.** angiotensin I, angiotensin II, renin, aldosterone.
- **C.** renin, angiotensin I, angiotensin II, aldosterone.
- **D.** aldosterone, renin, angiotensin I, angiotensin II.

166. Blood pressure is:

- **A.** higher in systole than in diastole.
- **B.** higher in diastole than in systole.
- **C.** roughly equivalent in systole and diastole.
- **D.** higher in either diastole or systole, depending on the phase of the cycle.

GO ON TO NEXT PAGE.

167. The passage implies that sympathetic input induces its greatest effect on peripheral resistance by causing contraction of the:

A. veins.
B. aorta.
C. arterioles.
D. capillaries.

Passage V (Questions 168–174)

All muscles convert the chemical energy of adenosine triphosphate into mechanical work. There are three major classes of muscle: striated, cardiac, and smooth.

Striated muscles get their name from well-developed cross-striations that are caused by the patterned arrangement of contractile proteins. These muscles are under voluntary control and are innervated by the somatic motor neurons, which transmit a signal to the motor end plate of muscle fibers through the neurotransmitter acetylcholine. Striated muscles are sometimes called skeletal muscles because they are attached to the skeletal system by tendons and are responsible for motion. Each striated muscle fiber is an elongated individual multinuclear cell. Several muscle fibers are innervated by branches of a single motor neuron, producing a motor unit. All of the fibers in a motor unit contract when their motor neuron is stimulated. Muscles used for fine control tend to have fewer fibers in a motor unit than muscles that function for strength. Muscles used to sustain tension for long periods often have motor units associated with neurons that fire in an asynchronous fashion. As one motor unit contracts, another is relaxed, and fatigue of the total muscle is retarded.

Smooth muscles lack striations and are not under voluntary control. They are innervated by the autonomic nervous system. Smooth muscles from various sources differ in many details, but share some features. In general, smooth muscle fibers are uninuclear, spindle shaped, and considerably smaller than skeletal muscle fibers. Compared with skeletal muscle, smooth muscles contract slowly and develop less tension. They are located in the arteries and arterioles, the air passages of the lung, and various tissues of the gastrointestinal and reproductive systems.

Cardiac muscle has properties intermediate to those of smooth and skeletal muscles. The cells are striated, but branched, and contain a single nucleus. Neighboring cells are connected by intercalated disks within which are gap junctions that facilitate the passage of electric currents and small molecules from one cell to another. Therefore, a piece of heart tissue behaves as a single unit when subjected to an electric current. This behavior allows the heart to beat in a synchronous fashion.

168. Myoblasts are precursor muscle cells. During embryonic development, a group of myoblasts fuse. These cells might be destined to become:

A. skeletal muscle.
B. smooth muscle.
C. cardiac muscle.
D. all of the above.

169. The heart contracts in a synchronous fashion because the muscle fibers:

A. contract without voluntary input.
B. have striations.
C. are connected by intercalated disks.
D. have branched cells.

170. Which of the following statements about muscles is **NOT** true?

A. During evolution, muscles developed specific properties to perform specific tasks.
B. Striated muscles are connected to bone by tendons.
C. A person can will his heart to skip beats.
D. Smooth muscle contraction or relaxation influences blood pressure.

171. Syn- is a prefix meaning with, or together. Cyt- refers to cells. Some muscles have syncytium. Syncytium is likely to be found in:

A. striated muscle.
B. smooth muscle.
C. cardiac muscle.
D. all muscles.

172. Poliovirus destroys motor neurons in the anterior horn of the spinal cord. Infection with poliovirus depresses the function of:

A. striated muscle.
B. smooth muscle.
C. cardiac muscle.
D. any of the above.

173. Goose bumps are an involuntary response formed in reaction to low temperature. Cold stimulates the arrector pili muscles, which are associated with hair follicles, to contract. Arrector pili muscles are an example of:

A. striated muscle.
B. smooth muscle.
C. cardiac muscle.
D. skeletal muscle.

174. Curare competes with acetylcholine for receptor sites along motor end plates. Administration of curare to a person:

A. causes striated muscles to relax.
B. causes striated muscles to contract.
C. has no effect on striated muscles.
D. induces tetany.

GO ON TO NEXT PAGE.

Passage VI (Questions 175–180)

Water is the most important inorganic substance in the body. In humans, 70% of the fat-free mass is composed of water. The water of the body is divided into two major components; intracellular fluid and extracellular fluid. The latter is conventionally further divided into blood fluid and interstitial fluid. Blood fluid includes all of the water in blood that is not intracellular or, in other words, the fluid that remains after the white and red cells are removed. When blood is collected in the presence of an anticoagulant and the red and white cells are removed by centrifugation, the blood fluid obtained is called plasma. If the blood is first allowed to coagulate and the cells become trapped in the coagulum, the blood fluid fraction is called serum. For the remainder of this passage, blood fluid will be called plasma.

Approximately 55% of the total body water is intracellular fluid, 36% is interstitial fluid, and 9% is plasma. Although the plasma component is quantitatively the least significant, it is the fraction that is considered most often. It is the most readily available fraction; therefore, it is used for diagnostic purposes and as a route to introduce soluble substances into the other water compartments. It is also the fraction most subject to change through interaction with the substances entering the body through the digestive system, leaving normally through the excretory system, or leaving abnormally through a punctured or ruptured blood vessel.

All body water is in osmotic equilibrium. Therefore, water loss or gain in one compartment causes reflected changes in the other compartments. Although the osmotic pressure is the same in all three compartments, the composition of the intra- and extracellular fluids is different. It has been hypothesized that the composition of intracellular fluid approximates the composition of the seawater in which life first arose, whereas the composition of plasma approximates the composition of seawater when the first multicellular organisms enclosed themselves within a membrane that separated them from the external sea. However the difference arose, the cells work hard to maintain their internal ionic composition, whereas the various homeostatic mechanisms, primarily involving the excretory systems and bone, function to maintain the plasma composition.

The graph compares the ionic composition of seawater, blood plasma, interstitial fluid, and intracellular fluid.

175. A laboratory reports that the normal plasma K^+ concentration is 4 ± 0.5 mEq/L. A value of 3.8 mEq/L is obtained for a patient. From these data and the information given above, it would be safe to conclude that the patient's total body K^+ levels are:

    A. normal.
    B. depleted.
    C. either normal or depleted.
    D. increased.

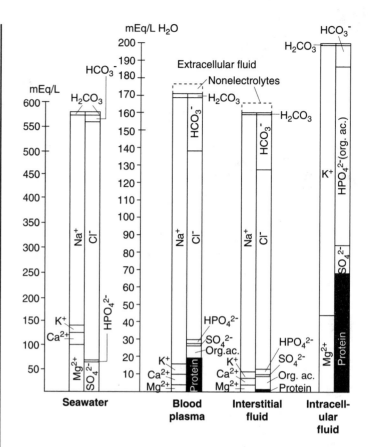

(Reprinted with permission from Gamble JL: Chemical Anatomy, Physiology, and Pathology of Extracellular Fluid. Cambridge, MA, Harvard University Press, copyright 1942 by JL Gamble, copyright 1947, 1954 by the President and Fellows of Harvard College, copyright renewed 1970 by James L. Gamble, Jr., copyright renewed 1975 by Elizabeth Gamble.)

176. Assuming that the composition of intracellular fluid and blood plasma is related to the composition of seawater at the time of the evolution of these fluid compartments, in the period between the evolution of extracellular fluid and the present, the Na^+ composition of seawater has increased by an approximate factor of:

    A. one.
    B. two.
    C. three.
    D. four.

177. In blood plasma, the concentration of Cl^- plus HCO_3^- most closely approximates that of which cation?

    A. Mg^{2+}
    B. CA^{2+}
    C. K^+
    D. Na^+

178. The plasma concentration (in millequivalents per liter) of:

    A. anions is greater than that of cations, plus uncharged substances.

    B. cations is greater than that of anions, plus uncharged substances.

    C. cations equals that of anions.

    D. cations, anions, plus uncharged substances in plasma equals the concentration of cations, anions, plus uncharged substances in intracellular fluid.

179. The plasma concentration (in milliosmoles per liter) of:

    A. anions is greater than that of cations, plus uncharged substances.

    B. cations is greater than that of anions, plus uncharged substances.

    C. cations equals that of anions.

    D. cations, anions, plus uncharged substances in plasma equals the concentration of cations, anions, plus uncharged substances in intracellular fluid.

180. The normal pH of blood plasma is 7.4. The concentration of plasma H^+ (in millequivalents per liter) is approximately:

    A. 100 times less than that of plasma K^+.

    B. 1000 times less than that of plasma K^+.

    C. 10,000 times less than that of plasma K^+.

    D. 100,000 times less than that of plasma K^+.

Passage VII (Questions 181–190)

Lipids are a heterogenous class of biologically important compounds that share the property of hydrophobicity. They include fats, oils, phospholipids, glycolipids, steroids, and naturally occurring waxes.

These various lipids can be different chemically and have diverse biologic functions. Fats and oils are esters of fatty acids and glycerol, forming triacylglycerides. They differ in state at room temperature: oils are liquid, fats solid. The primary factors accounting for this difference are the length and the degree of saturation of the acyl moieties. The more unsaturated it is or the fewer carbons it has, the lower the melting point of the triacylglyceride. With the exception of milk and dairy products, the natural fats and oils typically encountered have acyl groups consisting of 16 or more carbons. Therefore, they differ in degree of saturation. The fats and oils primarily store reserve energy. Generally, fats are found in animals and oils in plants. These are the primary forms of ingested lipid.

Phospholipids have substituted phosphoric acid esters on carbon three of glycerol, but are otherwise similar to fats or oils. The lecithins are a group of phospholipids in which the phosphate is bonded to diacylglycerol and choline in a phosphodiester bond. Sphingolipids are lipids in which fatty acyl groups are bound to sphingosine rather than glycerol. They may contain phosphate groups and belong to the phospholipid class, or they may be substituted with complex carbohydrates and belong to the glycolipid group. The phospho- and glycolipids are found in high concentrations in membranes. Steroids are substituted alicyclic hydrocarbons that have three six-membered rings as well as a five-membered ring. Included among the steroids are cholesterol, many hormones, bile acids and salts, and other compounds. Waxes are esters of higher fatty acids and high–molecular-weight alcohols and are found as the protective coatings on the skins and fur of mammals, the leaves and fruit of plants, and in certain animal oils, such as that of the sperm whale.

181. Triacylglycerides:

    A. are solid at room temperature if they contain fatty acids with several alkene bonds.

    B. can be hydrogenated if they do not contain alkene bonds.

    C. are soluble in water.

    D. undergo alkaline hydrolysis to yield soaps.

182. The phosphate moiety of the phospholipids makes the molecule:

    A. detergent-like.

    B. more hydrophobic.

GO ON TO NEXT PAGE.

C. more positively charged.
D. more stable.

183. All lipids:

A. share similar functional groups.
B. have similar biologic roles.
C. are relatively soluble in nonpolar organic solvents.
D. contain long-chained fatty acid moieties, which may be either saturated or unsaturated.

184. Cholesterol:

A. can be saponified.
B. is a hormone.
C. is a phospholipid.
D. is a steroid.

185. Which of the following lipids yields glycerol on complete hydrolysis?

A. A sphingolipid
B. A phospholipid
C. A steroid hormone
D. Cholesterol

186. How could an unsaturated fatty acid be converted into a saturated one?

A. $KMnO_4$, OH^-, heat
B. OH^-, H_2O, heat, then H_3O^+
C. H_2, Ni, pressure
D. O_3, then Zn^{2+}, H_2O

187. Choline is found as a product on the hydrolysis of:

A. lecithins.
B. all phospholipids.
C. sphingolipids.
D. triacylglycerides.

188. Which lipid has the following generalized structure?

$$
\begin{array}{l}
\text{C-O-C-R1} \\
\quad | \quad \overset{||}{O} \\
\text{C-O-C-R2} \\
\quad | \quad \overset{||}{O} \\
\text{C-O-P-O-R3} \\
\qquad \overset{||}{O}
\end{array}
$$

A. A steroid
B. A lecithin
C. An oil
D. A fat

189. Consider a micelle composed of phosphotidylcholine. Which part of the molecule forms the hydrophilic part of the molecule?

A. The fatty acid esterified on carbon one of glycerol
B. The fatty acid esterified on carbon two of glycerol
C. The glycerol backbone itself
D. The phosphocholine moiety

190. The following structural unit is found in:

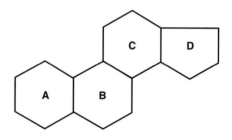

A. testosterone.
B. a lecithin.
C. a sphingolipid.
D. a wax.

174

Aldehydes and ketones are in equilibrium with their enol forms; a proton strays from a carbon to the oxygen, and the double bond shifts:

$$-C-C=O \rightleftharpoons -C=C-OH \rightleftharpoons -C=C-O^-$$
$$\qquad | \qquad\qquad\qquad\qquad\qquad$$
$$\qquad H$$

Aldo form   Enol form   Enolate ion

This type of resonance is called keto-enol tautomerism. Tautomerism is an important phenomenon used by organic chemists and in nature to direct certain reactions. In the aldo form, the electrophilic properties of the oxygen draw electrons from the carbonyl carbon, leaving it with a weak positive charge. However, in the enol form, the oxygen shares two electrons with hydrogen, leaving the carbon more negatively charged:

$$-C:O \qquad -C\,O\,H$$
$$\sigma_+ \ \sigma_- \qquad \sigma_- \quad \sigma_+$$

Usually, the equilibrium favors the aldo or keto form because this carbanion is a stronger nucleophile than the oxygen. An exception to this generalization is phenol, which favors its hydroxyl form.

191. The carbonyl carbon on an aldehyde or ketone has:

    A. a slightly positive charge.
    B. a slightly negative charge.
    C. no charge at all.
    D. none of the above.

192. Aldehydes and ketones:

    A. tend to be susceptible to nucleophilic attack.
    B. tend not to be susceptible to nucleophilic attack.
    C. do not act as Brönsted acids.
    D. are compounds that contain nitrogen.

193. What is the order of importance of resonance contributors of the following?

$$CH_2=CH-C=O \rightleftharpoons {}^+CH_2-CH=C-O^- \rightleftharpoons CH_2-CH=C-O^+$$
$$\qquad\quad | \qquad\qquad\qquad\qquad | \qquad\qquad\qquad\qquad |$$
$$\qquad\quad H \qquad\qquad\qquad\qquad H \qquad\qquad\qquad\qquad H$$
$$\qquad\quad 1. \qquad\qquad\qquad\qquad 2. \qquad\qquad\qquad\qquad 3.$$

    A. $1 > 2 > 3$
    B. $2 > 1 > 3$
    C. $3 > 2 > 1$
    D. $2 > 1 > 3$

194. The observation that phenol is favored over its keto form is best explained by the:

    A. loss of the aromatic structure of the benzene ring in the keto form.
    B. decreased nucleophilic properties of oxygen.
    C. decreased pKa of the enolic proton in phenol.
    D. pH of phenolic solutions.

195. Acetylene reacts with water. The primary product is:

    A. hydroxyethylene.
    B. acetone.
    C. vinyl alcohol.
    D. ethanol.

GO ON TO NEXT PAGE.

Passage IX (Questions 196–205)

In 1906, the Russian scientist Tswett defined chromatography as a procedure for separating dyes based on repeating adsorption and desorption in successive layers of some adsorptive medium. The name was coined based on the observation that the dyes separated into differently colored bands. The term chromatography has since been applied to all processes of separation in which a selective process is repeated many times on some carrier material, even though the materials used have no color. Several types of chromatography exist, including gas, ion-exchange, gel, paper, thin-layer, and reverse-phase chromatography. All of these techniques partition the sample between a stationary phase and a mobile phase. The compounds are separated according to their relative attraction to the two phases. Those most attracted to the stationary phase remain relatively stationary, whereas those with the greatest affinity for the mobile phase move more readily with the mobile phase.

In gas chromatography, the sample to be analyzed is volatilized and the vapor is partitioned between a high–molecular-weight stationary phase and a helium or nitrogen mobile phase. In ion-exchange chromatography, the stationary phase is charged and the compounds to be separated are of the opposite charge. The compounds are moved off of the charged stationary matrix by changing their charge (e.g., changing the pH of the eluting solution in separating proteins) or by increasing the concentration of ions with the same charge. In either case, compounds with a lesser attraction to the stationary phase move most rapidly, and those with a higher attraction are left behind. In gel chromatography, the solid matrix consists of microscopic hollow sphere-like beads that have pores leading to the interior of the bead. The bead-like gels are available with different pore sizes, and separation occurs based on molecular weight. Larger molecules penetrate fewer beads and migrate faster than smaller molecules, which enter more beads and therefore have a longer route to travel. In paper and thin-layer chromatography, the stationary phase is not charged, but is polar. Because of its polarity, this phase attracts water. The mobile phase is a mixture of relatively nonpolar solvents. As the mobile phase passes over the compounds to be separated, the compounds partition between the water phase, which is bound to the stationary matrix, and the mobile, organic phase in proportion to their relative solubility. In effect, a nearly infinite number of continuous, repetitive extractions occur between the two phases. In reverse-phase chromatography, the stationary phase is nonpolar and the mobile phase is polar. Although it is given a different name, reverse-phase chromatography is normally performed on glass plates using a thin layer of nonpolar adsorbent material and is in effect a special type of thin-layer chromatography.

Thin-layer chromatography differs from paper chromatography in that a slurried adsorbent material is spread in a thin layer on a glass plate. A wide variety of adsorbents may be used. Silica gel and alumina are the most common. Both of these have hydroxyl groups and are therefore polar. The advantages of thin-layer chromatography over paper chromatography are that the separation times are faster, the sample spot tends not to spread as much, and a wide range of test reagents can be used that might char or otherwise destroy the paper.

To conduct the procedure, a few microliters of a solution of the mixture to be separated is applied at the point of origin. The plate is placed in a beaker, jar, or some other type of equipment that permits the mobile phase to travel up the plate, through the point of origin, and toward the other end of the plate. The figure below illustrates the separation of a sample containing a mixture of three compounds with different polarities. Compound a is the most polar, b is intermediate, and c is the least polar. The sample is run along with samples of known composition to aid in identification. The distance traveled by a substance relative to the distance traveled by the solvent is known as the R_f value.

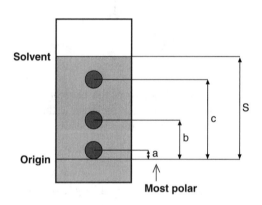

$$R_f = \frac{\text{Distance spot A moves from the origin}}{\text{Distance solvent S moves from the origin}} = A/S$$

$R_f(a) = a/S$

$R_f(b) = b/S$

$R_f(c) = c/S$

196. The four samples below were subjected to thin-layer chromatography on silica gel. Which has the lowest R_f value?

    A. Ethanol
    B. Ethane
    C. Phenol
    D. Benzene

197. The four samples below were subjected to thin-layer chromatography on silica gel. Which has the greatest R_f value?

    A. Ethanol
    B. Ethane

C. Phenol
D. Benzene

198. The four samples below were subjected to thin-layer chromatography on nonpolar adsorbent material. Which has the greatest R_f value?

A. Ethanol
B. Ethane
C. Phenol
D. Benzene

199. The following pairs of compounds were subjected to reverse-phase thin-layer chromatography on alumina. Which set would be separated most efficiently?

A. Benzene and acetylene
B. Ethanol and butanol
C. Ethanol and butane
D. Leucine and valine

200. A compound was subjected to thin-layer chromatography. The solvent traveled 10 cm, and the compound traveled 2 cm. What is the R_f value of the compound?

A. 2
B. 1
C. 0
D. 0.2

201. How is thin-layer chromatography analogous to extraction processes? Both processes involve:

A. time-consuming and laborious mixing of solvents.
B. the use of a solid support medium.
C. the distribution of solute between two immiscible solvents.
D. no similarities.

202. In thin-layer chromatography, but **NOT** in paper chromatography:

A. a slurried adsorbent material is spread on a glass plate.
B. a solid support medium is employed.
C. compounds are separated on the basis of their polarity.
D. the mobile phase is generally a mixture of relatively nonpolar solvents.

203. The various chromatographic techniques share the property of:

A. using differences in color to determine the degree of separation.
B. partitioning the sample between a stationary phase and a mobile phase.
C. applying the sample to be chromatographed in a solution.
D. having a polar solid phase and a less polar mobile phase.

204. Thin-layer chromatography can be performed in one dimension, as in the previous illustration, or in two dimensions. To run the second dimension, a square plate rather than a rectangular plate is used, and the sample is applied toward one edge. After the sample is run in the first dimension, the plate is turned 90° and subjected to a second chromatographic separation at a right angle to the first. When this second dimension is run, what is most likely to be changed?

A. The nature of the adsorbent material
B. The temperature at which the separation is conducted
C. The polarity of the solvent
D. The chamber in which the separation is conducted

205. You have a sample with a suspected molecular weight of several hundred daltons. You want to confirm the weight, but the only technique available is thin-layer chromatography. You think that if you run your sample along with another sample of known molecular weight, you may be able to determine the weight of the first sample using thin-layer chromatography. To do so, what adsorbent material do you choose?

A. Silica gel
B. Alumina
C. A nonpolar substance
D. A bead-like gel

GO ON TO NEXT PAGE.

206. Many physiologic functions are regulated by calcium ions. Therefore, it is of critical importance that blood calcium ion levels be maintained within narrow limits. In humans, bone is an important reservoir for calcium. The plasma level of calcium is regulated by two hormones. One degrades bone and releases calcium into the blood; the other stimulates the deposit of calcium into bone. These hormones are:

    A. thyroid, which releases calcium from bone, and calcitonin, which deposits calcium into bone.

    B. thyroid, which deposits calcium into bone, and calcitonin, which releases calcium from bone.

    C. parathyroid, which releases calcium from bone, and calcitonin, which deposits calcium into bone.

    D. parathyroid, which deposits calcium into bone, and calcitonin, which releases calcium from bone.

207. Exposure of a person to stress causes increased sympathetic nerve activity. This activity induces which of the following responses?

    A. Decreased heart rate

    B. Increased urine output

    C. Increased glycogenolytic activity

    D. Contraction of bronchioles

208. HCl is secreted in the stomach by which of the following?

    A. Parietal cells

    B. Chief cells

    C. Mucosal cells

    D. None of the above

209. Arteries differ from veins in that only veins have:

    A. an internal elastic lamina.

    B. a tunica media.

    C. valves.

    D. a tunica adventitia.

210. Sperm is produced in which of the following testicular structures?

    A. Interstitial cells

    B. Epididymis

    C. Seminiferous tubules

    D. Tunica vaginalis

211. Mutations in somatic genes that result in altered activities of enzymes in the tricarboxylic acid cycle almost invariably:

    A. are dominant.

    B. are recessive.

    C. are sex linked.

    D. occur in mitochondrial genes.

212. Heating an amide in an aqueous base:

    A. oxidizes the acid component to the corresponding ketone or aldehyde.

    B. reduces the acid component to the corresponding ketone or aldehyde.

    C. deprotonates the amide component to the corresponding amine.

    D. hydrolyzes the ester to the corresponding amine and acid.

213. Heptane is not soluble in aqueous solutions, even if they are basic or acidic. This property is a reflection of the fact that heptane is:

    A. not reactive.

    B. hydrophilic.

    C. hydrophobic.

    D. amphoteric.

214. Which of the following observations about the infrared spectrum would indicate that the reaction below had occurred?

    A. The appearance of an O-H stretch

    B. The disappearance of a C=O stretch

    C. The appearance of an aliphatic C-H stretch

    D. The appearance of an aldehyde C-H stretch

215. A compound gives the following nuclear magnetic resonance (NMR) spectra.

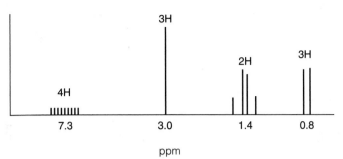

ppm

This compound is:

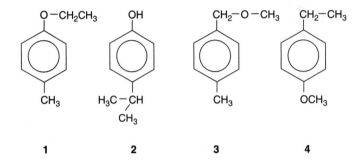

1   2   3   4

A. 1.
B. 2.
C. 3.
D. 4.

216. The products of the hydrolysis of a triacylglyceride by NaOH are:

A. glycerol and the Na salt of a fatty acid.
B. glycerol, the Na salt of phosphoric acid, and the Na salt of a fatty acid.
C. glycerol and the Na salt of phosphoric acid.
D. sphingosine and the Na salt of a fatty acid.

217. Which of the following is a ketohexose?

A. D-Glucose
B. D-Mannose
C. D-Fructose
D. L-Mannose

218. Which of the following compounds is most susceptible to electrophilic attack by nitronium ions?

1   2   3   4

A. 1
B. 2
C. 3
D. 4

219. Which of the following compounds is a reducing sugar?

I

II

III

IV

GO ON TO NEXT PAGE.

A. I
B. II
C. III
D. IV

STOP. IF YOU FINISH BEFORE TIME IS
CALLED, CHECK YOUR WORK. YOU MAY
GO BACK TO ANY QUESTION IN THIS TEST
BOOKLET.

ANSWER SHEET

Verbal Reasoning

1. Ⓐ Ⓑ Ⓒ Ⓓ
2. Ⓐ Ⓑ Ⓒ Ⓓ
3. Ⓐ Ⓑ Ⓒ Ⓓ
4. Ⓐ Ⓑ Ⓒ Ⓓ
5. Ⓐ Ⓑ Ⓒ Ⓓ
6. Ⓐ Ⓑ Ⓒ Ⓓ
7. Ⓐ Ⓑ Ⓒ Ⓓ
8. Ⓐ Ⓑ Ⓒ Ⓓ
9. Ⓐ Ⓑ Ⓒ Ⓓ
10. Ⓐ Ⓑ Ⓒ Ⓓ
11. Ⓐ Ⓑ Ⓒ Ⓓ
12. Ⓐ Ⓑ Ⓒ Ⓓ
13. Ⓐ Ⓑ Ⓒ Ⓓ
14. Ⓐ Ⓑ Ⓒ Ⓓ
15. Ⓐ Ⓑ Ⓒ Ⓓ
16. Ⓐ Ⓑ Ⓒ Ⓓ
17. Ⓐ Ⓑ Ⓒ Ⓓ
18. Ⓐ Ⓑ Ⓒ Ⓓ
19. Ⓐ Ⓑ Ⓒ Ⓓ
20. Ⓐ Ⓑ Ⓒ Ⓓ
21. Ⓐ Ⓑ Ⓒ Ⓓ
22. Ⓐ Ⓑ Ⓒ Ⓓ
23. Ⓐ Ⓑ Ⓒ Ⓓ
24. Ⓐ Ⓑ Ⓒ Ⓓ
25. Ⓐ Ⓑ Ⓒ Ⓓ
26. Ⓐ Ⓑ Ⓒ Ⓓ
27. Ⓐ Ⓑ Ⓒ Ⓓ
28. Ⓐ Ⓑ Ⓒ Ⓓ
29. Ⓐ Ⓑ Ⓒ Ⓓ
30. Ⓐ Ⓑ Ⓒ Ⓓ
31. Ⓐ Ⓑ Ⓒ Ⓓ
32. Ⓐ Ⓑ Ⓒ Ⓓ
33. Ⓐ Ⓑ Ⓒ Ⓓ

34. Ⓐ Ⓑ Ⓒ Ⓓ
35. Ⓐ Ⓑ Ⓒ Ⓓ
36. Ⓐ Ⓑ Ⓒ Ⓓ
37. Ⓐ Ⓑ Ⓒ Ⓓ
38. Ⓐ Ⓑ Ⓒ Ⓓ
39. Ⓐ Ⓑ Ⓒ Ⓓ
40. Ⓐ Ⓑ Ⓒ Ⓓ
41. Ⓐ Ⓑ Ⓒ Ⓓ
42. Ⓐ Ⓑ Ⓒ Ⓓ
43. Ⓐ Ⓑ Ⓒ Ⓓ
44. Ⓐ Ⓑ Ⓒ Ⓓ
45. Ⓐ Ⓑ Ⓒ Ⓓ
46. Ⓐ Ⓑ Ⓒ Ⓓ
47. Ⓐ Ⓑ Ⓒ Ⓓ
48. Ⓐ Ⓑ Ⓒ Ⓓ
49. Ⓐ Ⓑ Ⓒ Ⓓ
50. Ⓐ Ⓑ Ⓒ Ⓓ
51. Ⓐ Ⓑ Ⓒ Ⓓ
52. Ⓐ Ⓑ Ⓒ Ⓓ
53. Ⓐ Ⓑ Ⓒ Ⓓ
54. Ⓐ Ⓑ Ⓒ Ⓓ
55. Ⓐ Ⓑ Ⓒ Ⓓ
56. Ⓐ Ⓑ Ⓒ Ⓓ
57. Ⓐ Ⓑ Ⓒ Ⓓ
58. Ⓐ Ⓑ Ⓒ Ⓓ
59. Ⓐ Ⓑ Ⓒ Ⓓ
60. Ⓐ Ⓑ Ⓒ Ⓓ
61. Ⓐ Ⓑ Ⓒ Ⓓ
62. Ⓐ Ⓑ Ⓒ Ⓓ
63. Ⓐ Ⓑ Ⓒ Ⓓ
64. Ⓐ Ⓑ Ⓒ Ⓓ
65. Ⓐ Ⓑ Ⓒ Ⓓ

Physical Sciences

66. Ⓐ Ⓑ Ⓒ Ⓓ
67. Ⓐ Ⓑ Ⓒ Ⓓ
68. Ⓐ Ⓑ Ⓒ Ⓓ
69. Ⓐ Ⓑ Ⓒ Ⓓ
70. Ⓐ Ⓑ Ⓒ Ⓓ
71. Ⓐ Ⓑ Ⓒ Ⓓ
72. Ⓐ Ⓑ Ⓒ Ⓓ
73. Ⓐ Ⓑ Ⓒ Ⓓ
74. Ⓐ Ⓑ Ⓒ Ⓓ
75. Ⓐ Ⓑ Ⓒ Ⓓ
76. Ⓐ Ⓑ Ⓒ Ⓓ
77. Ⓐ Ⓑ Ⓒ Ⓓ
78. Ⓐ Ⓑ Ⓒ Ⓓ
79. Ⓐ Ⓑ Ⓒ Ⓓ
80. Ⓐ Ⓑ Ⓒ Ⓓ
81. Ⓐ Ⓑ Ⓒ Ⓓ
82. Ⓐ Ⓑ Ⓒ Ⓓ
83. Ⓐ Ⓑ Ⓒ Ⓓ
84. Ⓐ Ⓑ Ⓒ Ⓓ
85. Ⓐ Ⓑ Ⓒ Ⓓ
86. Ⓐ Ⓑ Ⓒ Ⓓ
87. Ⓐ Ⓑ Ⓒ Ⓓ
88. Ⓐ Ⓑ Ⓒ Ⓓ
89. Ⓐ Ⓑ Ⓒ Ⓓ
90. Ⓐ Ⓑ Ⓒ Ⓓ
91. Ⓐ Ⓑ Ⓒ Ⓓ
92. Ⓐ Ⓑ Ⓒ Ⓓ
93. Ⓐ Ⓑ Ⓒ Ⓓ
94. Ⓐ Ⓑ Ⓒ Ⓓ
95. Ⓐ Ⓑ Ⓒ Ⓓ
96. Ⓐ Ⓑ Ⓒ Ⓓ
97. Ⓐ Ⓑ Ⓒ Ⓓ

98. Ⓐ Ⓑ Ⓒ Ⓓ
99. Ⓐ Ⓑ Ⓒ Ⓓ
100. Ⓐ Ⓑ Ⓒ Ⓓ
101. Ⓐ Ⓑ Ⓒ Ⓓ
102. Ⓐ Ⓑ Ⓒ Ⓓ
103. Ⓐ Ⓑ Ⓒ Ⓓ
104. Ⓐ Ⓑ Ⓒ Ⓓ
105. Ⓐ Ⓑ Ⓒ Ⓓ
106. Ⓐ Ⓑ Ⓒ Ⓓ
107. Ⓐ Ⓑ Ⓒ Ⓓ
108. Ⓐ Ⓑ Ⓒ Ⓓ
109. Ⓐ Ⓑ Ⓒ Ⓓ
110. Ⓐ Ⓑ Ⓒ Ⓓ
111. Ⓐ Ⓑ Ⓒ Ⓓ
112. Ⓐ Ⓑ Ⓒ Ⓓ
113. Ⓐ Ⓑ Ⓒ Ⓓ
114. Ⓐ Ⓑ Ⓒ Ⓓ
115. Ⓐ Ⓑ Ⓒ Ⓓ
116. Ⓐ Ⓑ Ⓒ Ⓓ
117. Ⓐ Ⓑ Ⓒ Ⓓ
118. Ⓐ Ⓑ Ⓒ Ⓓ
119. Ⓐ Ⓑ Ⓒ Ⓓ
120. Ⓐ Ⓑ Ⓒ Ⓓ
121. Ⓐ Ⓑ Ⓒ Ⓓ
122. Ⓐ Ⓑ Ⓒ Ⓓ
123. Ⓐ Ⓑ Ⓒ Ⓓ
124. Ⓐ Ⓑ Ⓒ Ⓓ
125. Ⓐ Ⓑ Ⓒ Ⓓ
126. Ⓐ Ⓑ Ⓒ Ⓓ
127. Ⓐ Ⓑ Ⓒ Ⓓ
128. Ⓐ Ⓑ Ⓒ Ⓓ
129. Ⓐ Ⓑ Ⓒ Ⓓ
130. Ⓐ Ⓑ Ⓒ Ⓓ
131. Ⓐ Ⓑ Ⓒ Ⓓ
132. Ⓐ Ⓑ Ⓒ Ⓓ
133. Ⓐ Ⓑ Ⓒ Ⓓ
134. Ⓐ Ⓑ Ⓒ Ⓓ

135. Ⓐ Ⓑ Ⓒ Ⓓ
136. Ⓐ Ⓑ Ⓒ Ⓓ
137. Ⓐ Ⓑ Ⓒ Ⓓ
138. Ⓐ Ⓑ Ⓒ Ⓓ
139. Ⓐ Ⓑ Ⓒ Ⓓ
140. Ⓐ Ⓑ Ⓒ Ⓓ
141. Ⓐ Ⓑ Ⓒ Ⓓ
142. Ⓐ Ⓑ Ⓒ Ⓓ

Biological Sciences

143. Ⓐ Ⓑ Ⓒ Ⓓ
144. Ⓐ Ⓑ Ⓒ Ⓓ
145. Ⓐ Ⓑ Ⓒ Ⓓ
146. Ⓐ Ⓑ Ⓒ Ⓓ
147. Ⓐ Ⓑ Ⓒ Ⓓ
148. Ⓐ Ⓑ Ⓒ Ⓓ
149. Ⓐ Ⓑ Ⓒ Ⓓ
150. Ⓐ Ⓑ Ⓒ Ⓓ
151. Ⓐ Ⓑ Ⓒ Ⓓ
152. Ⓐ Ⓑ Ⓒ Ⓓ
153. Ⓐ Ⓑ Ⓒ Ⓓ
154. Ⓐ Ⓑ Ⓒ Ⓓ
155. Ⓐ Ⓑ Ⓒ Ⓓ
156. Ⓐ Ⓑ Ⓒ Ⓓ
157. Ⓐ Ⓑ Ⓒ Ⓓ
158. Ⓐ Ⓑ Ⓒ Ⓓ
159. Ⓐ Ⓑ Ⓒ Ⓓ
160. Ⓐ Ⓑ Ⓒ Ⓓ
161. Ⓐ Ⓑ Ⓒ Ⓓ
162. Ⓐ Ⓑ Ⓒ Ⓓ
163. Ⓐ Ⓑ Ⓒ Ⓓ
164. Ⓐ Ⓑ Ⓒ Ⓓ
165. Ⓐ Ⓑ Ⓒ Ⓓ
166. Ⓐ Ⓑ Ⓒ Ⓓ
167. Ⓐ Ⓑ Ⓒ Ⓓ
168. Ⓐ Ⓑ Ⓒ Ⓓ
169. Ⓐ Ⓑ Ⓒ Ⓓ

170. Ⓐ Ⓑ Ⓒ Ⓓ
171. Ⓐ Ⓑ Ⓒ Ⓓ
172. Ⓐ Ⓑ Ⓒ Ⓓ
173. Ⓐ Ⓑ Ⓒ Ⓓ
174. Ⓐ Ⓑ Ⓒ Ⓓ
175. Ⓐ Ⓑ Ⓒ Ⓓ
176. Ⓐ Ⓑ Ⓒ Ⓓ
177. Ⓐ Ⓑ Ⓒ Ⓓ
178. Ⓐ Ⓑ Ⓒ Ⓓ
179. Ⓐ Ⓑ Ⓒ Ⓓ
180. Ⓐ Ⓑ Ⓒ Ⓓ
181. Ⓐ Ⓑ Ⓒ Ⓓ
182. Ⓐ Ⓑ Ⓒ Ⓓ
183. Ⓐ Ⓑ Ⓒ Ⓓ
184. Ⓐ Ⓑ Ⓒ Ⓓ
185. Ⓐ Ⓑ Ⓒ Ⓓ
186. Ⓐ Ⓑ Ⓒ Ⓓ
187. Ⓐ Ⓑ Ⓒ Ⓓ
188. Ⓐ Ⓑ Ⓒ Ⓓ
189. Ⓐ Ⓑ Ⓒ Ⓓ
190. Ⓐ Ⓑ Ⓒ Ⓓ
191. Ⓐ Ⓑ Ⓒ Ⓓ
192. Ⓐ Ⓑ Ⓒ Ⓓ
193. Ⓐ Ⓑ Ⓒ Ⓓ
194. Ⓐ Ⓑ Ⓒ Ⓓ
195. Ⓐ Ⓑ Ⓒ Ⓓ
196. Ⓐ Ⓑ Ⓒ Ⓓ
197. Ⓐ Ⓑ Ⓒ Ⓓ
198. Ⓐ Ⓑ Ⓒ Ⓓ
199. Ⓐ Ⓑ Ⓒ Ⓓ
200. Ⓐ Ⓑ Ⓒ Ⓓ
201. Ⓐ Ⓑ Ⓒ Ⓓ
202. Ⓐ Ⓑ Ⓒ Ⓓ
203. Ⓐ Ⓑ Ⓒ Ⓓ
204. Ⓐ Ⓑ Ⓒ Ⓓ
205. Ⓐ Ⓑ Ⓒ Ⓓ
206. Ⓐ Ⓑ Ⓒ Ⓓ

207. Ⓐ Ⓑ Ⓒ Ⓓ

208. Ⓐ Ⓑ Ⓒ Ⓓ

209. Ⓐ Ⓑ Ⓒ Ⓓ

210. Ⓐ Ⓑ Ⓒ Ⓓ

211. Ⓐ Ⓑ Ⓒ Ⓓ

212. Ⓐ Ⓑ Ⓒ Ⓓ

213. Ⓐ Ⓑ Ⓒ Ⓓ

214. Ⓐ Ⓑ Ⓒ Ⓓ

215. Ⓐ Ⓑ Ⓒ Ⓓ

216. Ⓐ Ⓑ Ⓒ Ⓓ

217. Ⓐ Ⓑ Ⓒ Ⓓ

218. Ⓐ Ⓑ Ⓒ Ⓓ

219. Ⓐ Ⓑ Ⓒ Ⓓ

CHAPTER 13

Scoring of the Practice MCAT

- Obtaining Raw and Scaled Scores

- Significance of the Conversion to MCAT Scaled Scores

- Analysis of the Verbal Reasoning Section

- Analysis of the Science Sections

- Analysis of the Writing Sample Section

The new Medical College Admission Test (MCAT) was introduced in 1991 to overcome concern that the examination promoted rote memorization rather than thinking skills. To a large degree, the examination writers have achieved this goal, and for this reason, examinees can no longer prepare for the MCAT simply by memorizing facts. This chapter provides an analysis of the sample test in Chapter 12, allowing you to identify areas for content review.

This chapter contains:

- The answer key for the practice MCAT

- A table for converting the percent scores to the MCAT 15-point scale

- An analysis of the Verbal Reasoning section

- An analysis of the Physical Sciences and Biological Sciences sections

- An analysis of the Writing Sample section

● ● ●
OBTAINING RAW AND SCALED SCORES

MCAT Practice Exam Answer Key—Obtaining a Raw Score

Using the following answer key, mark the incorrect answers on the answer sheet. Subtract the number of questions answered incorrectly from the total number of questions in each section to obtain the raw (percent) score in the Verbal Reasoning, Physical Sciences, and Biological Sciences sections. The Writing Sample is scored separately.

PRACTICE MCAT ANSWER KEY

Item	Answer	Item	Answer	Item	Answer
Verbal Reasoning		28.	B	56.	B
1.	D	29.	C	57.	C
2.	A	30.	C	58.	A
3.	B	31.	B	59.	B
4.	B	32.	A	60.	B
5.	B	33.	A	61.	A
6.	A	34.	A	62.	C
7.	C	35.	B	63.	C
8.	A	36.	D	64.	B
9.	C	37.	C	65.	C
10.	C	38.	B	**Physical Sciences**	
11.	C	39.	A	66.	C
12.	B	40.	B	67.	C
13.	C	41.	B	68.	A
14.	D	42.	C	69.	C
15.	B	43.	C	70.	C
16.	C	44.	C	71.	B
17.	B	45.	D	72.	C
18.	B	46.	B	73.	D
19.	A	47.	B	74.	C
20.	B	48.	B	75.	B
21.	D	49.	A	76.	B
22.	C	50.	C	77.	B
23.	C	51.	D	78.	A
24.	C	52.	D	79.	B
25.	D	53.	B	80.	B
26.	B	54.	A	81.	C
27.	C	55.	B	82.	C

(Table continued on the following page)

83.	B	121.	C	158.	A
84.	B	122.	A	159.	C
85.	C	123.	D	160.	A
86.	A	124.	C	161.	C
87.	C	125.	C	162.	B
88.	A	126.	B	163.	C
89.	D	127.	D	164.	C
90.	D	128.	D	165.	C
91.	C	129.	A	166.	A
92.	D	130.	B	167.	C
93.	D	131.	C	168.	A
94.	A	132.	D	169.	C
95.	B	133.	D	170.	C
96.	A	134.	A	171.	A
97.	C	135.	A	172.	A
98.	B	136.	D	173.	B
99.	C	137.	B	174.	A
100.	D	138.	B	175.	C
101.	D	139.	A	176.	C
102.	B	140.	C	177.	D
103.	D	141.	A	178.	C
104.	D	**Biological Sciences**		179.	D
105.	C	142.	C	180.	B
106.	C	143.	D	181.	D
107.	A	144.	B	182.	A
108.	C	145.	B	183.	C
109.	A	146.	B	184.	D
110.	C	147.	D	185.	B
111.	B	148.	C	186.	C
112.	C	149.	A	187.	A
113.	C	150.	B	188.	B
114.	D	151.	B	189.	D
115.	B	152.	A	190.	A
116.	B	153.	B	191.	A
117.	B	154.	B	192.	B
118.	C	155.	B	193.	A
119.	A	156.	B	194.	A
120.	D	157.	D	195.	D

196.	B	204.	C	212.	D
197.	C	205.	D	213.	C
198.	B	206.	C	214.	B
199.	C	207.	C	215.	D
200.	D	208.	A	216.	A
201.	C	209.	C	217.	C
202.	A	210.	D	218.	D
203.	B	211.	B	219.	B

Converting Raw Scores to MCAT Scaled Scores

Table 13–1 converts the total raw score for each section to an MCAT scaled score. First, find the range of raw scores for each section that corresponds to the number of questions answered correctly, then look at the scaled score in the row next to the range. This number is the scaled score for that section. Next to the scaled score column is a column showing the percentile rank for the raw score range. The percentile rank indicates the percentage of students who scored either above or below the score. For instance, if a student had a scaled score of 8 on the Verbal Reasoning section, the associated percentile rank of 34–43 means that 34% of students scored below this score and 57% scored above it. The percentile rank allows students to compare their scores against those of other students. The relationship between percentile rank scaled and raw score will vary from exam to exam.

● ● ●

TABLE 13-1. MCAT Raw Scores, Scaled Scores, and Percentile Ranks

Verbal Reasoning			Physical Sciences			Biological Sciences		
Raw Score	Scaled Score	Percentile Rank	Raw Score	Scaled Score	Percentile Rank	Raw Score	Scaled Score	Percentile Rank
			71–77	13–15	97–99	71–77	12–15	91–99
			66–70	12	91–95	66–70	11	80–89
61–65	11–15	79–99	61–65	11	83–89	61–65	10	70–78
56–60	10	59–74	56–60	10	75–81	56–60	9	59–68
51–55	9	45–56	51–55	9–10	67–74	51–55	9	49–57
46–50	8	34–43	46–50	9	59–65	46–50	8	39–47
41–45	7	27–33	41–45	8	49–57	41–45	8	30–37
36–40	6	19–25	36–40	8	40–48	36–40	7	22–29
31–35	5	14–18	31–35	7	30–38	31–35	6	15–21
26–30	4	9–12	26–30	6	19–28	26–30	5	9–14
21–25	4	4–7	21–25	5–6	9–17	21–25	4	4–8
0–20	1–3	1–3	0–20	1–4	1–8	0–20	1–3	1–3

• • •

SIGNIFICANCE OF THE CONVERSION TO MCAT SCALED SCORES

The relation between raw scores and scaled scores is U shaped. In other words, it takes fewer correct answers at the lower and higher ends of the scale to increase the scaled score than it does in the middle of the scale.

The inflection point in the Verbal Reasoning section is particularly low. In other words, fewer correct answers are needed to increase the scaled score at the high end, especially when compared with the science sections. For example, if a student has a raw score of 60 in Verbal Reasoning, her scaled score is 10. On the other hand, if her raw score is 65, then her scaled score is 15. An increase of five correct answers, or only 8% of the sixty-five total answers, translates into a five-point, or 33%, increase in the scaled score.

Similar relations are found in the science sections, although the effect is not as dramatic. For example, a student who has the same raw score of 60 in the Physical Sciences section would have a scaled score of 10. However, in this case, the addition of five correct answers would increase the scaled score by only one point, to 11.

This example illustrates another point, previously mentioned in Chapter 11, that whenever a scaled score is used, there must be a transition point between scores. If, in this last example, the raw score increased from 60 to 66, rather than to 65, the scaled score would be 12 rather than 11. The difference in this case is just one correct answer.

The practical importance of the relation between scaled scores and the number of questions answered correctly is twofold. First, it is important to use every means available to answer every question correctly. Chapter 15 describes test-taking techniques that can help to improve a student's MCAT score. For instance, if a student is running out of time, he can fill in all of the blanks with Bs. A student who uses this approach will answer at least 27% of the questions correctly. One more correct answer, however arrived at, can increase the scaled score by a full point at any point on the scale. Secondly, at either extreme of the scale, only a few correct answers can increase the scaled score by several points.

A student whose practice MCAT score is lower than she wanted should remember that a better score might depend on answering only a few more questions correctly. A person who scores 7 or 8 across the board may have missed only 10 more questions in each section of the test compared with someone who achieves a score of 10 across the board. This difference translates into only about 13% of the questions on the examination.

A student whose score on the practice MCAT is between 7 and 10 probably can add two points to her scaled MCAT score after a thorough review. However, a student who scores less than 7 on the practice MCAT should plan to work harder to improve her actual MCAT score. A section score of 2–5 indicates problems that may go beyond mere content weakness.

There are many reasons for scores this low. These range from reading or learning disabilities that can hamper a person's review and affect his test-taking abilities to an inability to concentrate during the examination. The first problem usually requires the services of a professional learning disabilities specialist, but the latter problem is the most common cause of poor MCAT scores. Inability to concentrate is usually manifested as anxiety, which is readily treated. Most individuals can reduce their anxiety through adequate preparation. If a student reviews the content material completely and realizes that only slightly more than one-half of the questions need to be answered correctly to obtain a fairly good score, then she should have the confidence required to maintain her concentration during the examination.

Even when they are fully prepared for the test, some students cannot reduce their anxiety to manageable levels. These students may benefit from the stress reduction techniques discussed in Chapter 17.

● ● ●
ANALYSIS OF THE VERBAL REASONING SECTION

Circle the number of each missed question listed below. The questions are divided into four categories according to the performance criteria described in the *MCAT Student Manual* (Association of American Medical Colleges, Washington DC). The questions that meet each of these criteria are listed after the description of that criterion. The four criteria are arranged in order from least to most difficult in terms of the cognitive skills needed to answer the questions.

1. **Comprehension.** These questions test the ability to recognize key information or concepts contained in a passage. Some questions test material explicitly stated in the passage; other questions test valid inferences that may be drawn from the passage. These criteria are met by questions 1, 2, 3, 4, 5, 6, 7, 8, 9, 10, 11, 12, 13, 14, 15, 16, 17, 19, 20, 21, 22, 23, 24, 25, 26, 27, 28, 29, 30, 31, 32, 33, 34, 35, 36, 37, 38, 39, 40, 41, 43, 44, 45, 46, 47, 49, 51, 53, 54, 55, 56, 57, 59, 60, 62, and 65. **Total number of questions in Category 1:** 56.

2. **Evaluation.** These questions require the student to consider the accuracy, consistency, relevance, or reliability of information contained in the passage. These criteria are met by questions 42, 48, and 61. **Total number of questions in Category 2:** 3.

3. **Application.** These questions require the student to use her understanding of the passage to solve a problem or interpret a hypothetical situation outside the immediate scope of the passage. These criteria are met by questions 18, 50, 52, 58, and 63. **Total number of questions in Category 3:** 5.

4. **Incorporation of new information.** These questions require the student to reevaluate the content of the passage in light of new information. These criteria are met by question 64. **Total number of questions in Category 4:** 1.

Most of the questions on the practice MCAT are Category 1. A typical MCAT examination also contains primarily Category 1 questions. Many students consider Category 1 questions the easiest to answer. Answering two-thirds of these questions correctly will lead to a score of 7 or 8 on this section. To achieve a double-digit score, a student must do well with this type of question as well as with questions at higher cognitive levels.

A person with college-level reading ability should be able to answer Category 1 questions with little difficulty. An inability to answer these questions, given adequate testing time, may indicate a fundamental problem with reading comprehension. People who have trouble with Category 1 questions also typically score low on other measures of reading ability, such as standardized reading tests. These students may lack sufficient training in reading English. On the other hand, some students can score well on this section, given adequate testing time, but not under the stringently timed conditions of the MCAT. These students may use inappropriate test-taking strategies (e.g., wasting time reading nonessential parts of the passages, reading passages too many times), or they may have some psychologically or physiologically based reading disability, which may vary from disabling anxiety to dyslexia.

Students who have inadequate test-taking skills usually respond rapidly to training. A few hours of test-taking instruction from a learning skills professional can improve a student's ability to work through the passages. With adequate training and practice, some students have increased their reading scores by as much as nine points over a 6-week period. Chapter 15 discusses techniques for improving speed in analyzing passages and questions and answering difficult questions. Students who work to improve their test-taking ability often experience a concomitant reduction in anxiety that improves their ability to concentrate and results in a further improvement in their score.

Students who lack basic skills or have acute psychologic or physiologic problems face a different challenge. Basic skills can be improved through a course in English composition and additional reading. Diagnosis of a psychologically or physiologically based reading disability requires analysis by a professional, and affected students may need to take the MCAT under special conditions. Fortunately, few students have these problems.

A student's scoring potential is diagnosed as follows:

- A student whose score is 9 or greater should have no problem with the Verbal Reasoning section of the MCAT. To gain more experience, the student can take other simulated examinations. Even students whose scores are consistently high may benefit from the following exercise. Determine the cognitive level of each missed question. If most of the missed questions occur at the higher cognitive levels, analyze what each question really asks and why the answer chosen is incorrect. This analysis may provide insight into the type of reasoning required and lead to better performance on the MCAT. Test-taking techniques for the Verbal Reasoning section are outlined in Chapter 15.

- A student who scored 7 or less should take other simulated examinations to determine whether this score is consistent. If it is, he should take the examinations again, but not under timed conditions. If his score improves significantly, he may have inadequate test-taking skills. The test-taking suggestions given in Chapter 15 can help. After he masters this material, he should take a practice verbal reasoning test under stringently timed conditions. For the most meaningful comparison, the second test should be taken from a book that contains several examinations, one of which the student has already taken. Taking two examinations from one source increases the likelihood that the examinations are at similar levels of difficulty. The most likely outcome will be a dramatic improvement in score (e.g., 9 or greater). If this improvement occurs, the student should continue as described earlier for students who score in this range initially. A student whose score remains low should seek professional help, for example, from a learning skills expert at her college or university.

● ● ●
ANALYSIS OF THE SCIENCE SECTIONS

When analyzing scores on the science sections of the practice MCAT, both the content areas and the cognitive levels of the questions must be considered. The questions on the practice examination are grouped first by content area and then by cognitive level. The questions are arranged according to the major content areas described in the *MCAT Student Manual*. Bloom's *Taxonomy of Cognition* was used to group the questions by cognitive level. The breakdown of the groups is followed by an explanation of how to use this information for review.

Content Area

The major content areas of questions on the practice MCAT follow:

Physical sciences

CHEMISTRY

1. **Stoichiometry:** Question 69. **Total number of questions:** 1.

2. **Electronic structure and the periodic table:** Questions 81, 82, 83, 84, 85, 86, 87, and 88. **Total number of questions:** 8.

3. **Bonding:** Questions 73, 74, 75, 76, 77, 78, 79, 80, 118, 119, 120, 121, and 122. **Total number of questions:** 13.

4. **Phases and phase equilibria:** Questions 123, 124, 125, 126, 127, 128, and 131. **Total number of questions:** 7.

5. **Acids and bases:** Questions 66, 67, 68, 70, 71, 72, 129, 132, and 133. **Total number of questions:** 9.

6. **Thermodynamics and thermochemistry:** Question 130. **Total number of questions:** 1.

7. **Electrochemistry:** Question 134. **Total number of questions:** 1.

PHYSICS

1. **Force and motion, gravitation:** Question 135. **Total number of questions:** 1.

2. **Equilibrium and momentum:** Questions 93, 94, 95, 96, 97, 98, 99, 100, 101, 102, 103, 104, 105, 106, and 107. **Total number of questions:** 15.

3. **Work and energy:** Questions 89, 90, 91, 92, and 138. **Total number of questions:** 5.

4. **Wave characteristics and periodic motion:** Questions 113, 114, 115, 116, and 117. **Total number of questions:** 5.

5. **Sound:** Questions 139 and 140. **Total number of questions:** 2.

6. **Electrostatics and electromagnetism:** Questions 108, 109, 110, 111, and 112. **Total number of questions:** 5.

7. **Electric circuits:** Question 137. **Total number of questions:** 1.

8. **Light and geometrical optics:** Questions 141 and 142. **Total number of questions:** 2.

9. **Atomic and nuclear structure:** Question 136. **Total number of questions:** 1.

Biological sciences

BIOLOGY

1. **Microbiology:** Questions 155, 156, 157, 158, 159, and 160. **Total number of questions:** 6.

2. **Nervous and endocrine systems:** Questions 206 and 207. **Total number of questions:** 2.

3. **Circulatory, lymphatic, and immune systems:** Questions 161, 162, 163, 164, 165, 166, 167, 175, 176, 177, 178, 179, 180, and 209. **Total number of questions:** 14.

4. **Digestive and excretory systems:** Question 208. **Total number of questions:** 1.

5. **Muscle and skeletal systems:** Questions 168, 169, 170, 171, 172, 173, and 174. **Total number of questions:** 7.

6. **Respiratory and skin systems:** Questions 143, 144, 145, 146, 147, 148, and 149. **Total number of questions:** 7.

7. **Reproductive system and development:** Question 210. **Total number of questions:** 1.

8. **Genetics and evolution:** Questions 150, 151, 152, 153, 154, and 211. **Total number of questions:** 6.

ORGANIC CHEMISTRY

1. **Biologic molecules:** Questions 181, 182, 183, 184, 185, 186, 187, 188, 189, 190, and 216. **Total number of questions:** 11.

2. **Oxygen-containing compounds:** Questions 191, 192, 193, 194, 195, and 212. **Total number of questions:** 6.

3. **Hydrocarbons:** Questions 213, 217, 218, and 219. **Total number of questions:** 4.

4. **Separations and purifications:** Questions 196, 197, 198, 199, 200, 201, 202, 203, 204, and 205. **Total number of questions:** 10.

5. **Use of spectroscopy in structural identification:** Questions 214 and 215. **Total number of questions:** 2.

Check the answer sheet against the question numbers listed after each subcategory and determine the percent score by dividing the number of questions answered correctly by the total number of questions listed at the end of each subcategory. This analysis identifies relative strengths and weaknesses in each content area. For example, in the chemistry section, if a student answered only five of the thirteen questions on bonding correctly (38%), he should review this area intensely. On the other hand, if he answered 12 of these 13 questions correctly (92%), he probably understands this material well and needs only regular review of the topic. A score of 50% or greater indicates a fairly strong understanding of the basic material, whereas a score of 33% or less indicates the need for more intense study.

The use of appropriate review materials helps students to retain what they know and refamiliarize themselves with what they have forgotten over time. It is not wise to neglect areas of relative strengths because forgetting details can lead to a lower score. On the other hand, it is important to concentrate on areas in which the score is 33% or less. Relearning science material is a time-consuming process. See Chapter 14 for further information on interpreting scores and scheduling review time.

A student who scores poorly on both science sections probably has reading or test-taking problems or is completely unfamiliar with the content material. The analysis described in the discussion of the Verbal Reasoning section can help to identify the problem. A student who misses many questions at lower cognitive levels probably lacks content knowledge and would benefit from a content-based review course or some refresher science courses at the undergraduate level.

Cognitive Level

In this section, the science questions on the practice MCAT are arranged according to cognitive level, using Bloom's scale. Interpretation is provided to help students evaluate their potential performance and plan their preparation for the actual MCAT.

1. **Knowledge.** Answering a question at this level requires rote memorization and simple recollection of fact. Most standardized test questions are at this level. Most MCAT questions that fall into this category are either stand-alone questions or questions that relate to informational passages. These passages present information in the format of a textbook or a journal article. The questions assume some background knowledge, but also contain information that may be new. Questions that can be assumed to be answerable on the basis of background knowledge are included in this cognitive level. Questions at this level generally require the least time to answer, so completing them rapidly allows more time to work on questions at higher, more difficult levels of cognition. Questions at this level are 70, 71, 72, 76, 77, 78, 79, 80, 82, 88, 94, 123, 124, 125, 129, 130, 133, 139, 140, 141, 142, 143, 144, 145, 148, 149, 152, 153, 154, 157, 163, 165, 166, 167, 178, 179, 181, 183, 184, 187, 190, 192, 203, 206, 207, 208, 209, 210, 212, 214, 215, 217, and 219. **Total number of questions: 53.**

2. **Comprehension.** Answering a question at this level requires interpretation of what is read. These questions are also commonly found associated with informational passages. However, the questions pertain to facts that are not likely to be known to the average undergraduate student and therefore must be answered by closely reading and correctly interpreting the information in the passage. Questions at this level are 74, 75, 81, 83, 84, 93, 96, 97, 98, 99, 100, 101, 102, 108, 109, 110, 111, 122, 126, 128, 137, 146, 150, 151, 156, 161, 162, 164, 169, 170, 172, 173, 176, 177, 180, 182, 185, 188, 189, 191, 196, 197, 198, 200, 201, 202, 211, 213, and 216. **Total number of questions: 49.**

3. **Application.** Answering a question at this level involves the use of familiar information in a new setting, usually by asking the student to apply previously known information to solve a specific new problem. Data are often presented in tables or graphs that must be analyzed to obtain a specific answer. To do well on this type of question, a student should know how to solve specific types of problems (e.g., how to balance a half-cell equation, what equations are used to describe inertia). Students should also pay close attention to the problem-solving methods described in Chapter 15. Because of limitations imposed by the examination format, timing restrictions, and level of knowledge tested, these problem-solving exercises are usually easier to solve than classroom exercises. Questions at this level are 66, 67, 68, 73, 85, 86, 87, 89, 90, 91, 92, 95, 103, 104, 105, 106, 107, 112, 113, 114, 115, 116, 117, 120, 127, 131, 132, 134, 135, 136, 138, 175, 193, 199, 204, 205, and 218. **Total number of questions: 37.**

4. **Analysis.** To answer questions at this level, a student must identify errors in logic or differentiate among facts, opinions, assumptions, hypotheses, and conclusions. These questions tend to be the most frustrating to students, who may believe that their knowledge is not being tested. However, these questions test reading comprehension and critical thinking abilities. These questions are commonly associated with passages that describe a research study. The student is expected to understand the rationale for the study as well as the validity of the methods and conclusions. Questions at this level are 69, 147, 155, 158, 159, 160, 168, 171, 174, and 194. **Total number of questions: 10.**

5. **Synthesis.** Questions at this level require the student to create something new to solve a problem. Questions on standardized examinations, such as the MCAT, rarely achieve this level of cognition. Questions at this level are 118, 119, 121, 186, and 195. **Total number of questions:** 5.

It is important to track the number of questions missed at each cognitive level, as in the content section. A student who generally misses questions at the higher cognitive levels probably has poor reading and critical thinking skills. On the other hand, missing many questions at lower cognitive levels indicates a lack of content knowledge.

A well-informed student can achieve a maximum score of 7 or 8 on the basis of content alone, primarily working at the level of rote memorization. Similarly, a student with minimal content knowledge, but acute test-taking and critical thinking skills, can also score within this range. However, to achieve a double-digit score, a student must both know facts and be able to reason well and read critically. The problem-solving skills described in Chapter 14 suggest specific methods for working through these questions. Following these suggestions can lead to a higher score.

● ● ●
ANALYSIS OF THE WRITING SAMPLE SECTION

Self-scoring of this section is not advised because it is difficult to be objective. Students should ask someone who is familiar with the MCAT to score this section. If a student does not know anyone who is familiar with the MCAT, she can ask someone with an English degree or major to score this section. Chapter 11 describes the scoring for the Writing Sample.

Unlike the other sections of the MCAT, it is not important to attain a high score on the essay section. However, it is important not to get a low score. The writing section is used primarily to exclude candidates. For this reason, it is important to score at least M, or better yet, N or O. Chapter 15 offers suggestions for writing the essays.

CHAPTER 14

Review Methods and Study Skills for the MCAT

REVIEW METHODS

Chapters 12 and 13 provide a full practice Medical College Admission Test (MCAT) and describe scoring methods. Chapter 13 describes both the percentage and scaled scores for the practice MCAT. This chapter describes a structured method for preparing for the MCAT.

Pretesting

Students who took the practice MCAT have already taken an important step. Students who did not take the practice MCAT should take the practice test before continuing with this chapter. The ideal pretest can be broken down into significant parts to pinpoint the student's strengths and weaknesses (e.g., in the practice MCAT, scores can be derived for microbiology and the nervous and endocrine systems in the Biological Sciences section). Students should take the practice MCAT, then perform a simple percentage scoring of the entire test as well as a percentage scoring for each subsection.

Scoring the Pretest

Students can use their scores to identify their strengths and weaknesses according to the following scale:

90%–100%	Very strong
80%–90%	Strong
70%–80%	Passing
60%–70%	Barely passing
50%–60%	Not passing, but the student understands the basics of the subject
40%–50%	Fairly weak
30%–40%	Weak
20%–30%	Very weak; student does not understand the basics of the subject
Below 20%	Within guessing range; student does not know the subject

For example, based on this scale, a student might find that her percentage score is 55% for the Verbal Reasoning section, 30% for the Physical Sciences section, and 60% for the Biological Sciences section. These scores indicate that the student's strongest area is Biological Sciences and her weakest area is Physical Sciences. This information is valuable, but does not help the student to plan an effective review. The subsection scores are more helpful for this type of planning.

The same scale can be used to analyze the scores for each of the subsections within the test. For example, if a student has the following scores for three subsections of the Biological Sciences section—circulatory, lymphatic, and immune systems, 45%; digestive and excretory systems, 25%; and respiratory and skin systems, 65%—the student's weakest area is digestive and excretory systems, and his strongest area is respiratory and skin systems.

In determining how to proceed, the student must consider two factors. The first factor is where the scores fall on the scale shown earlier. If most of the scores are between 40% and 60%, then the student has achieved the ideal initial level of performance and is ready to increase his scores by conducting a thorough review. However, if some or all of the student's scores are between 15% and 40%, then a review of these topics is not adequate. The student must learn or relearn this material. A score within this range indicates that the student does not fully understand the material. Attempting to memorize it will only lead to frustration and failure.

The results of this assessment determine the second factor, allocation of time for review. Students with scores of 40% to 60% require less time for review than students with lower scores. Students with extremely low scores should allocate substantial time for study. These students may benefit from a refresher course as well. The student should also evaluate his other activities. With class and study hours, paid work, social activities, volunteer work, household responsibilities, and personal business, the average student has little time to review for the MCAT. To allow more time for review, many students take a light academic course load in the semester or quarter before the MCAT is administered.

A score of 40% to 60% or greater indicates that the student understands the material well. A lower score indicates that the student does not know or understand the major principles or concepts. Therefore, if a student has limited time for review, she should concentrate on subjects on which her pretest score is 40% to 60%. The student should study the general principles of subjects on which her pretest score is less than 40%. On subjects on which she scores greater than 60%, she should focus on incorporating more details into her knowledge base.

Using Time Wisely

The most important element to control in any review is time. The student should use the percentage scores to determine how much time to spend on each subject and each subsection. The student should spend more time on subjects on which her pretest score is 40% to 60% than on subjects on which her score is higher or lower. The section on time management describes how to create an effective study schedule.

Reinforcing the Review

Studies show that as much as 50% of what a person sees or hears is forgotten within 1 hour. This process usually continues until, at the end of 2 weeks, approximately 80% of the memory is forgotten. The only way to prevent this process from occurring is to reinforce the memory.

Knowledge can be reinforced in many ways, but the best method is to use review notes. Review notes are short, concise notes taken from text or lectures. Review notes are similar to a table of contents from a textbook. A table of contents usually follows an outline format (e.g., main subject headings above major subheadings) and includes just enough information to identify the topics of the chapters or sections. Although review notes are similar, they do not necessarily follow a strict outline format. The format for review notes should reflect the student's learning and note-taking style. Review notes should be about 1% of the volume of the original material. Thus, a 1000-page textbook yields approximately 100 pages of original notes and 10 pages of review notes.

Using Review Notes

Review notes offer four benefits.

1. Review notes are brief and easy to carry and consult throughout the day.

2. The process of creating review notes forces the student to think about the material and pinpoint what he really does and does not understand. Additionally, because he writes review notes in his own words, a student is likely to remember the material.

3. Continual review reinforces the material in the student's memory.

4. By using these notes, a student can determine how much of the material he remembers. In most cases, the student can assign a rough numeric value to the subject matter to identify how much he remembers. (For example, the heart has four chambers. If a student can name all four, then he has mastered 100% of the knowledge of this subject. If he can name only two, then he has mastered 50% of the knowledge, and so on.)

The student should treat the results of this review in the same way as the results of a pretest. When a student has mastered more than 40% of the knowledge, he should review text notes to learn more details. When the student has mastered less than 40%, he should consult the text book and focus on general principles or concepts.

Performing a Distributed Practice Review

A distributed practice review is the single most effective means of retaining information. To perform a distributed practice review, the student simply reviews the material several times over an extended period of time. In contrast, most students perform mass practice, better known as cramming, at some point during their undergraduate studies. When students cram, the information is stored in short-term memory and quickly forgotten. It is not practical or possible to cram all of the information covered on the MCAT.

The distributed practice review process begins at the start of the formal review. The following scenario shows how to conduct a distributed practice review.

> After a student takes the practice MCAT, scores it, and evaluates her scores, she determines that she will need 10 weeks to review for the MCAT. She allocates more time to areas of relative strength (scores of 40%–60%) and less time to subjects in which she scores above or below this range. The first area for review is gastrointestinal biology, followed by organic molecules, cardiovascular biology, work and force from physics, and so on. She sets aside the first week to review the first two topics and the second week to review the next two.
>
> As she reviews gastrointestinal biology and organic molecules, she creates review notes from the review materials or textbook. At the end of the week, after completing the initial review of these topics, the student reviews the material again, using the review notes. The next week, she repeats this process for cardiovascular biology and the physics topics. At the end of this week, the student reviews all of the topics covered over the last 2 weeks. The student continues this process, each week reviewing new topics, making review notes, and reviewing the material from all previous weeks. At the end of the last week, she reviews everything covered during the review period. If there is time, she completes this final review one or two more times before the date of the examination.

Obviously, this process requires a significant amount of work. However, neglecting this part of the review process diminishes the effectiveness of the overall review. There is no substitute for performing a structured, thorough review. One student might be able to perform this review in less time than another student, or may have a slightly better memory, but in the long run, every student must review all topics thoroughly.

● ● ●
TIME MANAGEMENT

Time management is simply the management of your time to most effectively accomplish your goals. The key word in this statement is "effectively." Good time management is effectively using the time allotted for each activity. Therefore, effective time management depends on advance planning and proper budgeting of time. For this reason, "cramming" has no place in higher education. Only by effectively managing his time is a student able to learn and review the necessary information. Cramming does not help because it is a short-term memory process.

Each student must spend as much time as necessary to perform a complete review for the MCAT. Each student has a different background, and some students must spend more time on subjects that others find easy. Each student must know her weaknesses and strengths and work on the weaknesses.

Developing an effective review schedule requires four steps:

1. Determine how much time is needed for review. Based on the results of pretesting, a student should be able to determine how many weeks to allocate for review. Most students achieve aggregate scores of 40% to 60% on the practice MCAT. With scores in this range, the minimum review time is approximately 14 weeks. It is important to allow adequate time for review, and to avoid overestimating how much can be accomplished in a given amount of time.

2. Review the calendar. The student should check his calendar for the review period and determine whether he can take a light academic load during this time.

He should also check his work schedule, research assignments, social activities, and other obligations to determine how he can allow more time for review by changing the time allotted for other activities.

3. Establish a schedule. After the student eliminates as many time-consuming activities as possible, she should create a study schedule. The schedule must include regular activities, such as classes and work. If possible, the student should check the syllabus for each class to determine when midterm and final examinations are scheduled and allow additional time to study for them. The next step is to block out time each week to review for the MCAT. Many students make the mistake of overscheduling. It is important to leave free time each day to accommodate emergencies. A schedule must be flexible. *Table 14–1* shows a weekly schedule that allows time for classes, study, and review.

4. Reevaluate the schedule as time passes. The task of scheduling is not done just once. Weekly, or even daily, the student should assess how well the review is progressing. For example, is it taking longer than planned to complete a topic? If so, more time should be allocated for review. There may not be enough time to complete this topic and review another topic. Taking time from the other topic might be justified if the current topic is an important one. However, many students continue to review a topic and then learn that there is not enough time to review another topic that is equally important. Giving one topic additional time at the expense of another topic may be the best use of the student's time, or it may not. All students must make choices about the use of time; these choices are the essence of time management.

The key to success for many students is the ability to create a schedule that helps them to reach their goals. *Table 14–1* shows a schedule that reflects the various activities in a week. Additional points to consider in developing a schedule include how a student studies and his preferred study times. Some students do best when studying or reviewing on their own; others do better when studying in a group. Students who prefer to study in a group must plan around the group members' schedules. Also, people function differently at different times during the day. Determine your ideal study times and take this factor into consideration when planning a schedule.

Developing a schedule and then failing to follow it is a waste. Everyone has the urge to delay tasks, especially those that require intense concentration, hard work, and an extensive commitment of time. Reviewing for the MCAT requires all of these. A simple three-step method for overcoming the urge to procrastinate is:

1. Get ready. Plan what you will review.

   - Get out the books or text materials that are needed for review.
   - Have all necessary supplies (e.g., pens, paper) at hand.
   - Plan how much time each topic requires for review.

2. Do it. Do not procrastinate!

   - Begin studying at the predetermined time.
   - Keep working until the planned material is covered.

3. Put it away. After the review is finished, stop!

   - Do not use the time allotted for other activities to "make up" unfinished reviewing.
   - If the time is planned effectively, then it will not be necessary to continue working on an activity past the time allocated.

● ● ●

TABLE 14–1. Sample Review Schedule

Time	Monday	Tuesday	Wednesday	Thursday	Friday	Saturday	Sunday
8:00 A.M.	C		C		C		L
9:00 A.M.	C	C	C	C	C	S	
10:00 A.M.		C	S	C	S	S	
11:00 A.M.	C	S	C		C	S	
12:00 A.M.	L	L	L	L	L	L	L
1:00 P.M.	W	W		W			S
2:00 P.M.	R	R	R	R	R	L	S
3:00 P.M.	R	R	R	R	R	L	S
4:00 P.M.	L	L	L	L	L		S
5:00 P.M.	L	L	L	L	L	L	L
6:00 P.M.	S		S	S	S	S	W
7:00 P.M.	S	S	S	S	S	W	W
8:00 P.M.	S		S		L	W	W
9:00 P.M.		R		R	L	W	W
10:00 P.M.	S	S		S	L	W	W
11:00 P.M.	Z	Z	Z	Z	Z	Z	Z
12:00 P.M.	Z	Z	Z	Z	Z	Z	Z

C = class hours (i.e., time spent in class and on laboratory work); L = living hours (i.e., time spent meeting other obligations, such as extracurricular activities, volunteer work, sports, social engagements, and household tasks); R = review hours (i.e., time spent reviewing for the MCAT); S = study hours (i.e., time spent preparing for class assignments and examinations; rule of thumb is to plan 2 hours of study for each hour of class time); W = work hours (i.e., time spent at a paid job); Z = sleep hours.

● ● ●
STUDY GROUPS

Participating in a study group can be an effective way to prepare for the MCAT. The ideal study group has five to seven members. Leadership rotates through the group weekly or biweekly. The leader of the group is responsible for the following:

- Scheduling group meetings
- Setting the meeting agenda
- Chairing meetings
- Assigning tasks to group members
- Appointing the next leader

One way to assign tasks to group members is to divide reading assignments among the group members. For instance, if the group has five members, each member is assigned one chapter from a textbook. Each member reads all five chapters, but spends more time on her chapter's topic. To prepare for the next group meeting, each student may:

● Create detailed charts, graphs, or notes for the group

● Create questions to test the group

● Meet with faculty, teaching assistants, or tutors to learn more about the topic

● Use the library or other resources to obtain additional information about the topic

At each meeting, the members share their notes, questions, and other materials. This process dramatically increases the amount of time devoted to the review process because each person collects information and shares it with the group. This cooperative process makes study groups so effective and useful.

●●●
NOTE-TAKING TECHNIQUES

Note taking is one of the most important study skills that students can learn. The importance of developing and using review notes was discussed earlier. Taking notes helps students to organize, understand, and retain information. Everyone takes notes differently, and a key component of taking good notes is to adjust the process to reflect the content. For instance, it would be ridiculous to take notes in the same way for a calculus class as for a history class.

The ideal way to take notes is to adjust to the demands of the subject and create notes that contain the key information needed to achieve good grades or test scores. This section describes note-taking formats for both lectures and text materials. Students should remember the following points:

● Taking notes is a process of condensing a volume of information to make it more manageable and understandable.

● Creating effective notes takes time and effort. A student should allow time to develop notes based on the difficulty of the subject and his ability to comprehend the material.

● Students should periodically evaluate whether note taking is accomplishing the intended goal of making the material clear and meaningful.

● Notes are a tool. Like any tool, the more a person uses them, the more studied she becomes in their use. Notes should be reviewed at least once or twice each week.

● When taking notes, a student should use the techniques that work for him and discard those that do not. However, students should not be afraid to experiment. There is no correct way to take notes, and a technique that works with one subject may not work with another.

The note-taking methods described in this section are similar, but they have slightly different purposes. Each student should choose a system that works for her. Some students may take part of one system and apply it to another, and others may add parts of a system to their current note-taking system. Each student should use a system that is compatible with her learning style and the information being reviewed. It is a good idea to try one of the systems, evaluate the results, and then decide what changes to make.

Taking Lecture Notes

Many students take a lecture review course for the MCAT. The most important part of taking notes during lectures is to listen effectively. Listening is a complex skill that must be learned through practice. One way to practice is to watch a telecourse shown on public television and pay close attention. It is important not to take notes at first. The student should try to identify the main ideas and supporting details given in the lecture. After a few sessions, she should begin to take notes using one of the methods described in this section. Eventually, the student's listening and note-taking skills become automatic. A student with good listening skills has more time to think about what is being said and to note any discrepancies or omissions.

Students can listen more actively by following these steps:

- Prepare for class by reviewing the material covered in previous lectures and anticipating what will be covered in the lecture for that day.

- Read any material assigned before the class to become familiar with the topic, identify important points, and formulate questions.

- Take notes on the main ideas covered during the lecture. Two methods for taking notes from lectures are:

The TQLR Method

T = Tune in. The student prepares to listen by preparing his mind for what he is about to hear.

Q = Question. The student formulates questions (e.g., "What is about to happen? What should I be looking for in this lecture?").

L = Listen. The student listens and notes the main ideas and supporting details.

R = Review. The student fills in missed information and summarizes the lecture.

The TQLR method is a simple, straightforward note-taking technique. The emphasis is on preparing for what is about to happen, thinking, and determining which information should be recorded.

The 5R Method

The 5R method is a more formal system of note taking than the TQLR method. It requires the student to divide the page into two columns: one column 2.5 inches wide, and one 6 inches wide. The student then performs the five "Rs" of taking notes: record, reduce, recite, reflect, and review.

1. **Record** the lecture as fully and meaningfully as possible in column B.

2. **Reduce** the information in column B to summaries in column A.

Column A 2.5 inches	Column B 6 inches

● ● ●

FIGURE 14–1. Format for the 5R lecture note-taking format.

3. **Recite** (aloud) the main ideas, questions, and significant details from column A without referring to column B.

4. **Reflect** on the notes, and attempt to develop analogies and inferences, and discern meaning.

5. **Review** the notes frequently.

Figure 14–2 shows notes from a lecture recorded using the 5R method. This lecture dealt with arrhythmias.

Taking Textbook Notes

Taking notes from written material requires an active approach to reading. Reading actively means reading with a purpose. A reader must identify his purpose when reading any material. For example, the reader's purpose may be to get information, to understand, to criticize, to create, or to review. The student adjusts his reading speed according to the purpose.

For difficult material, a reading rate of 100 to 200 words per minute is not unusual. For easier material, the rate can increase to hundreds of words per minute, and for the easiest material, 1000, 2000, or even 3000 words per minute is possible. However, the student must adjust her reading rate so that she understands and remembers the material. Another important factor is the student's reading comprehension skills. These skills include the ability to grasp the main ideas, the ability to distinguish important from unimportant details, and the ability to evaluate the author's point of view and intent. If the student cannot perform these tasks while reading, she cannot take effective notes. A reading comprehension class can help students to improve these skills.

Finally, a poor vocabulary reduces progress in reading. To improve their vocabularies, students should consult a dictionary frequently. Several techniques are available to improve vocabulary. One technique is to write new words on index

Column A	Column B
Main idea: Arrhythmias, abnormal heartbeat	Arrhythmias (dysrhythmias) 　—abnormal cardiac rhythms 　—sinus beats at abnormal rate
Main details: 3 different kinds	—Atrial flutter 　—rapid regular rhythm 　—220–350/min
Question: Effect on blood flow?	—Atrial fibrillation 　—rapid irregular rhythm 　—350–1000/min —AV block 　—1st degree 　　—1:1 conduction 　—2nd degree 　　—2:1, 3:2, etc., conduction 　—3rd degree 　　—complete block

● ● ●

FIGURE 14–2. Example of notes taken using the 5R lecture note-taking format.

cards. Below the word, the student writes a sentence using the word in each of its meanings. On the other side of the card, the student writes the definitions of the word. The student reviews these cards whenever she has time. First, the student looks at the word and tries to remember its definition. If she cannot remember the definition, she reads the sentences and sees if they trigger a memory of the definitions. If the sentences do not help, the student reads the definitions on the back of the card. When the student knows the definition of a word, she puts the card away. She keeps cards with unfamiliar words for further study. Following these suggestions helps the student to become an efficient and effective reader. After the student improves her reading skills, she is ready to use the note-taking techniques for text material.

The SQ3R Method

The SQ3R method is the oldest known organized method for taking notes. This method is similar to the 5R lecture method. In the SQ3R method, S stands for survey. In the survey step, the student skims the reading material to identify important information. Q stands for question, which is the pivotal step. The student converts chapter headings and subheadings to questions. For instance, if a chapter in a biology review book is titled, "The Skeletal System," then the student should ask, "What is the skeletal system?" The student should also ask more detailed questions (e.g., How does the skeletal system relate to other biologic systems? What are its main components?).

S = Survey. Skim the reading assignment, noting chapter headings, introductory and summary paragraphs, graphs, charts, and glossaries.

Q = Question. Write questions based on the survey step by converting chapter headings and subheadings to questions. Focus questions on the main ideas.

R = Read. Read purposefully based on the questions you have created, pacing the reading rate to the difficulty and importance of the material covered.

R = Recite/Reflect. Recite answers to the questions without looking at the text. Use examples, check answers, and write outline notes using questions and answers for each chapter. Reflect on the material covered, noting areas of weakness. Reread those sections.

R = Review. Skim the notes, then try to recall the main ideas and important supporting details without referring to the notes.

The Text Mapping Method

With this method, the student develops a graphic representation of the text material (*Figure 14–3*). This method is especially useful for students who learn best by visualizing concepts, facts, and relations. It is also useful for material that is best understood graphically (e.g., bonding relations in chemistry, many concepts in physics).

A map is constructed as follows.

1. Identify the starting point of the map by locating the primary thesis, or main idea, of the reading assignment. Write the title or main idea in the center of the paper.

2. Identify secondary categories by skimming the material for information that supports the main idea. Group and label the information. Limit categories to a maximum of six or seven.

3. After determining the categories, design the map. When the secondary categories are drawn around the main idea, the basic structure is complete.

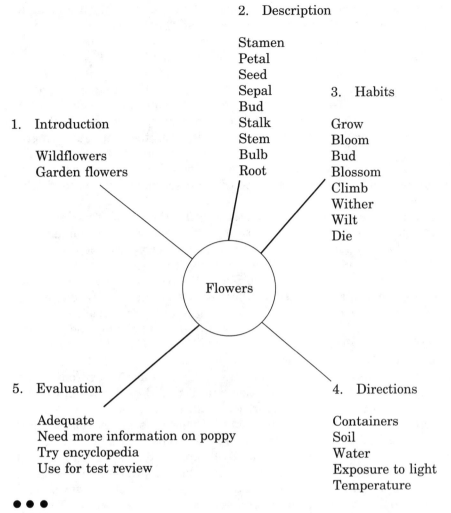

2. Description

Stamen
Petal
Seed
Sepal
Bud
Stalk
Stem
Bulb
Root

3. Habits

Grow
Bloom
Bud
Blossom
Climb
Wither
Wilt
Die

1. Introduction

Wildflowers
Garden flowers

Flowers

5. Evaluation

Adequate
Need more information on poppy
Try encyclopedia
Use for test review

4. Directions

Containers
Soil
Water
Exposure to light
Temperature

● ● ●

FIGURE 14-3. Example of notes taken using the textbook mapping note-taking format.

4. Read the chapter for details. After reading, and from memory, complete the map. Review the map by covering up details and reciting them from memory.

● ● ●
PROBLEM-SOLVING METHODS

Problem solving is an important study and test-taking skill. Students make five major errors in problem solving when taking examinations. The most prevalent type is computational errors. Computational errors occur when students skip steps in problem solving, do not find errors, or do not check their work. It is easy to see how this type of error occurs, especially in a high-pressure, timed situation, such as the MCAT. These errors often involve simple mistakes (e.g., adding when subtracting is required, misplacing the decimal point when converting a fraction to a whole number). These errors can be prevented by performing all steps when solving a problem and by allowing time after each mathematic question to check the work.

The second common problem-solving error that students make is using the wrong formula or equation. These errors usually occur because students memorize formulas, rather than learn them, and often do not understand that a formula is an explanation of a part of reality, whereas an equation is a tool for defining that part of reality. To avoid these errors, students should learn and understand formulas and equations, not just memorize them. They should also question whether a specific answer is possible, given the limitations of the formula that they are using to solve the problem. For example, if the student calculates an answer in millimeters and the multiple choice answers are all given in grams, then the student is using the wrong formula or equation to solve the problem.

The third error is answering the wrong problem or question. Students make this error because they misinterpret the problem or question. For example, a student may think that a question associated with a table is asking him to calculate the incidence of disease over time, which is shown on one axis, when the question is actually asking for the incidence by age, which is shown on the other axis. To prevent this type of error, students should list the known and unknown factors in the problem. They should then determine what information is needed to solve the problem (not all information is useful). They should plan solutions before starting to solve the problem.

The fourth error occurs when students restrict, or limit, the problem. This error takes two forms: putting inappropriate limits or restrictions on a problem, and not seeing limits that do exist. For example, a student might read a question that asks him to describe the effect of reduced atmospheric oxygen on respiration rate. He thinks that this question means that there is no effect on the volume of gas exchange in the lungs, which should also be affected by a decrease in available oxygen. These errors can be avoided by listing all information given about the problem, determining what the problem is asking you to do, and solving the problem based on the information given.

The final problem-solving error is giving up too soon. Students often think that there is only one way to solve a problem and do not analyze problems from different angles. They try the most obvious solution, and if that does not work, give up because they are afraid to try a novel approach. Additionally, they make assumptions about a problem that are not true or are based on erroneous information. For example, if a question asks the student to determine the mass of an object in zero gravity, she thinks about the equation for mass. She applies the data from the problem to the equation, finds that there is no corresponding answer choice, and gives up. She does not evaluate what her answer means in light of the choices given, and guesses, rather than attempt to solve the problem using another method. To overcome these errors, the student should realize that problems can be solved in more than one way and that the logical approach is not always the best. Before solving a problem, students should recognize their assumptions before solving a problem, and use metacognitive methods to monitor their thinking processes. They should ask themselves questions (e.g., Why do I see this? How do I know this? What if I'm wrong?). They should question even their basic assumptions. They should write out their thoughts and problem-solving steps so that they can review them for errors.

In addition to the solutions described for each type of problem-solving error, there is a general method for improving problem-solving skills. This method involves four steps:

1. **Analyze the problem.** The student diagrams or writes out the process described in the problem, and analyzes this process. For example, does the problem deal with a written description of the trajectory of a projectile in comparison to another projectile on a different trajectory? If so, she sketches how the two items are related. In this way, she can see the situation at a glance. Drawing or writing saves time by eliminating the need to reread the problem. The diagram or written explanation should indicate the given values and their associated units. Each value should be labeled clearly.

   The unknown factor and its units should also be labeled. In some cases, the unknown factor should be defined immediately because its definition may indicate that another variable must be determined first. If the variable that must be calculated is known from the beginning, the student can easily formulate an appropriate plan for solving the problem.

2. **Develop a plan.** Before performing any calculations, the student should plan out the solution. Calculating without thinking the problem through generates more data, making the solution more difficult to find. Most students try to solve the problem before they fully grasp what the problem is asking. Planning at this point saves time later.

   In planning the solution, the student should think of relations and formulas that connect the unknown factor with the given data. It is generally best to work backward, selecting equations that involve the unknown factor and determining whether they can be combined with the given data to solve the problem. Look for additional given data if the solution cannot be seen immediately. For example, if C = A + B and both A and B are provided, then C is also known. Including C as given data may lead to the solution to the problem.

3. **Perform the necessary calculations.** The student should solve for the unknown factor, insert the appropriate values, and perform the necessary calculations. Check the units of each value carefully, making sure that they are all within the same unit system. For example, if the answers are expressed in millimeters and some of the values in the problem are given in meters, then it will be necessary to convert these values before performing the calculation.

4. **Evaluate the answer.** After calculating an answer, be sure to check whether the answer derived for the unknown factor makes sense in terms of the original analysis of the problem. If the answer calculated is not even close to the answer choices, then you probably made an error in the calculation process. Reevaluate the problem and determine whether you made a simple mathematical error or whether your entire approach to solving the problem was incorrect. Based on this analysis, either recalculate the solution or reread the problem, looking for information or data that was overlooked the first time.

This problem-solving process is oriented toward problems that require a calculation. However, these four steps can be applied to any problem. This method can be used even in the Verbal Reasoning section of the MCAT. In this situation, the student analyzes the reading passage, plans how to answer the associated questions, applies the plan, and evaluates how well the plan worked.

● ● ●
MNEMONICS

Mnemonic devices can help many people to remember information. Several types are used, but mnemonic devices are best remembered when the individual takes the time to create them. People who use mnemonics must repeat them many times to commit them to long-term memory. Some common mnemonic devices, with examples, follow:

1. **Acronyms.** An acrostic, or acronym, is a set of initial letters from a group of words. When written in a specific order, these initial letters form a word, phrase, or abbreviation. For example:

   N(A)PP

   Nitrogenous base

   (A)

   Pentose monosaccharide

   Phosphate groups

This mnemonic describes the basic elements of a nucleotide. The letter A was added to make the mnemonic sound like the word "nap." This is the simplest type of acrostic mnemonic. It provides a means to remember these items, but is not as effective as the following examples.

CAPS

Central nervous system

Autonomic nervous system

Peripheral nervous system

Sense organs

This acronym describes the four major parts of the nervous system. It is a better mnemonic device than the previous example because it provides some sense of relative importance of the items listed. The central nervous system controls the other systems and is the clearinghouse and processing center for the messages that enter the brain from the other parts of the nervous system. The autonomic nervous system is the workhorse of the nervous system. It controls movement and the internal regulation of the body. The peripheral nervous system sends information to the central and autonomic nervous systems. The sense organs provide essential information to the central nervous system, monitor the environment, and allow the central nervous system to communicate with other central nervous systems (i.e., people).

BATTL(E) S(O)AP

Bone marrow

Adenoids

Thymus

Tonsils

Lymph nodes

(E)

Spleen

(O)

Appendix

Peyer's patches

This mnemonic defines the organs of the immune system. It is effective for two reasons. First, BATTLE SOAP is a memorable phrase because it presents a unique image. Second, this phrase relates to the topic. The immune system protects the body by fighting foreign invaders and removes the debris of dead cells and other products. Thus, the immune system engages in battle with invaders and acts as a "soap."

2. **Epi-acronyms.** Students can use epi-acronyms to remember more complex concepts. Epi-acronyms can take several forms, including short poems, song lyrics (set to popular music), or nonsense sentences. The classic example is the well-known metered rhyme to help students recall the 12 cranial nerves.

On old Olympic towering tops, a Finn and German viewed some hops.

On	**Olfactory** (cranial nerve I)
Old	**Optic** (cranial nerve II)
Olympic	**Oculomotor** (cranial nerve III)
Towering	**Trochlear** (cranial nerve IV)
Tops	**Trigeminal** (cranial nerve V)
A	**Abducens** (cranial nerve VI)
Finn	**Facial** (cranial nerve VIII)
And	**Acoustic** (cranial nerve VIII)
German	**Glossopharyngeal** (cranial nerve IX)
Viewed	**Vagus** (cranial nerve X)
Some	**Spinal accessory** (cranial nerve XI)
Hops	**Hypoglossal** (cranial nerve XII)

This popular epi-acronym is an easily remembered nonsense rhyme that lists the cranial nerves in order, from one to twelve. The following epi-acronym has some of the same features.

DR. PAGE and **DR. PIC** Do PatienT Rounds in a PickUp

DR. PAGE	**D**NA and **R**NA **P**urines are **A**denine and **G**uanin**E**
DR. PIC	**D**NA and **R**NA **P**yrimidine **I**s **C**ytosine
Do PatienT	**D**NA **P**yrimidine is **T**hymine
Rounds in a PickUp	**R**NA **P**yrimidine is **U**racil

This silly epi-acronym reviews the purines and pyrimidines found in DNA and RNA. Its silliness does not make this mnemonic less useful; in fact, some of the best mnemonics are silly or off-color poems or songs.

Epi-acronyms are especially appropriate for long lists of items. Complex phrases are often easier to construct and remember than simple words and phrases because more cue words are available to combine into vivid images. Students should create epi-acronyms that contain memorable images and that reflect the material being reviewed. The act of creating these mnemonics helps to commit these items to memory.

2. **Onomatopoeias.** An onomatopoeia is a word whose sound suggests its meaning (e.g., bang, pow). Although it can be difficult to create, an onomatopoeia can make an excellent mnemonic. For example:

TAP-TaP-TOPP

Thyroid

Adrenal cortex

Parathyroid

Thymus

(a)

Pituitary

Testes

Ovaries

Pancreas

Pineal

This mnemonic lists the glands of the endocrine system. The sound that is being mimicked is water dripping from a faucet into a sink. This image relates to the topic, in that these glands release hormones slowly, almost drop by drop, into the body.

By inference, mnemonics are the work of individuals. Some mnemonics can be shared with others, but most are too idiosyncratic or specialized to be of value to others. Each student should create his own mnemonics for the concepts, facts, and information he has trouble remembering. Mnemonics work well with information that can be listed or ordered, but are not useful for other types of information. When reviewing material, students should consider whether the information could be turned into a mnemonic.

● ● ●

MEDICAL TERMINOLOGY

Many medical terms contain Greek and Latin elements. Being able to translate these words into simple English is a vital and effective part of test taking. Most of these terms can be translated into simple English words if the Greek or Latin prefix, suffix, or root is known. The prefixes, suffixes, and roots in *Tables 14–2, 14–3, and 14–4* apply to thousands of words.

● ● ●

TABLE 14–2. Prefixes

Term	Meaning	Example
a-	without	apnea
ab-	deviating	abnormal
abdomin/o-	about the abdomen	abdominal
acr/o-	concerning extremities	acromegaly
ad-	to, toward	adduction, advance
aer/o-	air	aerophobia
amb/i-	both, both sides	ambilateral
an-	without	anesthesia
anis/o-	unequal	anisocoria
ante-	before	antepyretic
anti-	against	antidote, antipyretic
bi-	two	bicycle

• • •

TABLE 14-2. Prefixes *(Continued)*

blephar/o-	eyelid	blepharedema
brad/y-	slow	bradycardia
calcane/o-	heel	calcaneal
carcin/o-	cancerous, or malignant, tumor	carcinoma
cardi/o-	having to do with the heart	cardiomegaly
cheil/o-	lips	cheilotomy
circum-	around	circumocular
col/o-	pertaining to colon	colocentesis
com-	together, with	composite
con-	with	congenital
contra-	against	contraceptive
cost/o-	pertaining to the ribs	costectomy
crypt/o-	hidden	cryptorchidism
cyt/o-	pertaining to cells	cytology
de-	away, from	deciduous, deter
dis-	to free of, separate, undo	disease
dys-	painful, faulty, diseased, bad, difficult	dysmenorrhea
electr/o-	electric impulses	electrocardiogram
epi-	over	episplenitis
epi-	on	epilogue
equi-	equal, equally	equivalent
ex-	out of	expel
glyc/o-	sweet, sugar	glycogen
hemi-	half	hemigastrectomy
homo-	same, equal, like	homogenized
hyper-	above, more than normal, over, too much	hyperactive, hypercritical
hypo-	below, less than normal, under, too little	hypodermic, hypotrophy
in-	in, into, not	inspiration
infra-	below, under	inframammary
inter-	between	intercostal, interstate
mal-	bad, poor	malformation, malfunction
mes/o-	middle, mean	mesoderm
meta-	beyond, after, occurring in a series	metacarpal

(Table continued on the following page)

• • •

TABLE 14-2. Prefixes *(Continued)*

mis-	wrong	mistake
mon/o-	alone, one	monolith
non-	not	nonentity
ob-	against	objection
omni-	all, everywhere	omniscient
over-	above	overbearing
poly-	many	polymorphous
pre-	before	precede
pro-	before, in front of, forward	prognosis, propel
retro-	backward	retrograde
re-	back, again	regress
semi-	half, partly	semicircle
sub-	under, below	subabdominal, submarine
super-	above, beyond	superabduction
supra-	on, higher in position, outside, further	supralumbar
sym-	together, joined	sympodial
trans-	across, beyond, over	transcend, transposition
un-	not	unneeded

• • •

TABLE 14-3. Suffixes

Term	Meaning	Example
-able, -ible	able to	usable
-algia	pain	cardialgia
-cele	herniation	encephalocele
-centesis	surgical puncture	abdominocentesis
-dyn/ia	pain	cephalodynia
-emia	blood	xanthemia
-er, -or	one who does	competitor
-fy	to make	dignify
-iasis	pertaining to a pathologic condition (an infestation)	cholelithiasis
-iatr-	indicating a medical professional	podiatrist

• • •

TABLE 14–3. Suffixes *(Continued)*

-ism	the practice of	rationalism
-ist	one who is occupied with	feminist
-itis	inflammation	acrodermatitis
-less	without, lacking	meaningless
-log/o-	study	cardiologist
-logue	a type of speaking or writing	prologue
-ness	the quality of	aggressiveness
-oid	like, resembling	lipoid
-oma	tumor	adenoma
-opia	vision	diplopia
-orrhagia	bursting forth of blood	gastrorrhagia
-osis	condition	acrocyanosis
-ptosis	prolapse, downward displacement	hysteroptosis
-scop/o-	examine	microscope
-ship	the art or skill of	statesmanship
-tude	the state of	rectitude

• • •

TABLE 14–4. Roots

Term	Meaning	Example
acromi/o	pertaining to the embryonic sac	acromial
aden/o	referring to glands	adenitis
alges/i	sensitivity to pain	algesimeter
amni/o	amnion	amniocentesis
angi/o	relating to the blood or lymph vessels	angiospasm
ankyl/o	stiff, not movable	ankylosis
anter/o	toward the front, in front of	anterior
appendic/o	appendix	appendicitis
arch	to rule	monarch
arteri/o	having to do with arteries	arteriosclerosis
arthr/o	joints	osteoarthropathy
aut/o	self	automobile

(Table continued on the following page)

• • •

TABLE 14-4. Roots *(Continued)*

belli	war, warlike	belligerent
bene	good	benevolent
bi/o	life	biology
blast/o	pertaining to the process of budding by cells or tissue	neuroblast
bronch/o	bronchus	bronchocele
burs/o	referring to the bursae (small pouches, or sacs) of the body	bursitis
carp/o	pertaining to the wrist	carpoptosis
caud/o	downward, toward the tail	caudal
cephal/o	head	cephalodynia
cerebr/o	a part of the brain	cerebrum
cervic/o	cervix	cervicectomy
chir/o	hand	chirospasm
chlor/o	green	chloremia
chol/e	gall, bile	cholelith
chondr/o	cartilage	osteochondritis
chrom/o	color	chromoblast
chron	time	chronology
clys/o	washing, irrigation	coloclysis
cocc/o	spherically shaped family of bacteria	cocci
colp/o	pertaining to the vagina	colpitis
condyl/o	rounded process occurring on many bones	condylectomy
cor/e, core/o	pupil	corectopia
corne/o	cornea	corneitis
cortic/o	cortex	cortical
crani/o	pertaining to the skull	cranioplasty
cyan/o	blue, blueness	acrocyanosis
cycl/o	ciliary body	cycloplegia
cyst/o	bladder	cystectomy
dacry/o	tear	dacryorrhea
dactyl/o	fingers, toes	dactylomegaly
dent/o	tooth	interdental
derm/o, dermat/o	pertaining to the skin	acrodermatitis, dermopathy
dextr/o	right	dextrogastria
di/a	through	diagnosis

• • •

TABLE 14-4. Roots *(Continued)*

dic	to say	indicative
dipl/o	double	diplocardia
dips/o	thirst	polydipsia
dors/o	back	dorsal
drom/o	running	syndrome
duoden/o	pertaining to the first part of the small intestine	duodenum
ect/o	outer, on the outside	ectoderm
ectas/ia, ectas/is	dilation, stretching	gastrectasia
ectomy	excision, removal	gastrectomy
ectop/o	out of place	ectopic
edema	excess fluids in cells or tissues	pseudoedema
emesis	vomiting	hyperemesis
encephal/o	pertaining to the brain	encephalitis
end/o	inner, inside	endoderm
enter/o	pertaining to the small intestine	gastroenteric
erythr/o	red	erythroderma
esophag/o	esophagus	esophagostomy
esthesi/o	feeling or sensation	esthesioscopy
eu	well, easy (opposite of dys)	eupepsia
external	exterior, on the outside	posteroexternal
extra	outside, beyond	extraarticular
fac	to make, to do	artifact
femor/o	femur	pubofemoral
fibr/o	fibrous, fiber	myofibroma
gangli/o	collection of nerve cell bodies	ganglion
gastr/o	stomach	megalogastria
gen/o	genesis (formation or beginning)	pyogenic
gingiv/o	pertaining to the gums	gingivitis
gloss/o	tongue	glossitis
gnos/ia	knowledge	prognosis
gram/o	record	electrocardiogram
graph	writing	telegraph
graph/o	instrument that records, any pictorial device	electrocardiogram
gynec/o	women	gynecology

(Table continued on the following page)

• • •

TABLE 14-4. Roots *(Continued)*

hem/o, hemat/o	blood	hemangiitis, hematolysis
hepat/o	pertaining to the liver	hepatoscopy
heter/o	different	heteronia
hidr/o	sweat	hidrocystoma
hist/o	tissue	histolysis
humer/o	pertaining to the bone of the upper arm	humerus
hydr/o	water, fluid	hydrocephalus
hyster/o	pertaining to the uterus	hysterectomy
intr/a	within	intracellular
ir/o, irid/o	iris	iritis, iridocele
is/o	equal	isometric
ischi/o	the part of the hipbone the body rests on when sitting	ischiorectal
kerat/o	cornea	keratocele
kinesi/o	movement, motion	kinesialgia
lacrim/o	pertaining to tears	lacrimal
lapar/o	abdominal wall	laparectomy
laryng/o	pertaining to the larynx	larynx
later/o	the side	lateral
leps/y	attack, seizure	narcolepsy
leuk/o	white	leukoderma
lip/o	fat	lipoma
lith/o	calculus, stone	lithogenesis
lumb/o	pertaining to the loin	lumbar
lymph/o	pertaining to the lymph	lymphostasis
lys/o	dissolution, loosening	myolysis
macr/o	large	macrocyte
malac/o	soft, softening	malacotomy
mania	madness	megalomania
medi/o	middle	medial
megal/o	large, enlarged	acromegaly
melan/o	black	melanoderma
men/o	menstruation	dysmenorrhea
mening/o	pertaining to the membranes that envelope the brain and spinal cord	meningitis
metr/o, meter	instrument	speedometer
metr/o	uterus	metrorrhea

● ● ●

TABLE 14-4. Roots *(Continued)*

micr/o	small	microcephalus
mort	to die	mortal
muc/o	resembling mucus	mucoid
mult/i	many, more than one (opposite of mon/o)	multiglandular
my/o	referring to the muscles	myocarditis
myc/o	fungus	mycelial
myel/o	spinal cord, bone marrow	myelitis
narc/o	sleep	narcotic
nas/o	nose	nasoantritis
ne/o	new	neogenesis
necr/o	pertaining to death	necrocytosis
nephr/o	kidney	nephroptosis
nerv	nerve	nervous
neur/o	denoting nerves, relating to the nervous system	neurology
noct/i	right	noctiluca
null/i	none	nullify
nyct/o	night	nyctalgia
oo/ovo	egg or ovum	ooblast
omphal/o	umbilicus (navel)	omphalitis
onych/o	referring to the nails	onychoid
oophor/o	referring to the ovary	oophorectomy
ophthalm/o	pertaining to the eye	ophthalmitis
orchid/o	pertaining to the testes	orchidalgia
orrhaphy	suturing, stitching	ureterorrhaphy
orrhea	flow, discharge	pyorrhea
orrhexis	rupture	hysterorrhexis
oste/o	bone	osteopathy
ostomy	forming an opening	gastroduodenostomy
ot/o	ear	otorrhea
otomy	incision	duodenotomy
pancreat/o	denoting the pancreas	pancreatic
par/a	beside, beyond, near, abnormal	parahepatitis
par/o	to bear	multipara
paralysis	loss of movement	acroparalysis
path/o	disease	adenopathy

(Table continued on the following page)

• • •

TABLE 14-4. Roots *(Continued)*

pelv/i	referring to the pelvis	pelvimetry
penia	decrease in	leukocytopenia
peps/o	digestion	dyspepsia
per	through	perforate
peri	around	periarticular
pex/o	fixation	oophoropexy
phag/o	eat	bradyphagia
phalang/o	bones of the fingers and toes	phalangitis
pharmac/o	drugs, medicine	psychopharmacology
pharyng/o	pertaining to the pharynx	pharyngocele
phas/o	speech	paraphasia
phil/o	strong attraction to	hydrophilia
phleb/o	vein	phlebosclerosis
phob/o	abnormal fear	hydrophobia
phon/o	voice, sound	dysphonia
phor/o	eye	exophoria
phren/o	personality	schizophrenia
plas/o	formation, change (of molding)	dysplasia
plasm/o	growth, formation	neoplasm
plast/o	surgical repair	arthroplasty
pleg/o	paralysis	iridoplegia
pleur/o	covering the lungs	pleurocele
pne/o	breathe, breathing	pneopneic
pneum/o	air	pneumothorax
pneumon/o	referring to the lungs	pneumonia
pod/o	foot	podalgia
pol/y	too many, too much	polyuria
port	to carry	deport
post, poster/o	after, behind	postcibal, posterior
prim/i	first	primipara
proct/o	rectum	proctology
pseud/o	false	pseudocyesis
psych/o	mind	psychoanalysis
pub/o	pubis	suprapubic
py/o	pus	pyocele

● ● ●

TABLE 14-4. Roots *(Continued)*

pyel/o	renal pelvis	pyelitis
pyr/o	heat, fever	pyrexia
rach/i, rachi/o	spine	rachialgia
rect/o	rectum	rectocele
ren/o	kidney	renal
retin/o	pertaining to the retina	retinal
retr/o	behind	retrocolic
rhin/o	pertaining to the nose	rhinorrhea
salping/o	pertaining to the fallopian tubes	salpingostomy
sanguin/o	blood	consanguinity
scapul/o	scapula	scapulalgia
schiz/o	split	schizophrenia
scler/o	hard	angiosclerosis
sept/o	infection	aseptic
sinistr/o	left	sinistral
spasm	involuntary musclar contraction	neurospasm
spermat/o	referring to spermatozoa	spermatogenesis
spir/o	breath	inspiration
splen/o	pertaining to the spleen	splenectomy
spondyl/o	spine	spondylitis
staphyl/o	bunch of grapes	staphylococci
stasis	stopping	menostasis
stern/o	sternum	sternopericardial
stomat/o	mouth	stomatitis
strept/o	twisted	streptococci
syn	together, joined	syndactylism
syphil/o	referring to syphilis	syphilitic
tach/y	fast, rapid	tachycardia
ten/o	tendons	tenoplasty
therap/o	referring to treatment	hydrotherapy
therm/o	heat	thermal
thorac/o	pertaining to the chest, thorax	thoracic
thromb/o	blood clot	thrombocyte

CHAPTER 15

Test-Taking Techniques for the MCAT

MULTIPLE-CHOICE TESTS

The best preparation for taking the Medical College Admissions Test (MCAT) is to study and review the subject matter areas tested. This chapter describes test-taking strategies and techniques that can also improve your MCAT score.

All standardized, multiple-choice tests, such as the MCAT, Scholastic Aptitude Test (SAT), Graduate Record Examination (GRE), and United States Medical Licensing Examination (USMLE) have inherent weaknesses. Constructing a multiple-choice test involves considerable effort and expertise and trade-offs must be made. This situation is analogous to the process of designing and building a sailboat. If the sailboat maker wants the boat to go faster, he must add more sail, but more sail means that the boat needs more keel to prevent it from tipping over in the water. If more keel is added, the boat has more drag in the water and, as a result, goes more slowly. Thus, the sailboat maker must make choices in the sail-to-keel ratio of each boat.

People who construct tests face a similar situation. For instance, validity is an important consideration in the creation of a test. For a test to be valid, it must distinguish between different levels of knowledge. The test should have some type of scale that can identify students with thorough to poor knowledge of the subject matter. A question, such as the following one, can be answered by all students and would not be valid because it cannot discriminate between students.

Question: Who invented the light bulb?

A. Thomas Edison

B. Ronald Reagan

C. Mickey Mouse

D. Snow White

Answer: **A**

On the other hand, the following question would be too difficult for most students to answer. This question also would not be valid because it does not distinguish between levels of knowledge.

Question: Who invented the safety pin?

A. Eli Whitney

B. Lord Grade

C. Thomas Edison

D. John Carleton

Answer: **D**

Students can benefit from knowing and understanding the constraints under which tests are created. Students can use this knowledge to identify correct answers, even when the information is unfamiliar.

● ● ●
DEFINING WORDS IN QUESTIONS

Questions usually have two parts: terminology and simple English words. Most students do well when questions are focused primarily on the terminology, but not as well when they focus on other words. *Table 15–1* shows simple English words that often appear in questions as well as their usual meaning on tests.

Rather than defining these words, *Table 15–1* lists the sense of the words as they are used in multiple-choice questions. This table is not a definitive list of all words used to create questions, but it contains enough examples to show how to interpret these words in questions.

It is important to interpret words and phrases in questions accurately. For example:

Question: A characteristic of virus X is that it:

A. grows on blood agar

B. is highly virulent

C. is blue

D. has no DNA

Answer: **C**

Answer C is the only one that gives the physical appearance, shape, or size of the virus, the sense of "characteristic" given in *Table 15–1*.

● ● ●
TEST-TAKING TECHNIQUES

Every student should learn as much as possible about how tests are constructed and should develop test-taking strategies. This knowledge allows students to take an active rather than a passive approach to testing. These students look for weak-

● ● ●
TABLE 15–1. Common Defining Words and Phrases
Found in Questions

Word or Phrase	Meaning
Acute	Sudden, severe problem
Affect(s)	Change from one thing to another
Association (of) (with)	Always linked with item
Can cause	Nearly always
Cause(s)	Leads to
Change(s)	Make different from before
Characteristic(s)	Physical appearance, shape, or size
Chronic	Long-term, mild
Define(s) (ed)	Name it
Describe(s) (d)	Physical appearance, shape, or size
Develop(s) (ed)	Created or made by
Effect(s)	Next thing to happen
Expect(s) (ed)	Will happen
Factor(s)	Parts, sections, or action
Feature(s)	Physical appearance, shape, or size
Finding(s)	Result
Function(s) (ed)	Works by
Identify	Name it
Include(s) (ed)	All
Indicate(s)	Could mean
Initial	First or start from
Involve(d)	Includes (all)
Label(ed)	Name it

● ● ●

TABLE 15–1. Common Defining Words and Phrases
Found in Questions *(Continued)*

List(s)	Name them
Main(ly)	First or only
Match(es)	The same as
May (have) (be)	Not always
May cause	Sometimes
Common manifestation	Physical appearance, shape, or size
Most probable	Logical choice
Most common type	Physical appearance, shape, or size
Most common cause	Number one
Most frequently	Number one
Most appropriate	Least harmful or next step
Most common	Number one
Most likely	Will occur
Name(s)	Number one
Often	Nearly always
Outline(s)	Name all
Pattern(s)	Shape or size
Phase(s)	Steps from one to ?
Probable	Will happen
Recall(s)	Name it
Recite(s)	Name in order
Regard (to)	Related to
Require(d)	Needed (absolutely)
Response(s)	Reaction to
Reveal(s) (ed)	Shows
Select(s) (ed)	Name first item
State(s) (ed)	Name it
Statement(s)	Opinion
Suggest(s)	Means
Symptom(s)	Series of items
Treat(s) (ed) (ing)	Helps or aids
Which	One
Would expect	Will happen
Would	Will

nesses and errors in test construction that make choosing an answer easier. They also adjust their test-taking strategy to reflect how the questions are asked. They do not treat each test the same way; they approach each test individually. For example, a well-prepared student may start at the end of the test because she finds easier questions there, whereas a less knowledgeable student always starts with the first question.

The test-taking strategies described in this chapter are divided into a series of dos and don'ts for both before and during the test. Some of the techniques apply to multiple-choice tests in general, whereas others apply to the MCAT specifically.

In general, there are three reasons why a multiple-choice question is missed. The most common reason is lack of knowledge. The student may not know the answer or even recognize the topic. Although these questions are frustrating, they should account for few of the missed questions if a thorough review has been done. Approximately 20% to 30% of the questions missed will probably fall into this category. Because these questions are missed as a result of gaps in knowledge, additional review should correct the problem.

The second reason why a question is missed is misreading or misinterpreting the question. Approximately 60% to 70% of missed questions are included in this category. For example, the student may not have realized that the question asked for an exception, or she may have read it too quickly and not noticed that the question asked for the "afferent" and not the "efferent" receptor. To avoid these errors, it is necessary to read slowly and be sure that the answer chosen is the best answer to the question being asked, not the answer to a question that the student thinks is being asked.

The final type of error is failing to analyze the question or answers correctly. In this case, the student probably knows the topic, but focuses on the wrong information. For example, the following question contains two pieces of essential information. Either one can help to eliminate two of the answers, but only one can distinguish between the final two answers.

Question: A bacterium is isolated from the sputum of a 12-year-old boy. The organism Gram stains negative and ferments lactose. It is believed that the patient was infected while in the hospital for a routine appendectomy. The organism is most likely:

A. *Clostridium tetani.*

B. *Klebsiella pneumoniae.*

C. *Escherichia coli.*

D. *Staphylococcus.*

Answer: **B**

The question contains five pieces of information:

1. The organism was found in the sputum.

2. The patient is a 12-year-old boy.

3. The organism Gram stains negative.

4. The organism ferments lactose.

5. The infection occurred in the hospital.

The two essential pieces of information are that the organism Gram stains negative and that it was isolated from the sputum. Being gram-negative eliminates answers A and D, because they are both gram-positive organisms. Because the organism was isolated from the sputum, it infects either the respiratory or upper gastrointestinal tract. Of the two remaining answers, only B, *Klebsiella pneumoniae*, predominantly attacks one of these tracts. Answer C, *Escherichia coli*, primarily infects the urinary or lower gastrointestinal tract. For this reason, it is not as likely to be the pathogen in question. However, a student might choose answer C if he placed greater weight on the importance of the infection having occurred during an appendectomy, because the appendix is clearly in the same region as the lower gastrointestinal and urinary tracts. For this situation to occur, however, the surgeon would have to cut through part of the bowel or another structure where *E. coli* would be present. The question states that the operation was routine, so this possibility is eliminated.

● ● ●
BEFORE THE TEST

Do Prepare Mentally and Physically

Preparing mentally for the MCAT is similar to a runner's preparation for a marathon race. This preparation has three components: attitude, practice, and assessment.

First is the development of a mental outlook that allows only success. An athlete's psychological state or motivation has a tremendous effect on his performance. This idea can be applied in many other areas. A student's positive attitude on the day of a test can make the difference between a grade of A or B. Conversely, a negative attitude can significantly impair performance. Unfortunately, many people find it easier to question their ability than to motivate themselves to succeed. Each student should work to overcome self doubt with positive mental images and anxiety-reduction techniques.

The second component of preparation is practice. A runner who is preparing for a marathon runs a few miles each day, completes longer runs on weekends, and completes a few marathon-length runs before a race. Students must practice too. They should answer a dozen or so questions each day, work on entire Physical Sciences, Biological Sciences, or Verbal Reasoning sections on weekends, and complete a practice MCAT at least twice before the test. This type of practice increases the student's ability to concentrate and analyze questions.

The third component of preparation is assessment. Runners assess their performance by measuring how much their running time improves. The shorter the time, the better. Students who are preparing for the MCAT should also assess their improvement. However, runners are not only concerned with their speed, but also with improved performance. For example, was it new running shoes or a new diet that made the difference? Students should ask themselves whether a higher score is the result of greater knowledge of the content material or improved test-taking skills. The answers to such questions should guide content review, testing practice, or both.

In analyzing test performance, students should not focus solely on how many questions they answer. They should also be concerned with the questions they miss. Analyzing missed questions is an essential step in improving results. Despite its importance, many students do not perform this step.

In addition to preparing mentally for the exam, students should prepare physically by getting enough sleep and exercising regularly. The MCAT requires a full day of concentration, and getting enough rest is part of the mental and physical preparation. Students should also exercise regularly to increase physical endurance and relieve stress and anxiety.

Do Select the Best Test Site

Students often do not consider where they should take the MCAT. Most can choose from several sites. Two factors should be considered when choosing a test site:

1. How many students will be taking the test at the site

2. The physical environment of the site

The number of students taking the examination can affect the administration of the MCAT. At some sites, so many students take the test that administrative tasks (e.g., signing in students, assigning seats, distributing and collecting examinations) take longer. As a result, students at these sites may finish the last section of the test as late as 5:00 or 6:00 P.M., when most other students are finished by 4:00 P.M. Students who finish later must sustain their energy and concentration for a longer period.

The physical setting of the test site can affect performance. Seating accommodations vary significantly. Some tests are given in rooms with theater-style seating, with small, pop-up desktops that leave little room for spreading out the test and writing on the answer sheet. Other tests are given in laboratory rooms that have little soundproofing. The smallest sounds can be heard throughout these rooms, which can be distracting.

The ideal site is a room that has tables with chairs, is reasonably soundproof, and has adequate lighting. Tables with chairs allow students to spread out their materials and sit comfortably, reducing fatigue. Soundproofing limits distractions, and adequate lighting reduces eyestrain. The best way to locate an ideal site is to talk to students who have taken the test. Students should speak to their peers or fellow members of prehealth or premedical clubs to determine which testing site is best.

After selecting a site, the student should visit it before the test. Visiting the site in advance allows the student to measure travel time to the site and determine where to park.. Students who live far from the site may decide to stay at a nearby hotel the night before the test. Limiting travel time guarantees that the student will be on time for the test, and may reduce anxiety caused by driving in traffic.

Do Take Everything You Need on the Day of the Test

It is a good idea to take the following items to the testing site:

- A wristwatch
- The ticket for admission to the test site
- Photo identification (e.g., a drivers' license)
- Pencils, an eraser, and pens with black ink
- Lunch
- A pillow or inflatable cushion to sit on
- A sweater
- Candy bars (to be eaten in the afternoon when blood glucose levels are low)

Do Read the Registration Packet

The MCAT application packet contains a 56-page booklet that describes the rules and regulations for the MCAT. Students should be familiar with these rules, especially as they pertain to conduct during the test. The section on reporting of scores contains an important point. The student has a right to have her test scored manually. The MCAT is scored by machine and errors can occur. For instance, a student might change an answer without fully erasing the other answer. The machine may read this answer as a double mark, and count it as incorrect. Students should consider having their test scored manually if they believe their scores are not accurate.

Don't Stay Up All Night Cramming for the Test

Chapter 14 describes a review schedule for the MCAT, based on the results of the diagnostic MCAT. Students who follow the recommended review process do not need to cram at the last minute. Cramming is unnecessary and self-defeating. College students may be able to cram for a midterm or final examination in one or more subjects, but the MCAT covers 2 years of coursework in chemistry, biology, and physics. Attempting to cram for the Verbal Reasoning or Writing Sample section is a waste of time. The MCAT is a complex, difficult, but manageable examination. No amount of cramming can substitute for a well-planned review.

Don't Take Drugs or Medications to Stay Awake

If it is inappropriate to cram before the MCAT, it is even more inappropriate to attempt to stay awake to cram by using drugs. Whether legal or illegal, there is no good reason to consume drugs. In fact, the most likely result of resorting to drugs is drowsiness and fatigue on the day of the test. On the day of the test, it is also a good idea to avoid consuming too much coffee or other caffeine-containing drinks. Caffeine can increase anxiety.

Don't Panic

A student who has performed a thorough review should not be intimidated by the MCAT. The material tested is taken from subjects that the student has studied for more than 2 years in the classroom and has reviewed for months before the test. Nothing new or foreign should appear on the examination.

DURING THE TEST

Do Scan Each Question and Answer Set

Take a few seconds to scan the question and answer set to determine the subject (e.g., genetics, translational motion, acid–base balance). Knowing what subject is being tested helps the student to focus his attention. Another method to aid in concentration is to read the last sentence in long questions. This last sentence usually asks the actual question. Determining that the question is asking for the structure of an organic compound or the substrate for a certain enzyme, for example, helps the student to look for key words in the rest of the question or in the passage.

Do Read the Directions Completely

Each set of questions is prefaced by a set of directions. It is important to note what the directions do and do not ask the student to do. Most directions ask students to choose the one best answer, not the correct answer. In other words, there may be two or more correct answers, but only one best answer.

Do Monitor How Much Time You Spend on Questions

Time management during the test is a vital part of doing well. Taking too long to answer some questions means that insufficient time will be available for others. Some students run out of time with 10 to 20 questions unanswered. Then they must guess to answer those questions.

In the Verbal Reasoning, Biological Sciences, and Physical Sciences sections of the MCAT approximately 77 seconds is allocated for reading the passage and answering each associated question. One way to use this time well is to check the time before starting each passage, count the number of questions, and multiply this number by 2 minutes. For example, a passage with 10 questions should take less than 20 minutes to complete. A student who takes more than 20 minutes to complete a 10-question passage should try to work more quickly.

There is no differential weighing of questions. In other words, longer or more complex questions count exactly as much as shorter, simpler questions. Also, questions are not grouped by level of difficulty. A student who runs out of time with 10 to 20 questions unanswered probably could have answered some fraction of those questions easily, given time to read and consider the answers. On the other hand, questions that take more time to answer are usually more difficult and, by inference, missed more frequently. Some questions are too difficult to answer in the allotted 2 minutes; the best approach is to give each question its 2 minutes, eliminate some answers, make a reasonable guess, and move on to the next question.

Running out of time is the most common timing error that students make. A less common, but potentially serious, timing error is to work too quickly. Because most questions ask for the best answer, more than one answer may be correct. For example, in the following question, three of the answers are correct, but only one is the best answer.

Question: The human kidney is composed of approximately 1 million nephrons. Each nephron is composed of a glomerulus, arterioles, and a renal tubule. The most important functional component of the renal tubule is:

A. Bowman's capsule.

B. the distal convoluted tubule.

C. the proximal convoluted tubule.

D. the loop of Henle.

Answer: **A**

The best answer to this questions is A, Bowman's capsule. The other three answers are components of the renal tubule. However, the phase "most important functional component" makes A the best choice because it is in Bowman's capsule that the major function of the renal tubule, filtration, occurs.

A student who reads this question too quickly might choose answer B, the distal convoluted tubule, because it is the final component of the renal tubule before the collecting duct. The distal convoluted tubule is the site where the final product of filtration leaves the renal tubule, but it is not the "most important functional component."

This type of question presents concepts and facts in subtle ways. Each answer should be analyzed and rejected only if it is clearly not the best answer.

Do Look for Absolute or Qualified Answers

Some words (e.g., "always," "all," "never") are clues to false statements. On the other hand, statements that contain qualifying words such as "usually," "most," "some," "may," "if," or "frequently," are usually true. Science is based on hypotheses and theories that are approximations of reality and are difficult to define as always being true. Qualified answers express this imprecision and are more often correct.

Do Consider Whether the Question is Asking for a General or Specific Answer

When a question tests a general idea, concept, fact, or set of facts, the most general answer is often the best answer. For example:

Question: The basic active component(s) of the endocrine system is (are):

A. tyrosine.

B. cholesterol.

C. hormones.

D. sex steroids.

Answer: **C**

In this question the correct answer, hormones, is the most general. The other answers are either precursors of hormones (answers A and B) or a specific set of hormones (answer D). Because the question asks about a broad concept, "the basic active component," it is logical to assume that the most general answer is best.

When a question is specific, the most specific answer is usually correct. For example:

Question: In obstructive jaundice, the yellowing of the skin and sclera of the eye is produced by:

A. increased urine excretion.

B. the leaking of conjugated bilirubin into the circulation.

C. decreased urine excretion.

D. viral hepatitis.

Answer: **B**

The correct answer, B, gives a specific explanation for the yellowing that is produced in association with jaundice; the other answers do not. Answers A and C are unrelated to jaundice, but even if they were related, they would be incorrect because neither directly produces yellowing. The most that either increased or decreased urine excretion could do is cause the accumulation or loss of some chemical product that, in turn, could cause yellowing. Answer D is related to jaundice, but does not directly produce yellowing. The damage to the liver cells seen in viral hepatitis causes conjugated bilirubin to accumulate and leak into the circulation, producing yellowing.

In this specific question, the most specific answer is correct. The only other possibly correct answer, D, is involved in the process that produces yellowing in jaundice, but does not cause yellowing. Viral hepatitis creates the situation that leads to an excess of conjugated bilirubin, which causes the yellowing.

Do Look For Two Answers That Cover the Possible Range of Choices or That Are Opposite One Another

Sometimes an answer is the opposite of the correct answer. For instance, two answers might be "in the heart" and "not in the heart." These two answers present the full range of possibilities regarding location within or outside the heart. The two answers are also the opposite of one another.

The student should assume that one of these answers is potentially the best answer. He should concentrate his initial analysis of the question on determining whether one of these answers is the best answer or whether they are both incorrect. Only after making this judgment should he go on to evaluate the other answers.

For example:

Question: A 28-year-old man is involved in an automobile accident that injures part of his spinal cord. As a result of the accident, he has developed spastic paralysis. This paralysis indicates damage to the:

A. basal ganglia.

B. upper motor neuron.

C. lower motor neuron.

D. primary afferent nerve fiber.

Answer: **B**

In this question, answers B and C represent the range of possibilities. Presumably, the student knows that the human nervous system contains only these motor neurons. The two answers are also the opposite of one another. Therefore, the student should evaluate these answers before considering the other answers.

Do Eliminate Upper and Lower Values for Questions With Numbers for Answers, and Do Estimate Answers

Most MCAT questions with number answers are physics questions. Following a few simple steps can focus attention on the most likely answers. First, the highest and lowest value answers are usually incorrect, so it is best to evaluate the middle values. With these two answers in mind, the student should perform a quick calculation of the problem, rounding the values in the question up or down to estimate the answer. This estimate should be compared with the two remaining answers to determine whether one of them is fairly close to the estimate. If one answer is close, it is probably correct. For example:

Question: Two trains are heading in opposite directions after leaving Kansas City. One train travels at a constant speed of 90 mph and the other at 80 mph. Train A left Kansas City at 8:00 A.M. and Train B left at 8:45 A.M. After 4.5 hours, Train A has traveled 360 miles. How far did Train B travel in the same time?

A. 325 miles

B. 375 miles

C. 405 miles

D. 480 miles

Answer: **C**

   This question is not difficult, but performing the necessary calculations may take longer than the allotted 2 minutes. To answer this question, a student might consider various physics equations involving speed or distance. However, some simple calculations can help the student arrive at the correct answer quickly. First, the student chooses one of the speed values and multiplies it by the time span. For example, choosing 80 mph leads to a value of 360 miles (80 mph $\times$ 4.5 hours = 360 miles). Because Train A traveled 360 miles, this answer is incorrect. Next, multiplying 4.5 hours by 90 mph produces a value of 405 miles (90 mph $\times$ 4.5 hours = 405 miles). Answer C, 405 miles, is the correct answer.

   This solution is satisfactory, but this question can be answered with one multiplication step. The difference in the speed of the two trains is 10 mph. Multiplying this difference (10) by 4.5 hours equals 45 miles. Because Train A traveled 360 miles, the answer should equal 360 plus or minus 45. No answer is 315 miles (360 $-$ 45 = 315), but answer C is 405 miles (360 + 45 = 405), making it the best choice.

   Most mathematic problems can be solved in more than one way. The best approach is to find the easiest, simplest method. After stating the problem in its simplest form, the student should perform the necessary steps to calculate the answer. Trying to solve the problem without analyzing it may lead to false starts, overworking the problem, and lost time.

   After an answer is chosen in a mathematic question, it is a good idea to work backward. In other words, once a value for X (or any unknown value) is selected, the student should substitute the answer X and recalculate the equation. With the correct value for X, the answer derived should balance out the other parts of the equation. This technique takes a few seconds, but can identify answers that appear correct, yet are mathematically incorrect.

Do Translate Scientific Terminology into Common English Words

Chapter 14 lists the major prefixes, suffixes, and root words used to create nearly all of the terminology used in the biologic and health fields. Using this list to translate scientific terms into simple English can be helpful when answering biologic and organic chemistry questions on the MCAT. The following question illustrates this principle:

Question: The primary lesion in osteoarthritis is in the:

A.   bone.

B.   synovium.

C.   cartilage.

D.   synovial fluid.

Answer: **C**

   Understanding that "lesion" means a "hole, cut, or damage" eliminates answer D because a hole cannot occur in fluid. Translating "osteo-" as "bone" and "-arthritis" as "inflammation of the joints," which are primarily cartilage, narrows the choices to answers A and C. Translating "primary" as "first" and rereading the question as "Where does the first hole, cut, or damage occur in the bone–joint inflammation disease process?" leads to answer C. It makes sense that a hole would first occur in the soft tissue of the cartilage rather than in the harder tissue of the bone.

Do Look for Grammatical Consistency

Multiple-choice questions and answers can often be read as a complete sentence. However, sometimes mistakes are made in the other choices. These errors can lead to errors in usage or to awkwardly phrased question–answer combinations. For instance, if a question ends in "a" and one of the answers is "apple," this answer is obviously incorrect.

Tests do not usually contain such obvious mistakes; however, students should look for questions and answers that do not match. For example, if a question is written to correspond with an answer that starts with a verb, answers that start with a noun are incorrect.

A more common error in usage is a lack of agreement in number. For example, if a question asks for a single-item answer, plural answers can be eliminated. As an example, consider the following question:

Question: Organs that are involved in the regulation of blood pressure, fluid volume, and acid–base balance are the:

A. testes.

B. kidneys.

C. adrenal glands.

D. heart.

Answer: **B**

Answer D is a single item, and the question is asking for a plural answer. "Heart" might have been a possible answer because this organ is involved with blood pressure and fluid volume, but the test-wise test taker would immediately consider this answer incorrect because of the lack of agreement in number.

Do Look for Long or Unusually Short Answers

Long answers are often correct because the best answer may have to be qualified. For this reason, if one answer is three sentences long and the others are one sentence long, then the three-sentence answer is probably correct. Even if the longest answer is incorrect, the student should evaluate it first, because it has a good chance of being correct. For example:

Question: Pyruvate dehydrogenase kinase:

A. is a cAMP-dependent enzyme.

B. activates pyruvate dehydrogenase.

C. is a subunit of the pyruvate dehydrogenase complex and inhibits pyruvate dehydrogenase by phosphorylating it.

D. is normally activated by pyruvate.

Answer: **C**

The longest answer in this question is C. This answer defines pyruvate dehydrogenase kinase and explains its function. This information is more important and significant than the information provided in the other three answers. The next best answer is B, which also explains the function of this item, albeit incorrectly.

Whereas long answers tend to be correct, short answers tend to be incorrect. It is often difficult to write more than two challenging incorrect answers, and additional incorrect answers tend to be short. If three answers are two sentences long and one answer is one-half a sentence long, the shorter answer is probably incorrect.

Do Make Sure to Mark the Correct Answer

It is best to allow a few minutes at the end of each section of the MCAT to review the answer sheet to determine whether the correct answer is marked for each question. Correct answers should be marked on the test booklet and then, at the end of each section, checked against the question numbers. This simple check can identify mismarked answers in time to correct them. It can also detect more significant errors, such as shifting down one or more questions on the answer sheet when marking an answer. In this situation, a student may read question 25, choose an answer, and accidentally mark the answer on the question sheet line for question 26. If not corrected, this shift would affect all subsequent answers.

Don't Be Afraid to Change an Answer

The conventional wisdom is that the first answer chosen is the best choice. Students have heard this advice from their peers and many of their teachers. However, studies dating as far back as the 1920s show that changing an answer leads to an increase in the number of questions answered correctly. A recent study at the University of Michigan Medical School found that of the nearly 2000 answers that were changed by students in six courses, 67% of the changes were from incorrect answers to correct answers. Only 33% of the changed answers were from correct answers to incorrect answers.[1]

In contrast to such studies, the evidence in favor of not changing answers is anecdotal. For example, a student takes a test, receives the score, and finds that he missed 10 questions. During the test, he had changed the answers on 10 questions. Further, he sees that three of the questions he missed were ones he changed during the test. He vows not to change an answer again. However, he did not realize that seven of the answers he changed were changed to correct answers, twice as many as he missed by changing answers.

Of course, answers should not be changed on a whim. Changes should be based on fresh insight or a better analysis of the question. Changes are often made after a student reevaluates a question. Between the first and second reading of the question, the student's subconscious mind has probably been working on the question and has arrived at a better answer.

Don't Underestimate Your Ability

A student who has difficulty answering a question on a familiar topic may question his knowledge or testing skills. Difficulties encountered with subsequent questions can further erode the student's confidence. In this situation, students begin to second-guess themselves and their abilities. They see more in a question than

---

[1]Whitehouse BA, Davis WK: A majority of medical students improve multiple choice test scores by changing first answers on answer sheets. *Acad Med* 68(5):333–5, 1995.

is actually there and believe that answers that they know to be true are too obvious or simple to be correct.

Students facing this situation should remember two points: First, no one answers every question right, even the best students, who earn double-digit scores on the MCAT. For this reason, students must know when to make a reasonable guess and move on to the next question. Second, students who have done reasonably well in their undergraduate premedical courses and have completed a focused review for the MCAT should do well on the MCAT. They should face the MCAT with the confidence that they have the knowledge and analytical skills needed to answer most of the questions correctly.

● ● ●
MARKING KEY ELEMENTS OF MULTIPLE-CHOICE QUESTIONS

This section describes methods for marking questions and answers to highlight important facts or focus on key elements.

Circle Important Directions

It is important to understand each set of directions. For example, are the questions associated with a passage, graph, or table, or do they stand alone? Circle these directions and refer to them when choosing answers. In addition, circle the words or phrases in the question that define what the question is asking. For example, does the question ask for a definition or a description of a process?

It is easy to become confused by questions that ask for the exception or least likely answer. Circling these directions helps the student to focus his attention on the answer that is false or untrue. This process can be especially helpful for students who miss these negatively phrased questions because they concentrate on finding the best correct answer and do not see that the negatively phrased question is asking for the best incorrect answer. Circling the negative words helps to correct this tendency.

Underline Key Concepts or Facts

A difficult task in answering questions on the MCAT is quickly identifying important information in the associated passage, graph, or table. So much information may be provided that, in the short time allotted, the student has trouble defining what is necessary to answer the question. This problem can be compounded if the student does not identify important points while reading the material. Often, a student decides that one fact is important and another is not while reading the data initially. However, if she does not note this decision, when she reads the questions, she may return to the data and reread the same points. This practice wastes time and effort. A simple way to avoid this problem is to underline the key data on the first reading. If the student must return to the passage, she can immediately locate important points, saving time and energy.

Mark True and False Choices

Marking T (true) or F (false) next to each answer choice is useful for two reasons. First, it helps to eliminate errors in marking answers on the answer sheet. For example, in a question that is asking for the best correct answer, an F marked next to one or more answers reminds the student that these answers are not correct. Second, a type of question format that is found on the MCAT has a standard question stem followed by a series of Roman numeral items. The Roman numerals then appear as answer choices. The following question is an example of this format. It has been marked according to the suggestions given earlier.

Question: Eukaryotic cells contain a number of organelles that assist them in producing energy, synthesizing proteins, and performing other vital functions. Which two of the following <u>organelles</u> are (NOT) directly involved in <u>energy metabolism</u> in these cells?

F **I.** Nucleus

F **II.** Golgi apparatus

T **III.** Mitochondria

F **IV.** Nucleolus

F **A.** I and III

F **B.** II and III

F **C.** III and IV

T **D.** I and II

Answer: **D**

In this example, the key words are underlined and the negative word ("not") is circled. In addition, Ts and Fs are marked, not only by the answer choices, but also by the Roman numerals. With this type of question, marking the Roman numerals is more important than marking the answer choices. The Fs marked by the numerals I, II, and IV and the T marked by numeral III simplify selection of the correct answer. However, this question asks the student to identify two organelles that are not involved in energy metabolism. In other words, both of the choices must not be involved in producing energy. Therefore, any answer that includes III is incorrect. The only answer that does not include III is D.

Circle Words Repeated in the Choices

Circling repeated words in answers is the most powerful marking and test-taking technique. It is not always possible for the author of the question to provide four equally challenging answers. Instead, the answers may include one or more choices that differ only slightly from the correct answer. Including similar answers is meant to make choosing an answer confusing. However, for this reason, one of the answers that includes the repeated word or phrase is probably correct.

Three types of repeated word groups are found in questions. The first type has two or three answers that include the same word or phrase. For instance, if two answers contain the phrase "following an increase in atmospheric pressure," then one of these is the correct answer and the other is probably incorrect. In the second type, there is more than one set of repeating words or phrases, but one set provides more information and, therefore, carries more weight. For example, the following question contains two repeating word groups, but they are of unequal weight. The words repeated in A and B are not as important as the phrase repeated in answers C and D. Thus, the correct answer is probably either C or D.

Question: Respiration is the exchanging of gases in the lungs. Oxygen (O_2) enters the lungs, and carbon dioxide (CO_2) is expired. The <u>major physical regulator</u> of this process is:

F   **A.** increases in lung volume.

F   **B.** increases in atmospheric pressure.

T   **C.** a gas's tendency to move from higher to lower pressure areas.

F   **D.** a gas's tendency to move from lower to higher pressure areas.

Answer: **C**

In this example, the key words are marked, the answer choices are classified as either T or F, and the repeated elements in the answer are circled.

In the last type of repeated word group, two groups of words appear in more than one answer but the word groups are of equal weight. For instance, if two answers include the phrase "decreased level of ..." and the other two answers include "increased level of ...," there is no way to distinguish between these two groups based on the repeating elements. Therefore, when evaluating these answers, the student should first consider whether the question is related to an increase or a decrease in the value discussed. If the level should be increasing, then both answers that mention a decrease are incorrect.

Look for Words or Phrases Repeated in the Question and Answers

An answer that contains a word or phrase that appears in the question is usually correct. The word or phrase had to be repeated in order to make the answer correct. If the word or phrase appears in more than one answer, then one of those answers is probably correct.

● ● ●
THE VERBAL REASONING AND SCIENCE SECTIONS

In the Verbal Reasoning, Physical Sciences, and Biological Sciences sections of the MCAT, additional test-taking methods can increase efficiency and help the student analyze the material more effectively. These methods are similar for all sections, although some slight differences between the Physical Sciences and Biological Sciences sections and the Verbal Reasoning section are described. The term "passage" is used to define text passages that appear in the Verbal Reasoning and science sections as well as the tables, graphs, and illustrations that appear in the science sections.

Skim Each Passage to Determine the Topic

One problem associated with the MCAT is that so many potential content areas are used as the basis for questions. The Physical Sciences and Biological Sciences sections encompass physics, biology, and organic and inorganic chemistry. The Verbal Reasoning section draws material from more than 20 areas. For this reason, the student will be familiar with some topics and unfamiliar with others. A student can optimize his score by skimming each passage before starting to answer the questions.

First, the student should look at each passage and determine its topic. Then he should number each passage according to his familiarity with the subject matter. After this assessment, the passage newly assigned number one might be the fifth passage on the test. By the same token, the first passage in the test might be assigned number eight.

After completing this process, the student should read the new number one passage. This practice aids the student in two ways. First, the student is more likely to answer questions correctly when the material is familiar. This system allows her to work on familiar passages first and less familiar passages last. If the student runs out of time, she will not complete the last few passages, which will probably yield the fewest questions answered correctly. Second, the easier passages usually take less time to complete, so by completing them first, the student may have more time to work though the last few passages. This extra time may make a big difference in how many questions she answers correctly.

Skim the Questions

After skimming each passage, the student should evaluate the questions in the same way. She should skim the questions before reading the passage in depth. She should then determine what is being asked in each question and answer as many questions as possible without referring to the passage. On average, two or three of the nine or ten questions associated with the passage can be answered based on general knowledge of the subject.

The student should mark questions that require information from the passage (e.g., by circling the entire question) and underline or circle key points. The student can then refer to these key points when reading the passage. For example, in the following question from a passage that deals with epidemiology, key points are marked.

Question: Based on the <u>information provided in the passage</u>, the <u>incidence rate</u> of the <u>disease</u> described can be calculated as:

A. 0.25.

B. 0.35.

C. 0.50.

D. 0.70.

Answer: **None**

The words "incidence rate" and "disease" are underlined in this question. To determine the incidence rate of a disease, it is necessary to know the number of people who had the illness during the last year. The number is divided by the total number of individuals at risk for the illness. With this information in mind, a student could skim the passage to find the two values needed to calculate the incidence rate. In other words, it is not necessary to read the entire passage to answer this question.

Make Margin Notes

Annotating the text passages for the Physical Sciences and Biological Sciences sections is useful, but margin notes are most helpful in the Verbal Reasoning section. As the student skims the text passage, he should make brief comments on the information contained in each paragraph. One method is to write the standard newspaper questions: who, what, when, where, why, and how. A more complex method is to use abbreviations to mark important points (e.g., def. for a definition; ex. for example; op. for an opinion; con. for the conclusion; mi. for the main idea; sp. for a supporting fact or detail) and to write more detailed comments based on the information presented in the text.

In the following passage, comments are noted and important points are underlined.

The history of the internment of Japanese-Americans during World War II is a <u>highly controversial issue.</u> Basically, two diametrically opposed paradigms have developed. The first is forcefully presented by Japanese-Americans themselves. They reason that the <u>internment was unlawful</u> and <u>inspired by racism.</u> They cite the fact that <u>German-Americans and Italian-Americans</u> were <u>not rounded up, en masse,</u> as they were and placed in concentration camps in the wilderness.

On the other side are those who believe that the <u>internment was justified by the wartime emergency</u> and the proximity of most Japanese-Americans to military bases, ports, and other important sites ripe for sabotage on the West Coast. They also condemn the use of the term "concentration camps" to describe what they <u>prefer to call "relocation centers."</u> They argue that, unlike camps in Europe, <u>no mass executions or slave labor</u> were performed in the relocation centers.

Japanese-Americans counter that they were <u>forced to leave their homes at gunpoint</u> and were taken to remote areas, to <u>camps surrounded by barbed wire and guard towers</u> manned by military troops. They further state that they were not allowed to leave and had to <u>suffer great hardships of weather and disease</u> because they were forced to live in hastily constructed barracks, without proper heating or sanitary facilities.

●●●
GUESSING STRATEGIES

Every student must occasionally guess. Even with the best preparation, some questions are too difficult, or time may limit analysis. Even when guessing, however, students can use strategies to improve their scores. Because there is no penalty for incorrect answers, every student should answer every question, even if forced to guess. The next section describes points to consider when guessing.

Eliminate Incorrect Answers

Guessing is most effective if one or more answers can be eliminated. It is nearly always possible to eliminate at least one answer, using knowledge, test-taking skills, or both. Eliminating answers requires time to analyze the question; however, it is important that every question is given some time, no matter how brief, for analysis.

Choose the Highest Unknown Answer

Choosing the highest unknown answer is a simple, highly effective method for guessing when some answers can be eliminated. In this situation, "highest" refers to the physical placement of the answers on the page, with A at the top and D at the bottom. For example, if answers C and D have been eliminated, the highest answer that is left is A. As another example, if answers A and C are eliminated, the highest answer left is B. Normally, if two answers are left and a student guesses randomly, the odds of choosing the correct answer are 50/50, or 50%. With this technique, the odds increase to 60%–65%, or an increase of 10%–15%. This difference could increase a student's score on the MCAT by one or two scaled points. The following answer group is an example of this process:

F **A.** increases.

F **B.** decreases.

   C. remains the same.

   D. not known.

Answers A and B have been marked as false, leaving answers C and D. Because C is the highest answer left, it should be chosen. It is important to select the highest answer consistently. If the highest unknown answer is not chosen consistently, then the odds of choosing the correct answer decrease significantly.

Choose B Consistently When All Answers Are Unknown

Most students know about this guessing method. When they run out of time or cannot eliminate any answers, they must guess. However, choosing the same answer consistently improves the odds of guessing correctly. Answer B is recommended because of the percentage of times that B is the correct answer. On the MCAT, A is correct 26% of the time, B is correct 27% of the time, C is correct 24% of the time, and D is correct 23% of the time. For this reason, B is a slightly better choice than A, and is clearly better than either C or D. However, in order to benefit from this technique, the student must choose B for all questions for which no answers are eliminated. On the other hand, if any answers are eliminated, the student should choose the highest answer. This method increases the odds of choosing the correct answer when guessing from 27% to 40%–45% when one answer is eliminated and to 60%–65% when two answers are eliminated. For this reason, it is important to allow time to evaluate and eliminate some answers.

● ● ●
THE WRITING SAMPLE SECTION

Test-taking strategies for the Writing Sample section of the MCAT are different from those described for multiple-choice questions. Writing an essay requires a different set of skills and abilities than choosing an answer from a list of possibilities. The best preparation is to practice writing essays before taking the MCAT. Students who attend schools that use essays as a major form of testing and assessment should have little trouble with the writing sample section. However, most students attend colleges and universities that use multiple-choice, true–false, and other short testing methods to assess performance. These students are often intimidated by the Writing Sample section. To prepare for the MCAT, the student should write 15 to 20 practice essays. The essays should be evaluated by someone familiar with the scoring methods described in Chapter 11 (e.g., a professor or advisor). The student's goal is not to get the highest possible score, but to score at or above the mean. On the scoring scale of J through T, the student should score at least N or O.

The next section describes methods for improving performance on the Writing Sample section of the MCAT. These techniques should be integrated into the student's practice sessions because they provide a practical, systematic approach to analyzing the steps required in writing the essays. These techniques are described as a series of dos and don'ts.

Do Manage Your Time

Because students have only 60 minutes to write both essays in the Writing Sample section, managing time is an important factor in improving performance. Problems with time management involve both working too quickly and working too slowly. Students who work too quickly often do a cursory reading of the essay topic and question, and then begin writing without planning what they want to say or how they will answer the question. These students start off with an idea, write a paragraph or so about it, and then cannot finish the essay. They waste time rewriting what they have written to correct the essay. The essay may then be disjointed, sloppy, and unclear, and may receive a low score.

Students who work too slowly try to write too much and often cannot finish because they run out of time. These students think about the topic and question, but start before they have completely outlined what they plan to write. They write at length about the points they wish to address, but do not limit the examples or information that supports their arguments. These students may achieve a higher score than students who work too quickly, but are penalized for not completing the essay.

To avoid these problems, students should allocate their time as shown in *Table 15–2.*

Read the Topic and Question, Underlining the Main Points

The essay questions on the MCAT follow a specific pattern. For this reason, it is important to review and understand the topic. As described in Chapter 11, the topics present an either/or situation, in which the student must agree or disagree with the author. The student should underline the points that present this conflicting information.

The question about the topic is divided into three parts. The first part asks the student to explain or interpret the statement. The second part asks the student to describe an example opposite to the statement. The third part asks the student to propose a resolution to the conflict between initial statement and its opposite.

Do Write Down Everything You Know About the Topic

The student should think about the topic and quickly write down all of the ideas, facts, and examples that come to mind. This process is known as brainstorming. For example, consider this topic:

● ● ●

TABLE 15–2. Allocation of Time

Time	Task
2 minutes	Read the topic and question
10 minutes	Brainstorm ideas and write outline
13 minutes	Write the essay
5 minutes	Edit and correct the essay

To be prepared for war is one of the most effectual means of preserving peace.
George Washington

Based on this quote by George Washington, the student might list the following points:

- About Washington: 1776; Revolutionary War; first president; general.
- About war: only governments have power to wage war; wars fought for land, economics; millions killed in history; money spent on defense, armies, weapons; wars still happened.
- About peace: M. Gandhi; Martin L. King; Switzerland; United Nations.

Do Write an Outline

After noting all of the ideas that come to mind, the next step is to develop an outline to use in writing the essay. In its simplest form, an outline is three sentences long. The first sentence contains the thesis of the essay, the second sentence states the antithesis of this idea, and the third describes a synthesis of the thesis and antithesis. Based on the ideas listed in the previous example, these sentences could be:

- Thesis: George Washington, general of the Revolutionary Army and the first president of the United States, obviously felt that preparing for war would preserve peace, because he must have thought that no enemy would dare attack a nation that had a strong defense in place.
- Antithesis: Others in history, most notably Gandhi and Martin Luther King, have advocated nonviolent means to achieve social and national changes. Gandhi's use of nonviolent protests led to the withdrawal of British authority from India.
- Synthesis: A strong defense can often protect a nation and, therefore, preserve peace, but this is not true in all circumstances. Nations that are threatened rather than intimidated by another nation's power may strike out of a sense of self-preservation.

Do Use the Rule of 3s

After the outline is done, it is fairly simple to finish the essay. Students should follow the rule of 3s: the essay should contain at least three paragraphs; each paragraph should have an opening sentence (i.e., the three written in the outline); and each paragraph should contain at least three sentences (i.e., the opening sentence; an example, or proof, based on the opening sentence; and a transition or concluding sentence). Following this process will produce a well-constructed, concise essay. In most cases, the essay will earn the mean score.

Writing more can improve a student's score. If the student has time, he can provide further examples or support for the arguments presented in the thesis, antithesis, or synthesis sentences. The following example shows the final essay that might be written for this topic:

George Washington, general of the Revolutionary Army and the first president of the United States, obviously felt that preparing for war would preserve peace, because he must have thought that no enemy would dare attack a nation that had a strong defense in place.

This viewpoint preceded Washington and continues to this day. One of the more ambitious recent forms of this ideal is the Star Wars antimissile defense system that was started by President Reagan. The philosophy behind this ideal holds that power can be used to intimidate other nations, making them think twice before attacking.

Others in history, most notably Gandhi and Martin Luther King, have advocated nonviolent means to achieve social and national changes. Gandhi's use of nonviolent protests led to the withdrawal of British authority from India. In effect, peace was preserved in India without resorting to either war or the use of intimidation. In fact, the large British defensive system in India proved completely inadequate when dealing with this nontraditional form of warfare. Another argument against the idea that a strong defense can preserve peace is a situation when other nations are not intimidated by the defender's power. This situation occurred in World War II, when the Japanese attacked the United States. At the time, the United States was a larger nation, with a larger population, a larger economy, and a larger navy and army. Japan attacked because they felt that they had no choice. Their economy needed more raw materials if it was to expand and grow, but the United States was limiting their ability to acquire those materials. Thinking that they had nothing to lose, the Japanese attacked, knowing that their chances of success were limited.

While a strong defense can often protect a nation and, therefore, preserve peace, this is not true in all circumstances. Nations that are threatened rather than intimidated by another nation's power may strike out of a sense of self-preservation. Additionally, significant changes have been made to nations without the advent of war, leaving military defenders helpless and bewildered. To preserve peace requires a strong defense, balanced by a nation's willingness to negotiate, communicate, and clearly define its goals, ambitions, and national interests. In this way, other nations will respect this nation and have realistic expectations about its potential use of deadly force.

Do Double-space

The essays must be written in black ink, so erasing is not possible. For this reason, it is a good idea to double-space to leave room for corrections or additions. Also, it is important to write or print as legibly as possible, because the essays will be copied and sent to the reviewers for scoring. Additions and other changes may be overlooked if they are not indicated clearly.

Do Proofread and Review the Essay for Errors

The final step in writing the essays is to proofread them and make any necessary corrections (e.g., spelling or grammatical changes). To make the essay as neat as possible, it is important to keep changes to a minimum, but students should not be afraid to cross out sentences or even paragraphs that are awkward or weak.

Don't Forget the Topic

If the student has prepared a good outline before starting to write, then the essay should be a clear, unified statement about the topic, with paragraphs flowing from point to point. Without an outline, the student may stray from the topic and write about something else. Mean to high scores are given to students who answer the question, not to students who write beautiful, passionate essays that do not answer the question.

Don't Be Afraid to Express an Opinion

Some students believe that they should not express an opinion on the topic. This belief is inaccurate. If a student has an opinion on the topic, she should express it and support it with examples or other information that shows her knowledge. However, students should not manufacture an opinion to impress the reviewers; nor should they claim to know more about the topic than they do.

CHAPTER 16

MCAT Review Courses and Materials

- Self-Study for the MCAT
- MCAT Preparation Programs

A double-digit score on the Medical College Admission Test (MCAT) is an important part of the medical school application. A high score demonstrates to admission committees that a student has the basic knowledge and skills needed to succeed in medical school. It validates a good grade point average (GPA) and can help to overcome a low GPA. There is also a strong correlation between achieving a high MCAT score and passing the United States Medical Licensing Examination (USMLE) tests. Therefore, it is important to make every effort to score well on the MCAT. Students should get some exposure to the MCAT before taking it, but it is not wise to take the test for practice. The student's last two scores and the number of times the student sat for the test are reported to schools. Admissions committees tend to disfavor students who have made more than three attempts to pass.

Students prepare for the MCAT in two basic ways:

1. Self-study with the aid of published materials
2. Structured study with a full-fledged MCAT preparation program

• • •
SELF-STUDY FOR THE MCAT

This book describes the structure and scoring of the MCAT and provides a sample MCAT with the answers and a guide for analyzing the results. The book also describes how to use study materials and how to take the test. These chapters provide all of the background material necessary to perform well on the MCAT. The authors have used this type of material for more than a decade to help hundreds of students prepare for the MCAT. However, this material is not designed to provide either content review or extensive practice in taking the MCAT. Both of these components are also necessary for success.

Several books provide content review or simulated examinations. These books differ with respect to the space that they devote to either process. Moreover, the simulated examinations differ in the degree that they reflect the philosophy, difficulty, and style of questions found on the real MCAT. However, all of these books provide feedback and reinforce content review.

The following books are primarily devoted to content review:

- Flowers JL, Silver T: *MCAT: The Princeton Review.* New York, Random House, 1995, $50.00, 1045 pages, paperback. This first edition has a 15-page overview section. The rest of the book is devoted to content review, with questions and answers provided at the end of each section.

- Hassan AS, et al: *A Complete Preparation for the MCAT: The Betz Guide,* 7th ed. Baltimore, Williams & Wilkins, 1996, $49.50, 1000+ pages, paperback. This book is the updated version of a classic review edited by James L. Flowers, MD, who is still a contributor. Several of the authors have conducted their own MCAT preparation courses or have been intimately involved with the MCAT for years. The book provides general information about the MCAT, but primarily provides content material, with questions and answers, and a final section with 22 MCAT-style passages, also with questions and answers.

The following volumes are hybrids that devote significant space to content review, but also contain simulated MCAT examinations, with answers and explanations.

- Alvarez JA: *Best Test Preparation for the Medical College Admission Test (MCAT).* Piscataway, NJ, Research & Education Associates, 1994, $39.95, 1002 pages, paperback. The first six chapters provide a content review of the various MCAT subjects. This section is followed by six tests with answers and explanations. The appendix lists medical schools in the United States and Canada.

- Bosworth S, et al: *ARCO MCAT SuperCourse,* 2nd ed. New York, Prentice Hall, 1994, $35.00, 697 pages, paperback. The first 6 pages provide a general overview of the test. The next sections provide content review for each area covered on the MCAT. Each section has a short summary, with practice problems and answers. Unit 5 has three practice MCAT examinations with an answer key. The final 12 pages describe the content of the various medical school courses and residency programs.

The following books offer little content review, but contain one or more simulated examinations with answers and explanations:

- Flowers JL, Silver T: *Princeton Review—Annotated Practice MCAT, 1997 Edition.* New York, Random House, 1996, $20.00, paperback. This book contains a short section describing the MCAT and practice examinations with explanations.

- Rothstein R, et al: *Kaplan MCAT All-In-One 96/97 Edition.* New York, Bantam Doubleday Dell, 1996, $34.95, paperback. This book is accompanied by a computer disk containing a half-length simulated MCAT test. The first 36 pages describe medical school admissions. The next nine pages describe the MCAT. The next section provides a short practice test, with explanations, followed by a full-length simulated test with answers and explanations.

- Seible H, et al: *MCAT,* 7th ed. Hauppage, NY, Barron's Educational Services, 1991, $12.95, 471 pages, paperback. This book contains four examinations, with answers and explanations. A brief introduction describes the MCAT.

-

Students who study independently need to rely on these published materials for guidance. Before committing to an expensive and time-consuming commercial program, students should take the simulated test from this book and at least two other books (to compensate for differing levels of difficulty), under timed conditions.

Students who score 7 or higher after taking these simulated examinations before studying probably do not need a commercial review program. These students have the fundamental knowledge required to do well on the MCAT. They may need to review some material or learn some new material, but a score of 7 suggests that these are limited gaps. The best approach is to conduct a complete self-study by reviewing material and becoming familiar with the test. This book can be used as a guide for self-study (see Chapters 14 and 15). Conducting a review as described in this book, improving testing skills, and reviewing content with one of the books mentioned above should be sufficient to help a student achieve a high MCAT score.

On the other hand, students who score less than 7 and identify areas of content deficiency need an organized content review. The best approach may be to use a commercial course. Effective programs contain a wealth of easily accessible, clearly presented, didactic coursework. These programs offer advice and experience that are not available otherwise. Many students hesitate because of the cost of these programs. However, it is important to weigh the cost against the possible benefit. For example, paying $700 for a course is far less expensive than reapplying to medical school the next year or attending a foreign school.

● ● ●
MCAT PREPARATION PROGRAMS

Most areas of the United States are serviced by one to three national programs and often by one or more smaller regional programs. The national programs are often effectively marketed and tend to have a wealth of educational resources. However, the quality of instruction may vary from site to site because these companies tend to rely on students as instructors or group leaders. Therefore, a company may offer a good program at one site and a lesser program at another site. The regional programs also vary in quality, but they tend to offer programs of the same quality year after year because they service a limited number of sites.

Students should go to the closest sites; talk to the personnel, even if they are not teaching; determine what is offered; review the materials that are distributed during the program; and evaluate the sincerity and competence of the staff. It is also helpful to talk to friends who have taken courses to determine the advantages and disadvantages of each course. However, it is important to remember that individual needs vary. Commercial programs include:

National Programs

- *Kaplan.* The Kaplan program was started decades ago by Stanley Kaplan. The company has become part of a conglomerate, which is both a strength and a weakness. Kaplan has multiple centers, which often makes attendance convenient. Although they offer live class reviews, they are limited, largely conducted by students, and variable in quality from site to site. The strength of the Kaplan centers is their multimedia libraries that house up-to-date and well-crafted study materials. In addition, they provide home study materials. In general, Kaplan courses are best suited for individuals who are self-starters and are looking primarily for content review. For more information about the Kaplan programs, call 1 (800) KAP-TEST.

- *Princeton Review.* Princeton Review also has centers throughout the United States. One advantage is that class size is limited to 12 students. Instruction is provided by students who have variable teaching skills. They also offer a variety of study materials and emphasize their software package *Caduceus Project.* For more information, call 1 (800) 995-5565.

- *Columbia Review.* Columbia Review was started in 1985 by Stephen Bresnick, MD, then a medical student at the University of California, San Diego. Although most heavily represented in California, Columbia Review now has centers across the United States. They claim to offer more live lectures than any other major program and although the science lectures and tutorials are also conducted by students, the reading and writing components are taught by college or university English instructors. They also provide study and take-home materials, but their literature states that they "do not utilize impersonal (audio and video tape-recorded) teaching methods used by other programs." For more information, call 1 (800) 300-PREP.

- *Graduate Admissions Preparation Service.* Graduate Admissions Preparation Service offers take-home preparation programs. These programs consist of text material and cassettes. Students can purchase an entire MCAT course or parts. This option allows students to limit costs and also provides flexibility. However, students have no interaction with faculty and other students, and the material can become outdated quickly. For information, call 1 (800) 676-2202.

Regional Programs

In addition to national programs, many regional programs are available. Some of these programs are limited to a single site, and some have several sites. Some offer a superior course at a modest price. Others may be inferior. These programs typically advertise in school newspapers, post flyers, or provide information to pre-health advisors. The following programs are available in California:

- *Hyperlearning.* Hyperlearning got its start at the University of California, Irvine, by Todd Bennett, the current director of Berkeley Review. It has grown and now has centers in Southern and Northern California. It offers a balanced content skills approach and ranks among the better regional programs. For more information, call 1 (800) MD-BOUND.

- *Berkeley Review.* Berkeley Review is headquartered in Northern California. It is philosophically and academically similar to Hyperlearning. For more information, call (510) THE-TEST.

CHAPTER 17

Relaxation Training to Reduce Anxiety

- How to Perform the Training Exercise
- Relaxation Training Exercise

Everyone experiences anxiety. In its mildest form, anxiety is characterized by a general feeling of discomfort. Physical signs include a slight increase in heart rate and blood pressure, dry mouth, sweaty palms, and a slight impairment of mental abilities, such as concentration and memory. In its most severe form, anxiety causes overpowering feelings of dread and fear. Pronounced increases in heart rate and blood pressure are accompanied by profuse sweating, nausea, frequent urination, and severe headaches. In some cases, the anxiety is so debilitating that the individual appears physically ill and cannot get out of bed. In a person with severe anxiety, mental ability may be dramatically impaired.

Most people experience anxiety when they must perform a task under timed or observed conditions. A classic example of this type of anxiety is test anxiety, which occurs when an individual is preparing for or taking an examination. Whether the test evaluates manual skill (e.g., a driving test) or mental ability (e.g., a midterm examination), test anxiety affects everyone to some degree.

Unfortunately, for some students, test anxiety is so severe that all of their preparation for the Medical College Admission Test (MCAT) is useless. These students lose confidence in themselves, begin to question their ability, and make mistakes. Anxiety may not have a significant effect on test performance, but even a small difference in performance can reduce a student's score from 10 to 9.

Anxiety can be controlled in many ways. All of these approaches are based on the simple idea that a person cannot have two conflicting emotional responses at the same time. Therefore, to control anxiety, it is necessary to replace it with another emotional response, such as tranquility.

Mild forms of anxiety can be controlled through meditation, yoga, breathing exercises, or prayer. More severe forms of anxiety require more sophisticated methods, such as relaxation training, cued desensitization, biofeedback, and drug therapy.

All of these methods substitute another emotion for anxiety. Relaxation training can alleviate all but the most severe forms of anxiety. This training combines physical and mental elements. The person slowly contracts and then relaxes muscles throughout his body while he thinks about a relaxing mental image. The next section describes how to perform a relaxation training exercise.

It is best to perform this exercise at least eight times, with two to three sessions scheduled per week. This exercise helps participants to learn how to control their ability to relax and overcome anxiety. As a measure of their performance, participants count their heartbeats before and after each session. The heart rate should be reduced by 10%–15%.

After a few sessions, most people begin to experience relaxation, increased self-confidence, and decreased anxiety. Participants stop using the audiotape as they internalize the process. During a stressful time (e.g., taking the MCAT), they use their training to overcome anxiety.

• • •
HOW TO PERFORM THE TRAINING EXERCISE

Record the exercise on a cassette tape, using your voice or a friend's. The more closely you follow the instructions, the more quickly you will learn to relax, even in difficult situations. Try to avoid going to sleep during the training exercise. The training is most effective if you are not fatigued or unable to pay attention.

The next section contains the text for the training exercise. Read and record this text, speaking slowly and carefully.

• • •
RELAXATION TRAINING EXERCISE

To begin, it is important that you feel comfortable. Loosen any tight clothing and remove any uncomfortable jewelry. (Pause.) Move your body around until you feel comfortable. (Pause.)

The purpose of this training exercise is to help you recognize and control relaxation by comparing tension and tension release. As an example, close your eyes and you will immediately feel the tension release after the cessation of brightness, movement, and color. If you keep your eyes closed for a few seconds, you can feel the relaxation begin to flow through your body. This exercise helps you to learn how to achieve that feeling of relaxation whenever you want. (Pause for about 5 seconds.)

Now open your eyes. Feel the tension building up again. The tension isn't bad, but this example shows that you have the ability, at least to a small degree, to control how your body feels. It's easier to focus on your feelings with your eyes closed, so please close your eyes for the remainder of the exercise.

Concentrate now on the tension and release associated with breathing. Take a deep breath and hold it. Focus on the feeling of tension and anxiety. Hold it. You can feel tenseness building. Now let go—all at once, not slowly. Don't force it. Just let it flow out.

Notice that as your breath flows out and you begin to breathe again, you feel more relaxed. Notice that each time you exhale, more tension fades and you feel more relaxed.

Now, each time you exhale, say the word "calm" to yourself, and consider each breath a step toward greater relaxation. Breathe naturally for a minute or so, focusing on the increasing calm you feel each time you exhale and say the word "calm." (Pause for about 60 seconds.)

Notice, also, that as you relax, your muscles begin to feel heavier and heavier. It's a pleasant heaviness. As you learn to relax your muscles, your mind will become more serene. As the tension flows out of your muscles, tension flows out of your mind. It's a pleasant feeling. As tension slips away, your mind feels clearer, sharper, and more aware. The fogginess disappears. (Pause for 5–10 seconds.)

We're going to ease the tension in your body now with several tension and relaxation cycles. Start with your dominant hand: the right one if you are right-handed and the left one if you are left-handed.

As I mention the various parts of your body, tense them until they are uncomfortable. Don't hurt yourself or cause cramps; just tense the body part and hold it for about 5–10 seconds. Then release it all at once. It's important to let go all at once and let the tension leave of its own accord.

Start now with your hand. Tense it. Hold it. Focus on the feeling of hardness, of tension, of tightness. Your fingers are digging into your palms. Now release it. Let it go. Let the tension melt away. Feel the tension flow out, and feel the warmth replacing it as the life-giving blood flows in, bringing a tingling feeling, a pleasant feeling, the feeling associated with waking up after a restful night's sleep.

Tense your hand again, but this time, try to maintain the relaxation in the rest of your body. Just focus on your hand. As you learn to control your body's ability to relax, you will learn to control the tension and relaxation in various parts of your body. Right now, practice tensing your hand. Hold it for a slow count of 10. Notice the contrast between your hand and the rest of your body as you count to 10. When you reach 10, relax and let the tension go. Let the relaxation from the rest of your body flow in as the tension is released. (Pause for about 10 seconds.)

Now, let's practice with your other hand. Tense it, squeeze hard, and feel the tension building up. Your fingers are pushing into your palms. Squeeze harder. Now let go. Feel your fingers straighten out as the tension leaves them and the warmth flows in. Focus on that warmth. Let it flow throughout your hand. Enjoy it for a few seconds. (Pause for 10–20 seconds.)

Now that you're becoming more skilled at controlling your tension and relaxation, we're going to practice with your whole body. We'll begin with your toes and move up your body. As I mention each part, tense it. Continue tensing each part of your body until your whole body is tense. Then, on my signal, let it go all at once. You'll feel complete relaxation. Focus on the feeling. As you let go, release all of the tension that has built up.

Let's begin with your toes. Tense them. Tense your left toes and your left foot. Tense your right toes and your right foot. Feel the tension moving up your calves. Tense your calves by pointing your toes down or up, whichever is comfortable. Now tense your thighs. Allow the tension to move upward into your buttocks and pelvis.

As the tension moves up, focus on each muscle. The tension is moving into your stomach. Now clench both of your hands. Feel the tension moving up your forearms and biceps. As the tension moves from your shoulders and stomach into your chest, take a deep breath. Hold it to increase the tension in your chest. The tension is moving into your jaw. Clench your teeth and your face. Squint your eyes. Feel the tension flowing into your eyebrows and up your forehead to the top of your scalp. Now hold it.

When I count to three, relax—all at once—and exhale. One. Two. Three. Release. Breathe out. Let your muscles droop. Let them relax. (Pause for 5 seconds.) Continue breathing naturally. Focus on your breathing. Each time you exhale, feel a little more tension leave. As you relax more and more, you'll feel heavier and heavier, but it's pleasant heaviness.

Imagine a bit of goose down floating on a windless day. As your anxieties flow out, imagine that you're floating and drifting like that bit of down. It's a pleasant, comfortable feeling. You have no tension, no worries, and no fears.

Now, imagine that you're that piece of soft down. As you inhale and exhale, imagine that you're floating up and down. As you become more relaxed, your breathing will slow down. Just relax and breathe smoothly, easily, and only when necessary. (Pause for about 60 seconds.)

As you continue to relax your body, you may notice that your mind is also relaxing. It's not becoming dull or unresponsive; it's becoming clearer and brighter. You're becoming more aware of your whole body, and it feels pleasant to be relaxed. Imagine your blood flowing to every part of your body, to every organ and muscle, to every cell, bringing relaxation to your whole body via the flow that spreads warmth.

Some people like to find a place in their body where they can store that warmth. Whenever they begin to feel anxious or tense, they can call on the warmth to relieve the tension and help them face the situation more relaxed and more aware. Some people like to store their warmth in their chest, others at the back of their head, others in their stomach, and others in the tip of one of their fingers. This skill is difficult to learn, but many people report that it is worth the effort.

As you relax now, let your imagination find a spot that feels comfortable and safe, and store your warmth there. The next time you feel anxious, and the anxiety is interfering with your ability to perform, take a deep breath and repeat the word "relax" or "calm." You'll begin to feel the relaxing warmth flowing to your shoulders, neck, stomach, and forehead.

As you practice, you'll find that tension and anxiety begin in specific places and you'll be able to focus the warmth and serenity on those areas. Petty annoyances will not turn into headaches or stomachaches. The warmth of relaxation is healing.

Now, let's take your awareness and let it move up your body. For each group of muscles, pause and let the relaxation flow in. Let any tension that you find there melt. Let the warmth flow in to ease the tension.

Focus on your toes and your feet, first one foot and then the other. It's a pleasant, comfortable feeling. If you feel any tension, let it go. Move slowly up your calves and relax. (Pause for 5 seconds.)

Now focus on your knees and thighs. They're so relaxed that you can almost feel the blood flowing through them. (Pause for 5 seconds.) Focus on your right hand and forearm. Let them droop. Let them relax. Let the tension flow smoothly out your fingertips. (Pause for 5 seconds.) Now do the same with your left hand. Just let it relax. Focus on the warmth, and let your body relax on its own. Don't force it. Just allow it to relax.

Now focus on your shoulders and the muscles in your neck. With each breath, imagine that the tension is flowing out. Focus on the feeling of relaxation. Let it spread through your shoulders and neck and up your neck to your scalp and head. Focus on that feeling of relaxation. (Pause for 10 seconds.)

Let the relaxation and warmth move up into your jaw. Just let the tension flow out. Don't keep your mouth tightly closed. Let your jaw droop a little. The relaxation is spreading throughout your face. (Pause for 10 seconds.)

As you finish this training session, concentrate on how good it feels to be so completely relaxed. It's the kind of peaceful feeling people occasionally have in the morning as they wake up. Don't hurry. Just relax and enjoy the feeling. Relaxed. Calm. Serene. You're at peace with yourself, your surroundings, and your hopes and dreams. Today, and from now on, you can keep that serenity and peace of mind with you. (Pause for about 60–100 seconds.)

As I count backward from 10, allow the muscle tension to return. Not too much. Not too fast. Don't let the serenity leave. Let the serenity and awareness exist together. Be aware, be confident, and be serene. As I count backward, open your eyes when I reach five. When I reach one, stretch and feel refreshed, relaxed, and ready to face the challenges ahead. Ten. Nine. Eight. Seven. Six. Five. Open your eyes. Four. Three. Two. One. Stretch, and turn off the tape, if necessary.

Appendices

Appendix A summarizes the admission requirements for medical schools in the United States and Puerto Rico. In addition, the mean grade point average (GPA) and Medical College Admission Test (MCAT) scores for the 1994–95 class are given. Also provided are the class size, the number of out-of-state matriculants in the 1994 class, and the earliest and latest days for application.

Appendix C lists the fees and resident and nonresident tuition rates for medical schools in the United States and Puerto Rico. It is important to consider fees as well as tuition. Note that in some schools fees are as large or larger than tuition. In other schools fees are only used to pay for incidental expenses, such as anatomic specimens. The full name and address of each school are given in Appendix A. The state universities of California, New York, and Texas are each considered as a single entity because tuition is the same and fee differs only slightly.

APPENDIX A. Addresses and Admission Requirements for Medical Schools in the United States and Puerto Rico

School Name and Address	Admission Requirements (Courses)	Mean GPA	MCAT Score				Class Size	Number of Out-of-State Acceptances	AMCAS Dates	
			Verbal Reasoning	Physical Sciences	Biological Sciences	Mean			Earliest	Latest
Alabama										
Office of Medical Student Services/Admissions VH100 University of Alabama, School of Medicine Birmingham, AL 35294-0019 (205) 934-2330	General biology or zoology (with lab), 8 semester hours; inorganic chemistry (with lab), 8 semester hours; organic chemistry (with lab), 8 semester hours; general physics (with lab), 8 semester hours; college mathematics (must include calculus), 6 semester hours; English composition and literature, 6 semester hours	3.51	9.9	9.4	9.7	9.7	166	34	June 15	November 1
Office of Admissions 2015 MSP University of Southern Alabama College of Medicine Mobile, AL 36688-0002 (205) 460-7176	General biology (with lab), 8 semester hours; general chemistry (with lab), 8 semester hours; organic chemistry (with lab), 8 semester hours; general physics (with lab), 8 semester hours; humanities, 8 semester hours; English composition or literature, 8 semester hours; college mathematics, 8 semester hours; calculus, recommended	3.6	9.4	9.1	9.3	9.3	66	6	June 15	November 15
Arizona										
Admissions Office University of Arizona College of Medicine Tucson, AZ 85724 (602) 626-6214	General biology or zoology, 2 semesters or 3 quarters; general chemistry, 2 semesters or 3 quarters; organic chemistry, 2 semesters or 3 quarters; physics, 2 semesters or 3 quarters; English composition and literature, 2 semesters or 3 quarters	3.5	9.4	8.6	9.3	9.1	100	0	June 15	November 1
Arkansas										
Office of Student Admissions Slot 551 University of Arkansas for Medical Sciences, College of Medicine 4301 West Markham Street Little Rock, AR 72205 (501) 686-5354	Biology, 2 semesters; general chemistry, 2 semesters; organic chemistry, 2 semesters; physics, 2 semesters; mathematics, 2 semesters; English, 3 semesters	3.5	9.0	8.0	8.0	8.3	143	2	June 15	November 15
California										
Admissions Office University of California, Davis School of Medicine Davis, CA 95616 (916) 752-2717	English, 1 year; biologic sciences (with lab), 1 year; general chemistry (with lab), 1 year; organic chemistry (with lab), 1 year; physics, 1 year; mathematics, to integral calculus	...	10.5	11.2	11.4	11.0	93	0	June 15	November 1

(Table continued on the following page)

School Name and Address	Admission Requirements (Courses)	Mean GPA	MCAT Score				Class Size	Number of Out-of-State Acceptances	AMCAS Dates	
			Verbal Reasoning	Physical Sciences	Biological Sciences	Mean			Earliest	Latest
Office of Admissions University of California, Irvine College of Medicine PO Box 4089 Irvine, CA 92717-4089 (714) UCI-5388 or (800) 824-5388	Biology or zoology, 1 year lower-division and 0.5 year upper-division coursework (excluding botany and biochemistry); general chemistry, 8 semester hours; organic chemistry, 8 semester hours; physics, 8 semester hours; calculus, 1 quarter; biochemistry, 4 semester hours	3.5	9.2	10.4	10.7	10.2	92	0	June 15	November 1
Office of Student Affairs Division of Admissions University of California, Los Angeles School of Medicine Center for Health Sciences Los Angeles, CA 90024-1720 (310) 825-6081	English and composition, 1 year; physics (with lab), 1 year; chemistry (inorganic, quantitative, and organic), 2 years; biology, 2 years, including 1 year upper-division coursework; mathematics, 1 year (introduction to calculus recommended); biochemistry, recommended; Spanish, recommended	3.57	...	...	...	...	145	10	June 15	November 1
Office of Admissions 0621 Medical Teaching Facility University of California, San Diego School of Medicine 9500 Gilman Drive La Jolla, CA 92093-0621 (619) 534-3880	Biology, 1 year, excluding botany and biochemistry; chemistry, 2 years, including 1 year organic; physics, 1 year; mathematics, 1 year (calculus, statistics, or computer science); English, competence	3.62	...	...	...	...	122	4	June 15	November 1
School of Medicine, Admissions C-200 Box 0408 University of California, San Francisco San Francisco, CA 94143 (415) 476-4044	Biology (with lab), 12 quarter hours (includes vertebrate zoology); general chemistry (with lab), 12 quarter hours; organic chemistry, 8 quarter hours; physics (with lab), 12 quarter hours	3.7	11.0	11.0	11.0	11.0	141	31	June 15	November 1
Associate Dean for Admissions Loma Linda University, School of Medicine Loma Linda, CA 92350 (909) 824-4467	General biology or zoology (with lab), 8.5 hours; general or inorganic chemistry (with lab), 8.5 hours; organic chemistry (with lab), 8.5 hours; physics (with lab), 8.5 hours; English, sufficient for baccalaureate degree	3.57	9.3	8.9	9.2	9.1	159	68	June 15	December 1
Office of Admission University of Southern California School of Medicine 1975 Zonal Avenue Los Angeles, CA 90033 (213) 342-2552	Biology (with lab), 2 semesters or 3 quarters; inorganic chemistry (with lab), 2 semesters or 3 quarters; organic chemistry (with lab), 2 semesters or 3 quarters; general physics (with lab), 2 semesters or 3 quarters	3.5	10.0	10.0	10.0	10.0	136	...	June 15	November 1
Office of Admissions RM154 Stanford University, School of Medicine 851 Welch Road Palo Alto, CA 94304-1677 (415) 723-6861	Biologic science (with lab), 1 year; chemistry, including organic (with lab), 2 years; physics (with lab), 1 year; calculus, physical chemistry, behavioral sciences, and biochemistry, strongly recommended	3.6	10.0	11.0	11.0	10.7	86	43	June 15	November 1

MCAT Score

School Name and Address	Admission Requirements (Courses)	Mean GPA	Verbal Reasoning	Physical Sciences	Biological Sciences	Mean	Class Size	Number of Out-of-State Acceptances	AMCAS Dates Earliest	AMCAS Dates Latest
Colorado										
Medical School Admissions C-297 University of Colorado School of Medicine 4200 East 9th Avenue Denver, CO 80262 (303) 270-7361	General biology (with lab), 8 semester hours; general chemistry (with lab), 8 semester hours; organic chemistry (with lab), 8 semester hours; general physics (with lab), 8 semester hours; mathematics (college algebra and trigonometry), 6 semester hours; English literature, 6 semester hours; English composition or creative writing, 3 semester hours	3.7	9.9	9.9	9.9	9.9	126	18	June 15	November 15
Connecticut										
Office of Admissions and Student Affairs Room AG-062 University of Connecticut, School of Medicine 263 Farmington Avenue Farmington, CT 06030-1905 (203) 679-2152	General biology or zoology (with lab), 8 semester hours; general chemistry (with lab), 8 semester hours; organic chemistry (with lab), 8 semester hours; general physics (with lab), 8 semester hours	3.5	...	...	...	9.7	81	11	June 15	December 15
Office of Admissions Yale University School of Medicine 367 Cedar Street New Haven, CT 06510 (203) 785-2643	General biology or zoology (with lab), 6–8 semester hours; general or inorganic chemistry (with lab), 6–8 semester hours; organic chemistry (with lab), 6–8 semester hours; general physics (with lab), 6–8 semester hours	...	10.8	11.1	11.2	11.0	100	88	June 1	October 15
District of Columbia										
Office of Admissions George Washington University School of Medicine and Health Sciences 2300 Eye Street, NW Washington, DC 20037 (202) 994-3506	Biology or zoology (with lab), 8 semester hours; inorganic chemistry (with lab), 8 semester hours; organic chemistry (with lab), 8 semester hours; physics (with lab), 8 semester hours; English composition and literature, 8 semester hours	3.4	9.0	10.0	10.0	9.7	157	154	June 15	December 1
Office of Admissions Georgetown University, School of Medicine 3900 Reservoir Road, NW Washington, DC 20037 (202) 687-1154	Biology (with lab), 2 semesters or 3 quarters; inorganic chemistry (with lab), 2 semesters or 3 quarters; organic chemistry (with lab), 2 semesters or 3 quarters; general physics (with lab), 2 semesters or 3 quarters; college mathematics, 2 semesters or 3 quarters; English, 2 semesters or 3 quarters	3.51	10.0	10.0	10.0	10.0	185	181	June 15	November 15

(Table continued on the following page)

School Name and Address	Admission Requirements (Courses)	Mean GPA	MCAT Score				Class Size	Number of Out-of-State Acceptances	AMCAS Dates	
			Verbal Reasoning	Physical Sciences	Biological Sciences	Mean			Earliest	Latest
Admissions Office Howard University College of Medicine 520 W Street NW Washington, DC 20059 (202) 806-6270	Biology or zoology, 8 semester hours; general chemistry, 8 semester hours; organic chemistry, 8 semester hours; general physics, 8 semester hours; college mathematics, 6 semester hours; English, 6 semester hours	...	7.6	7.2	7.3	7.4	122	112	June 15	December 15
Florida										
Chairman, Medical Selection Committee J. Miller Health Center University of Florida, College of Medicine Box 100216 Gainesville, FL 32610 (904) 392-4569	Biology (with lab), 8 semester hours; inorganic chemistry (with lab), 8 semester hours; organic chemistry (with lab), 8 semester hours; general physics (with lab), 8 semester hours	3.66	...	...	...	9.3	85	0	June 15	December 1
Office of Admission University of Miami School of Medicine PO Box 016159 Miami, FL 33101 (305) 547-6791	English, 6 semester hours; chemistry (with lab), 8 semester hours; physics (with lab), 8 semester hours; general biology or zoology, 6 semester hours; other science courses, 6 semester hours; biochemistry, strongly recommended	3.56	9.5	9.2	9.5	9.4	139	9	June 15	December 15
Office of Admissions Box 3 University of South Florida College of Medicine 12901 Bruce B. Downs Boulevard Tampa, FL 33612-4799 (813) 974-2229	General biology (with lab), 2 semesters; general chemistry (with lab), 2 semesters; organic chemistry (with lab), 2 semesters; general physics (with lab), 2 semesters; mathematics, 2 semesters; English, 2 semesters	3.7	9.5	9.6	9.8	9.6	96	0	June 15	December 1
Georgia										
Medical School Admissions Room 303 Woodruff Health Center Administration Building Emory University School of Medicine Atlanta, GA 30322-4510 (404) 727-5660	Biology (with lab), 8 semester hours; inorganic chemistry (with lab), 8 semester hours; organic chemistry (with lab), 8 semester hours; physics (with lab), 8 semester hours; English, 6 semester hours; humanities, social, or behavioral sciences, 18 semester hours	3.62	9.9	9.7	9.9	9.8	114	59	June 15	October 15
Mary Ella Logan, MD Associate Dean for Admissions Medical College of Georgia School of Medicine Atlanta, GA 30912-4760 (706) 721-4792	Biology (with lab), 1 year; inorganic chemistry (with lab), 1 year; advanced chemistry (with lab), 1 year (must include 1 semester or 2 quarters of organic chemistry); physics (with lab), 1 year; English, sufficient for baccalaureate degree; biochemistry, highly recommended	...	9.7	9.2	9.4	9.4	180	2	June 15	November 1

MCAT Score

School Name and Address	Admission Requirements (Courses)	Mean GPA	Verbal Reasoning	Physical Sciences	Biological Sciences	Mean	Class Size	Number of Out-of-State Acceptances	AMCAS Dates Earliest	AMCAS Dates Latest
Office of Admissions and Student Affairs Mercer University School of Medicine Macon, GA 31207 (912) 752-2542	General biology (with lab) 1 year; general or inorganic chemistry (with lab), 1 year; organic chemistry or organic biochemistry sequence (minimum of 1 semester or 2 quarters organic; with lab), 1 year; general physics (with lab), 1 year	...	8.9	8.0	8.6	8.5	54	0	June 15	December 1
Admissions and Student Affairs Morehouse School of Medicine 720 Westview Drive, SW Atlanta, GA 30310-1495 (404) 752-1650	Biology (with lab), 8 semester or 12 quarter hours; inorganic or general (with lab), 8 semester or 12 quarter hours; organic chemistry (with lab), 8 semester or 12 quarter hours; physics (with lab), 8 semester or 12 quarter hours; college mathematics, 6 semester or 10 quarter hours; English, 6 semester or 10 quarter hours	...	6.9	6.8	7.2	7.0	34	12	June 15	November 15
Hawaii										
Office of Admissions University of Hawaii John A. Burns School of Medicine 1960 East-West Road Honolulu, HI 96822 (808) 956-5446	Biology or zoology (with lab), 8 semester hours; chemistry (with lab), 12–16 semester hours (must include 8 semester hours of organic chemistry); physics (with lab), 8 semester hours	3.44	9.6	9.3	9.6	9.5	56	1	June 15	December 1
Illinois										
Office of the Dean of Admissions University of Chicago Pritzker School of Medicine 924 East 57th Street Chicago, IL 60637 (313) 702-1939	Biology or zoology (with lab), 1 year; inorganic chemistry (with lab), 1 year; organic chemistry (with lab), 1 year; physics (with lab), 1 year	3.51	10.0	10.3	10.3	10.2	104	57	June 15	November 15
Office of Admissions Finch University of Health Sciences, Chicago Medical School 3333 Green Bay Road North Chicago, IL 60064 (708) 578-3206/3207	Biology or zoology (with lab), 1 year; inorganic chemistry (with lab), 1 year; organic chemistry (with lab), 1 year; general physics (with lab), 1 year	3.2	9.0	9.0	9.0	9.0	165	117	June 15	December 15
Office of Medical College Admissions Room 165 CME M/C 783 University of Illinois College of Medicine 808 South Wood Street Chicago, IL 60612 (312) 996-5635	Bachelor's degree	...	9.3	9.2	9.3	9.3	300	25	June 15	December 1

(Table continued on the following page)

School Name and Address	Admission Requirements (Courses)	Mean GPA	MCAT Score				Class Size	Number of Out-of-State Acceptances	AMCAS Dates	
			Verbal Reasoning	Physical Sciences	Biological Sciences	Mean			Earliest	Latest
Associate Dean of Admissions Northwestern University Medical School 303 East Chicago Avenue Chicago, IL 60611 (312) 503-8206	135 quarter or 90 semester hours	3.51	9.7	9.6	9.8	9.7	173	89	June 15	November 15
Office of Admissions 524 Academic Avenue Rush Medical College of Rush University 600 South Paulina Street Chicago, IL 60612 (312) 942-6913	Biology or zoology, 8 semester hours; inorganic chemistry, 8 semester hours; organic chemistry, 8 semester hours; general physics, 8 semester hours	...	9.0	9.0	9.0	9.0	121	12	June 15	November 15
Office of Student and Alumni Affairs Southern Illinois University School of Medicine PO Box 19230 Springfield, IL 62794-9230 (217) 782-2860	90 semester hours	...	9.2	8.3	8.9	8.8	72	1	June 15	November 15
Office of Admissions, Room 1752 Loyola University Medical Center Stritch School of Medicine 2160 South First Avenue Maywood, IL 60153 (708) 216-3229	Biology or zoology (with lab), 1 year; inorganic chemistry (with lab), 1 year; organic chemistry (with lab), 1 year; physics (with lab), 1 year; biochemistry can substitute for part of the organic chemistry	3.57	...	...	...	...	130	64	June 15	October 15
Indiana										
Medical School Admissions Office Fesler Hall 213 Indiana University, School of Medicine 1120 South Drive Indianapolis, IN 46202-5113 (317) 274-3772	Biology (with lab), 1 year; general chemistry (with lab), 1 year; organic chemistry (with lab), 1 year; physics (with lab), 1 year	3.59	9.4	9.4	9.4	9.4	280	17	June 15	December 15
Iowa										
Director of Admissions 100 Medicine Administration Building University of Iowa College of Medicine Iowa City, IA 52242-1101 (319) 335-8052	Biologic sciences, an introductory plus an advanced course (not botany); chemistry, an introductory course in organic chemistry that follows a complete general course; physics, a complete introductory course; mathematics, college algebra and trigonometry or advanced algebra if college algebra and trigonometry were completed in high school	3.6	9.5	9.3	9.7	9.5	175	15	June 15	November 15

MCAT Score

AMCAS Dates

School Name and Address	Admission Requirements (Courses)	Mean GPA	Verbal Reasoning	Physical Sciences	Biological Sciences	Mean	Class Size	Number of Out-of-State Acceptances	Earliest	Latest
Kansas										
Associate Dean for Admissions University of Kansas, School of Medicine 3901 Rainbow Boulevard Kansas City, KS 66160-7301 (913) 588-5245	General biology or zoology (with lab), 2 semesters; inorganic chemistry (with lab), 2 semesters; organic chemistry or organic biochemistry sequence (with lab), 2 semesters; physics (with lab), 2 semesters; calculus, statistics, or computer science, 1 semester; English, 2 semesters; credits sufficient for a liberal arts degree	3.5	9.0	8.0	9.0	8.7	175	13	June 15	November 1
Kentucky										
Admissions, Room MN-102 Office of Education Chandler Medical Center University of Kentucky College of Medicine 800 Rose Street Lexington, KY 40536-0084 (606) 323-6161	Biology (with lab), 2 semesters; general chemistry (with lab), 2 semesters; organic chemistry (with lab), 2 semesters; physics (with lab), 2 semesters; English, 2 semesters; emphasis on spoken communication	3.44	9.0	9.2	8.7	9.0	96	5	June 15	November 1
Office of Admissions School of Medicine Health Science Center University of Louisville Louisville, KY 40292 (502) 852-5193	General biology (with lab), 2 semesters; general or inorganic chemistry (with lab), 2 semesters; general physics (with lab), 2 semesters; college mathematics, 2 semesters or 1 semester calculus; English, 2 semesters	3.5	8.9	8.7	8.7	8.8	136	12	June 15	November 1
Louisiana										
Admissions Office Louisiana State University School of Medicine in New Orleans 1901 Perdido Street New Orleans, LA 70112-1393 (504) 568-6262	Biology or zoology (with lab), 8 semester hours; general or inorganic chemistry (with lab), 8 semester hours; organic chemistry (with lab), 8 semester hours; physics (with lab), 8 semester hours; proficiency in written and spoken English	3.4	8.9	8.4	8.6	8.6	175	0	June 15	November 15
Admissions Office Louisiana State University School of Medicine in Shreveport PO Box 33932 Shreveport, LA 71130-3932 (318) 674-5190	Biology or zoology (with lab), 8 semester hours; general or inorganic chemistry (with lab), 8 semester hours; organic chemistry (with lab), 8 semester hours; physics (with lab), 8 semester hours; English, 6 semester hours	3.4	9.0	8.4	8.9	8.8	100	0	June 15	November 15
Office of Admissions Tulane University School of Medicine 1430 Tulane Avenue, SL67 New Orleans, LA 70112-2699 (504) 588-5187	Biology or zoology (with lab), 8 semester or 12 quarter hours; inorganic chemistry (with lab), 8 semester or 12 quarter hours; organic chemistry (with lab), 8 semester or 12 quarter hours; physics (with lab), 8 semester or 12 quarter hours; English, 6 semester or 9 quarter hours	~3.5	9.5	9.5	9.5	9.5	148	122	June 15	December 15

(Table continued on the following page)

265

MCAT Score

School Name and Address	Admission Requirements (Courses)	Mean GPA	Verbal Reasoning	Physical Sciences	Biological Sciences	Mean	Class Size	Number of Out-of-State Acceptances	AMCAS Dates Earliest	AMCAS Dates Latest
Maryland										
Committee on Admissions Johns Hopkins University School of Medicine 720 Rutland Avenue Baltimore, MD 21205-2196 (410) 955-3182	General biology (with lab), 8 semester hours; general chemistry (with lab), 8 semester hours; organic chemistry (with lab), 8 semester hours; general physics (with lab), 8 semester hours; humanities and social and behavioral sciences, 24 semester hours; calculus, 4 semester hours	...	...	...	...	...	118	104	July 1	November 1
Committee on Admissions Room 1-005 University of Maryland School of Medicine 655 West Baltimore Street Baltimore, MD 21201 (410) 706-7478	Biologic sciences, 8 semester hours; inorganic chemistry, 8 semester hours; organic chemistry, 6 semester hours; general physics, 8 semester hours; English, 6 semester hours	3.5	...	...	...	9.0	145	25	June 15	November 1
Admissions Office Room A-1041 Uniformed Services University of the Health Sciences F. Edward Hébert School of Medicine 4301 Jones Bridge Road Bethesda, MD 20814-4799 (301) 295-3101	General biology (with lab), 8 semester hours; general or inorganic chemistry (with lab), 8 semester hours; organic chemistry (with lab), 8 semester hours; physics (with lab), 8 semester hours; calculus, 6 semester hours; English, 6 semester hours	3.4	9.9	9.8	9.8	9.8	~165	...	June 15	November 1
Massachusetts										
Admissions Office Building L, Room 124 Boston University School of Medicine 80 East Concord Street Boston, MA 02118 (617) 638-4630	Biology (with lab), 1 year; inorganic chemistry (with lab), 1 year; organic chemistry (with lab), 1 year; physics, 1 year; humanities, 1 year; English composition or literature, 1 year	...	9.0	9.0	9.3	9.1	135	89	June 15	November 15
Administrator of Admissions Harvard Medical School 25 Shattuck Street Building A-210 Boston, MA 02115-6092 (617) 432-1550	Biology (with lab), 1 year (courses should deal with cellular and molecular aspects as well as the structure and function of living organisms); chemistry (with lab), 2 years (full-year courses in general or inorganic and organic chemistry meet this requirement; other options that adequately prepare students for the study of biochemistry and molecular biology in medical school are acceptable); physics, 1 year; mathematics, 1 year of calculus; expository writing, 1 year (may be met with writing, English, or nonscience courses that involve expository writing); HST program requirements are the same, except that calculus through differential equations and calculus-based physics are required; a course in biochemistry is encouraged	3.7	10.5	11.3	11.3	10.8	168	156	June	October 15

MCAT Score / AMCAS Dates

School Name and Address	Admission Requirements (Courses)	Mean GPA	Verbal Reasoning	Physical Sciences	Biological Sciences	Mean	Class Size	Number of Out-of-State Acceptances	Earliest	Latest
Associate Dean for Admissions University of Massachusetts Medical School 55 Lake Avenue, North Worcester, MA 01655 (508) 856-2323	Biology (with lab), 1 year; inorganic chemistry (with lab), 1 year; organic chemistry (with lab), 1 year; physics (with lab), 1 year; English, 1 year	3.5	10.0	10.0	10.0	10.0	100	0	June 15	November 15
Office of Admissions Tufts University School of Medicine 136 Harrison Avenue, Stearns 1 Boston, MA 02111 (617) 956-6571	Biology (with lab), 1 year; inorganic chemistry (with lab), 1 year; organic chemistry (with lab), 1 year; physics (with lab), 1 year; English, facility in the use of speech and composition; a course in classic genetics is recommended	...	9.1	9.6	9.8	9.5	168	122	June 15	November 1
Michigan										
Office of Admissions A-329 Life Sciences Michigan State University College of Human Medicine East Lansing, MI 48824-1317 (517) 353-9620	Biological sciences (with lab), 6 semester or 9 quarter hours (lab must be 2 semester or 3 term credits); inorganic and organic chemistry (with lab), 8 semester or 12 quarter hours (lab must be 3 semester or 5 term credits); physics (with lab), 6 semester or 9 quarter hours; English composition and literature, 6 semester or 9 quarter hours; psychology or sociology, 6 semester or 9 quarter hours; nonscience courses, 18 semester or 27 quarter hours (may include English, psychology, or sociology requirements)	...	9.7	8.6	9.1	9.1	116	19	June 15	November 15
Admissions Office M4130 Medical Science I Building University of Michigan Medical School Ann Arbor, MI 48109-0611 (313) 764-6317	Biology (with lab), 6 semester hours; General inorganic and organic chemistry (with lab), 8 semester hours; biochemistry, 3 semester hours; physics (with lab), 6 semester hours; English composition and literature, 6 semester hours; nonscience or humanities courses, 6 semester hours	3.6	10.0	11.0	11.0	10.3	122	53	June 15	November 15
Director of Admissions Wayne State University School of Medicine 540 East Canfield Detroit, MI 48201 (313) 577-1466	General biology or zoology (with lab), 12 semester hours; inorganic chemistry (with lab), 8 semester hours; organic chemistry (with lab), 8 semester hours; general physics (with lab), 8 semester hours; English, 8 semester hours	3.5	8.8	9.1	8.8	8.9	257	20	June 15	December 15
Minnesota										
Admissions Committee Mayo Medical School 200 First Street SW Rochester, MN 55905 (507) 284-3671	Biology or zoology, 1 year; chemistry (with lab), 2 years (must include organic chemistry); physics (with lab), 1 year; biochemistry, 1 course	3.67	>10.0	>10.0	>10.0	>10.0	42	37	June 15	November 15

(Table continued on the following page)

267

School Name and Address	Admission Requirements (Courses)	Mean GPA	MCAT Score Verbal Reasoning	MCAT Score Physical Sciences	MCAT Score Biological Sciences	MCAT Score Mean	Class Size	Number of Out-of-State Acceptances	AMCAS Dates Earliest	AMCAS Dates Latest
Office of Admissions, Room 107 University of Minnesota, Duluth School of Medicine 10 University Drive Duluth, MN 55812 (218) 726-8511	General biology or zoology (with lab), 8 semester or 12 quarter hours; general physics (with lab), 8 semester or 12 quarter hours; general inorganic chemistry (with lab), 8 semester or 12 quarter hours; organic chemistry (with lab), 8 semester or 12 quarter hours; English composition, 6 semester or 9 quarter hours; humanities, 8 semester or 12 quarter hours (at least 1 upper-division course); behavioral science (with lab), 8 semester or 12 quarter hours (at least 1 upper-division course); mathematics, through differential and integral calculus or upper-division statistics, preferably biostatistics	3.45	9.0	8.7	9.0	8.9	50	6	June 15	November 15
Office of Admissions and Student Affairs Box 293-UMHC University of Minnesota, Minneapolis, Medical School 420 Delaware Street, SE Minneapolis, MN 55455-0310 (612) 624-1122	General biology or zoology (with lab), 2 quarters; general or inorganic chemistry (with lab), 2 quarters; organic chemistry (with lab), 2 quarters; general physics (with lab), 3 quarters; English, 3 quarters; behavioral science, social sciences, or other liberal arts courses, 27 quarter hours; calculus or upper-level statistics; biochemistry, genetics, psychology, and liberal arts, strongly recommended	3.55	10.0	10.0	9.0	9.7	185	15	June 15	November 15
Mississippi										
Chairman, Admissions Committee University of Mississippi School of Medicine 2500 North State Street Jackson, MS 39216-4505 (601) 984-5010	General biology or zoology (with lab), 8 semester or 12 quarter hours; general physics (with lab), 8 semester or 12 quarter hours; general inorganic chemistry (with lab), 8 semester or 12 quarter hours; organic chemistry (with lab), 8 semester or 12 quarter hours; advanced science, 8 semester or 12 quarter hours; mathematics, 6 semester or 9 quarter hours; English, 6 semester or 9 quarter hours	3.6	9.0	9.0	9.0	9.0	100	0	June 15	November 1
Missouri										
Office of Admissions MA202 Medical Sciences Building University of Missouri, Columbia, School of Medicine 1 Hospital Drive Columbia, MO 65212 (314) 882-2923	English composition, 6 semester hours (may including writing-intensive courses); college algebra, 3 semester hours, or exemptions resulting in calculus eligibility; general biology (with lab), 8 semester hours; inorganic chemistry (with lab), 8 semester hours; organic chemistry (with lab), 8 semester hours; general physics (with lab), 8 semester hours	3.6	9.3	9.2	9.4	9.2	97	2	June 15	November 15

School Name and Address	Admission Requirements (Courses)	Mean GPA	MCAT Score Verbal Reasoning	Physical Sciences	Biological Sciences	Mean	Class Size	Number of Out-of-State Acceptances	AMCAS Dates Earliest	Latest
Council on Selection University of Missouri, Kansas City, School of Medicine 2411 Holmes Kansas City, MO 64108 (816) 235-1870	6-year baccalaureate–medical program	...	...	...	...	...	99	13	August 1	December 1
Nancy McPeters Admissions Committee Saint Louis University School of Medicine 1402 South Grand Boulevard St. Louis, MO 63104 (314) 577-8205	General biology or zoology (with lab), 8 semester hours; inorganic chemistry (with lab), 8 semester hours; organic chemistry (with lab), 8 semester hours; general physics (with lab), 8 semester hours; English, 6 semester hours; other humanities and behavioral science, 12 semester hours; biochemistry, strongly recommended	3.61	9.8	9.9	10.0	9.9	151	102	June 15	December 15
Office of Admissions, 8107 Washington University School of Medicine 600 South Euclid Avenue St. Louis, MO 63110 (314) 362-6857	Biologic science, 1 year; general or inorganic chemistry, 1 year; organic chemistry, 1 year; mathematics, 1 year (through differential and integral calculus)	3.77	10.9	11.6	11.6	11.4	123	113	June 15	November 15

Nebraska

School Name and Address	Admission Requirements (Courses)	Mean GPA	Verbal Reasoning	Physical Sciences	Biological Sciences	Mean	Class Size	Number of Out-of-State Acceptances	Earliest	Latest
Office of Admissions Creighton University 2500 California Plaza Omaha, NE 68178 (402) 280-2798	General biology (with lab), 8 semester hours; inorganic chemistry (with lab), 8 semester hours; organic chemistry (with lab), 8–10 semester hours; general physics (with lab), 8 semester hours; English, 6 semester hours	3.56	8.9	8.6	8.9	8.7	112	101	June 15	December 1
Office of Academic Affairs Room 4004, Conkling Hall University of Nebraska College of Medicine 600 South 42nd Street Omaha, NE 68198-4430 (402) 559-4205	Biology (with lab), 8–10 semester hours; inorganic chemistry (with lab), 8–10 semester hours; organic chemistry (with lab), 8–10 semester hours; physics (with lab), 8–10 semester hours; humanities or social sciences, 12–16 hours (minimum of 3 courses); calculus or statistics; English composition or writing, 1 course	3.6	9.5	8.8	8.2	8.8	118	1	June 15	November 15

Nevada

School Name and Address	Admission Requirements (Courses)	Mean GPA	Verbal Reasoning	Physical Sciences	Biological Sciences	Mean	Class Size	Number of Out-of-State Acceptances	Earliest	Latest
Office of Admissions and Student Affairs University of Nevada School of Medicine Mail Stop 357 Reno, NV 89557 (702) 784-6063	Biology, 12 semester hours (must include 3 semester hours upper-division credit); inorganic chemistry, 8 semester hours; organic chemistry, 8 semester hours; physics, 8 semester hours; behavioral science, 6 semester hours (must include 3 semester hours upper-division credit)	3.4	...	...	...	9.6	52	5	June 15	November 1

(Table continued on the following page)

School Name and Address	Admission Requirements (Courses)	MCAT Score					Class Size	Number of Out-of-State Acceptances	AMCAS Dates	
		Mean GPA	Verbal Reasoning	Physical Sciences	Biological Sciences	Mean			Earliest	Latest
New Hampshire										
Admissions Dartmouth Medical School 7020 Remsen, Room 306 Hanover, NH 03755-3886 (603) 650-1505	General biology, 8 semester hours; inorganic chemistry, 8 semester hours; organic chemistry, 8 semester hours; physics, 8 semester hours; calculus, 3 semester hours; proficiency in written and oral English	...	9.0	9.0	9.9	9.3	88	76	June 15	November 1
New Jersey										
Director of Admissions University of Medicine and Dentistry of New Jersey Medical School, Newark 185 South Orange Street Newark, NJ 07103 (201) 982-4631	Biology or zoology (with lab), 8 semester hours (exclusive of botany and invertebrate zoology); organic chemistry (with lab), 8 semester hours; other chemistry (with lab), 8 semester hours; general physics (with lab), 8 semester hours; English, 6 semester hours; mathematics, recommended, but not required	3.35	9.4	9.7	9.8	9.6	170	18	June 15	December 15
Office of Admissions University of Medicine and Dentistry of New Jersey—Robert Wood Johnson Medical School 675 Hoes Lane Piscataway, NJ 08854-5635 (908) 235-4576	Biology or zoology (with lab), 2 semesters; inorganic chemistry (with lab), 2 semesters; organic chemistry (with lab), 2 semesters; physics (with lab), 2 semesters; college mathematics, 1 semester; English, 2 semesters (must include 1 semester of college writing; college-approved writing-intensive courses may substitute for English)	3.47	9.0	9.4	9.7	9.4	138	20	June 15	December 15
New Mexico										
Office of Admissions and Student Affairs University of New Mexico School of Medicine Basic Medical Sciences Building, Room 107 Albuquerque, NM 87131-5166 (505) 277-4766	General biology (with lab), 8 semester hours; general or inorganic chemistry (with lab), 8 semester hours; organic chemistry (with lab), 8 semester hours; general physics (with lab), 6 semester hours; biochemistry, calculus, and Spanish, strongly recommended	3.40	...	...	...	8.9	73	6	June 15	November 15
New York										
Office of Admissions A-3 Albany Medical College 47 Scotland Avenue Albany, NY 12208 (518) 262-5521	Biology or zoology (with lab), 6 semester or 9 quarter hours; inorganic chemistry (with lab), 6 semester or 9 quarter hours; organic chemistry (with lab), 6 semester or 9 quarter hours; general physics (with lab), 6 semester or 9 quarter hours; proficiency in written and oral English	3.5	9.3	9.0	9.1	9.1	131	76	June 15	November 15

School Name and Address	Admission Requirements (Courses)	Mean GPA	Verbal Reasoning	Physical Sciences	Biological Sciences	Mean	Class Size	Number of Out-of-State Acceptances	Earliest	Latest
Office of Admissions, Albert Einstein College of Medicine of Yeshiva University, Jack and Pearl Resnick Campus, 1300 Morris Park Avenue, Bronx, NY 10461, (718) 430-21006	Biology (with lab), 8 semester hours; general chemistry (with lab), 8 semester hours; organic chemistry (with lab), 8 semester hours; physics (with lab), 8 semester hours; college mathematics, 6 semester hours (may include statistics and computer science); English, 6 semester hours	…	9.4	10.1	10.0	9.8	177	99	June 15	November 15
Admissions Office, Room 1-416, Columbia University, College of Physicians and Surgeons, 630 West 168th Street, New York, NY 10032, (212) 305-3595	Biology, 1 year (mammalian preferred); general chemistry, 1 year; organic chemistry, 1 year; physics, 1 year; English, 1 year	…	10.6	11.0	10.8	10.8	150	103	June 15	October 15
Office of Admissions, Cornell University Medical College, 445 East 69th Street, New York, NY 10021, (212) 746-1067	General biology or zoology, 6 semester hours; general chemistry, 6 semester hours; organic chemistry, 6 semester hours; general physics, 6 semester hours; English, 6 semester hours	3.53	10.5	10.5	10.5	10.5	101	61	June 15	October 15
Director of Admissions, Mount Sinai School of Medicine, Annenberg Building, Room 5-04, 1 Gustave L. Levy Place, Box 1002, New York, NY 10029-6574, (212) 241-6696	Biology, 1 year; inorganic chemistry, 1 year; organic chemistry, 1 year; physics, 1 year; mathematics, 1 year; English, 1 year	3.5	9.5	9.5	9.5	9.5	115	47	June 15	November 1
Office of Admissions, Room 127, Sunshine Cottage, New York Medical College, Valhalla, NY 10595, (914) 993-4507	Biology (with lab), 8 semester hours; inorganic chemistry (with lab), 8 semester hours; organic chemistry (with lab), 8 semester hours; physics (with lab), 8 semester hours; English, 6 semester hours	…	9.7	10.1	10.4	10.1	183	141	June 15	December 1
Office of Admissions, New York University School of Medicine, PO Box 1924, New York, NY 10016, (212) 263-5290	Biology (with lab), 6 semester hours; inorganic chemistry (with lab), 6 semester hours; organic chemistry (with lab), 6 semester hours; general physics (with lab), 6 semester hours; English, 6 semester hours; biochemistry, recommended	…	10.0	11.0	11.0	10.7	160	75	August 15	December 1
Director of Admissions, University of Rochester, School of Medicine and Dentistry, Medical Center Box 601, Rochester, NY 14642, (716) 275-4539	Biology (with lab), 6–8 semester hours; general or inorganic chemistry (with lab), 6–8 semester hours; organic chemistry (with lab), 6–8 semester hours (1 semester of biochemistry may be substituted for a semester of organic chemistry; within a 2-year chemistry sequence, 1 year of lab is required); physics (with lab), 6–8 semester hours; English, 6–8 semester hours; humanities or social or behavioral science, 12–16 semester hours; biochemistry, recommended	…	9.9	9.0	9.0	9.0	98	63	June 14	October 15

(Table continued on the following page)

School Name and Address	Admission Requirements (Courses)	Mean GPA	MCAT Score				Class Size	Number of Out-of-State Acceptances	AMCAS Dates	
			Verbal Reasoning	Physical Sciences	Biological Sciences	Mean			Earliest	Latest
Director of Admissions State University of New York Health Science Center at Brooklyn Box 60M 450 Clarkson Avenue Brooklyn, NY 11203 (718) 270-2446	General biology or zoology (with lab), 1 year; inorganic chemistry (with lab), 1 year; organic chemistry (with lab), 1 year; general physics (with lab), 1 year; English, 1 year (if freshmen English is exempted, a more advanced course is required)	...	...	9.5	9.6	9.5	199	19	June 15	December 15
Office of Medical Admissions State University of New York at Buffalo CFS Building, Room 35 Buffalo, NY 14214-3013 (716) 829-3465	Biology (with lab), 2 semesters (not more than 1 semester of botany); chemistry (with lab), 3 semesters [at least 1 semester must be organic chemistry (with lab)]; general physics, 2 semesters; English, 2 semesters	...	9.6	9.7	9.7	9.7	135	1	June 15	December 1
Admissions Committee State University of New York Health Science Center at Syracuse, College of Medicine 155 Elizabeth Blackwell Street Syracuse, NY 13210 (315) 464-4570	Chemistry, 8–12 semester hours; [inorganic (with lab), 6–8 semester hours; organic (with lab), 6–8 semester hours]; biology or zoology (with lab), 6–8 semester hours; physics (with lab), 6–8 semester hours; English, 6 semester hours	...	9.0	9.0	9.0	9.0	149	7	June 15	December 1
Committee on Admissions Level 4, Room 147 Health Science Center State University of New York at Stony Brook, School of Medicine Stony Brook, NY 11794-8434 (516) 444-2113	Biology (with lab), 1 year; inorganic chemistry (with lab), 1 year; organic chemistry (with lab), 1 year; general physics (with lab), 1 year; English, 1 year	...	...	...	...	...	100	8	June 15	November 15
North Carolina										
Office of Medical School Admissions Bowman Gray School of Medicine of Wake Forest University Medical Center Boulevard Winston-Salem, NC 27157-1090 (910) 716-4264	General biology, 8 semester hours; general or inorganic chemistry, 8 semester hours; organic chemistry, 8 semester hours; general physics, 8 semester hours	...	10.0	9.3	9.5	9.6	108	52	June 15	November 1
Committee on Admissions Duke University School of Medicine Duke University Medical Center PO Box 3710 Durham, NC 27710 (919) 684-2985	Biology, 1 year; inorganic chemistry, 1 year; organic chemistry, 1 year; calculus, 1 year; English, 1 year; biochemistry, suggested	...	...	...	...	...	100	68	June 15	October 15
Associate Dean Office of Admissions East Carolina University School of Medicine Greenville, NC 27858-4354 (919) 816-2202	General biology or zoology (with lab), 1 year; inorganic chemistry (with lab), 1 year; organic chemistry (with lab), 1 year; physics (with lab), 1 year; English, 1 year	3.35	8.4	7.7	8.3	8.1	72	0	June 15	November 15

School Name and Address	Admission Requirements (Courses)	Mean GPA	MCAT Score				Class Size	Number of Out-of-State Acceptances	AMCAS Dates	
			Verbal Reasoning	Physical Sciences	Biological Sciences	Mean			Earliest	Latest
Admissions Office CB 7000 MacNider Hall University of North Carolina School of Medicine Chapel Hill, NC 27599-7000 (919) 962-8331	Biology or zoology (with lab), 8 semester hours; general chemistry, including qualitative and quantitative analysis (with lab), 8 semester hours; general physics (with lab), 8 semester hours; organic chemistry, 8 semester hours; English, 6 semester hours	...	9.8	9.1	9.3	9.4	160	10	June 15	November 15
North Dakota										
Secretary, Committee on Admissions University of North Dakota School of Medicine Box 9037 501 Columbia Road Grand Forks, ND 58202-9037 (701) 777-4221	General biology or zoology, 8 semester hours; inorganic and qualitative chemistry, 8 semester hours; organic chemistry (biochemistry may be substituted for the final semester or quarter), 8 semester hours; college physics, 8 semester hours; college algebra, 3 semester hours; psychology or sociology, 3 semester hours; English composition and literature, 6 semester hours	3.55	8.7	8.6	8.9	8.7	57	13	July 1	November 1
Ohio										
Associate Dean for Admissions and Student Affairs Case Western Reserve University School of Medicine 10900 Euclid Avenue Cleveland, OH 44106-4920 (216) 368-3450	Biology, 1 year of modern biology that emphasizes biochemical and quantitative concepts (courses in anatomy, botany, ecology, and taxonomy do not meet this requirement); chemistry, 2 years, including organic (courses with organic or biochemistry content are acceptable); physics, 1 year introductory; writing skills, 1 course in freshman expository writing (other courses with significant writing content are acceptable)	3.5	...	...	...	10.0	138	48	June 15	October 15
Office of Admissions Room E-251, MSB, ML 552 University of Cincinnati, College of Medicine 231 Bethesda Avenue Cincinnati, OH 45267-0552 (513) 558-7314	90 semester hours, providing the knowledge usually obtained in 1 year of biology, chemistry, organic chemistry, physics, and mathematics	...	9.3	9.5	9.7	9.5	162	27	June 15	November 15
Admissions Office Medical College of Ohio PO Box 10008 Toledo, OH 43699 (419) 381-4229	Biology, 1 year; inorganic chemistry, 1 year; organic chemistry, 1 year; physics, 1 year; college mathematics, 1 year; college English, 1 year	3.37	8.7	8.9	9.2	8.9	135	24	June 17	November 1
Office of Admissions and Educational Research Northeastern Ohio University College of Medicine PO Box 95 Rootstown, OH 44272-0095 (216) 325-2511	1 year university-level college or physics	...	9.4	8.8	9.1	9.1	15	0	June 15	November 1

(Table continued on the following page)

273

School Name and Address	Admission Requirements (Courses)	Mean GPA	MCAT Score				Class Size	Number of Out-of-State Acceptances	AMCAS Dates	
			Verbal Reasoning	Physical Sciences	Biological Sciences	Mean			Earliest	Latest
Admissions Committee 270-A Meiling Hall Ohio State University College of Medicine 370 West Ninth Avenue Columbus, OH 43210-1238 (614) 292-7137	Biology, 1 year; inorganic chemistry (with lab), 1 year; organic chemistry (with lab), 1 year; general physics, 1 year	3.5	10.0	10.3	10.3	10.3	210	42	June 15	November 1
Office of Student Affairs and Admissions Wright State University School of Medicine PO Box 1751 Dayton, OH 45401 (513) 873-2934	Biology, 1 year; chemistry (with organic), 2 years; physics, 1 year; college mathematics, 1 year; English, 1 year	...	...	...	...	...	90	12	June 15	November 15
Oklahoma										
Dotty Shaw Killam Admissions Coordinator University of Oklahoma College of Medicine PO Box 226901 Oklahoma City, OK 73190 (405) 271-2331	Vertebrate zoology or general biology (with lab), 1 semester; cell biology, embryology, histology, genetics, or comparative vertebrate anatomy, 1 semester; inorganic (general) chemistry, 2 semesters; organic chemistry, 2 semesters; general physics, 2 semesters; English, 3 semesters; psychology, sociology, anthropology, philosophy, humanities, or foreign language (any combination), 3 semesters; additional work in the social sciences, suggested	3.55	9.6	8.8	9.0	9.1	146	18	June 15	October 15
Oregon										
Office of Education and Student Affairs, L102 Oregon Health Sciences University 3181 SW Sam Jackson Park Road Portland, OR 97201 (503) 494-2998	Chemistry, 2 years (including general chemistry (with lab) and organic chemistry (with lab); introductory biochemistry recommended; MD/PhD students should take more advanced chemistry); biology, 1 year (genetics recommended; molecular biology recommended for MD/PhD students); physics (with lab), 1 year; college mathematics, 1 course; humanities, social science, and English (including composition), 1 year each	3.6	10.0	10.0	10.0	10.0	93	17	June 15	October 15
Pennsylvania										
Associate Dean for Admissions Jefferson Medical College of Thomas Jefferson University 1025 Walnut Street Philadelphia, PA 19107 (215) 955-6983	General biology (with lab), 1 year; inorganic chemistry (with lab), 1 year; organic chemistry (with lab), 1 year; general physics (with lab), 1 year	3.4	...	...	...	9.9	223	124	June 15	November 15

School Name and Address	Admission Requirements (Courses)	Mean GPA	MCAT Score				Class Size	Number of Out-of-State Acceptances	AMCAS Dates	
			Verbal Reasoning	Physical Sciences	Biological Sciences	Mean			Earliest	Latest
Admissions Office Medical College of Pennsylvania and Hahnemann University School of Medicine 2900 Queen Lane Philadelphia, PA 19129 (215) 991-8202	Organic chemistry (with lab), 2 semesters; inorganic chemistry (with lab), 2 semesters (may also take biochemistry); biology (with lab), 2 semesters; physics (with lab), 2 semesters; English, 2 semesters	3.5	9.2	8.1	8.1	8.4	302	154	June 15	December 1
Office of Student Affairs Pennsylvania State University College of Medicine PO Box 850 Hershey, PA 17033 (717) 531-8755	Biology, 1 year; inorganic chemistry, 1 year; organic chemistry, 1 year; physics, 1 year; calculus, behavioral science, genetics, and physical chemistry, recommended	3.5	8.9	9.0	9.5	9.1	107	51	June 15	November 15
Director of Admissions and Financial Aid Edward J. Stemmler Hall, Suite 100 University of Pennsylvania School of Medicine Philadelphia, PA 19104-6054 (215) 898-8001	Competence in general science and liberal arts	3.6	10.3	10.7	10.6	10.5	150	99	June 15	November 1
Office of Admissions 518 Scaiffe Hall University of Pittsburgh School of Medicine Pittsburgh, PA 15261 (412) 648-9891	Biology, exclusive of botany (with lab), 1 year; general or inorganic chemistry (with lab), 1 year; organic chemistry (with lab), 1 year; physics (with lab), 1 year; English, 1 year	3.52	...	...	...	10.4	131	55	June 15	November 1
Admissions Office Suite 305, Student Faculty Center Temple University School of Medicine Broad and Ontario Streets Philadelphia, PA 19140 (215) 707-3656	Biology (with lab), 8 semester hours; inorganic chemistry (with lab), 8 semester hours; organic chemistry (with lab), 8 semester hours; general physics (with lab), 8 semester hours; humanities, 6 semester hours	3.4	...	...	...	10.0	182	69	June 15	December 1
Puerto Rico										
Office of Admissions Universidad Central del Caribe School of Medicine Ramón Ruíz Arnau University Hospital Call Box 60-327 Bayamón, PR 00960-6032 (809) 740-1611	General biology or zoology, 8 semester hours; general chemistry, 8 semester hours; organic chemistry, 8 semester hours; general physics, 8 semester hours; college mathematics, 6 semester hours; English, 6 semester hours; Spanish, 6 semester hours; behavioral science, social science, or humanities, 6 semester hours	3.11	...	...	...	...	60	6	June 15	December 15
Admissions Office Ponce School of Medicine PO Box 7004 Ponce, PR 00732 (809) 840-2511	Biology, 8 semester hours; inorganic chemistry, 8 semester hours; organic chemistry, 8 semester hours; physics, 8 semester hours; college mathematics or trigonometry, 8 semester hours;	3.30	...	...	...	...	60	14	June 15	December 15

(Table continued on the following page)

School Name and Address	Admission Requirements (Courses)	Mean GPA	MCAT Score				Class Size	Number of Out-of-State Acceptances	AMCAS Dates	
			Verbal Reasoning	Physical Sciences	Biological Sciences	Mean			Earliest	Latest
	humanities (sociology, psychology, political science, economics, or anthropology), 6 semester hours; English, 12 semester hours; Spanish, 12 semester hours									
Central Admissions Office School of Medicine Medical Sciences Campus University of Puerto Rico PO Box 365067 San Juan, PR 00936-5067 (809) 758-2525, extension 5213	Biology, 8 semester hours; general chemistry (with lab), 8 semester hours; organic chemistry (with lab), 8 semester hours; physics (with lab), 8 semester hours; English, 12 semester hours; Spanish, 12 semester hours; behavioral and social sciences (sociology, psychology, political science, economics, or anthropology), 6 semester hours	3.50	6.0	7.0	7.0	6.7	108	4	June 15	December 1
Rhode Island										
Office of Admissions Box G-A212 Brown University School of Medicine Providence, RI 02912-9706 (401) 863-2149	Most students enter through the 8-year continuation program	...	...	...	...	...	...	...	August 15	March 20
South Carolina										
Office of Enrollment Services Medical University of South Carolina 171 Ashley Avenue Charleston, SC 29425 (803) 792-3281	No specific requirements	...	9.0	9.0	9.0	9.0	140	24	June 15	December 1
Associate Dean for Student Programs University of South Carolina School of Medicine Columbia, SC 29208 (803) 733-3325	General biology or zoology (with lab), 8 semester hours; inorganic chemistry (with lab), 8 semester hours; organic chemistry (with lab), 8 semester hours; general physics (with lab), 8 semester hours; college mathematics (a minimum of college algebra; calculus, recommended), 6 semester hours; English composition and literature, 6 semester hours	...	...	...	...	...	73	2	June 16	December 1
South Dakota										
Office of Student Affairs, Room 105 University of South Dakota School of Medicine 414 East Clark Street Vermillion, SD 57069-2390 (605) 677-5233	General biology or zoology (with lab), 1 year; general chemistry (with lab), 1 year; organic chemistry (with lab) or second-semester biochemistry, 1 year; general physics (with lab), 1 year; college mathematics (analytical geometry and calculus preferred)	3.63	9.1	8.5	8.9	8.8	50	7	June 15	November 15

MCAT Score

School Name and Address	Admission Requirements (Courses)	Mean GPA	Verbal Reasoning	Physical Sciences	Biological Sciences	Mean	Class Size	Number of Out-of-State Acceptances	AMCAS Dates Earliest	AMCAS Dates Latest
Tennessee										
Assistant Dean for Admissions and Records East Tennessee State University James H. Quillen College of Medicine PO Box 70580 Johnson City, TN 37614-0580 (615) 929-6221	Biology (with lab), 8 semester hours; general or inorganic chemistry (with lab), 8 semester hours; organic chemistry (with lab), 8 semester hours; physics (with lab), 8 semester hours; communications skills, 9 semester hours	3.4	9.1	8.6	8.8	8.8	60	8	June 15	December 1
Director, Admissions and Records Meharry Medical College School of Medicine 1005 D. B. Todd, Jr. Boulevard Nashville, TN 37208 (615) 327-6223	General biology or zoology (with lab), 8 semester or 12 quarter hours; general chemistry (with lab), 8 semester or 12 quarter hours; organic chemistry (with lab), 8 semester or 12 quarter hours; general physics (with lab), 8 semester or 12 quarter hours; English composition, 6 semester or 9 quarter hours	...	7.7	7.2	7.8	7.6	80	71	June 15	December 15
University of Tennessee, Memphis College of Medicine 790 Madisone Avenue Memphis, TN 38163-2166 (901) 448-5559	Biology (with lab), 8 semester hours (must include 4 semester hours of zoology); inorganic chemistry (with lab), 8 semester hours; organic chemistry (with lab), 8 semester hours; general physics (with lab), 8 semester hours; English composition and literature, 6 semester hours; electives, 52 semester hours	3.5	9.0	9.0	9.0	9.0	165	9	June 15	November 15
Office of Admissions Light Hall Vanderbilt University School of Medicine Nashville, TN 37232-0685 (615) 322-2145	Biology or zoology (with 2 hours of lab), 8 semester hours (no more than half may be botany); inorganic chemistry (with 2 hours of lab), 8 semester hours; organic chemistry (with 2 hours of lab), 8 semester hours; physics (with 2 hours of lab), 8 semester hours; English and composition, 6 semester hours	...	10.5	10.9	11.0	10.8	102	88	June 15	October 15
Texas										
Office of Admissions Baylor College of Medicine 1 Baylor Place Houston, TX 77030 (713) 798-4841	General biology (with lab), 1 year; general chemistry (with lab), 1 year; organic chemistry (with lab), 1 year; general physics (with lab), 1 year; English, 1 year	3.6	10.0	10.0	10.0	10.0	167	50	June 1	November 1
Associate Dean for Student Affairs and Admissions Texas A&M University Health Center, College of Medicine College Station, TX 77843-1114 (409) 845-7744	General biology (with lab), 1 year; additional biology, 1/2 year; inorganic chemistry (with lab), 1 year; organic chemistry (with lab), 1 year; general physics (with lab), 1 year; calculus, 1/2 year; English, 1 year	3.63	...	...	...	...	48	0	May 1	November 1

(Table continued on the following page)

277

School Name and Address	Admission Requirements (Courses)	Mean GPA	MCAT Score				Class Size	Number of Out-of-State Acceptances	AMCAS Dates	
			Verbal Reasoning	Physical Sciences	Biological Sciences	Mean			Earliest	Latest
Office of Admissions Texas Tech University Health Sciences Center School of Medicine Lubbock, TX 79430 (806) 743-2997	General biology or zoology (with lab), 2 years; inorganic chemistry (with lab), 1 year; organic chemistry (with lab), 1 year; physics (with lab), 1 year; English, 1 year	3.39	9.4	9.1	9.4	9.3	120	1	June 15	November 1
Office of the Registrar University of Texas Southwestern Medical Center at Dallas 5323 Harry Hines Boulevard Dallas, TX 75235-9096 (214) 648-2670	Biology, 2 years (with 1 year lab); inorganic chemistry (with lab), 1 year; organic chemistry (with lab), 1 year; physics (with lab), 1 year; calculus, 1/2 year; English, 1 year	...	10.0	10.2	10.6	10.3	196	22	April 15	October 15
Office of Admissions G-210, Ashbel Smith Building University of Texas Medical Branch at Galveston School of Medicine Galveston, TX 77555-1317 (409) 772-3517	Biology, 2 years (with 1 year lab); inorganic chemistry (with lab), 1 year; organic chemistry (with lab), 1 year; physics (with lab), 1 year; calculus, 1/2 year; English, 1 year	3.5	...	...	...	...	200	15	April 15	October 15
Office of Admissions, Room G-024 University of Texas, Houston, Medical School PO Box 20708 Houston, TX 77225 (713) 792-4711	Biology, 14 semester hours (with lab); inorganic chemistry (with lab), 8 semester hours; organic chemistry (with lab), 8 semester hours; physics (with lab), 8 semester hours; calculus, 3 semester hours; English, 6 semester hours	3.41	8.8	8.4	8.9	8.7	200	20	June 15	October 15
Medical School Admissions Registrar's Office University of Texas Health Center at San Antonio 7703 Floyd Curl Drive San Antonio, TX 78284-7701 (210) 567-2665	Biology, 14 semester hours (with 1 year lab); inorganic chemistry (with lab), 8 semester hours; organic chemistry (with lab), 8 semester hours; physics (with lab), 8 semester hours; calculus, 3 semester hours; English, 6 semester hours	3.58	9.0	9.0	9.0	9.0	199	19	April 15	October 15
Utah										
Millie M. Peterson Director, Medical School Admissions University of Utah School of Medicine 50 North Medical Drive Salt Lake City, UT 84132 (801) 581-7498	Chemistry (with lab), 2 years (must include inorganic and organic and coursework in qualitative and quantitative analysis); general physics (with lab), 1 year (heat, light, electricity, and magnetism); English composition or basic communication, 1 year	...	10.0	10.5	10.6	10.4	100	25	June 15	October 15

School Name and Address	Admission Requirements (Courses)	Mean GPA	MCAT Score Verbal Reasoning	MCAT Score Physical Sciences	MCAT Score Biological Sciences	MCAT Score Mean	Class Size	Number of Out-of-State Acceptances	AMCAS Dates Earliest	AMCAS Dates Latest
Vermont										
Admissions Office E-109 Given Building University of Vermont College of Medicine Burlington, VT 05405 (802) 656-2154	Biology or zoology (with lab), 1 year or 8 semester hours; general chemistry (with lab), 1 year or 8 semester hours; organic chemistry (with lab), 1 year or 8 semester hours; general physics (with lab), 1 year or 8 semester hours	3.3	...	...	...	8.9	91	57	June 15	November 1
Virginia										
Office of Admissions Eastern Virginia Medical School 721 Fairfax Avenue Norfolk, VA 23507-2000 (804) 446-5812	Biology (with lab), 1 year; general chemistry (with lab), 1 year; organic chemistry (with lab), 1 year; physics (with lab), 1 year	3.32	9.2	8.9	9.6	9.2	100	40	June 15	November 15
Medical School Admissions Virginia Commonwealth University Medical College of Virginia MCV Station, Box 565 Richmond, VA 23298-0565 (804) 786-9629	Biology (with lab), 2 semesters; general chemistry (with lab), 2 semesters; organic chemistry (with lab), 2 semesters; general physics (with lab), 2 semesters; English, 2 semesters	3.4	...	...	...	9.7	173	54	June 15	November 15
Medical School Admissions Office University of Virginia School of Medicine Charlottesville, VA 22908 (804) 924-5571	Biology (with lab), 1 year; general chemistry (with lab), 1 year; organic chemistry (with lab), 1 year; physics (with lab), 1 year	3.56	10.0	10.5	10.2	10.2	139	41	June 15	November 15
Washington										
Admissions Office (SM-22) Health Science Center T-545 University of Washington Seattle, WA 98195 (206) 543-7212	Biology, 8 semester hours; chemistry, 12 semester hours (any combination of inorganic, organic, biochemistry, or molecular biology courses); physics, 4 semester hours; other science, 8 semester hours (may be satisfied by taking courses in any of the above categories); Proficiency in English, basic mathematics, and informational technologies; biochemistry and molecular biology, strongly encouraged	3.58	9.9	10.0	10.3	10.0	166	15	June 15	November 1
West Virginia										
Admissions Office Marshall University School of Medicine 1542 Spring Valley Drive Huntington, WV 25755 (304) 696-7312	General biology or zoology (with lab), 8 semester hours; inorganic chemistry (with lab), 8 semester hours; organic chemistry (with lab), 8 semester hours; physics (with lab), 8 semester hours; English composition and rhetoric, 6 semester hours; behavioral or social science, 6 semester hours	3.5	8.6	7.5	8.0	8.0	49	3	June 15	November 15

(Table continued on the following page)

279

School Name and Address	Admission Requirements (Courses)	Mean GPA	MCAT Score				Class Size	Number of Out-of-State Acceptances	AMCAS Dates	
			Verbal Reasoning	Physical Sciences	Biological Sciences	Mean			Earliest	Latest
Office of Admissions and Records West Virginia University Health Science Center PO Box 9815 Morgantown, WV 26506 (304) 293-3521	Biology (with lab), 8 semester hours; inorganic chemistry (with lab), 8 semester hours; organic chemistry (with lab), 8 semester hours; general physics (with lab), 8 semester hours; English, 6 semester hours; behavioral or social sciences, 6 semester hours; calculus, biochemistry, and cell biology, recommended	3.55	8.6	8.5	8.8	8.6	88	7	June 15	November 15
Wisconsin										
Office of Admissions and Registrar Medical College of Wisconsin 8701 Watertown Plank Road Milwaukee, WI 53226 (414) 257-8246	Biology (with lab), 8 credits; general chemistry (with lab), 8 credits; organic chemistry (with lab), 8 credits; physics, 8 credits; English, 6 credits (should stress composition); mathematics, course in high school or college algebra	...	9.5	9.6	9.6	9.6	213	100	June 15	November 15
Admissions Committee Medical Sciences Center, Room 1205 University of Wisconsin Medical School 1300 University Avenue Madison, WI 53706 (608) 263-4925	General zoology or biology (with lab), 1 semester; advanced zoology or biology (with lab), 1 semester; inorganic chemistry (with lab), 2 semesters; organic chemistry (with lab), 2 semesters; general physics (with lab), 2 semesters; mathematics, 2 semesters; college algebra and trigonometry	...	9.4	9.5	9.7	9.5	143	20	June 15	November 1

AMCAS = American Medical College Admissions Service; GPA = grade point average; MCAT = Medical College Admission Test; HST = Health Sciences and Technology Program.

APPENDIX B. Acceptance to Medical School by Major
(1994–95 Entering Class)

Undergraduate Major	Percentage of All Applicants Accepted	Percentage of Applicants From Each Major Accepted
Interdisciplinary studies	0.6	53.6
History	1.3	51.8
Economics	1.3	48.5
Philosophy	0.5	48.3
Biomedical engineering	1.1	48.0
English	1.5	47.0
Chemical engineering	0.9	46.5
Political science	0.9	46.3
Other biological sciences	2.1	46.5
Physiology	2.1	46.5
Physics	0.7	44.3
Foreign language	0.8	44.2
Biochemistry	5.0	43.3
Double nonscience majors	2.2	42.9
Other preprofessional majors	0.5	42.6
Anthropology	0.7	42.4
Chemistry	5.8	41.8
Psychobiology	1.0	40.8
Premedical	1.9	40.8
Other and not stated	14.2	39.8
Mathematics	0.8	39.7
Natural sciences	0.5	38.8
Electrical engineering	1.2	38.3
Sociology	0.5	36.7
Chemistry and biology	0.6	36.2
Double science majors	1.3	35.7
Biology	37.5	35.3
Microbiology	2.3	33.6
Psychology	5.5	33.5
General science	0.4	33.3
Nursing	0.9	25.1
Pharmacy	0.7	22.4
Medical technology	0.6	21.6
Total	100.0	. . .
Mean	. . .	38.2

APPENDIX C. Tuition and Fees for Medical Schools in the United States and Puerto Rico

School	Fees (Dollars)		Tuition (Dollars)	
	Application	Other	Resident	Nonresident
Alabama				
University of Alabama	50	2357	5335	16,005
University of Southern Alabama	25	567	5808	11,616
Arizona				
University of Arizona	0	66	6760	...
Arkansas				
University of Arkansas	10	733	6996	13,992
California				
University of California, all five campuses	40	7800–8281	0	7699
Loma Linda University	55	805	20,965	20,965
Stanford University	55	607	23,124	23,124
University of Southern California	50	1216	25,052	25,052
Colorado				
University of Colorado	60	1529	10,139	45,780
Connecticut				
University of Connecticut	60	3125	7825	17,400
Yale University	55	175	22,000	22,000
District of Columbia				
George Washington University	55	720	30,200	30,200
Georgetown University	60	...	22,500	22,500
Howard University	25	788	14,000	14,000
Florida				
University of Florida	20	...	8172	21,172
University of Miami	50	110	21,940	21,940
University of South Florida	20	0	8245	21,245
Georgia				
Emory University	50	700	19,500	19,500
Medical College of Georgia	0	249	4527	13,581
Mercer University	25	...	17,850	17,850
Morehouse	45	1811	15,000	15,000
Hawaii				
University of Hawaii	0	87	5710	19,840

Illinois

University of Chicago-Pritzer	55	1645	20,625	20,625
Finch University-Chicago Medical School	65	100	27,615	27,615
University of Illinois	30	1114	7890	23,136
Loyola University of Chicago	35	235	24,157	24,157
Northwestern University	50	0	24,291	24,291
Rush Medical College of Rush University	45	1536	21,900	21,900
Southern Illinois University	50	1205	10,035	30,105

Indiana

Indiana University	35	174	8987	20,554

Iowa

University of Iowa	20	399	8088	20,988

Kansas

University of Kansas	40	220	8240	19,398

Kentucky

University of Kentucky	0	330	7090	16,720
University of Louisville	15	0	7300	16,930

Louisiana

Louisiana State University, New Orleans	50	150	6774	. . .
Louisiana State University, Shreveport	50	151	6776	14,676
Tulane University	65	1060	25,020	25,020

Maryland

Johns Hopkins University	60	2064	20,500	20,500
University of Maryland	40	1700	10,292	19,957
Uniformed Services University	0	0	0	0

Massachusetts

Boston University	95	375	28,900	28,900
Harvard	70	1533	22,300	22,300
University of Massachusetts	50	1470	8792	. . .
Tufts University	75	305	27,670	27,670

Michigan

Michigan State University	50	825	13,233	29,079
University of Michigan	50	175	14,963	24,063
Wayne State University	30	350	9286	18,242

Minnesota

Mayo Medical School	60	0	9925 AZ, FL, and MN	19,800
University of Minnesota, Duluth	0	588	14,092	28,184

(Table continued on the following page)

University of Minnesota, Minneapolis	50	558	14,092	28,184

Mississippi

University of Mississippi	0	115	6600	12,600

Missouri

University of Missouri, Columbia	0	495	11,027	20,750
University of Missouri, Kansas City	25	455	11,792	23,795
Saint Louis University	100	874	23,040	23,040
Washington University	50	0	23,525	23,525

Nebraska

Creighton University	50	770	21,698	21,698
University of Nebraska	25	1107	9890	18,450

Nevada

University of Nevada	45	1616	6597	14,376

New Hampshire

Dartmouth	55	1765	22,360	22,360

New Jersey

UMDNJ-New Jersey Medical School	50	1106	12,795	16,791
UMDNJ-Robert Wood Johnson Medical School	50	1106	12,795	16,791

New Mexico

University of New Mexico	25	32	4392	12,653

New York

Albany Medical College	70	0	21,885	23,042
Albert Einstein Medical College	70	1100	23,400	23,400
Columbia University	65	1500	22,369	22,369
Cornell University	65	750	21,300	21,300
Mount Sinai School of Medicine	75	825	21,000	21,000
New York Medical College	60	415	24,150	24,150
New York University	75	3070	20,900	20,900
University of Rochester	65	1310	21,500	21,500
State Universities of New York (SUNY), all four campuses	60–65	130–359	8450	17,100

North Carolina

Bowman Gray	50	...	17,400	17,400
Duke University	55	1331	19,500	19,500
East Carolina University	35	793	1876	19,308
University of North Carolina	55	690	1874	19,308

North Dakota

University of North Dakota	35	318	8460	22,338

Ohio

Case Western Reserve University	50	590	21,800	21,800

University of Cincinnati	25	498	10,110	18,117
Medical College of Ohio	30	585	9036	12,288
Northeastern Ohio University	30	699	9255	18,510
Ohio State University	30	606	8352	24,816
Wright State University	30	639	11,552	16,352
Oklahoma				
University of Oklahoma	50	307	6567	16,227
Oregon				
Oregon Health Sciences University	60	2097	13,466	28,339
Pennsylvania				
Jefferson Medical College	65	0	22,625	22,625
Medical College of Pennsylvania (MCP) and Hahnemann University (HU)	55	541 (MCP) 1310 (HU)	20,250 (MCP) 21,300 (HU)	20,250 (MCP) 21,300 (HU)
Pennsylvania State University	40	998	15,476	22,020
University of Pennsylvania	55	1129	23,230	23,230
University of Pittsburgh	50	415	17,556	23,478
Temple University	55	358	19,416	24,559
Puerto Rico				
Universidad Central del Caribe	50	789	15,000	22,000
Ponce	50	1763	15,673	23,504
University of Puerto Rico	15	516	5000	10,500
Rhode Island				
Brown University	60	1548	22,704	22,704
South Carolina				
Medical University of South Carolina	45	3252 resident; 8672 nonresident	2508	6818
University of South Carolina	20	50	6790	17,120
South Dakota				
University of South Dakota	15	2535	7803	16,670
Tennessee				
East Tennessee State University	25	313	8580	14,452
Meharry Medical College	25	1896	15,120	15,120
University of Tennessee, Memphis	25	472	8424	14,884
Vanderbilt University	50	1210	18,300	18,300
Texas				
Baylor College of Medicine	35	1559	6550	19,650
Texas A&M University	45	1100	6550	19,650
Texas Tech University	40	864	6550	19,650

(Table continued on the following page)

University of Texas, all four campuses	0	250–534	6550	19,650
Utah				
University of Utah	40	427	6125	13,513
Vermont				
University of Vermont	65	450	13,730	25,900
Virginia				
Eastern Virginia Medical School	80	1819	12,500	22,000
Virginia Commonwealth University	75	868	9457	23,317
University of Virginia	50	822	8184	19,352
Washington				
University of Washington	35	. . .	7458	18,833
West Virginia				
Marshall University	30 resident; 50 nonresident	360	7354	17,080
West Virginia University	30	6040 resident; 14,216 nonresident	1640	4550
Wisconsin				
Medical College of Wisconsin	50	35	11,909	22,000
University of Wisconsin	35	. . .	12,138	17,581

Index

Page numbers in *italics* refer to illustrations; numbers followed by (t) indicate tables.

AACOMAS (American Association of Colleges of Osteopathic Medicine Application Service), 112
AAMC (Association of American Medical Colleges), goals for "underrepresented" minorities, 35, 77
AAMC Curriculum Directory, 88, 103
AAMC Directory of American Medical Education, 103
Academic achievements, in medical school admission, 34
Academic record, on application form, *62–63,* 64
Acceptance; *see* Admission
Acknowledgment postcard, for AMCAS application, 64
Acronyms, as mnemonic devices, 213–214
Acrostics, as mnemonic devices, 213–214
Action words, 70–71
Admission, 1–118
  see also Application process
  criteria for, 21–22
  under early decision programs, 73, 74(t)–76(t)
  early provisional, 9
    programs of, 10(t)–12(t)
  failure in, options after, 105–118
  increasing chances of success with reapplication, 105–106
  requirements for, 32–35, 259(t)–280(t)
    minimal, 6
    for osteopathic schools, 112
    sources of information on, 103
  skewed standards for, 35
  state of residency and, 19–20, 20(t)–21(t), 76–77, 80, 82(t)–84(t)
  undergraduate major and, 33, 281(t)

Advanced placement classes, 7, 9
Advisors, premedical, 18
Affirmative action, 33
Aging population, 29
Akron, University of, combined baccalaureate–MD program, 12(t)
Alabama, combined baccalaureate–MD program in, 10(t)
  medical schools in, addresses and admission requirements for, 259(t)
  resident status and, 20(t)
  tuition and fees for, 282(t)
Alabama, University of; *see* University of Alabama
Alaska, residency and admissions in, 20(t)
Albany Medical College, address and admission requirements for, 270(t)
  combined baccalaureate–MD program, 11(t)
  mean MCAT score of accepted students at, 79(t)
  out-of-state students accepted by, 82(t)
  tuition and fees for, 284(t)
Albert Einstein College of Medicine, address and admission requirements for, 271(t)
  mean MCAT score of accepted students at, 78(t)
  out-of-state students accepted by, 82(t)
  tuition and fees for, 284(t)
Allied Health Directory 1995–1996, 107
Alternative curricula, 23
AMCAS; *see* American Medical College Application Service
American Academy of Family Physicians, address of, 104
American Association of Colleges of Osteopathic Medicine

Application Service (AACOMAS), 112
American Board of Family Practice, address of, 104
American Board of Internal Medicine, address of, 104
American College of Emergency Physicians, address of, 104
American College of Surgeons, address of, 104
American Medical College Application Service (AMCAS), 57
  address of, 60
  application form of, 60–64, *61–63*
  application process through, 57–60, *58*
American Medical Student Association, address of, 104
American Society of Contemporary Medicine and Surgery, address of, 104
American University of the Caribbean, 118(t)
Answer key, for practice MCAT, 190–193
Anxiety, 194–195
  relaxation training to reduce, 254–257
Application packet, for MCAT, 124
  rules and regulations covered in, 233
Application process, 57–104
  for AMCAS schools, 57–60, *58*
    form used for, 60–64, *61–63*
  early decision, 73, 74(t)–76(t)
  interview in, 90–104
    see also Interview
  letters of recommendation in, 88–90, *91–96*
  for non-AMCAS schools, 60
  for osteopathic schools, 112
  personal statement in, 65–71
  repeating, after rejection, 105–106